END-USER COMPUTING

CONCEPTS, ISSUES, AND APPLICATIONS

END-USER COMPUTING

CONCEPTS, ISSUES, AND APPLICATIONS

■

edited by

R. Ryan Nelson
University of Houston

WILEY

John Wiley & Sons, Inc.

New York   •   Chichester   •   Brisbane   •   Toronto   •   Singapore

Library of Congress Cataloging-in-Publication Data

End-user computing.

   Bibliography: p.
   Includes index.
   1. End-user computing.   I. Nelson, R. Ryan.
QA76.9.E53P35   1989   658.4'038   88-27688
ISBN 0-471-61359-2 (pbk.)

Printed in the United States of America

10 9 8 7 6 5 4 3 2 1

To My Parents,
Eileen S. and William R. Nelson

PREFACE

As organizational computing enters its fourth decade, a number of sociotechnical changes appear to be taking place, leaving the management of information systems (IS) in a state of transition. Once the sole domain of large, highly centralized IS groups, computers are now permeating the entire organization via a trend toward **end-user computing (EUC)**. Indeed, there seems to be a growing interest in EUC among virtually all circles of IS development and usage. The underlying reasons for this (e.g., improved productivity, reduction of backlog, and reduction in maintenance requirements) assure us that it is not a passing phenomenon but a very real, and useful, development.

Recognizing this trend, many colleges of business administration now include a course on the subject within their IS area of concentration. However, despite an abundance of literature aimed at the advancement of EUC, the arduous task of collecting and organizing such material can be overwhelming.

This book was specifically designed to address this problem. Twenty articles have been selected from leading sources such as the *MIS Quarterly, Harvard Business Review, Journal of Management Information Systems, Communications of the ACM, IBM Systems Journal*, and others. The articles have been carefully organized under five subheadings:

- End-User Computing: What Is It?
- Organizational Support for EUC
- The Development of User-Centered Systems
- The Management of EUC
- Cases and Applications in EUC

Each section is designed to characterize recent developments in EUC from five different perspectives.

The book can be used in several ways:

1. As a supplementary text in the EUC course.

   This collection of articles in effect presents a collage of various perspectives on EUC and therefore could be used with another EUC text to provide a broader perspective. Although the number of EUC textbooks is limited, a variety of EUC-related books have been published and are referenced in the EUC bibliography contained at the end of this book.

2. As the main text in an EUC course.

   As noted in point one above, the number of EUC textbooks is presently limited. This book could address the textbook market while others are

being developed. In addition, many EUC courses include hands-on application development with 4GL software products such as FOCUS, and/or
case development in "real-world settings". The book would be appropriate as the main text in a course that takes either one (or both) of these
approaches. It would also be useful in those courses that are based on
current literature alone.

3. As a supplementary text in an IS course.

    Many IS textbooks devote only a single chapter to EUC. This book could
    be used to provide enhanced EUC coverage.

4. As a reference tool for practitioners.

    Practitioners often find it difficult to identify the leading works in a
    discipline or specific area of study such as EUC. This collection and
    organization of articles should provide a useful tool for IS professionals
    and end users alike.

    The following learning and instructional aids are provided with this book:

☐   Each section is preceded by an introduction describing the central theme
    of the articles grouped within the section and their importance to the
    understanding and advancement of EUC.
☐   Each article is followed by a set of questions designed to be useful in
    generating individual thought and/or class discussion.
☐   A cross-referenced bibliography is provided to help students, faculty, and
    practitioners who wish to pursue some areas of EUC in more depth.

ACKNOWLEDGMENTS

A number of people have contributed to the preparation of this book. Thanks are due, first of all, to the authors of the articles that are included. I would like to express my appreciation to these authors and to their publishers for allowing us to reprint them. In addition, I am especially grateful to Professor Hugh Watson of The University of Georgia for his support and guidance. Hugh was the first to promote the idea of an EUC reader and was an invaluable asset throughout the life of the project. I would also like to thank Joe Dougherty and his staff at John Wiley & Sons for providing an environment that I could be productive within. Finally, a word of appreciation to my wife, Joelle, who spent many an evening as my research assistant on this project. I couldn't have made the deadlines without you.

CONTENTS

END-USER COMPUTING

CONCEPTS, ISSUES,
AND APPLICATIONS

Introduction to End-User Computing: Concepts, Issues, and Applications

■

Significant shifts have taken place in the world of information systems (IS) over the past decade. Ten years ago, the IS function maintained a virtual monopoly over the acquisition, deployment, and operation of an organization's information resources. Today, these responsibilities have been transferred to the end users, who ultimately use IS output. The following figures represent this transfer.

- In 1985, the International Data Corporation[1] could already count 39 computer keyboards for every 100 office workers in the United States and project a 78 to 100 ratio by 1990.
- Xerox Corporation estimates that in 1981, 25 percent of the company's computer resources were dedicated to end-user computing. By 1991, this percentage will triple.[2]
- Companies studied by Rockart and Flannery[3] experienced annual end-user computing (EUC) growth rates of 50 to 90%, while their traditional data processing systems were growing at a much smaller annual rate of 5 to 15%.
- Richard L. Nolan[4] cites a case in which an IS director's "control" over information resource expenditures fell from 100 to 60% from 1970 to 1980.

Three major forces explain much of the motivation behind the transformation process.

☐ **Hardware and software improvements** have greatly increased the availability, affordability, and usability of information technologies. Powerful microcomputers and minicomputers, fourth-generation software, and enhanced telecommunications capabilities are inducing many managers and their staff analysts to experiment with and implement numerous information systems.[5,6,7]

☐ **Enhanced computer-related skills** within the end-user community have motivated and enabled end users to use IS products and technologies.[5,8]

☐ An **organizational environment** conducive toward EUC has grown around the successful employment of EUC products and technologies as productivity enhancement tools. From an aggregate point of view, EUC has had a positive impact on the "bottom line" (i.e., profit margin) within many organizations and as a result has been viewed as a **strategic weapon** by top management.[9]

Organizations capable of responding quickly to and exploiting these technological, operational, and strategic forces are likely to gain significant competitive advantages over the next decade.

END-USER COMPUTING: CONCEPTS, ISSUES, AND APPLICATIONS

This book is intended to be used as an educational tool in the organization's mission toward competitive advantage. It is designed to help the reader (present/future manager/staff professional) understand how IS products and technologies can be used to improve personal as well as work unit productivity.

Some specific lessons to be learned from the work reported in this book include the following:

☐ EUC is not a passing phenomenon, but instead represents the infinite utilization of IS technology by end users. As such, EUC represents a series of product offerings that must be managed carefully to ensure proper diffusion within the organization.

☐ Organizations must provide a **technical and managerial infrastructure** on which applications can be overlaid. This infrastructure should facilitate the integration of microcomputer, minicomputer, and mainframe technologies within three organizational dimensions: personal, departmental, and organizational. To do so, such technical issues as telecommunications and networking need to be coupled with such managerial issues as training and strategy formulation.

☐ Finally, the coexistence of end-user and centralized computing requires a great deal of managerial attention. Issues such as ownership and responsibility will continue to arise and demand resolution.

Generally, most of the problems associated with EUC can be traced to deficiencies in our current understanding of how to effectively use EUC products and technologies in organizational activities. Education is the answer to these problems; the way to educate oneself is through the writings of leading academics and practitioners.

STRUCTURE OF THE BOOK

The 26 articles contained within this book were selected and organized based on, among other things, their ability to complement one another. Each section is designed to characterize the field of EUC from five different perspectives.

- Part 1 serves as an introductory section, highlighting the evolution of the EUC concept via several "classic" and/or connotative articles.
- Part 2 contains a set of readings that describe how organizations are currently supporting EUC via information centers and organization-wide training programs.
- Part 3 presents the various issues involved when developing EUC applications. Specific topics include the prototyping methodology, software selection, and the potential of both success and failure in the development of user-centered systems.
- Part 4 addresses the benefits versus risks issues through articles that prescribe EUC management strategies and their timing for adoption.
- Part 5 contains a series of four case studies on EUC. Although these cases are included at the end of the book, they provide an indication of how various organizations have put theory into practice and may be effectively discussed at virtually any point in a semester or quarter.

Following Part 5 is an in-depth bibliography, cross-referenced by section, which will help the reader who wants to pursue a specific EUC topic in more detail.

REFERENCES

1. International Data Corporation, cited in "The Paper Blizzard," *USA Today* (April 4, 1986), p. 1.
2. Benjamin, R. I., "Information Technology in the 1990's: A Long Range Planning Scenario," *MIS Quarterly*, Vol. 6, No. 2 (June 1982), pp. 11–31.
3. Rockart, J. F., and L. S. Flannery, "The Management of End-User Computing," *Communications of the ACM*, Vol. 26, No. 10 (October 1983), pp. 776–784.
4. Nolan, R. L., "Managing Information Systems by Committee," *Harvard Business Review*, Vol. 62, No. 4 (July–August 1982), pp. 72–79.
5. McLean, E. R., "End Users as Application Developers," *MIS Quarterly*, Vol. 4, No. 4 (December 1979), pp. 37–46.

6. Zmud, R. W., "Design Alternatives for Organizing Information Systems Activities," *MIS Quarterly*, Vol. 8, No. 2 (June 1984), pp. 79–93.

7. Zmud, R. W., and M. R. Lind, "The Use of Formal Mechanisms for Linking the Information Systems Function with End-Users," in *Managers, Micros and Mainframes*, ed. M. Jarke (New York: John Wiley & Sons, 1986), pp. 133–149.

8. Nelson, R. R., and P. H. Cheney, "Training End Users: An Exploratory Study," *MIS Quarterly*, Vol. 11, No. 4 (December 1987), pp. 547–559.

9. Alavi, M., R. R. Nelson, and I. R. Weiss, "The Management of End-User Computing: Critical Attributes for Organizational Success," *Proceedings of the 20th Annual Meeting of the Hawaii International Conference on Systems Sciences*, Kona, Hawaii (January 6–9, 1987).

I

END-USER COMPUTING: WHAT IS IT?

■

End-user computing (EUC) is a complex and highly diverse phenomenon—in large part because the community in which it is used is itself complex and diverse. Although the **first** "end user(s)" can theoretically be traced to the **first** computer, EUC, as it is commonly referred to today, has grown out of the rapid advances in technology since those early days. For example, the last decade alone has seen such technological developments as

☐ The introduction of the personal computer (PC) to corporate America.
☐ Personal productivity software (e.g., spreadsheets, database management systems, and word processing).
☐ Fourth-generation languages.
☐ Peripheral devices, such as mice, touch-sensitive CRTs, and laser printers.
☐ Telecommunications and PC networking.

Unquestionably, EUC has benefited from technology over the years, but would it be more accurate to say that (1) EUC is a function of a **technology push**, or (2) EUC as a function of a **demand pull**? The four articles contained in this section may help to answer this question by describing the concept of EUC from a connotational point of view. Collectively, these articles offer definition, classification, and surveys of the field over the past 10 years, while also addressing future directional issues so the reader can gain some perspectives on the EUC phenomenon early in the book.

For example, consider the following:

The demand for new or expanded computer-based information systems far exceeds the capacity of many IS departments to meet it. Assuming that a massive expansion of IS personnel is not feasible, one solution is to make existing computer professionals more productive; efforts in this direction have met with a fair measure of success. Another approach is to allow end users, who ultimately use the computer's output, to function as their own developers. In this way, the programmer "middle man" is eliminated, and users can create and modify their own applications as the need arises. Not only does this help relieve the IS department's development workload, but it also helps lessen the maintenance load. However, to accomplish this transfer of application development from IS professional to IS user, certain key variables must be understood.

The article by Ephraim McLean, "End Users as Application Developers" (Reading 1) discusses these variables, including the nature of the development process, a user classification scheme, and the scope and orientation of systems. McLean's article is recognized by many as being "the first of its kind," an article espousing the potential of EUC to meet the growing needs of the organization.

"Directions and Issues in End-User Computing," by Raymond Panko (Reading 2) is another good definitional piece, and therefore a good place to begin to understand the EUC phenomenon. Panko explores the rise of EUC over the years into a very large and complex "market." The author's marketing perspective is based on two key concepts: (1) demand-driven services, and (2) market segmentation.

When EUC first exhibited signs of rapid growth (early 1980s), several studies were undertaken to answer questions such as: What is actually happening in the world of EUC? Will its growth be as explosive as the predictions? "A Field Study of End-User Computing: Findings and Issues," by David Benson (Reading 3), is one such study. In his article, Benson examines some of the differences between those who use the mainframe environment and those who use microcomputers. Software used, the varieties of applications developed, and the training background of end users are examined, as well as some of the problems encountered and some of the early results. Finally, five critical issues are identified that those interviewed saw as needing resolution in the near future.

The use of technology by top-level managers represents the apex of end-user computing within the organization. Senior executives of large corporations have customarily relied on functional staff for the information on which to base key decisions. The task of gathering data and preparing analyses has been too time-consuming and cumbersome to be left to the executives themselves. Today, however, improved technology, coupled with a heightened analytic orientation among top managers, is beginning to change the pattern by which a company funnels information upward. In fact, as John Rockart and Michael Treacy report in their article, "The CEO Goes On-Line"

(Reading 4), in some companies the responsibility for using such data-based support has moved into the executive office itself and, perhaps more important, the top managers of these companies have become active participants in the process—not merely final consumers of its output.

1

End Users
as Application
Developers

■

E. R. McLean

INTRODUCTION

Throughout the world, business organizations are becoming increasingly more complex. They are becoming larger, with expanding product and service lines. They are operating in a rapidly changing, frequently turbulent external environment. Their organizational structures are cycling between the extremes of centralization and decentralization. And finally, the time horizons for decisions are becoming both shorter and longer. More timely information, needed to make better current decisions, is becoming vitally important; and, at the same time, long range planning horizons are being extended many years into the future.

To help cope with this complexity, managers are beginning to recognize the potential of computers and information processing technology. This technology, long used to serve the transaction based, operational needs of the organization, is now "coming out of the closet" and being applied to a wide range of managerial problems.

However, for many organizations, this potential is only that—just potential. The reality has lagged far behind the promise. Highly sophisticated and powerful hardware is being used with decade-old programming languages and software. Managers who wish to tap into the information base

Reprinted by special permission of the MIS Quarterly, *Volume 3, Number 4, December 1979. Copyright 1979 by the Society for Information Management and the Management Information Systems Research Center at the University of Minnesota.*

of their organizations are frustrated by the long delays encountered and by the need to have to deal with programmer intermediaries in order to have their requests met. They long to have the data processing function more responsive to their needs; a central, routine part of the way of doing business, not a thing apart.

POTENTIAL SOLUTIONS

In response to this challenge, a number of developments are occurring. Data processing departments are attempting to expand their staffs to meet this demand. They are introducing tools and techniques to make their present staffs more productive. Finally, they are beginning to transfer the applications development function itself to the user groups. But each of these developments is not without its problems.

Expanded Staffs

In spite of the expanded demand for data processing services, the solution of expanding the number of DP professionals is meeting stiff resistance. For one, many senior managers feel that their DP departments are already too big, and requests for additional programmers and analysts are not being approved.

In those cases when approval is granted, it is frequently impossible to find and hire people with the requisite skills. Where the job market for programmers was fairly stable until two or three years ago, it has now heated up considerably; and companies are engaged in ruinous competition for experienced personnel. Large, well-managed companies that had only 5 to 10 percent turnover a few years ago are now experiencing programmer turnover rates of 25 to 35 percent. This, of course, compounds the problem because not only are companies unable to expand their DP staffs, but their present staffs are likely to be less effective due to the debilitating effects of this high turnover.

Improved Productivity

A second trend is the attempt to make existing DP professionals more productive. Such developments as high level languages, interactive programming support, database management systems, and preprogrammed application modules have all been used to enhance programmer productivity.

By and large, these efforts have met with a fair measure of success. In fact, it is highly problematical whether many of today's large scale, sophisticated systems would have ever seen the light of day had it not been for these tools. They are clearly beneficial and further gains in the future can be anticipated.

However, the chief value of these techniques is for applications that are already fairly well defined; systems where the users' requirements have already been analyzed and specified. But it is precisely at the "front end" where many of the problems occur. The task of successfully translating users' needs into detailed systems specifications is frequently a black art, and few of the present DP productivity aids are of much help in this critical first phase. End users are still faced with the problem of conveying their requirements to the systems designer—requirements that are, in all likelihood, not clearly understood by the user himself and are, in any event, likely to change several times before the end of the useful life of the application. Therefore, to eliminate this translation step, it would be highly desirable for the user to be able to take over the functions of the designer.

End Users as Developers

While not lessening the importance of the DP productivity techniques referred to above, it is in this area of end-user involvement in the development process that the greatest gains are likely to occur. If the "middle man"— the analyst or programmer—could be eliminated, then the user would be able to define his or her requirements directly. Time consuming conferences could be eliminated and misunderstandings about systems requirements minimized. Of perhaps even greater importance is the benefit that would accrue once an application went into production.

The so-called "maintenance problem" is an important concern of many DP managers, but it is misnamed. Maintenance of application programs bears little resemblance to hardware maintenance. Whereas the latter is aimed primarily at "fixing bugs," program maintenance is largely concerned with responding to changing user and environmental requirements.[1] Therefore, if users could specify directly the changes that are needed, without having to seek the assistance of the DP department, this "maintenance problem" could be greatly reduced.

Of course, these benefits cannot be realized unless the capability to support them is available. The software to allow users to function as application developers is only now beginning to come into existence. More will be said about this later.

As far as hardware is concerned, recent technological advances have far outstripped our ability to take full advantage of them. Luckily, this has meant that the cost of using computers "inefficiently" in order to achieve greater managerial effectiveness is not very great. However, even here much must be done in the way of human factoring so that the hardware/software interface presents a friendly user environment. *Easy-to-use interactive systems are essential if users are to become developers.*

USER CLASSIFICATION

Before continuing, it may be helpful to make some definitions and distinctions about users. For instance, from the standpoint of the compiler writer, all applications programmers are "users." Similarly, to the full time applications developer, all part time programmers (*e.g.*, engineers, analysts) may be "users." Therefore, for the purposes of this article, the following classification scheme is adopted.

- ☐ DP professionals (DPP)
- ☐ DP users (DPU). This second category is further divided into DP amateurs (DPA) and non-DP trained users (NTU).

This characterization is consistent with the framework for end users contained in the recent report of the CODASYL End-User Facilities Committee.[2] Also, the term "amateur" is not used in any pejorative sense, but merely to contrast this type of user with the full time DP professional.[3]

Stated most simply, the DP professional *writes code* for use by *others*. The DP amateur *writes code* for his or her *own use*, and the non-DP trained user *uses code written by others*. Of course, in practice these distinctions may not be nearly so clear-cut.

DP Professionals

If someone's full time activity is directed toward data processing—whether or not they actually are part of the DP department—they are considered DP professionals. This includes analysts, programmers, database administrators, project managers, operators, and so forth. It is this group that is experiencing the fitful growing pains mentioned earlier and to whom the DP productivity aids are being directed.

DP Users

DP amateurs and non-DP trained users comprise, at least potentially, the rest of the work force.

The *DP amateur* is most typically the engineer, financial analyst, or corporate planner who knows at least the rudiments of computing and can program in BASIC, FORTRAN, or APL. In addition to writing simple programs and using existing packages, he or she will frequently assist other less trained users or, in the case of large application development efforts, will function as a liaison between the DP professionals and the untrained users.

The *non-DP trained user* ranges all the way from the reservation clerk or bank teller to the senior manager or business professional. They have no programming knowledge at all and care about computing only to the extent that it helps them get their own work done.

Over time, it is possible that more and more DP users will acquire some programming experience. The rapid growth of personal or home computers, the increased prevalence of computing courses in high schools and colleges, the improved ease of use of many timesharing systems—these and other factors may well cause a significant shift in end user sophistication.

But it would be a serious mistake to base a development strategy on this assumption. Those who claim that soon "everybody" will know BASIC or APL—or even some yet to be developed very high level language—are simply naive or are engaged in wishful thinking. For the vast majority of users, the system will have to be adapted to them rather than *vice versa*.

This point is particularly difficult for many DP professionals to grasp and to appreciate. Because of their intimate and long standing association with computing, they have grown accustomed to the alien demands and accommodations that are required when working with computer systems. It is, therefore, hard for them to understand the frustration, or even terror, that many first time users experience when they approach the computer. What is very logical and obvious to a DP professional can be very confusing and mysterious to the manager attempting to find out a critical item of information locked away somewhere in the system.

Therefore, when these same DP professionals propose "user-oriented" facilities, they are often subconsciously proposing systems that are more suited to their own needs and abilities than to those of the real end user. As Gingras[4] has pointed out, this psychological difference between designers and users can have a significant effect on the way systems are designed, with the frequent result that users are forced to adjust to the designer's perspective rather than the reverse. This helps explain, at least partially, the greater progress that has been made in developing DP productivity aids as opposed to facilities aimed at supporting end users. The former have been created *by* DP professionals *for* DP professionals, and, by extension, to DP amateurs. The latter requires DP professionals to reorient their way of thinking and develop a user perspective—a difficult task at best.

THE DEVELOPMENT PROCESS

The preceding section characterized the types of data processing users; this section will do the same for the DP development process. This is necessary because there are some important distinctions that should be made with regard to the way systems are, or should be, developed and the purposes for which they are intended. As the circumstances differ, so do the respective roles played by DP professionals and DP users. Failure to recognize these factors can cause serious problems, especially in those efforts where the end user is to be heavily involved in the development process. These factors deal with the orientation, nature, and scope of systems.

System Orientation

The purpose or orientation of an application can have a crucial bearing on how it is developed. Although for many people "programming is programming," software developed for sale or to meet some contractual requirement may differ markedly from applications created to meet some inhouse need. In fact, it can be argued that there are at least three separate and distinct types of software development efforts: (1) software for sale; (2) software to support transaction based systems; and (3) software to support management. These distinctions are similar to those identified by Powers and Dickson in their 1973 study of MIS project management.[5]

1. **Software for Sale**. Under the general area of software for sale are all of the compilers, utilities, and systems software produced by equipment vendors; proprietary software packages; systems to fulfill government contracts; turnkey and contracted for, tailor made systems; and even inhouse corporate systems where the "customer" is a subsidiary or division.
2. **Transaction Based Systems**. For many organizations, transaction based systems comprise the majority, if not the totality of their data processing activity. Payroll, general ledger, order entry, demand deposit accounting, claims processing, inventory management—these and many other general specific industry applications are examples of this second area.
3. **Management Information Systems**. MIS, or as it is now more fashionable to say, decision support systems[6], are aimed at supporting management decision making, broadly defined. These systems may or may not be linked to the organization's transaction based systems, but their chief characteristic is their discretionary nature. As was pointed out in McLean and Riesing[7], the only basis for the existence of such systems is their usefulness in serving the end user.

Nature of the Development Process

What then are the implications of these distinctions? In many ways, types one and two are quite similar. If "DP professional" is substituted for "vendor" and "DP user" for "customer," the development process is very much alike in both cases. For want of a better word, I will call these first two types an *adversary development* relationship. In contrast, I will call the third type *cooperative development*.

Adversary Development

In using the term "adversary," I do not mean to suggest hostility, although this has been known to occur, merely that an arm's length relationship exists between developers and users. These two parties may, but frequently do not, share the same objectives. For instance, the developer may wish to limit the number of options available in order to minimize the programming cost. Also, proposed changes in the agreed upon specifications are usually met with great resistance. On the other hand, the user may want features that were never clearly delineated at the outset or may express disappointment with various aspects of the finished product. Often the disagreement centers on what exactly was specified in the vendor contract or promised by the DP department.

In this environment, the importance of a thorough, comprehensive, and detailed design phase cannot be overemphasized. Time spent at the front end in clarifying and refining the systems specifications will be repaid many times over downstream. Tools such as Structured Design,[8,9] HIPO,[10,11] PSL/PSA,[12] and entity-relational approaches[13,14,15] are all helpful in assisting developers and users to define in unambiguous terms what exactly the system will look like when completed. Ideally, to the extent that these tools are computer-based, (e.g., PSL/PSA), they may lead in time to the automatic generation of code, thus eliminating the errors and misunderstandings that inevitably creep in when specifications must be translated into code.

To date, it has been assumed that almost all systems are of the "adversary" type, although some may quarrel with the label I have given them. The underlying assumption of such systems is that there is a reasonably stable, well defined set of requirements that diligence and skill can ferret out; and, to the extent that this design effort is successful, the maintenance requirements once the system goes into production will be markedly reduced. Therefore, most of the development tools and techniques of the last decade have been aimed at improving this process. But these assumptions, and the corresponding emphasis on the design phase, can be seriously misleading for the third, and newest, type of development activity.

Cooperative Development

At the core of cooperative development is the premise that the developer and user share the same set of objectives; namely, the improvement in management decision making. Rather than an arm's length relationship existing, they are all on the same team; or, as this article suggests, the developer and user should be one and the same person(s). Rather than focusing on systems *efficiency*, the object is managerial *effectiveness*.

Because of this, the development process is much different. For one, the determination of the "real" requirements is a dynamic, not static, process. No amount of effort devoted to the design phase will produce a complete set of specifications, because the needs of management change over time. Thus DP professionals who lament that "management can't make up their minds," or "they don't know what they want," or "why didn't they ask for that at the beginning?" are still thinking in terms of type one and two systems, and the adversary relationship that accompanies them.

In cooperative development, the lines between design, installation, and maintenance are considerably blurred, reflecting the changing, dynamic nature of the process. It is a serious mistake to invest a significant amount of time and effort in attempting to improve and refine the specifications developed during the design phase because these requirements will change. This is in sharp contrast to adversary development where such front end efforts are amply repaid. The reason for these changing requirements are at least threefold.

Changing Nature of Systems

First, few managers fully understand their present systems, manual or otherwise, and the information necessary to support these activities. To demand such insight is, in most cases, unrealistic. Many managers function quite effectively with only an intuitive sense of the business and its needs.

Second, in those cases where management *does* understand and can articulate exactly what it wants, external events will cause this to change over time. New legal, market, environmental, and regulatory requirements will continually force change and modification—that is "maintenance."

Third, even in those rare cases where the manager is knowledgeable and the environment stable, change will occur because growth and learning take place. The better a system is, the more it will be used; and the more it is used, the more likely there are to be demands for enhancements and extensions—again, "maintenance."

Therefore, in light of the above, rather than deplore the growing maintenance burden, at least for user oriented systems, it should be recognized that it is a vital sign that the patient is alive and well. In those systems where there are few or no maintenance requests, it is not usually a sign of a superior design job, but instead of a little used system.

To develop applications of this third type, therefore, requires the ability to get systems up and running quickly, and then modify them as the need dictates. As Robert Kendall of IBM has put it: "Install it first, and program it later." To the extent that such prototyping tools do exist[16], this becomes possible. Many organizations have used APL in this way, creating working prototypes in weeks rather than months or years[7]. Only when the application stabilizes, and with management support systems this may never occur, does the issue of efficiency of execution, and possible recoding in COBOL or PL/1, come up for consideration. Also, as techniques emerge which allow users to generate their own reports or make their own modifications, the maintenance burden, at least as perceived by the data processing department, may lessen considerably.

System Scope

In undertaking applications development, the size or scope of the application has a large bearing on how the work should be performed, and by whom. For purposes of discussion, I will classify systems as personal (minor), departmental (intermediate), or corporate (major).

Personal Applications

Personal applications are, as the name implies, designed to serve the personal computing needs of an individual. This includes queries, simple calculations, and other *ad hoc* DP activities. They draw upon capabilities, facilities, and data that are already in place. It is this latter area, data, that separates personal applications development from "personal computing" as exemplified by the rapidly growing home computer market. The applications are personal, but in an organizational, data dependent setting.

Although currently quite small, this type of development activity has the potential to become extremely large, the critical factor in this growth being the ease with which the computing resources can be accessed. Depending upon the preferences of the individual user, this might include using existing high level languages like APL and BASIC; database accessing packages like MARK IV,[17] RAMIS,[18] and Query-By-Example,[19,20,21] application specific facilities like EXECUCOM's[22] Interactive Financial Planning System, and even natural language processing capabilities.[23]

The key factor, however, is that these features be provided in a friendly user, highly forgiving environment. This requires the ability to move conveniently among system resources and to access data, library routines, preprogrammed modules, language capabilities, and other features without reference to JCL or other highly detailed protocols.

If this personal applications development can be successfully supported, it could well have the apparently conflicting result of *expanding* the use of data processing, while at the same time *reducing* the demands on DP professionals to support this use.

This "off loading" of work is very much like what has happened in the telephone industry. With direct distance dialing, the work of placing a call has been transferred from the long distance operator to the caller, with a resulting decrease in the number of operators who would otherwise be required, accompanied by an increase in the total volume of calls.

Departmental Applications

Department applications span the field from the one time, *ad hoc* requirements described above, to the full blown corporate wide systems to be discussed below. These applications are the ones that generate most of the demands for what is presently, and erroneously, called maintenance. They provide the reports, both routine and special, the queries, the analyses, and the many other items of computer-based data that form the backbone of a department's management information system. However, because these applications are usually closely linked with corporate systems and databases, any modification or extension of them requires the assistance of DP professionals—and thus the maintenance problem.

Even when the applications are highly local in character, there are still the problems of interfacing with corporate systems and of successfully using corporate supplied computer resources. At the same time, the need for easy to use systems is just as great here as is true with the personal applications development discussed above. This desire for locally adaptive systems, with the end user as the primary developer, and yet coupled to corporate wide systems is probably the main reason behind the trend toward distributed data processing. Fundamental to the DDP approach is the idea that users can once again regain control of the information systems that are vital to their functioning.

But one often mentioned concern among DDP proponents is the lack of DP expertise within user organizations. Without careful planning and a cadre of DP professionals, they argue, the users will not be able to obtain the results they want. As should be apparent, this concern is a variant of the problem discussed earlier: the psychology of the DP professional getting in the way of a user oriented solution.

In fairness, most of the systems being distributed today *do* require the involvement of DP professionals, locally as well as centrally. Without their expertise, serious problems can and do arise. But it is to change this situation that is precisely the thesis of this article. The growth of departmental applications, whether or not they are centralized, decentralized, or distributed, should not have to wait for the availability of skilled DP professionals. Capabilities should exist, or be developed, that will allow these end users to act on their own behalf.

Corporate Applications

Corporate or company wide applications are still the central data processing activity of most organizations. These systems are designed to meet external as well as internal requirements and have many of the characteristics of the transaction based operational systems discussed earlier. The analysis, design, and implementation of these systems is performed by DP professionals; but the involvement of end users is frequently crucial. Such systems invariably require the cooperation of user departments to ensure their successful functioning; and, the more knowledgeable and committed this cooperation is, the more likely it is that the application will be successful. In addition, such systems frequently serve as the basis for the above mentioned management information systems. Queries and *ad hoc* reports, no matter how easy to prepare, are worthless if the underlying data are missing, inaccurate, or out of date.

To develop these large corporate applications, tools, and development aids like ADF,[24] DMS,[25] and SPF[26] can be helpful in enhancing the DP professional's productivity. Prototyping can be accomplished through the use of APL or possibly one of the very high level languages currently being researched.

To aid in the design specification phase, PSL/PSA[12] can be an important documentation tool, serving as a communication link between developers and users. Also, once the application is in operation, this same documentation helps to support the maintenance effort.

To aid in accomplishing the systems analysis that must precede the design phase, techniques like Business Systems Planning[27] and, more recently, BIAIT (Business Information Analysis and Integration Technique[28]) both offer valuable insights to users as to what applications they should be under-taking and how these applications should relate to one another.

Summary and conclusions

The expansion of data processing activities is pressing the limits of the human resources available to sustain this growth. Data processing professionals, until recently the only individuals capable of defining and developing new com-puter-based applications, are in short supply. However, top management is reluctant to expand their DP staffs, feeling that the costs may not be justified by the benefits; and, even when management is agreeable, qualified people are very hard to find.

One solution to this problem is to make the existing DP personnel more productive. A number of development aids have been used in one way or another to assist the DP professional in developing, and maintaining, applica-tions in a more timely and cost effective fashion. These tools, and others like them, have been quite successful in enhancing DP productivity and further gains can be expected.

Another way to attack this problem is to transfer the development task from the DP professional to the DP user. The end users, some with DP skills (the "DP amateur") but most with none (the "non-DP trained user"), are in the best position to understand the needs of the business, at least intuitive-ly, but they need a means of translating this understanding into working applications. Up until now, this has meant dealing with an intermediary, the analyst or programmer, in order to obtain the desired results. But with new approaches and techniques, the user may be able to take over this task direct-ly.

Of course, the scope and orientation of the application under considera-tion has a large bearing on the approaches to be used and the personnel to be involved. For personal and departmental applications, end users should be able to make simple queries, generate reports, and undertake other types of analyses entirely on their own without the intervention of DP professionals. To the extent that this is achievable, a large part of the "maintenance prob-lem" is transferred from the DP department to the user groups. But this main-tenance activity is misnamed. Most of maintenance is not correcting bugs; it is extending and enhancing the features of the system—an activity that users are in a much better position to do, *if they have the proper tools*.

In addition to the scope of an application, its orientation is also important. There are crucial differences between software developed in an "adversary" environment and in a "cooperative" one. In "adversary" development, time spent on carefully defining the specifications during the design phase is repaid many times over during the implementation phase. "Cooperative" develop-ment, on the other hand, is needed for systems designed to support manage-ment decision making. Developers and users must share the same objectives and, hopefully, can even be the same individuals. Here the specifications *cannot* be completely defined during the design phase because they change over time. Improvements in user understanding, changes in external events, desires to improve system functioning—these and many other factors make it impossible to specify all features in advance. For these types of systems, prototyping tools become extremely valuable. The ability to get something up and running quickly, and then modify it as the need dictates, can be critical to the success of such systems.

Underlying all of the above is the notion that end users can play an important part in the development of many types of applications. To accomplish this, however, many of the tools referred to must be improved and extended. For instance, several of the development aids mentioned above are APL based. But there is no consistent, overall architecture that brings these aids together and, equally important, allows them to interface with other system resources. Work is presently underway to accomplish this. The concept is appealing; much work needs to be done to make it a reality.

In conclusion, it should be stressed that there is no easy, single route to achieving the goal of the end user as an application developer. A number of tools already exist. Others have been proposed or are under development. This in itself is an encouraging sign. But equally important is the recognition of the fact that, if future growth in data processing is to occur, users must play a central role in this growth.

REFERENCES

1. Lientz, B. P., Swanson, E. B., and Tompkins, G. E. "Characteristics of Applications Software Maintenance," *Communications of the ACM*, Volume 21, Number 6, June 1978, pp. 466–471.

2. *A Status Report on the Activities of the CODASYL End User Facilities Committee*, February 1979, 48 pp.

3. Weinberg, Gerald M. *The Psychology of Computer Programming*, Van Nostrand Reinhold, New York, 1971, 288 pp.

4. Gingras, Lin. *The Psychology of the Design of Information Systems*, unpublished Ph.D. dissertation, Graduate School of Management, University of California, Los Angeles, California, 1977, 171 pp.

5. Powers, Richard F., and Dickson, Gary W. "MIS Project Management: Myths, Opinions, and Reality," *California Management Review*, Volume 15, Number 3, Spring 1973, pp. 147–156.

6. Keen, Peter G. W., and Scott Morton, Michael, S. *Decision Support Systems: An Organizational Perspective*, Addison-Wesley, Reading, Massachusetts, 1978, 264 pp.

7. McLean, Ephraim R., and Riesing, Thomas F. "MAPP: A Decision Support System for Financial Planning," *DATA BASE*, Volume 8, Number 3, Winter 1977, pp. 9–14.

8. Stevens, W. P., Myers, G. J., and Constantine, L. L. "Structured Design," *IBM Systems Journal*, Volume 13, Number 2, 1974, pp. 115–139.

9. Yourdon, Edward, and Constantine, Larry L. *Structured Design*, Yourdon Inc., New York, New York, 1975.

10. *HIPO—A Design Aid and Documentation Technique*, GC20-1851, IBM Corporation, Data Processing Division, White Plains, New York 10604.

11. Stay, J. F. "HIPO and Integrated Program Design," *IBM Systems Journal*, Volume 15, Number 2, 1976, pp. 143–154.

12. Teichroew, Daniel, and Hershey, Ernest A., III. "PSL/PSA: A Computer-Aided Technique for Structured Documentation and Analysis of Information Processing Systems," *IEEE Transactions on Software Engineering*, January 1977, pp. 41–48.

13. Chen, Peter. "The Entity-Relationship Approach to Logical Data Base Design," *The Q.E.D. Monograph Series on Data Base Management*, Q.E.D. Information Sciences, Inc., 141 Linden Street, Wellesley, Massachusetts, 02181, 1977.

14. Chen, Peter. "The Entity-Relationship Model: Toward a Unified View of Data," *ACM Transactions on Database Systems 1*, March, 1976, pp. 9–37.

15. Chen, Peter. "The Entity-Relationship Model—A Basis for the Enterprise View of Data," *Proceedings of the National Computer Conference*, AFIPS Press, 1977, pp. 77–84.

16. Berrisford, Thomas, and Wetherbe, James. "Heuristic Development: A Redesign of Systems Design," *Management Information Systems Quarterly*, Volume 3, November 1, March 1979, pp. 11–19.

17. *MARK IV/REPORTER: Product Description*, Informatics Inc. Software Products, 21050 Vanowen Street, Canoga Park, California 91304.

18. *RAMIS II Users Manual*, Mathematica Products Group Inc., Princeton Station Office Park, P.O. Box 2392, Princeton, New Jersey 08540.

19. Zloof, Moshe M. and de Jong, S. Peter. "The System for Business Automation (SBA): Programming Language," *Communications of the ACM*, Volume 20, Number 6, June, 1977, pp. 385–396.

20. Zloof, Moshe M. "Query-By-Example," *Proceedings of the National Computer Conference*, AFIPS Press, 1975, pp. 431–438.

21. Zloof, Moshe M. "Query-By-Example: A Data Base Language," *IBM Systems Journal*, Volume 16, Number 4, 1977, pp. 324–343.

22. *IFPS: Interactive Financial Planning System*, EXECUCOM, P.O. Box 9758, Austin, Texas 78766.

23. Harris, Larry R. "The Robot System: Natural Language Processing Applied to Data Base Query," *Proceedings of ACM 1978 Annual Conference*, Washington, D.C., December 1978, pp. 165–172.

24. *IMS Application Development Facility (ADF) General Information*, GB-21-9869, IBM Corporation, Data Processing Division, White Plains, New York 10604.

25. *Display Management System II, General Information Manual*, GH20-1251, IBM Corporation, Data Processing Division, White Plains, New York 10604.

26. *TSO-3270 Structured Programming Facility, General Information*, GH20-1638, IBM Corporation, Data Processing Division, White Plains, New York 10604.

27. *Business Systems Planning: Information Systems Planning Guide*, GE20-0527, IBM Corporation, Data Processing Division, White Plains, New York 10604.

28. Carlson, W. M. "The New Horizon in Business Information Systems," 1978 Northwest Systems Conference.

QUESTIONS

1. What was the impetus for end-user computing (EUC)? Aside from EUC, what other alternative courses of action were/are available?
2. Evaluate McLean's classification scheme for users.
3. What important distinctions need to be made with regard to the way

systems are, or should be, developed and the purposes for which they are intended? As the circumstances differ, how might the respective roles played by DP professionals and DP users tend to differ?

4. In undertaking applications development, what role does application size/scope have on how the work should be performed, and by whom?

5. Since the time this article was written, what important technological advances have been made to foster the growth of EUC?

2

Directions and Issues in End-User Computing

■

Raymond R. Panko

INTRODUCTION

The Computer Explosion

An explosion is taking place in the use of computers.

☐ In 1985, the International Data Corporation[1] could already count 39 computer keyboards for every 100 office workers in the United States.
☐ Many of these keyboards were shared, making the number of users even higher than keyboard counts would seem to indicate. For example, Future Computing found that the average personal computer in 1985 was shared by 2.3 people.[2]
☐ For 1990, International Data Corporation[1] projects 78 keyboards for every 100 office workers in the United States.

Although we have no comparable data for other countries, it appears that the use of computers is exploding in almost every industrialized country. It is hard to find an office anywhere that does not have at least one computer, and many offices have almost as many personal computers and terminals as they have employees.

Reprinted by special permission of INFOR, *Volume 25, Number 3, August, 1987, pp. 181–197.*

The Data Processing Era

Overall numbers tell only part of the story. More important than sheer growth is the fact that we are seeing *profound changes in the way that computers are being used*. Computing is not only bigger in the 1980s than it was in the 1960s and 1970s. It is something almost entirely different than it was in those early years.

During the 1960s and 1970s, a single application dominated corporate computing. This was data processing—the combination of clerical transaction processing and fixed-format management reporting. Although there are no statistics for the dominance of data processing in those early years, this lack of evidence exists because DP's dominance was so great and widely recognized that nobody bothered to document its ubiquity.

During the 1970s, office automation began to be touted as a partner for data processing. In the early 1960s, Ulrich Steinlilper coined the term *textverabeitung* (word processing) to indicate that the processing of words would eventually be as important as the processing of data. During the 1970s, word processing centers, records management centers, and other clerical OA departments began to be automated.

Office Demographics Analysis

In 1982 Panko and Sprague argued that DP and OA, instead of being very different, really shared a strong common bond in those early years. Specifically, both were implemented in one basic kind of office, which Panko and Sprague called the Type I office. In contrast, most newer applications were appearing in a very different kind of office, which Panko and Sprague called Type II. Roughly speaking, Type I offices are clerical offices that resemble paperwork assembly lines, while Type II offices handle the firm's nonroutine policy making and professional work—for example, the marketing department, the finance department, and the executive suite.

Data processing started in accounting departments and other Type I offices, while office automation started in word processing centers, records management centers, and yet other Type I offices. While word processing centers are different from accounting departments, the pace and nature of the work in these two departments (especially the importance of procedures in both kinds of departments) makes their automation far more similar to each other than to the automation of the staff and management offices that are the homes of most users of end user computing.[3]

On the basis of a preliminary analysis of office occupational data that was later expanded by Panko,[4] Panko and Sprague concluded that while computing had started in clerical Type I departments, its real future lay in Type II managerial and professional departments.

> Type I departments have only about a third of all office workers, and because most workers in Type I departments are clerical workers, Type I departments represent only about a quarter of all office salaries.[4]

Furthermore, because work in Type I offices is straightforward to describe and program, and because the repetitive nature of the work done in these offices permits the company to recoup its programming investment quickly, most early information systems development went into Type I departments. So when the computer explosion of the 1980s began to reach full swing, Type I departments had already gone through the first stage of automation, in which most of the easy gains had been mined. Type II departments were the virgin territory, and they represented a vast new continent to conquer.

In Type I clerical departments, data processing and clerical office automation were the two most important applications that could be implemented. In a study of Bureau of Labour Statistics data, Panko[5] estimated that clerical jobs that could be handled by data processing represented only 23 percent of all office employment. OA-oriented clerical jobs in Type I departments added only another four percent. These figures exclude secretaries, because most secretaries work in Type II departments such as finance; the clerical OA statistics did include typists, because this is the normal title given to word processing center operators.

In Type II managerial and professional departments, no single dominant application emerges. Use-of-time studies summarized by Panko[4] indicate that managers spend about half their days talking face-to-face, while professionals spend about 30 percent of their days in face-to-face communication. Although this is a large percentage of the work day, face-to-face communication is difficult to support electronically, when the rest of the day is considered, a very fragmented pattern of activities emerges.[4]

Both managers and professionals spend about 25 percent of the day reading and writing.

Both managers and professionals spend five to 10 percent of the day talking on the telephone.

Three other activities take up most of the rest of the day: analysis (both numerical and conceptual), looking for information, and managing personal activities and the activities of others.[6]

Managers and professionals are constantly interrupted in their work, switching tasks every few minutes. Although this finding is often attributed to Mintzberg,[7] it really comes from the earliest use-of-time studies.[8]

Secretaries in Type II departments also have extremely varied activities.[9,10] Less than half their days are spent typing. The secretarial job in the Type II department is very different from the typist job in Type I word processing centers.

Although these results map reasonably well into known patterns of personal computer use and the use of other office technologies, they suggest that data processing per se is only done in Type I departments, which have a small percent of the office workforce, and there is no a priori ground for believing that data extraction from corporate data bases will be a major need in Type II departments. Of course it will have some importance, but there is no reason to think that needs in Type II department are fed primarily or even largely by transaction data from DP applications.

The Type II managerial and professional department is a completely different environment with completely different needs. Its services are not likely to be simple extrapolations of past services like data processing. And because Type II departments represent the future of information systems, we need to understand these departments and their needs very thoroughly.

END-USER COMPUTING

The Rise of End-User Computing

The same year that Panko and Sprague[11] published their discussion for the importance of Type II managerial and professional departments, Benjamin[12] published a seminal study of computer use in a strategic business unit of the Xerox Corporation. As part of this study, he measured the importance of data processing, in terms of the percentage of central processing unit (CPU) cycles consumed by data processing.

> In 1970, to nobody's surprise, data processing consumed virtually 100 percent of all CPU cycles.
>
> In 1980, however, DP had slipped to a mere 60 percent of all CPU cycles.
>
> For 1990, Benjamin forecast that DP, despite constant growth, would shrink to a mere 25 percent of all CPU cycles.

Benjamin's results are often misquoted as being national estimates and national projections, but they were limited to a single strategic business unit of a single firm. An IBM Canada study the previous year,[13] for example, found DP at 75 percent of all use, instead of Benjamin's 60 percent. But many other firms that have looked closely at their own computer use have confirmed that non-DP applications, which Benjamin called end user computing (EUC) have risen in extreme importance in their firms. In 1986, one manager of end user computing, Ronald Brzezinski of Quaker Oats, expressed his company's 1984 analysis of EUC patterns this way:[14]

> A couple of years ago, we went through an assessment of all the money being spent at Quaker's information systems activity. We found that MIS was paying a lot of the bills but managing only 40% of the total dollar figure. . . . It was an eye-opener. So end-user computing had been there for a long time but sort of under covers. Now, it's brought out.

One of the reasons that the waning of data processing, relative to newer applications, has taken so long to be understood is that most information systems departments do not collect data in a way that makes EUC's importance visible.

First, on host computers (mainframes and minicomputers), accounting data is normally oriented toward resources used instead of the type of application performed.

Second, if host statistics are broken down by application, application information is rarely aggregated into an end user computing category for these hosts.

Third, even fewer information systems departments aggregate host EUC data with EUC data from other sources, such as personal computers.

The failure of many firms to understand the importance of end-user computing in their own firms is due to a failure in their own internal strategic information planning systems, not to the actual insignificance of user computing.

End-User Computing

Benjamin established the practice of calling applications beyond data processing "end-user computing", a practice that persists to this day. But end-user computing was originally a narrow application, in which employees outside of the information systems departments did their own work on host computers. In his original set of applications, several characteristics were nearly always present.

First, applications were normally built around data processing. A typical motivation for end-user computing is that end users—the people who ultimately use computers to do functional work such as marketing and finance—could get reports and build small applications quickly, without waiting months or even years for a request to IS to reach the top of the typical corporate backlog of DP applications.

Second, most early EUC applications were small and simple projects built by the ultimate users. This meant that they represented relatively few major control issues, although there was always concern that novice users would mislabel data or base analyses on the wrong data elements.

Third, end users were expected to be extremely self-reliant, that is, to do most or all of their own computer work, with only modest initial consulting, training, and hotline assistance from the central information systems departments.

These three characteristics, especially the second and third, are still viewed as central defining characteristics of end user computing. One end-user computing manager, Arnold Danberg of Transamerica Financial Services, gave the following definition of end-user computing[14]. Many other corporations use similar definitions.

> I would define end-user computing as an environment in which the user has free control and latitude over the process. He may use data that is interchanged through the mainframe of the MIS division, or he may create his own data. But he's in control, he's responsible for the product and the effectiveness of the use of the equipment.

Academicians often concur in defining end-user computing in terms of the second and third characteristics of early end-user computing—small application size and limited support.

The Corporate Response

Corporate interest in end-user computing did not begin in earnest until the PC shock of the early 1980s. A 1981 survey by Ball and Harris[15] could not even find end-user computing among the list of most important issues cited by information systems managers and professionals.

Once personal computers began to flood corporations, however, the situation changed dramatically. A 1983 survey by Dickson, et al.[16] saw end-user computing surge to the second position among the concerns listed by IS managers and professionals. End-user computing had caught management's attention.

IBM had long recommended that corporations establish special departments, called *information centers*, to manage end-user computing. Although different organizations give these units different names, the term "information center" has become the most accepted term, and that is the term we use in this paper. Readers should be cautioned, however, that some corporations reserve the term "information center" for the subunit that manages host-based data and decision support applications. These firms then give the unit that manages all of end user computing a broader name.

By 1985, more than half of all large corporations had already established information centers.[17–21] Today, a large majority of major corporations have information centers in place.

Many of these information centers have now grown beyond personal computers and host-based data and decision support applications, to embrace virtually all applications in Type II departments, including non-clerical office automation (such as electronic mail and personal work station applications), decision support systems (DSS), and executive information systems (EISs). Although only one known organization has specifically called its unit the "Type II Support Department", most firms have moved in this direction organically and have simply a de facto charter for Type II departmental support.

Now that information centers have become widespread and most organizations are coping reasonably well with the PC explosion and other aspects of end-user computing, there seems to be some waning of interest among corporate IS managers. Two recent studies, one in 1985[22] and one in 1986,[23] saw end-user computing and information centers much lower on manager's lists of top concerns. The 1985 survey saw end-user computing in fifth place, the 1986 survey in 12th place. The information center, which was rated as a separate issue, placed 12th in 1985 and 14th in 1986.

Some of this decline can be attributed simply to the success of information centers in dealing with many aspects of end-user computing. As a result of this success, EUC is less of a crisis to upper management than it used to be. But with waning interest, the information center may find itself with a more difficult time convincing IS and corporate management that end-user computing is a strategic issue—perhaps the most strategic issue in IS today—not simply something to be handled with low-level training and to be supported by low-level people in the IS organization.

Making this case will be especially difficult given the information center's small size relative to other IS units. Although EUC is probably larger than data processing in most firms today, only one information center staff member is needed for every 100 to 200 end users. As a result, information center staffs tend to be much smaller than systems analysis, programming, and even data entry operations in the average IS department. Small size tends to lead to low visibility and influence, and this is compounded by the relatively junior status of most information center heads. Unless senior IS management makes a conscious decision to treat end-user computing as one of the most critical strategic decisions facing it today, there is real danger that the information center will remain nothing but a training unit and that end-user computing will not be managed strategically.

In the next section, we will look more closely at end-user computing, including the applications that now seem to fall under the broad banner of end-user computing. In addition, we will look at the high diversity among different types of EUC projects and at the different support and control issues raised in different types of projects. After discussing the diversity that marks end-user computing, we will look at some major strategic alternatives for information centers as they plan their course through the next five years.

DIVERSITY IN END-USER COMPUTING

Diversity among Applications

As discussed earlier, EUC started with applications on corporate host computers, specifically data processing-related applications such as report generation. It also began with small and simple projects that needed only moderate support. Conditions have changed radically since those early days.

Figure 2.1[24] shows the major applications in end-user computing today. This "Computer-Application Matrix" emphasizes that applications tend to cut across PC-host lines. It was once true that certain applications were found almost exclusively on PCs, others almost exclusively on hosts. Today, this is no longer true, and the future will bring ever greater integration between PCs and hosts, blurring many of the remaining distinctions between PC applications and host applications.

In this figure, there are several *generic applications* that are often supported by stand-alone products:

Verbal communication includes all human-to-human communication involving words, including word processing, electronic mail, the telephone, and teleconferencing.

Analysis includes all tools for analyzing information, including pop-up calculators in desk accessories, general-purpose programs for spreadsheet

FIGURE 2.1
COMPUTER-APPLICATION MATRIX

		PC	Host Computer
Generic Applications	Verbal Communication		
	Analysis		
	Data		
	Activity Management		
	Graphics		
Hybrid Applications	Integrated Personal Productivity		
	DSS		
	EIS		
	Nonclerical Office Automation		

analysis, and special-purpose programs for financial analysis, statistics, and operations research.

Data applications include retrieval tools and applications development tools. In some cases, the data involved are corporate data from classical data processing systems. In other cases, they are personal and departmental applications outside of corporate systems.

Activity management applications include everything from personal calendar management and to-do list programs to sophisticated project management applications.

Graphics fall into two categories. *Analytical graphics* is for the presentation of numerical results. *Conceptual graphics* is used to present concepts and their relationships. Figure 2.1 is an example of conceptual graphics.

In addition to these general applications, there are several *hybrid applications* that combine several generic applications.

Integrated personal productivity applications combine such things as word processing, spreadsheet analysis, data management, graphics, activity management and electronic mail into a single integrated system.

Decision support systems (DSSs) are tailored to specific decisions. They combine the analysis, data management, and presentation tools (especially graphics) that are needed to support their specific decisions.[25]

Executive information systems (EISs) are tailored to the information needs of individual executives or small groups with similar information needs. EISs are normally confined primarily to data retrieval, but they are classified as hybrid applications first because they combine data from several sources, including corporate data, external commercial data banks, and even special studies done just for these EISs, and second because they usually have some presentation functions.

Office automation systems combine a rich set of verbal communication tools with such activity management tools as calendar management, to-do lists, and meeting scheduling.

These applications present strong challenges to traditional thinking about end-user computing.

Only some are oriented toward corporate data. In many cases, even projects that use some corporate data use these data only sparingly for part of their needs.

Some projects are fairly complex. DSSs and EISs, for example, often involved technical issues that few end users can handle. And, as we will see a little later, many applications are much larger than the traditional "small project" image that grew up in the early days of EUC.

Some projects are not developed by end users at all, because they are too complex (as in the case of DSSs), because they involve many users, only one of whom does the development, or simply because at least some ultimate users decline to do the work for a variety of reasons.

In other words, end-user computing has become extremely complex since its early days, and corporate planning for end-user computing must reflect this heterogeneity. EUC is no longer dominated by data processing-related activities.

Diversity in EUC Activities

When end-user computing first began, as noted earlier, most problems were small and were developed by the ultimate user. For these types of problems, certain management approaches were desirable, and information centers tried to create appropriate approaches for supporting and controlling these small user-developed projects.

Rockart and Flannery[3] criticized this view, arguing that information systems seemed to be focusing on only two application development *environments*—large projects developed by IS professionals and small user-developed projects. They called the development of large projects by the IS staff the *first environment*, and they referred to the small user-development projects as the *second environment*.

But, Rockart and Flannery argued, these are not the only two possibilities. Specifically, they presented data showing the existence of a *third environment* for project development, in which projects are still user-developed but are much larger than traditional second-environment projects. These larger projects have different management requirements than their smaller second-environment cousins, but few information centers seem to be developing specific management programs for large third-environment projects.

The author extended the environments model, as shown in Figure 2.2.[24]

FIGURE 2.2
PROJECT DEVELOPMENT ENVIRONMENTS

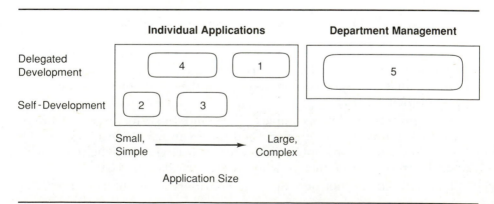

First, a fourth environment was proposed, in which development was not done by the ultimate user but was done by a third party. It could be argued that this is either not end-user computing or represents pathological behaviour on the part of the delegators, but there is strong evidence that delegation exists in EUC and is important.[3,26,27] There is also theoretical work on the importance of delegation and nonuse in the marketing literature[28,29] when use of a product is discretionary, as is usually the case in end-user computing. More pragmatically, delegated development raises different management issues than do either the second or third environments, because now the complexities of eliciting requirements comes into play. Eliciting requirements is even difficult for information systems professionals. For end users who develop systems for other end users, it is probably more difficult.

The first four environments shown in Figure 2.2 involve the development of individual applications. But the fifth environment needing a specific management program is the management of departments. Given current levels of computer use, nearly every manager now manages a department that is at least partially computerized, and partially computerized departments are probably more difficult to manage than fully computerized departments. Yet few firms give specific training in how to manage a computerized department or specify the roles of various department members, including the manager, secretaries, and professionals.

For each environment, the information center must develop a tailored *management mix* consisting of four components:[24]

Technological infrastructure development, including hardware, system software, application software, and communications. Users should be supplied with ready-to-use systems if possible, or clear standards for making selections if ready-to-use systems are not available.

Support in the forms of consulting, training, hotline assistance and other activities while the project is being developed.

Control in the form of rules and procedures for ensuring the proper development of applications and the protection of superpersonal interests in the department or the corporation as a whole.

Promotion to encourage not just the amount of EUC being done but also the identification and development of important projects that really need to be done but may not be done without strong prodding or even direct development by the information center.

Small User-Developed Activities (The Second Environment)

Many user-developed activities are still small in size and low in complexity. These include small spreadsheet models, word processing document creation, and similar small projects.

Many of these simple applications are developed by inexperienced users, so providing a ready-to-use technological infrastructure is very important. If a PC is used, it is good to have it assembled and tested by the information center, its application software installed on boot disks, and perhaps even a menu-driven front end added to it, to make the user's initial experiences easier.

Support should involve some initial consultation, to help users clarify their thinking about their application and what they need it to do for them. Then, good training should be provided, for the computer, its operating system, its application software, and the proper way to develop applications with the software (for example, good modeling practice in spreadsheet analysis). Finally, hotline assistance should be provided if users get into trouble. This prescription for support is given by almost every information center manager and article.

Control for small projects is a difficult topic, because extensive auditing is not likely to be achievable in practice, given the thinly stretched resources of most information centers today. Policies requiring self-testing and sections on good practice in the initial training are often used to try to build a general atmosphere of responsibility.

Larger User-Developed Applications (The Third Environment)

When Rockart and Flannery[3] studied users of host-based end-user computing, they found that a large percentage of projects were quite large, falling somewhere between central operational systems such as accounting systems and the traditional "small project" image of end-user computing projects. To keep things in perspective, their sample was highly biased toward such applications, so the specific percentages of large applications in their sample were very misleading. In addition, when Quillard et al.[30] looked at personal computing later, they did not find a high percentage of large projects. At the same time, large projects are very important when they do exist and are probably sufficiently commonplace to require both scholarly research and practical management approaches.

Because almost no empirical research has been done on large end-user developed applications, any discussion of the appropriate management mix must be purely speculative at this point, but certain issues can be identified as potentially important.

> Do the user-developers of those large applications need special application software that is more sophisticated than that needed by ordinary users?
>
> Do they have special needs for consulting in the initial development phase, for training in technical skills and development skills, and for general hotline assistance? When should the information center be willing to do small subtasks that are likely to be beyond the end user?
>
> Do they make certain design and development errors with any predictability, and how can these errors be avoided?
>
> How can projects be controlled to ensure timeliness, efficiency, correct-

ness, maintainability, and the other attributes needed in important applications of any kind in business? Is auditing an important tool, or can training and rules be sufficient?

If these applications are important to the firm and will not be done unless a user develops them, how can the information center promote the development of key applications by end users?

Delegated Development (The Fourth Environment)

In delegated development, someone other than the ultimate user develops the application. There are at least three major conditions under which delegated development occurs.

The project is a multiuser application, in which one person does the development for several others.

The project is beyond the capabilities of the ultimate user.

The ultimate user declines to do the development.

Although little empirical research has been done on any of these three forms of delegated development, we can again identify some potential research areas and practical concerns.

For multiuser projects, size is likely to be fairly large, so the general problems of large projects are likely to apply. In addition, two other issues are likely to be important.

How can the user-developer acquire the skills needed to elicit the requirements of the group—skills that are even difficult to teach to experienced IS professionals?

How can operational roles be assigned after development? Who will handle extensions to the development, who will be responsible for data integrity, who will handle data entry, and who will be responsible if the initial developer leaves the department?

Other issues appear for projects that should be done but lie outside the development skills of end users. In many organizations, there is a clear set of rules for developing data processing applications, but there is no way, other than end-user development, to create complex financial analysis models or other important applications that may be too difficult for end-user developers. The extent to which such important projects exist and are not being implemented despite their value is unknown, but if they are commonplace, then IS in general may be missing very important needs in the firm simply because these needs fall outside of the two realms of data processing applications and user-developable applications.

We need to know the prevalence of such applications.

We need to understand under what conditions the information center staff or some other IS groups should do the development or allow the affected department to contract out for development.

We need to know what needs analysis implications are raised in complex projects that are not data processing projects.

The third category of delegated development efforts comes when users use discretion to decline to do their own development and instead elect to delegate it to someone else. Information centers were initially established with the No Programming Dogma that prohibited delegation to the information center, because delegation for reasons of user preference would simply increase the backlog that was already excessive.[31]

But the convenience of the information systems department is not the only corporate consideration.

If users have one-time needs, is it fair to require them to learn how to use a complex hardware/software system?

Is it even fair if they are intermittent users who will have forgotten most of what they learned initially and will need retraining?

Also, what if they are regular users but have a one-time need to do some advanced development that would take long to learn how to do?

Under such conditions, the goal of *overall* corporate efficiency may require that delegation be done. Otherwise, the development effort may use excessive resources in other departments. At a minimum, the trade-offs between using information center resources or the resources of other departments should be faced explicitly.

In addition, refusing to do development within the information center may be killing important applications that need to be done but cannot be done by end users for lack of skills, as discussed earlier. While most firms are willing to build large data processing applications for which users lack the required skills, few firms have clear procedures for handling complex applications that fall outside of data processing, for example, the development of a complex financial planning model. Building these strategic applications for the firm may be critically important, and leaving them to end users on the grounds that they are not data processing would seem to be short-sighted.

Another basic set of issues in delegation is the breadth of managerial discretion in doing their jobs. In organizations that use management by objectives (MBO) or other results-oriented management evaluation approaches, it is not consistent with accountability to control how a manager may spend his or her budget. MBO implies high discretion, and when use of consumer products is discretionary,[28,29] there are always degrees of use and either nonuse or delegation. Delegation has been found in discretionary information systems products as well.[3,26,27] Again, there may be a basic conflict between IS goals and corporate goals. While user self-sufficiency is an important IS goal and is also an important general corporate goal, it must be balanced against the discretion that knowledge workers must have over what work they will do themselves and what work they will delegate.

Departmental Management (The Fifth Environment)

As noted at the start of the paper, more than half of all office workers now use computers. Yet few researchers or corporations seem to have thought clearly about the problems of departmental management. The author could find no empirical papers in this area, and even comments in the popular press were rare and embryonic.

Computerization means that new roles must be developed for a variety of planning, implementation, and operational needs.

> For planning the departmental technological infrastructure, the departmental manager must take the lead, but power users, ordinary users, and secretaries must have important inputs; it is also important that individuals, such as power users, do not dominate the process.

> Given limited resources, the departmental management must decide what applications should be implemented, including those that are needed but will not be developed spontaneously by users within the department.

> Project implementations must be managed to ensure that they comply with corporate standards. The departmental manager must ensure that good practice is being implemented.

> For simple technical tasks, power users are valuable but can be overloaded if care is not take to make secretaries and other support personnel competent to handle delegated work.

> Important departmental data and documents must be identified, as must important departmental models. Plans mus be made and executed to protect them from accidental damage, security violations, and loss of usefulness when key people leave must be put into place.

All of these roles need clarification at the corporate level, or different departments will implement them in ways that may or may not be appropriate. In addition, although training is given to individual users and power users, it seems to be less common to have training programs for managers of departments and to have training for secretaries that clarifies their roles and is based on new job assessments.

In general, departmental management in the end-user computing age is a major virgin territory for research. The pressing problems and traditional nature of individual applications has allowed attention to be diverted from this important problem for too long.

CONCLUSION

The major theme of this paper is that end-user computing is not only a very large "market" for information systems to serve. It is also an extremely complex market that cannot be attacked by any single strategy.

The use of the term *market* is deliberate. In business, managers are trained to consider the needs of their customers—their market—before considering technology or products. As information systems move toward being a "business within a business", it must develop this kind of business understanding of its customers.

Marketing thinking is based on two key concepts. The first is that services must be driven by data on user needs. This means that a great deal of research must be done on what services and tools are needed in Type II managerial and professional departments. We do not even have really solid demographic information, much less good information on what people do. For example, we do not even know how extensively people use corporate data when they do end-user computing. Overall, a great deal of both basic and targeted research needs to be done.

The second key concept of marketing is *segmentation*. Any large market is almost invariably a conglomeration of small market segments that each have specific needs and those needs are different from those of other segments. These segments must be identified, and a "marketing mix" consisting of product, price, promotion, and distribution must be developed for each segment. This paper has discussed possible ways of segmenting the EUC market, as well as proposing four parts to the *management mix* of end user computing, but the methods discussed are intuitive and not empirical. Empirical research may give entirely different results.

What we do know from marketing is that product dimensions rarely serve as good ways to understand markets. Just as Detroit lost ground when it tried to conceptualize the automobile market in terms of car sizes and styles instead of consumer aspirations and life styles, information center managers must not think in terms of PCs versus hosts or analysis programs versus word processing programs. Segmentation can be done in many ways, but it must always be done according to data on user work patterns and preference, rather than product distinctions.

End-user computing's very diversity and size raises new research issues, as well as planning problems for information systems management. EUC is so much more diverse than DP that the casual non-empirical way that IS departments have attacked IS planning in the past must give way to a more data oriented approach, just as general corporate planning must be more rational and data-oriented when corporations enter more complex markets.

REFERENCES

1. International Data Corporation (April 4, 1986), cited in "The Paper Blizzard", *USA Today*, p. 1.

2. *Computerworld* (March 25, 1985), pp. 1,4, "Shared Micros Commonplace".

3. Rockart, John F., and Lauren S. Flannery (October 1983), "The Management of End User Computing", *Communications of the ACM, Association for Computing Machinery*, pp. 776–784.

4. Panko, Raymond R. (September 1984), "Office Work", *Office: Technology and People*, Elsevier Science Publishers B.V., Amsterdam, pp. 205–238.

5. Panko, Raymond R. (January 1987b), "The Demographics of Office Work", Working Paper 87-1, Department of Decision Sciences, College of Business Administration, University of Hawaii, Honolulu.

6. Booz-Allen and Hamilton, Inc. (June 1980), *Booz-Allen Study of Managerial/Professional Productivity*.

7. Mintzberg, Henry (1971), "Managerial Work: Analysis from Observation", *Management Science*, Vol. 18, No. 2, pp. B97–B110.

8. Carlson, Sune (1951), *Executive Behaviour: A Study of the Workload and Working Methods of Managing Directors*, Stockholm.

9. Teger, Sandra L. (1983), "Factors Impacting the Evaluation of Office Automation", *Proceedings of the IEEE*, Vol. 71, No. 4, pp. 503–511.

10. Engel, G. H., J. Groppusa, R. A. Lowenstein, and W. G. Traub (1979), "An Office Communication System", *IBM Systems Journal*, Vol. 18, No. 3, pp. 402–431.

11. Panko, Raymond R., and Ralph H. Sprague (June 1982), "Toward a New Framework for Office Support", *Proceedings of the 1982 Conference on Office Information Systems*, Philadelphia, Association for Computing Machinery.

12. Benjamin, Robert I. (June 1982), "Information Technology in the 1990s: A Long Range Planning Scenario", *MIS Quarterly*, pp. 11–31.

13. (June 1981), "Supporting End User Programing", *EDP Analyzer* Canning Publications, Inc., Vista, CA.

14. *Computerworld* (August 18, 1986), pp. 41–55, "End-User Computing: MIS Answers the Call".

15. Ball, Leslie, and Richard Harris (March 1982), "SMIS Members: a Member Analysis", *MIS Quarterly*, pp. 19–38.

16. Dickson, Gary W., Robert L. Leitheiser, James C. Wetherbe, and M. Nechis (Sept. 1984), "Key Information Systems Issues for the 1980's", *MIS Quarterly*, pp. 135–147.

17. American Management Association (1985), *1985 AMA Report on Information Centers*, New York, cited in Crwth Computer Coursewares, "The Second Crwth Information Center Survey", *Crwth News for Better Training*, Vol. 3, No. 1, 1985.

18. Crwth Computer Coursewares (1985), "The Second Crwth Information Center Survey", *Crwth News for Better Training*, Vol. 3, No. 1.

19. The Diebold Group (1985), "Survey of MIS Budgets", New York, cited in Crwth Computer Coursewares, "The Second Crwth Information Center Survey", *Crwth News for Better Training*, Vol. 3, No. 1.

20. Guimares, Tor (July 15, 1984), "The Evolution of the Information Center", *DATAMATION*, pp. 127–130.

21. Melymuka, Kathleen (December 3, 1985), "The Information Center", *PC Week*, pp. 77–79.

22. Hartog, Curt, and Martin Herbert (December 1986), "1985 Opinion Survey of MIS Managers: Key Issues", *MIS Quarterly*, pp. 351–361.

23. Herbert, Martin, and Curt Hartog (November 1986), "MIS Rates the Issues", *DATAMATION*, pp. 79–86.

24. Panko, Raymond R. (1987), *End User Computing*, John Wiley & Sons.

25. Sprague, Ralph H. Jr. (December 1980), "A Framework for the Development of Decision Support Systems", *Management Information Systems Quarterly*, Vol 4, pp. 1–26.

26. Panko, Raymond R., and Rosemarie U. Panko (May 1981), "A Survey of EMS Users at DARCOM", *Computer Networks*, Vol. 5, No. 3, Elsevier Scientific Publishers, Amsterdam, pp. 19–34.

27. Culnan, Mary J. (March 1983), "Chauffeured Versus End User Access to Commercial Databases: The Effect of Task and Individual Differences", *MIS Quarterly*, pp. 55–67.

28. Twedt, Dik Warren (January 1964), "How Important to Marketing Strategy is the 'Heavy User'?", *Journal of Marketing*, Vol. 28, pp. 71–72.

29. Ehrenberg, A.S.C. (1972), *Repeat Buying: Theory and Applications*, North-Holland Publishing Company, Amsterdam, and American Elsevier, New York.

30. Quillard, Judith A., John F. Rockart, Eric Wilde, Mark Vernon, and George Mock (December 1983), "A Study of the Corporate Use of Personal Computers", CISR Working Paper No. 109, Center for Information Systems Research, Massachusetts Institute of Technology, Sloan School of Management, 77 Massachusetts Avenue, Cambridge, MA.

31. Alloway, Robert M., and Judith A. Quillard (June 1983), "User Managers' Systems Needs", *MIS Quarterly*, pp. 27–42.

QUESTIONS

1. Discuss the rise of end-user computing (How, when, and where did EUC begin?).

2. What impact has EUC had on the Type I versus Type II office?

3. Respond to (i.e., take a position and discuss) the following statement: "By 1990, DP will shrink to a mere 25% of all CPU cycles."

4. (a) Describe several *generic applications* that are often supported by stand-alone products.

   (b) Describe several *hybrid applications* that combine several generic applications.

5. In reference to the widespread diversity in EUC activities, describe five different environments surrounding EUC development efforts. For each environment, what managerial issues must be considered?

6. How might the principles of marketing be applied to end-user computing?

3

A Field Study of End-User Computing: Findings and Issues

■

David H. Benson

INTRODUCTION

The growth of end-user computing is one of the significant phenomena of the 1980s in the information management world. A recent study by the International Data Corporation predicted that four out of five administrative and professional workers will be using personal computing to support their work and personal activities by 1990.[1] In a study published in 1981, Rockart and Flannery referred to estimates that while current end-user computing consumed about ten percent of computer capacity in large corporations, such use would grow to consume seventy percent of an expanded capacity by the end of the decade.[2] *Business Week*, in November 1982, predicted that 26 million executives, professionals, and hobbyists would own microcomputers by 1985. In the same article, *Business Week* quotes an estimate from Dataquest, Inc. that the training industry will capture $3 billion of the $14 billion spent on personal computers by 1986.[3]

But what is actually happening in the world of end-user computing? Will its growth be as explosive as the predictions? Rockart and Flannery see lessons from the Gibson-Nolan stage theory[4] in the management of end user computing. They warn that while most companies are still (1981) in the "initiation" or early "contagion" stages of the curve, the most adverse

Reprinted by special permission of the MIS Quarterly, *Volume 7, Number 4, December 1983. Copyright 1983 by the Society for Information Management and the Management Information Systems Research Center at the University of Minnesota.*

effects of the "control" stage may ensue unless significant attention is paid to managing end-user computing.[2]

In the fall of 1982 the Center for the Study of Data Processing at Washington University in St. Louis, encouraged by its Corporate Affiliates, began a research project to examine the state and direction of end-user computing in the St. Louis corporate environment. The goal of the project was to gather information and gain perspective for planning educational programs for end users, and developing strategies for the management of end-user computing. With the growing demand for computing capabilities, input was needed directly from the managers who were either already involved in interactive computing or planning for such capability.

This article reports on a series of interviews carried out between December 1982 and March 1983 with managers and professionals in twenty locations. It attempts to describe the varieties of interactive computer use in this area by persons who are using either timesharing computer services, internal and external, or microcomputer facilities. It attempts to assess the growth patterns and amount of end-user computing, and to describe what corporate policy exists in the various settings. End-user education is also explored. Finally, the report defines certain critical issues that the phenomenon of end-user computing raises in the corporate setting.

Research approach

Because CENTER Affiliates provide contact with a wide variety of corporate and institutional settings, end users were reached through them. The Affiliates are the EDP (IS) departments of over thirty corporate and government bodies in the St. Louis area. Initial interviews were held with IS directors or their designees in eighteen of the affiliated organizations and one nonaffiliated corporation.

The interviews with EDP managers were to clarify the purposes of the study, obtain their cooperation in contacting end users, and obtain information concerning the corporate experience with end users. They were specifically asked for information regarding resources and support for end using and policy regarding the acquisition and use of microcomputers. The interviews were relatively unstructured and open-ended.

As a result of interviews with IS managers, 66 interviews with end-user managers and professionals were carried out in nineteen locations. Anywhere from two to six end users were interviewed per location. One additional end-user interview at a smaller company resulted from a contact made through an affiliated computer service organization.

Again, interviews were open-ended and relatively unstructured. However, in all cases these questions were asked: (1) Why did they begin to use computers interactively? (2) What training in the use of computers had they received or sought, if any? (3) What computer resources did they use, i.e., what hardware, what software? (4) What applications had they developed with the computer? (5) What direction did they see for interactive computing in their own setting or in their corporation? (6) What training or resources did they need to more effectively use the computer and what could a university setting appropriately provide to assist management in making effective use of computing?

While no random sampling techniques were used in the selection of those interviewed, the wide variety of settings and the broad spectrum of management levels and functional areas would seem to represent a fair sample of end users for this geographical area, if not the nation. A built-in bias must be recognized in that the access to end users was obtained through IS management. But, since the end users expressed a complete spectrum of attitudes toward traditional data processing, even this bias would not seem to threaten the validity of the sample.

DESCRIPTION OF THE END USERS INTERVIEWED

End users were interviewed in twenty locations. Eleven locations were manufacturing corporations among the Fortune 1,000. Other locations included three banks and financial organizations, two insurance companies, and one each retail merchandising, mining, transportation, and government operations. All but one organization have large management populations.

Table 3.1 gives the departmental distribution of the end users interviewed. As can be seen, twenty-seven, or fully forty percent, were from financial and accounting departments.

It is difficult to describe the organizational levels of those interviewed. Corporate job titles vary a great deal from one setting to another, and organization charts are not readily accessible. However, a rather subjective listing is attempted here, using a mixture of titles, location, size of office, and the intuition of experience. End users are divided into four classifications: top management, i.e., executive and senior vice president or corporate controller; upper-management, i.e., vice president or director of corporate manufactur-

TABLE 3.1
DEPARTMENTAL DISTRIBUTION OF 67 END USERS

Department	Number	Department	Number
Finance and Accounting	27	Auditing	1
Administration	7	Government Affairs	1
Planning and Forecasting	6	Legal	1
Personnel	5	Management Training	1
Manufacturing	5	Medical Examiner	1
Customer Service	5	Pricing	1
Research and Development	2	Tax	1
Actuarial Services	2		

ing; middle management, i.e., senior analyst, assistant vice president, assistant director, or manager of compensation; and lower management, i.e., accountants or entry level managers (see Table 3.2).

End users are also divided by the type of computing facility they use in Table 3.2. As can be seen, more microcomputer users were interviewed than mainframe users. This would indicate the current interest in microcomputers rather than the relative number of such users.

FINDINGS

History and Growth Patterns

End-user computing is in its infancy for any other than scientific or engineering applications. Between 1977 and 1980, five of the twenty companies installed some support for end using, including software and some file space. This support included such query and report writing software as GIS, RPG, and Mark IV, and such high-level programing languages as EASYTRIEVE and APL. Since 1980 seven other companies have installed, or are in the process of installing, end-user support. Most of these installations are high-level programming languages such as FOCUS, RAMIS, ADRS, and EXPRESS, and modeling packages such as IFPS.

Resource use has often been sporadic and isolated to date. In one company which has had end-user software for six years, there were only forty to fifty known users. In another company which installed IFPS last year, only five people were using it after six months. Nevertheless, the signs of overall rapid growth were in evidence. One IS department had instituted end-user training on a charge-out basis. There was a long waiting list for end-user training, which had actually become a profit center for the department. Another company installed FOCUS in early 1982 on a dedicated CPU and began to charge back its use directly to end users. Their monthly chargeback grew from $3,000 in July to $48,000 in November. A third company which

TABLE 3.2
MANAGEMENT LEVEL AND COMPUTING FACILITY USE OF THOSE INTERVIEWED

Management Level	Mainframe	Microcomputer	Both	Level Total
Top	4	3	0	7
Upper	3	8	2	13
Middle	14	20	2	36
Lower	7	3	1	11
Total	28	34	5	67

planned to train around 500 end users on RAMIS in 1982, had to train 1,200 and expects to train another 1,500 in 1983. Another very large corporation had twenty percent of its computer capacity in interactive use in 1978, almost exclusively for engineering and scientific applications. The corporation now projects that seventy percent of an expanded capacity will be interactive by 1985, mostly because of business end user growth.

In the midst of this process of mainframe software becoming accessible to end users, the microcomputer began to appear in the business office. Its advent and dispersion are as hard to trace as its use and acquisition are difficult, if not impossible, to control.

Personally owned microcomputers can be carried into the office and plugged into the wall socket. Some are acquired as "office equipment." In one case, a group of managers, tired of trying to manually perform an analysis, simply called a computer store and had an Apple II delivered by taxicab. "We got into some trouble for it, but it was here," they explained. After one MIS director stated confidently that no computer could be purchased without his approval and that he was approving none, four Apples were found in his company's trust department by this researcher. Another manager said that he knew of no microcomputers in his building. Down the hall in another office, a TRS-80 was visible on the desk. Because of this situation, dates and numbers given in this report are estimates provided mostly by MIS management.

Three companies acquired their first known microcomputers in 1980. Since then, twelve other companies have allowed or approved their use. Five other locations are still tacitly or explicitly trying to exclude microcomputers. One MIS director claimed there was simply no demand for them. Of the three companies that approved their first microcomputers in 1980, one still had only two in 1983, one had around forty, and one had over 100. Of four companies where MIS either placed or encouraged the use of microcomputers in 1982, three still had fewer than ten in 1983 and one had more than 100. Two of the former, however, planned significant additions of micros this year. The present status of microcomputers in the companies studied is listed in Table 3.3.

TABLE 3.3
NUMBER OF MICROCOMPUTERS
PER ORGANIZATION (JAN-MAR 1983)

Micros	Organizations
1	2
2-9	6
10-99	4
100-200	2
Over 200	1

The IBM Personal Computer (PC) has quickly become the dominant microcomputer hardware in the businesses studied. Of 34 personal computer users all but three were using three brands. Fifteen had IBM PCs, nine had Apples, six had TRS-80s, and one had both an IBM PC and an Apple. In all fifteen companies where microcomputers were allowed, the IBM PC was either the only personal computer or was one of those approved for use. This was not true of any other brand.

Applications

Managers have generally become direct users of computer technology in one of two ways. One way has been based on their need to capture, inquire of, and retrieve specific kinds of information relating to their jobs. The second way has grown from a need to analyze data and develop projections, models, and various kinds of "what if" procedures.

Data capture applications grew out of a general frustration with DP production reports and growing requests to the IS department for specific information. At most sites studied, this led to the installation of such inquiry languages and report generators as EASYTRIEVE, GIS, and RPG in the late 1970s or even early 1980s. However, the recent installations have tended to be more powerful and more user-friendly products, such as FOCUS and RAMIS. Examples of these applications include developing earning reports for corporate board meetings, tracking mortgages, cost reporting for specific cost centers, and tracking specific medical claims.

Simultaneously demands for computer power to perform analytical tasks grew, especially from financial analysts and planning departments. In response, software such as SAS and IFPS was installed in about half of the companies studied. In some companies, certain enterprising, computer literate analysts and planners have been able to develop models using such software as GIS and EASYTRIEVE. Examples of this kind of application are corporate budgets, financial forecasts, development of long-range plans, and the building of acquisition models.

The introduction of microcomputers was triggered primarily by these same application needs. But a striking contrast was found between applications initially used by microcomputer users compared to mainframe users. This contrast is demonstrated in the comparative figures shown in Table 3.4. It is clear that analytical applications drove the introduction of microcomputers.

The heavy proportion of end users in finance and accounting mentioned above might explain, in part, the heavy emphasis on analytical use of computer technology. It may also indicate the area of business management which takes most easily to the use of that technology.

It is interesting to note the domination of one piece of software—VISICALC. Twenty of 34 micro users employed VISICALC either primarily or exclusively. Eight others used it at least occasionally. Although nineteen

TABLE 3.4
INITIAL APPLICATION
BY PERCENTAGE OF TOTAL

	Mainframe	Microcomputer
Data Capture	60	29
Analysis	29	61
Word Processing	2	1
Graphics	2	4
Electronic Mail	5	0
Training	2	4

other software packages were in use, only DBase II with five users had significant spread. A mere seven of the 34 were hard-core programmers who did their own programming in BASIC, PASCAL, or FORTRAN.

The majority of end users developed further applications as they became more familiar with the technology. This is especially true of microcomputer users, probably because they have instant access to and total use of their hardware without adding measurably to costs. In total separate applications, those using microcomputers had almost twice the applications of mainframe users (97–51).

Although most microcomputer users began with analytical applications they quickly developed enough data files to make questions of data retrieval and file management urgent. A horror story example of this would be an inventory application which in two years expanded to 67 floppy disks. Six companies have gone to the use of hard disks for data storage as files have expanded, often using floppy disks as backups.

When microcomputer users get over the first euphoria from the power of their machine they often begin to chafe at the drudgery of data input. Their thoughts turn to the databases of the corporation and they begin to wonder how they can access those databases to unload the data they want directly into their microcomputer. But most of the companies so far have strict policies against this or are unsure of their technical capacity to do it. Only five managers had any direct access to corporate data through their microcomputer.

Microcomputer Cost Justification

Micro users are often required to demonstrate that a potential acquisition will pay back the company. This can be very difficult to do. A number of acquisitions have been justified on the basis that development costs, including hardware, were less than software development costs for the mainframe.

But most acquisitions have been justified in application and some of the payoffs have ultimately been rather dramatic. In one instance, the initial application was to develop an annual profit plan. With Apple and VISICALC, the development time was cut from three weeks to three days, and the parent company, feeling that the computer had already paid for itself, installed Apples in all its other profit centers. Similarly, six people used to work one month to develop a quarterly, manual, manpower accounting report. With a personal computer, one input operator now produces weekly reports. At another company, a five-year plan which cost $15,000 annually from a time-sharing service was converted to a TRS-80 for a one-time capital expense of less than $5,000. In a different case, use of an IBM PC, with access to economic reporting services, has cut outside computer services from $40,000 to $15,000 annually.

Perceived Problems

Stated worries of IS professionals concerning microcomputer documentation, data backup, and security were well founded. To most personal computer users, "documentation" was an unknown word. A few exceptional managers with some significant computer background have tried to document their programs. Some end users maintained that their programs did not need documentation since, with the software, they could be reconstructed in a very short time. Several, however, admitted that if they left the firm their applications would go with them as no one else could understand or maintain them. In any case, such things as data dictionaries and program libraries are almost unknown in the world of microcomputers as this study found it.

The use of backup disks usually begins after some accidental loss of a whole program, or a disk full of files. As to data security, disks are commonly kept at random in desk drawers, or in a file box next to the computer.

IS managers also fear that end users might become essentially programmers and thus sidetracked from their major career paths, without the credentials or desire to pursue a career in a computing specialty. One company, which was conducting its own survey of end users, had identified over twenty managers who had become essentially programmers (spending over 50% of their time in programming tasks). In the present study, such persons were the exception. There were only six documented cases of what might be called "amateur programmers," and only one of these was a microcomputer user.

The norm seems to be end users developing or using applications as tools for their own jobs. Even so, some managers using computers are concerned about its effect on their careers. One top manager stated, "Using a computer is essentially a clerical function. Executives and managers should tell their support people what they want from the computer." Many interviewees believed this to be a typical attitude in top management. Thus it is not surprising that some of the early end users in management are nervous. Some typical comments are: "Young managers don't want others to know they can use the computer." "I enjoy it, but I worry about what it will do to my career." "I don't want to become computer identified. It might lock me in a staff position." "If information is power, it hasn't worked yet." If these comments are indeed typical of the concerns of end users and if top management is indeed suspicious of computing as managerial behavior, the growth of end user computing might be slower than expected.

Support and Training

There was a general lack of a coherent policy concerning microcomputer use. Only eight of the twenty organizations studied had any stated policy about it. Three of these called for the MIS director's approval on all purchases (one of these, as mentioned above, has yet to approve any). Six policy statements provided a list of approved or preferred vendors. In no case did these exclude the purchase of hardware from nonapproved vendors. The policy statements were intended to establish consistency through discounts and vaguely worded promises of technical support. One MIS manager described technical support, "We will help them unpack it from the box, find the component connectors and show them where to plug it in the wall."

Twelve companies had some form of information center, but only two of these centers planned to support microcomputer users. In most cases the MIS departments had neither the manpower nor the resources to supply such support. A number of MIS departments did provide informal consultation and support. Usually one person in MIS took on this consultative role through personal interest or as a part of a much larger set of responsibilities.

Much more significant support was in place for end users of mainframe resources. The twelve companies that had information centers provided training, information, and consulting on data access, and in some cases, provided programming help for end user applications. Four companies had CPUs dedicated to end-user computing and three companies provided reserved disk space to registered end users. These information centers ranged from two-person consulting groups operating out of a data processing environment to full-fledged departments or support groups within distributed data processing centers.

One reason for inconsistent levels of support and unclear policy is that top management tends to be ignorant or indifferent about end-user development. As one MIS director said, "Top management is non-activist or anti-activist. The CEO is simply allowing end-user growth." Or, to quote another, "We are playing leap frog on a bottom-up movement. What we need is a top-down strategy." One CEO has simply put a hold on all resource expansion. No computer resource may be acquired without his express approval, and right now he is approving nothing. In this environment of top management indifference or even hostility, the MIS function finds itself under extreme, and sometimes impossible, pressure to cope. MIS managers have often attempted to provide support and reasonable control in a situation where they have neither resources nor authority to respond to growing pressure from end users.

Two significant exceptions to this general picture of top management

abdication were discovered. In one case, concerned MIS management organized a colloquium for top management with a national expert on end-user
computing. This resulted in an full study and a top-down strategy for end-
user management, now being put in place. The other exception was the
upshot of one CEO buying his own microcomputer. Convinced that his managers must become computer literate, he installed terminals in the offices
of his twelve senior vice presidents as an electronic mail network. Within six
months the network expanded to include all general managers and staff directors on an 800-terminal, vertically integrated network in three departments.
His support also led to the introduction of nearly 300 microcomputers in
1982.

Table 3.5 describes the training the end users have received. It demonstrates another contrast between mainframe and microcomputer users. The
general pattern for micro users has been to use software manuals to learn the
rudiments of an application package and then to proceed by trial and error.

Since almost none of the companies provide any training support for
microcomputers, these figures are not surprising. However, several questions
might be raised. If trial and error is not the most efficient means of learning
and if such issues as data security, back-up, and data integrity are important,
will not some training need to be put in place? If the information centers
will not, or cannot, offer such training, should the company seek outside
resources to provide it?

EDUCATION FOR END USERS

In each interview the end user was specifically asked what additional education he needed or wanted, and what education he felt was needed by company managers to make better use of computer technology. All but six had at
least one suggestion. A number of those interviewed could think only of the
learning needs of others. But a significant number of them expressed interest in further training for themselves, usually with the proviso that it would
not be too demanding on their time and that it would be financed by their
employer.

TABLE 3.5
TRAINING OF END USERS
BY PERCENTAGE

	Mainframe	Microcomputer
Self Trained	33	71
College Trained	24	18
Company Trained	29	0
Vendor Trained	9	4
DP Experience	5	7

Table 3.6 summarizes the responses. An attempt has been made to group them, yet be faithful to the specific suggestions offered. Education needs are categorized as advanced programs for the end users themselves and as those they felt were needed by others in the company.

The request for programming and systems analysis was generally *not* a request for highly technical training, though there was individual interest in such subjects as CMS, SAS, APL, and Assembler. Most of the requests dealt with general knowledge, such as how best to understand and organize a setting or a problem in order to deal most effectively with it through computer technology, or to develop a general understanding of programming skills rather than training in a particular language.

Microcomputer users were particularly interested in software orientation and data communication. In software they wanted to know what was available in specific applications, how to evaluate software and how to make software, and hardware, acquisitions without being at the mercy of vendors. Their interest in communications centered around technology and problems associated with linking stand-alone computers and related hardware.

Database management was the concern of both micro and mainframe users. In large part this was related to corporate database access and use.

In regard to training for others, introduction to computing was seen as covering a basic knowledge of computer technology, its capabilities and limitations. Some felt it should include orientation to structured thinking, or as one person said, "thinking in steps rather than using the 'big picture'." Most thought hands-on experience was essential and a few stressed instructions on controls and documentation.

It is interesting to note that six of the seven top managers interviewed named upper management training as a primary need. In addition to many

TABLE 3.6
SUGGESTIONS FOR END USER EDUCATION
(NUMBER OF MENTIONS IN PARENTHESES)

I. Advanced Programs for Present End Users
    A. Advanced programming and/or systems analysis (27)
    B. Software orientation (19)
    C. File management and database technology (12)
    D. Data communications (4)
    E. Update on technology (3)
    F. Computer graphics (1)
    G. Software conversions (1)

II. Computer Education for Managers and Professionals
    A. Introduction to computing (30)
    B. Computer training for upper management (23)
    C. Statistical education for use of analytical computer tools (4)
    D. Training IS professionals as trainers (3)

of the themes mentioned in introduction to computing such things as the management of, and planning for, technological change, and the use of computer technology as a tool for strategic planning were deemed crucial for upper management training.

CRITICAL ISSUES

Five closely related issues in the development of end-user computing, were mentioned again and again by those interviewed.

Security and Integrity

When a data processing department did all the managing of computing, though the security and integrity of data captured or reported might be questioned, the responsibility for it was clear. With the development of database management technology, computer professionals felt they were getting good control of this issue. But now, with the growth of end-user computing, a proliferation of databases threatens to bring new chaos to corporate information channels.

A number of managers interviewed are making reports "up the line" from data which they have developed and for which they are responsible. There have already been instances of conflicting reports using differing data sources or common sources with different results. If such confusion grows, it will almost surely bring new controls. But will the new controls cut off or cut back the growth of computing as a management tool, or will they provide means for establishing dependable data? And where will these controls reside? Can a centralized IS carry out the management of all the databases in an end-using environment?

Database Access for Microcomputers

Some IS managers are convinced that to provide access to corporate databases for micro users will lead to total chaos. Others believe that all microcomputer users should have access to corporate data to insure that the data they use is accurate. Microcomputer users themselves are ambivalent. While they would relish the time saving advantages of being able to download corporate data, they also like the total control they have over their own computer environment. The facts also point in two directions. While data directly entered from the corporate database will unquestionably be less error prone than data keyed in at the micro keyboard, many of the applications presently carried out on microcomputers use information not presently in the corporate database. And that is likely to continue to be true because the information is so local in nature that it is not cost-effective to centralize it. Otherwise, it is information so far down the system priority list it will be years before it is developed by a central IS facility.

Solutions to this issue may grow from clear definitions of what data is "private," specific to the individual work of the end user or the department, and what data is "corporate," of general importance for most of the corporation. Installation of intelligent terminals which can work both ways may be one solution. Microcomputer networks to facilitate management controls and shared applications and data in a limited part of the corporation may be another. Neither solution is currently much in evidence.

Education

A number of companies studied provide significant training to mainframe users. But this training is centered on learning to use certain software, and to a lesser degree, on accessing corporate data. Even locally controlled automation has ripple effects on its environment. Work patterns change, procedures change, even relationships between people change. Technological change can strongly affect people's attitude and feelings. Managers often introduce these changes without any preparation concerning the broader effects on themselves or the people who work with them. The data security and integrity issue will not be solved merely through external controls, nor is it a merely technical issue. The end user will need to understand data security and integrity, and will need to learn to exercise proper control within a specific environment. Education that goes beyond technical skills would seem both appropriate and essential. This kind of education may not be within the competence or mandate of an IS department.

The Role of Information Services

In a corporate setting where interactive computing is no longer under the direct control of IS, its role is still unclear, but several facets of that role are apparent. Since more and more managers and professionals throughout the corporation want to use corporate data for their own analytical and reporting needs, the traditional role of IS to capture, process, and manage transactional and production information will be, if anything, more valued. Surely, IS will also be called on to become more of a service organization, providing technical training and consultative help to those using both its facilities and information technology in general. To carry out effective control throughout the organization, it will also need to have the mandate and the consequent authority and resources to accomplish it. It would seem that only if the IS operation has direct access to top level decision making can it carry out such responsibilities.

Top-Level Planning

The key issue concerns the role of top management, indeed, the chief executive, to develop and plan for end user computing. Whereas in most companies studied senior management has tended to look the other way or has left the development of end-user computing to IS, the situation will soon demand top-level decisions. What a training director called "the reverse revolution" and others characterized as a bottom-up movement cannot continue long without disruption and chaos. All the issues described in this report carry implications that require policy decisions that will have to be made at the very highest levels of each organization. Some managers believe that such decisions would have to wait for another generation of top management, but it seems unlikely that the corporate world can wait that long. So the most crucial need may be for a program to educate top management about the "information revolution" already going on in their organizations and the need for careful strategic planning for future technological change. Such planning can ensure that the new and powerful tools already available and coming quickly over the horizon will be used to revolutionize the productivity of their company, and not its stability.

REFERENCES

1. "The Personal Computer in Large Organizations," International Data Corporation, Framingham, Massachusetts, 1982.
2. Rockart, F. and Flannery, L. S. "The Management of End User Computing," *Proceedings of the Second International Conference on Information Systems*, Cambridge, Massachusetts, December 1981, pp. 351–364.
3. *Business Week*, "Training: A Built-in Market Worth Billions," November 1, 1982, pp. 84–85.
4. Gibson, C. F. and Nolan, R. N. "Managing the Four Stages of EDP Growth," *Harvard Business Review*, Volume 54, Number 1, January–February 1974, pp. 76–88.

QUESTIONS

1. Why might the utilization of EUC-related resources be sporadic from one company to another?
2. Generally speaking, in what ways have managers become direct users of computer technology?
3. Which of the EUC-related problems cited by the IS professionals and end users in this study would be considered a "viable concern" today?
4. Based on the findings of this study, describe (a) the state of end-user training/education, and (b) the suggestions made for additional training/education.
5. Discuss five issues deemed critical to the development of end-user computing.

The CEO Goes On-Line

■

John F. Rockart
Michael E. Treacy

Computer terminals are no strangers to corporate offices. Clerks have had them for years. Middle managers are increasingly using them. So are key staff personnel. But the thought that the CEO and other top officers of a billion-dollar company might regularly spend time at their own terminals usually elicits an amused smile and a shake of the head. Somehow, the image of top executives hard at work at a keyboard just doesn't seem right.

After all, their day is supposed to be filled with meetings with key division officers, briefings, telephone conversations, conferences, speeches, negotiations. What is more, the classic research on what executives actually do shows them to be verbally oriented, with little use for "hard" information. According to Henry Mintzberg, "A great deal of the manager's inputs are soft and speculative—impressions and feelings about other people, hearsay, gossip, and so on. Furthermore, the very analytic inputs—reports, documents, and hard data in general — seem to be of relatively little importance."[1]

But consider:

☐ Ben W. Heineman, president and chief executive of Northwest Industries, spends a few hours almost every day at a computer terminal in his office. Heineman accesses reports on each of his nine operating companies and carries out original analyses using a vast store of data and an easy-to-use computer language. The terminal has become his most important tool for monitoring and planning activities.

☐ Roger E. Birk, president of Merrill Lynch, and Gregory Fitzgerald, chief financial officer, have access via computer terminals in their offices to a large number of continually updated reports on the company's worldwide operations. The system, to which a graphics capability has recently been added, was initiated by former president of Merrill Lynch and now Secretary of the Treasury Donald T. Regan as a vehicle for quickly generating information on the latest financial developments.

☐ John A. Schoneman, chairman of the board and CEO of Wausau Insurance Companies, and Gerald D. Viste, president and chief operating officer, use an on-line data base of information about their own business and those of competitors. At their terminals they develop numerical and graphic analyses that help determine the company's strategic direction.

☐ George N. Hatsopoulos, president of Thermo Electron, writes programs in the APL language to format data contained in several of his company's data bases. As a result, he can quickly study information about company, market, and economic conditions whenever he desires.

Although these examples do not yet represent common practice for senior corporate officers, they do suggest a trend toward greatly increased computer use in top-executive suites. In fact, during the past two years we have studied some 16 companies in which at least one of the three top officers, most often the CEO, directly accesses and uses computer-based information on a regular basis. In the pages that follow we present a status report on this rapidly growing phenomenon.

An INFORMATION SYSTEM FOR EXECUTIVES

Top managers' use of computers is spreading for three primary reasons: user-oriented terminal facilities are now available at an acceptable price; executives are better informed of the availability and capabilities of these new technologies; and, predictably, today's volatile competitive conditions heighten the desire among top executives for ever more timely information and analysis.

Whatever its specific causes, this trend is indisputably a measured response to a widely perceived need or set of needs. Our study indicates that the actual patterns of executive computer use represent variations on only a few basic themes. Though these patterns evolved independently and may appear quite different, their similarities are striking—so striking in fact that they suggest the emergence in a number of companies of a new kind of executive information support (or "EIS") system.

From our observations, we can generalize a simple model of EIS structure and development into which fit all the individual systems we have seen. This model helps illuminate both the process of executive information support and the factors that determine its success.

All EIS systems share . . .

A Central Purpose

Obviously, the top executives who personally use computers do so as part of the planning and control processes in their organizations. The provision of information to senior management for such purposes is certainly nothing new; the reason for EIS systems is to support a more effective use of this information. Those managers with terminals of their own have decided that they need a better understanding of the workings of their corporations. To achieve this, they have sought out the individually tailored access to the broader, more detailed sweep of data that only computers can provide.

A Common Core of Data

Although no two EIS systems are identical, each contains what we call a "data cube" (see Figure 4.1)—that is, data on important *business variables* (for example, the major general ledger accounting variables and, equally important,

FIGURE 4.1
THE DATA CUBE

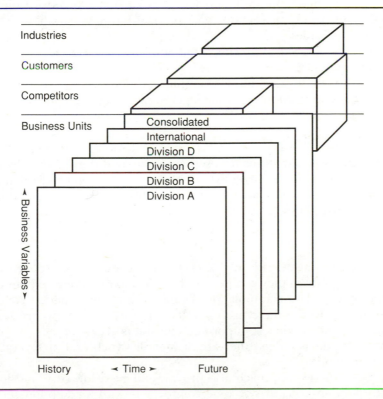

the nonfinancial substantive figures—such as unit sales by product line—that underlie and explain the accounting numbers) through *time* (budgeted, actual, and revised data on key variables is kept on a month-by-month basis for a number of past years, usually five, and is available in the form of projections for several years into the future) and by *business unit* (whatever the nature of those units—geographic, divisional, and functional).

What sets this data cube apart from information traditionally gathered by staff members and included in reports to top management is the sheer breadth of its cross-functional sources and the depth of its detail. With such inclusive information at their fingertips, executives can of course work through traditional accounting comparisons of "actual," "last year," and "budget" for a single business unit. But they can also look at a few variables, such as working capital and its major components, across time for a single subsidiary or at a single variable—say, a product line's performance in physical units as well as dollars—across all subsidiaries.

Further, a number of companies have extended these axes of data to include information, however incomplete, on major competitors, key customers, and important industry segments.[2] Much of this information can be purchased today in the form of any of the several thousand machine-processable data bases sold by information vendors. For competitive financial data, for example, one common source is Standard & Poor's Compustat tape, which provides ten years of data on 130 business variables for more than 3,500 companies.

Operating data from a growing number of industries are readily available from industry associations or other published sources. Some of these sources—customer surveys, market sampling, and the like—are fairly "soft," but they are accurate enough for managerial planning and control purposes.

Two Principal Methods of Use

The EIS systems in our study are used in two quite different ways by executives: (1) for access to the current status and projected trends of the business and (2) for personalized analyses of the available data. Let us look briefly at these two modes of use.

Status Access

When executives have "read only" access to the latest data or reports on the status of key variables, they can peruse the information requested but can do very little, if any, data manipulation. In industries where market conditions change rapidly, where there are many factors to watch, or where hour-to-hour operational tracking is important, the status access of this sort can be of great use. This is indeed the case at Merrill Lynch and at several other financial companies.

The status access approach also provides an easy, low-cost, and low-risk means to help an executive become comfortable with a computer terminal.

At Owens-Illinois, for example, the first stage in the development of an EIS system will—for just these reasons—provide only status access for the CEO and other senior executives. Moreover, taking this approach can send a clear signal throughout an organization that top management intends to put more emphasis than it had in the past on quantitative analysis in the planning and control process. As one CEO put it, "The terminal on my desk is a message to the organization."

Personalized Analysis

Executives can, of course, use the computer not only for status access but also as an analytic tool. At Northwest Industries, Wausau, and Thermo Electron, senior managers have chosen the contents of the data bases available to them and have learned to do some programming themselves. Instead of merely having access to the data, they are able to do creative analyses of their own.

The type of analysis performed differs from manager to manager. Some merely compute new ratios or extrapolate current trends into the future. Some graph trends of particular interest to gain an added visual perspective. Some work with elaborate simulation models to determine where capital investments will be most productive. All, however, enjoy a heightened ability to look at, change, extend, and manipulate data in personally meaningful ways. But to make this approach effective, executives must be willing to invest much of their own time and energy in defining the needed data and in learning what the computer can do.

A Support Organization

Finally, all the systems we observed depend on the provision of a high level of personal support to their executive users. This support is essential if those systems are to have a fair chance to demonstrate their full potential. Users require at least some initial training and ongoing assistance with computer languages. And they need help in establishing and updating data bases as well as in conceptualizing, designing, and improving their systems and their analyses.

In the organizations we observed, a group of EIS "coaches," often former consultants, gives EIS users continuing assistance. Their primary role is "to help" rather than "to do." Because such EIS coaches must be a different breed of expert from data processing analysts and because they need to be shielded from involvement in the normal run of EDP fire-fighting activities, the companies we studied have separated them organizationally from their regular data processing operations.

Northwest Industries: an example

Perhaps the most impressive example of an EIS system, both in design and use, is that at Northwest Industries (1980 sales: $2.9 billion). The development of this system began in 1976 when Heineman decided that he needed a specially tailored data base to aid him in monitoring, projecting, and planning the progress of his nine operating companies. A great believer in the advantages of "not being the captive of any particular source of information," Heineman wanted to be able to analyze various aspects of the business himself but saw little opportunity to do so without a computer-based system to reduce data-handling chores.

In January 1977, the six top executives at Northwest were given access to an experimental system through which they could retrieve more than 70 reports and perform such limited analyses as compound growth calculations, variance analysis, and trend projections. By February, Heineman had reached the limits of the system's capabilities and was demanding more.

Additional capabilities came in the form of a new access and analysis language, EXPRESS, which facilitated not only simple file handling and data aggregation but also extensive modeling and statistical analyses of data series. To complement these improved capabilities, Northwest has since added to its executive data base:

> 350 financial and operational items of data on planned, budgeted, forecasted, and actual monthly results for each operating company for the past eight and the next four years.
>
> 45 economic and key ratio time series.
>
> Several externally subscribed data bases, including Standard & Poor's Compustat and DRI services.

Northwest's EIS system with its extensive and continually growing data base is now used by almost all managers and executives at corporate headquarters to perform their monitoring and analytic functions. But the driving force behind the system and its most significant user remains Heineman. Working with the system is an everyday thing for him, a natural part of his job. With his special knowledge of the business and with his newly acquired ability to write his own programs, Heineman sees great value in working at a terminal himself rather than handing all assignments to staff personnel.

"There is a huge advantage to the CEO to get his hands dirty in the data," he says, because "the answers to many significant questions are found in the detail. The system provides me with an improved ability to ask the right questions and to know the wrong answers." What is more, he finds a comparable advantage in having instant access to the data base to try out an idea he might have. In fact, he has a computer terminal at home and takes another with him on vacations.

Supporting Heineman and other Northwest executives are a few information systems people who function as EIS coaches. They train and assist users in determining whether needed data are already available and whether any additional data can be obtained. They also help get new information into the data base, train users in access methods, and teach them to recognize the analytic routines best fitted to different types of analyses. Only for major modeling applications do these coaches actually take part in the system design and programming process.

THE PROMISE OF EIS SYSTEMS

Most of America's top managers still have no terminal-based access whatsoever. They find the idea of working at a terminal a violation of their managerial styles and their view of their roles. They are perfectly comfortable asking staff to provide both manual and computer-generated analyses as needed. What is more, EIS systems provide no clear, easily defined cost savings. In fact, we know of no system that a traditional cost-benefit study would justify in straight labor-saving terms. Why, then, are managers implementing them in growing numbers?

Three principal reasons suggest themselves. Most significant is the assistance EIS systems offer analytically oriented top executives in their search for a deeper understanding of their companies and industries. We believe that many top managers are basically analytic and that they are now both aware of the new tools offered by EIS and finding them to their liking. (For some of their specific comments, see Table 4.1.)

TABLE 4.1
WHAT TOP MANAGERS ARE SAYING ABOUT EIS SYSTEMS

"The system has been in infinite help in allowing me to improve my mental model of the company and the industry we're in. I feel much more confident that I am on top of the operations of our company and its future path."

"Your staff really can't help you think. The problem with giving a question to the staff is that they provide you with the answer. You learn the nature of the real question you should have asked when you muck around in the data."

"It saves a great deal of the time spent in communicating with functional staff personnel. Today, for an increasing number of problems, I can locate the data I want, and I can develop it in the form I want, faster than I could describe my needs to the appropriate staffer."

"Some of my best ideas come at fallow times between five in the evening and seven the next morning. Access to relevant data to check out something right then is very important. My home terminal lets me perform the analysis while it's at the forefront of my mind."

"Comparing various aspects of our company with the competition is a very fast way of defining the areas in which I should place most of my attention. The system allows me to do exactly that."

"I think graphically. It's so nice to be able to easily graph out the data in which I'm interested . . . And it's especially nice to be able adjust the display to see the data in the exact perspective that best tells the story."

"I've always felt that the answers were in the detail. Now, at last, I can pore through some of that detail. That's my style. It used to mean long nights and plenty of staff and lots of frustration. Now it's somewhat easier. And frankly, it also saves me a great deal of staff time that was formerly spent on routine charting and graphing."

"I bring a lot of knowledge to the party. Just scanning the current status of our operations enables me to see some things that those with less time in the company would not see as important. Although the resulting telephone calls undoubtedly shake up some of my subordinates. I think in the long run this is helpful to them, too."

"The system provides me with a somewhat independent source for checking on the analyses and opinions presented both for my line subordinates and by my functional staffs. There is a great deal of comfort in being relatively independent of the analyses done by others."

"By working with the data I originally thought I needed, I've been able to zero in on the data I actually need. We've expanded our data base significantly, but each step has led to better understanding of our company and its environment."

"Frankly, a secondary, but very real, advantage of the use of the system by me is the signal it gives to the rest of the company that I desire more quantitatively oriented management of the organization. I want my subordinates to think more analytically, and they are. I feel we're on the way to becoming a significantly better-managed company."

Second, EIS systems can be structured to accommodate the information needs of the individual manager. Although the Merrill Lynch system, for example, is principally geared for status access, Gregory Fitzgerald, the chief financial officer, often writes his own programs to carry out personally tailored analyses.

Finally, the systems can start small (less than $100,000), providing support to a single data-oriented member of the corporate office. In fact, an EIS system can begin either at a line-executive level or as a system for the sole use of a particular functional staff, such as finance or marketing (see Figure 4.2). It can then evolve as others become interested, adding the data sets and access methods appropriate to each new user. This pattern of growth marks a logical progression since the executives, personal assistants, and key functional staffs in the corporate office form, in effect, an "executive information support organization" *jointly* responsible for preparing and analyzing the data needed at the corporate level. EIS support of an individual user enhances the

FIGURE 4.2
A CONCEPTUAL MODEL OF EXECUTIVE INFORMATION SUPPORT

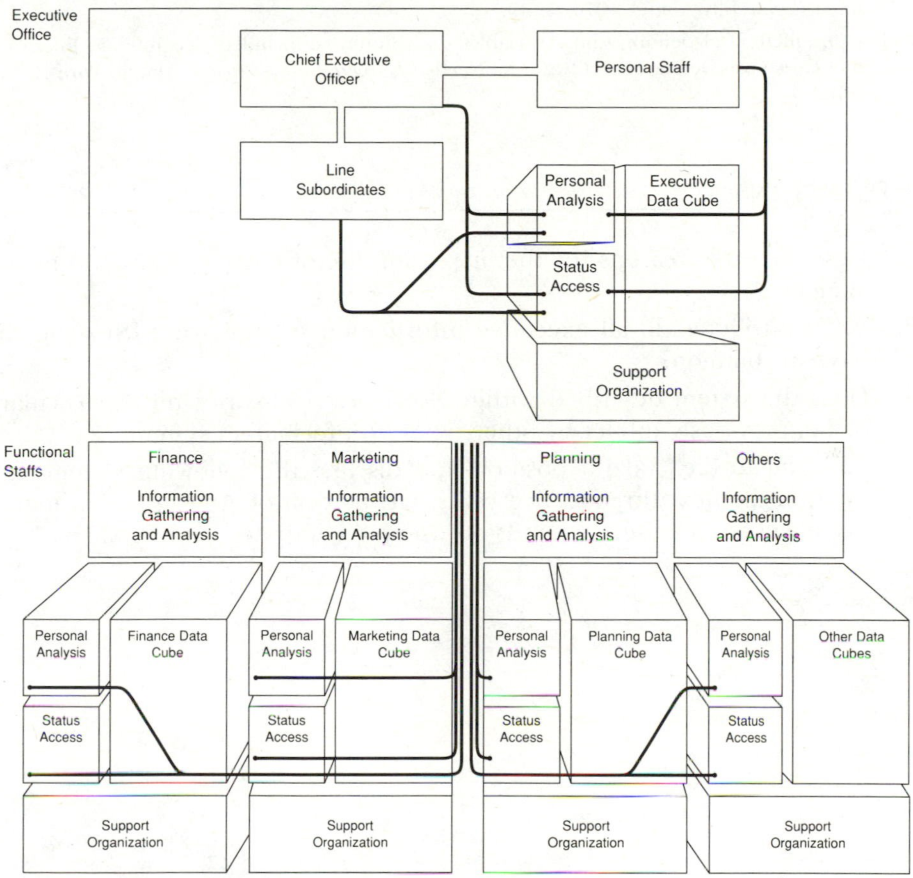

information processing capability of the entire corporate office, for the data needed by different members of the office tend to overlap.

But EIS systems have the added advantage that they need grow and develop only as additional individuals "buy in." Unlike the huge, one-shot, multimillion-dollar projects necessary for such classic data processing systems as order entry or manufacturing control, EIS systems can evolve by increments in precise step with the distinct needs of each corporate office.

Not all senior managers, of course, will find an EIS system to their taste, but enough user-friendly technology now exists to accommodate the needs of those who wish to master a more data-intensive approach to their jobs.

REFERENCES

1. See Henry Mintzberg, "Planning on the Left Side and Managing on the Right," *Harvard Business Review* July-August 1976, p. 49.
2. For one method of defining those variables that should be included, see John F. Rockart, "Chief Executives Define Their Own Data Needs," *Harvard Business Review* March-April 1979, p. 81.

QUESTIONS

1. Describe three reasons for the increasing use of computers by top management.
2. What attributes do all executive information systems (or EIS) seem to have in common?
3. Does the system described within Northwest Industries fill a particular niche, previously unmet by other types of information systems?
4. Respond to (i.e., take a position and discuss) the following statement: "Within the next three to five years, virtually all of America's top managers will become direct, hands-on users of computer-based systems."

II

ORGANIZATIONAL SUPPORT FOR EUC

∎

EUC support refers to activities that serve to enhance the development and growth of EUC within the organization. Many organizations have found that the proper mix and delivery of support activities can result in productivity gains, which can even be tailored to a particular area or areas of the organization (i.e., departmental, divisional, or corporatewide).

Examples of EUC-related support activities include the following.

1. Training and education—develop an ongoing, comprehensive training program that identifies and then addresses the needs of end users, management, and the IS professional.
2. Data access—enhance the end-user community's ability to obtain data needed for EUC applications.
3. Consulting—provides consultation services in the areas of EUC tool selection, cost justification of EUC applications, problem solving, modeling, and applications development.

This section is composed of two articles on the information center (IC), which has become the most common delivery mechanism for EUC support activities, and two articles dealing with EUC-related training within the organization.

The information center concept originated in the mid-1970s as IBM attempted to respond to the growing backlog of requests for IS service. IBM, like many firms, discovered that the IS organization was unable to respond to the large number of requests for new systems, while IS staff remained tied to the overwhelming task of maintaining existing ones. As a partial solution, information centers were installed at IBM and other firms to support end-user computing.

Based on the IBM approach, "Management Considerations for an Information Center," by L. W. Hammond (Reading 5), discusses what should be done in setting up an IC as part of an IS group. The IC is formally defined, and three key areas—the mission, organization and position, and staffing—are addressed. This article represents a seminal piece within the field and since its publication has been referred to as the "IBM/Hammond model."

The next article, "Information Centers: The IBM Model vs. Practice" by Houston Carr (Reading 6), describes how 20 firms operationalized the IC concept, comparing their information centers with the IBM/Hammond model. Carr explains how and why the 20 firms either agreed or disagreed with 46 specific propositions made by Hammond in his earlier article.

Although the contribution of effective training of users towards the success of EUC has been acknowledged by both practitioners and researchers in IS, very little research has been conducted in this area. Consequently, adequate guidelines for developing effective training procedures do not exist. The second pair of articles in this section are both descriptive and prescriptive in this regard.

"Training End Users: An Exploratory Study," by Ryan Nelson and Paul Cheney (Reading 7), presents and empirically evaluates a conceptual model of how training can impact the acceptance of information systems within the organization. Specifically, the training of end users is explored via an extensive field study of 100 middle- and upper-level managers from 20 companies.

Sein, Bostrom, and Olfman, in their article, "Training End Users to Compute: Cognitive, Motivational and Social Issues" (Reading 8), utilize an integrated training/learning framework to prescribe guidelines for EUC training. The framework proposes two training outcomes: that users form accurate initial mental models of the system, and that they have motivation to use the system. In addition, organizational support is considered essential to foster continued learning. Each dimension is discussed in detail, and prescriptions are proposed, then illustrated through examples and supported by research findings wherever possible.

Management Considerations for an Information Center

■

L.W. Hammond

An Information Center (IC) is a portion of the Information Systems (IS) development resource organized and dedicated to support the users of IS services in activities such as report generation and modification, data manipulation and analysis, spontaneous inquiries, etc. The fundamental premise underlying an IC is that if provided proper education, technical support, usable tools, data availability, and convenient access to the system, users may directly and rapidly satisfy a portion of their business area requirements that depend on an IS environment. With appropriate considerations given during the development of applications by IS project teams, an even larger portion of the user requirements could be satisfied. By that, I mean to suggest that most of the report generation requirements of a system could be accommodated by having application programs place information in a data base for users to manipulate in order to obtain their own reports. Support for the users would be provided through the IC. Designers of systems must understand the IC environment in order to generate good data bases for making reports.

The need for an IC environment becomes clear when you look at some of the factors that contribute to the frustration of users and developers with today's common IS project-oriented development environment. The user's environment is seldom static. Business requirements are subject to change at very little notice, although the IS project development environment strives for a stability of the requirements very early in the development cycle. An artificial stability is created when users agree to "freeze the specs" so the developers can "get on with the development of the system." In reality, user requirements do not freeze, and the long development cycle often creates a mismatch between what is needed by the user at the time the system is delivered and what is actually delivered.

A high percentage of this mismatch manifests itself in

- ☐ The difficulty in modifying the reports provided with the application (in terms of format, totaling rules, level of detail, frequency, data elements included, etc.)
- ☐ The inability to accommodate unplanned requests for information
- ☐ The lack of a capability to analyze historical data to aid in the decision-making and planning processes

Quite often, the alterations required are minor, but the IS schedule is not able to accommodate them in what the user considers a reasonable time frame (a day or two, not several weeks). This disparity leads to the user's view that IS

- ☐ Is not responsive
- ☐ Does not deliver what he/she needs
- ☐ Is inflexible

and the IS view that users

- ☐ Always change their minds about what they want and when
- ☐ Make unreasonable modification requests
- ☐ Do not appreciate the impact they have on other IS activities

When these views are considered, it is no wonder that frustration and conflict occur.

The proper implementation of an IC strikes at the heart of this conflict by recognizing this situation as real and relatively unavoidable but able to be solved if both users and IS will make some basic commitments relative to the report generation and data analysis components of the applications. IS must make a commitment to implement an IC with appropriate capabilities, packages, and data availability and to supply the users with education, hands-on support, debugging assistance, etc., and users must commit themselves to use the IC environment to do most of their spontaneous report generation and inquiry work. IS (and the IC staff) must make a commitment to provide the data interface in a usable form, and the users must make a commitment to privacy, security, and auditability requirements for usage of the data. Both sides must provide people who bring with them an appropriate set of skills to apply to the task. The IC staff provides the technical support and consulting services; the users provide the application knowledge, task requirements, and people to do the work.

The Information Center, then, is a new IS-user working relationship, a relationship built on cooperation and a joint dedication to getting the job done. This relationship is satisfying to users because it gives them more control over their jobs, provides timely solutions to their needs, gives them the support they need to develop this capability, and gives them the capability to ask the "next question." The phrase "next question" suggests that a characteristic of the spontaneous workload is that the answer to one question often leads to another question about an aspect of the problem that had not been considered before. This cycling typically continues for several iterations until they have enough information to form their response. The relationship is satisfying to the IS people because it reduces their frustration level and conflict with users, helps them solve problems the users want to have solved, reduces their application backlog, and eliminates a substantial portion of their maintenance load. It is satisfying to the organization as a whole because it utilizes a scarce and valuable resource in an effective and productive manner, provides access to information when it is valuable in the decision-making and planning processes, and promotes a healthy, cooperative, harmonious relationship between the user and IS communities.

THE INFORMATION CENTER CONCEPT

As stated earlier, an IC is a portion of the IS resource that has been organized and dedicated to support users in various IS activities. We now describe in more detail just what an IC is and the support it typically provides. Sections that follow will provide even more detailed discussions on these areas of management concern:

- User perspective
- Mission statement
- Justification
- Organization
- Staffing
- Physical facilities
- Data security
- Initial efforts
- Growth and expansion

Objective

The objective of an IC is to provide users access to data on their own terms so that they can solve their own business problems. It is typically accomplished by providing a set of packaged tools and data availability (with appropriate training and consulting support) to the users enabling them to gain the power of the computer in a relatively easy and timely fashion. Examples of such packages are:

- A Programming Language/Data Interface (APL/DI)—a data manipulation package
- A Departmental Reporting System (ADRS)—a report generation product
- Query-by-Example (QBE)—a query product
- SCRIPT/VS—a text-handling package
- Statistical Analysis System (SAS)—a statistical analysis package

The training and consultation are required to bring the users quickly to a level of confidence and proficiency with the tools so that they can develop solutions without having to involve IS personnel and to deliver that service in a time frame consistent with the users' needs and the value of the information to the users.

The type of work the IC is intended to support is the short job, the one-time query, the simple report, the minor change, etc. and *not* the work that requires the discipline of formal project development procedures. It is *not* a replacement for or a way around the longer schedules usually required to develop a *system*.

An IC is a formal organization within IS. It has a manager and staff, a mission statement and charter directing its efforts, and, usually, a set of objectives covering tangible measures (such as return on investment, revenue-to-expense ratios, budget headcount or budget dollars) and/or intangible measures (such as user satisfaction, quality of service, morale). The fact that the IC is placed within IS is important because it provides IS with the ability to monitor and control its usage and growth, include support requirements in personnel and equipment plans, and integrate the IC with the project-oriented development being done for all users. Placed too low, it will be viewed as belonging to the functional area into which it reports; placed too high, it will be seen as meant to serve only top IS management. Typical placement has the IC manager on the same level as an application development manager responsible for a specific functional area. In some cases within IBM, it is placed under a manager who also has managers for Data Administration and Data Management reporting to her/him. The desired effect of the placement of the IC within the organization is to

- Make the service and support available to users across the entire organization
- Give the IC equal status with application development
- Provide a management level focal point for the usage of and accountability for this resource

In addition to people (roles will be discussed later), the IC must have adequate hardware to support its operation. The basic hardware considerations include CPU, direct access storage devices (DASD), and terminals for convenient access. The required quantity of these resources must be based on your initial scope of operations with some consideration given to the first growth cycle. Generally, ICs start with only a few staff members supporting a few software packages for a small set of users; therefore, the initial requirements can be reasonably well determined.

The physical facilities to support an IC include space for staff offices, including a terminal in each office, a work area with several terminals for general use, and the availability of an education facility. This space is located in the IS area more often than in a user area even though a few heavy users of the IC may develop their own physical facilities to support their own efforts. The major consideration is that it be easily accessible to users. Physical security considerations should fit the need of the organization.

Personnel Requirements

There are several distinct roles which IC personnel fill. Very few people have the necessary skills to fill all the roles so most ICs acquire and develop staff to fill one or two rather specialized roles. The role of IC manager is perhaps the most intuitively obvious one. In addition to the traditional functions of personnel management, planning, projection and control of resources, development of tactical plans to implement the strategical direction set for the IC, and interfacing to other portions of the organization, it includes the responsibility to develop, with the users, a statement of the value of the IC to the organization on some regular basis.

There are several staff roles within the organization. First, there is the role of analyst or consultant. These people are usually the first that a user will work with in an IC. They are expected to help users assess the validity of using the IC approach to satisfy their needs and give guidance in the selection of the appropriate packages to use. They may assist users in their efforts to consider alternatives and to develop a business case justification and benefit projection. The next role to be filled is that of a product specialist who receives the user from the consultants. The function of these people is to help the users define a solution for their problem within the constraints of the packages they support. The consultants, of course, pass the user to the product specialist who best fits the user's needs. If a package not in his/her area of expertise is needed, the product specialist will call on other specialists to support the user as appropriate.

There are several other areas of support needed for both users and the IC staff. Usually some administrative support is provided by a person in a clerical position. This role includes secretarial support as well as control of the education facilities and schedules, keeping manuals up to date, preparation and distribution of a newsletter, etc. Two other roles remain to be mentioned. First, the technical support position includes responsibility for the installation and maintenance of the packages supported. Second, the education/training role consists of developing and presenting materials on the IC and the packages it supports.

It should be apparent that some people could fill two of the roles such as analyst and product specialist or product specialist and educator, but this should not be done if either job will adversely affect performance of the other with respect to responsiveness to user requirements. In a new IC, this overlap may be feasible because of the limited scope of the initial offerings. In a mature IC, the workloads are such that this is not practical. Please note, however, that everyone in the IC will be an educator or trainer at some time since the objective of the IC is to be as responsive as possible to user requests.

Finally, since this will represent a substantial commitment of resources on the part of IS, there must be a responsible attitude developed within the user community toward the use of the IC. This attitude can be accomplished through a series of actions. The most significant action you can take is to make sure the users realize what benefits they are receiving from their use of the facility and what it would mean to them if it were not available. A significant part of this action is to establish the cost they incur for the services they use. In order to provide this information, some form of measurement and charge-back accounting is necessary. In addition, charge back can provide some of the data necessary to

☐   Establish that the IC is not a free resource
☐   Monitor and control usage
☐   Establish and demonstrate the value of the IC
☐   Do capacity planning projections
☐   Determine productivity trends

The Information Center—A User's View

This section will discuss the IC from the viewpoint of the user of IS services. It will address the typical problems that now exist and how the IC meets those needs.

In today's environment, most business areas in an organization have computer-supported systems which help them perform their basic functions and produce most of their reports. Users may have been involved during the development of the systems, but typically, they now only supply data to the system, receive reports from the system, and interact with IS for error corrections, enhancements, and special reports. This activity constitutes only a small portion of their normal work activities so they do not develop a high level of expertise in IS. They do, however, develop a high level of expectation regarding IS service. In part, this attitude is fostered by their knowing quite a bit about the data that is contained within the system (since they supply it) and by their having some knowledge of query packages and report generators since those products are common at business meetings, frequently appear in business publications, and are usually taught as part of college classes. In fact, some of these packages are probably in use in the IS organization now.

Into this environment, let me now introduce a special request for information. The request could have come from someone within the organization or from outside the business area; perhaps from a source outside the corporation. The typical characteristics of this kind of request are that: the time frame to respond is short (hours or days); the request is not unreasonable; the data does exist to satisfy the request; but no *single* existing report contains all the data.

Therefore, a special report is needed to satisfy the request. The user has two options available: (1) get IS to write the special report program or (2) use a combination of fairly recent reports and compile the response manually. Both of these have drawbacks from the user's perspective. When IS writes special reports, it takes too long and costs too much. When it's done manually, out-of-date data or data from various sources may be used. This could introduce some inconsistencies into the response, and it probably means some overtime will be required to produce the response and continue with the daily activities of the organization.

Having set the stage, let me finish by changing from an abstract view of the situation to the user perspective. I will describe the situation just as the user of an IC would describe how an IC could be used to satisfy the request. The rest of this section consists of the description.

User Perspective

When the request comes into my department, we try to determine if we can handle it or not. Mostly, we look to see if the answer or the data to get the answer is in any of our existing reports or information. If we decide we can answer it, we next assess the resource (including computer services) we need to fill the request. If we need to use the computer and we need a report that does not exist, we go to the IC for help. Our IC provides a set of tools (software packages) and people to support us when we use the tools to solve our problems. They also supply us with education if we must train someone to use the tools they support. In addition, they have people we can talk to about our request who will help us determine which tool is most appropriate for our problem and how to structure the solution. We try to have someone in our organization trained on the tools all the time, but if we do not, the IC can usually teach us to use one in a half day or so.

We go to the IC with the request and some knowledge about the data we need but not where to find it or what it's called in the system. We expect the IC to help us get access to the data we need. Sometimes it means writing an extract program to make a data file for us, and sometimes we get sent to some other department that has data we need. Then, we must get their permission to access their data file. If we need help signing on to the terminal or in starting to use the tool we have selected, the IC staff is around to help. They are also around to help us figure out what we did wrong if the solutions we write do not work the way we expect. They have been helpful to us by telling us about techniques to help us manipulate the data and use new features of the packages to do our job better.

We usually find out, after we go through a version of the solution, that we didn't ask the right questions or really understand the request. We can go right back and change our "query" to include the new conditions and run it again instead of having to go through the development cycle with IS again. We sometimes see other questions which may be asked when we get the answer to the first one, so we change the program to get more, supportive data. When we give our response then, we can back it up with the information we used to develop it. Sometimes we even bring the person who asked the question with us when we run the "query" on the terminal so they can play the "what if" game and ask other questions that occur to them.

How much we can do is limited by the capability of the tools and the availability of the data we need. The IC staff can help us if we need to use other tools in conjunction with the primary one or if we need to include more data in our process.

Since we are using resources for which we will be charged, we develop a business case for our use of the facility. We also develop a statement of the actual benefits we realize from using the environment to solve our problems. The IC staff will assist us if we need help to do this, but it is our responsibility to do it.

In summary, we, as users of the IC, understand and accept the following as our responsibilities:

- ☐ Understand the problem from its business perspective
- ☐ Identify the data we need in a generic sense
- ☐ Know how to use the terminal
- ☐ Know how to use the packages the IC supports
- ☐ Do the work
- ☐ Develop a business case and benefit statement

We look to the IC to assist us by providing

- ☐ Education for the use of the IC facilities and training in the use of the supported packages
- ☐ Consultation, when we have a problem, to help us formulate a good approach to solve it
- ☐ Debug assistance if we run into trouble using a supported tool to solve our problem
- ☐ Data which is available in a usable format
- ☐ Special "user friendly" interfaces to tools or output generation capability when needed

The benefits to us from this facility are that

☐   We can respond to a wide variety of requests without excessive effort.
☐   We can do a better job of constructing the response.
☐   The cost is less and the time shorter than if we used IS development.
☐   Many other profitable uses of the center suggest themselves.
☐   IS has more time to do the large projects that are important to us for our future support and activities.

We also expect to help the IC maintain its ability to support us in the future by working with them to estimate our requirements for this type of service so they can do the proper job of capacity planning. We believe that it makes a stronger business case to top management if we present the case and support it with the IC staff.

Mission statement

The mission statement for the IC is a very significant document in terms of defining the function of the IC in the IS environment and the roles and responsibilities of both the staff and the users. The relationship between the IC and the IS development staff must also be defined in the document. It is a concise statement of what will be done, how it will be done, and by whom. It should state, in addition, what is *not* appropriate for the environment. There should be more details, perhaps as an appendix or a separate document, that describe the operating plan statement for the IC and indicate how the mission will be accomplished. The importance of these documents cannot be overemphasized since they will become the primary measurement standard against which performance will be judged and the final, authoritative criteria for providing support to users (or rejecting it if they try to abuse the facility or use it to evade standard justification or development procedures).

The relationship between the IC and the development group is one that deserves careful attention. These two IS functions must not be set up as competitive but rather as cooperative portions of the organization. Users should be able to approach either or both of the organizations with a work request and end up with a single, coordinated solution. This tone of cooperation must be woven throughout the mission statement document. Statements relating to the use of the IC within the scope of large projects and the splitting of the workload responsibilities between the IC and the project development group must be explicit in the document.

Sections of Mission Statement

The mission statement should be composed of three sections and be no more than three typed, moderately spaced sheets in length. The first section starts with a statement such as "The mission of the ABC Information Center is:" and then contains statements indicating what it is. Typical statements have included references to

☐ Creating an environment to assist people to use personal computing
    products
☐ Defining the cooperative interface between the IC and the project teams
☐ Planning expansion based on usage and user input
☐ Providing ongoing advice and consultation to personnel using the IC so
    they can make financially justified use of the facility
☐ Developing and maintaining a strategic statement for the usage of the IC
    environment
☐ "Marketing" the IC within the organization

Specific statements relative to the organization, such as being a product demonstration location in a marketing organization, are added along with statements to monitor and control usage (plan versus actual is most common).

The next section of the statement describes the steps that will be taken to accomplish the mission. Techniques and areas addressed have included

☐ Installation of hardware and software
☐ User needs and feedback surveys
☐ Technical competence of the IC staff
☐ Assisting users to do financial justifications
☐ Development and use of charge-back and measurement systems
☐ User training modules for packages
☐ Preparation of articles for publications

The third section must state the criteria for work appropriate to the IC and, in a generic sense, what is inappropriate. Criteria for acceptance usually include duration of effort, complexity of the task, level of user participation, and frequency of execution. A few more can be added to your own list. The most significant factor in the inappropriate category is that this is *not* a substitute for tasks that deserve/require project discipline. The problem several sites have encountered is that after users build some level of competence, they believe that they can develop *systems* faster and cheaper than the estimates IS provides, and in some cases, the users could make good on their statement. The problem is that systems developed this way lack many of the things necessary for an ongoing production system and have a heavy impact on operations and the maintenance effort if accepted into production. There are often problems with data compatibility, security, backup, and recovery to the extent that savings realized in development are more than eroded in production operations.

To digress from the topic briefly, the way to handle the above situation is to work with the user, the IC, and the IS project team to develop an approach that incorporates the discipline of the project team, meets the needs of the production environment, and incorporates the user's development skills with those of the project team to reduce the development estimate. Another approach is to let the user do it as a prototype system but have the pieces replaced with components developed by project teams as soon as possible, utilizing the user-IC portions where appropriate.

Operating Plan Statement

The operating plan statement is a more lengthy document (10–15 pages) and describes in detail the support the IC will provide to fulfill its mission. Specific portions of some existing documents include

- Background and mission
- Terms and definitions
- Roles and responsibilities
- Strategic direction
- Education
- Data security and availability
- Package selection
- Packages supported
- Potential package support
- Accountability for usage
- Charge-back considerations

JUSTIFICATION OF AN INFORMATION CENTER

Implementation of an IC must be a business decision. Executive management must be able to judge the return on investment for an IC in a manner similar to other IS and business opportunities. After initial justification, continuing cost/benefit analysis must be performed to ensure that the IC remains a profitable contributor to the business operation. This section will present several techniques and examples for both components of this activity.

In actual experience, the continuing analysis yields much stronger justification than the initial projections and usually exceeds them. In several centers, the benefits expected by only a small segment of the potential user community have been sufficient for the initial justification. Normal justification techniques work just as well for this project as they do for the more traditional ones. Within IBM, several sites have started by identifying the interactive software products they will initially support, surveying the business potential within the user community resulting from the use of tools, identifying the benefits that would be realized, and comparing them to the expected cost to establish an IC. One such survey for support of a query package such as ADRS and a presentation graphics offering that were located at a division headquarters identified over four million dollars per year of net benefits. A significant portion of that amount was attributed to redistribution of work among personnel to avoid extra hiring, and a portion was a reduction in money paid outside the organization for support services, artwork and printing, temporary clerical help, etc. Based on their initial results and the experience of several ICs, it is expected that an historical analysis will show that these benefits have been substantially realized.

Another location provided APL training, consulting, and tuning service to a group of heavy users of CPU resources. Over a two-month period, they reduced their usage 50 to 60 percent by improving their techniques and effectiveness, and by structuring their queries in APL/DI and ADRS rather than native APL. Still another site put two people into their personnel department and their facilities management department (one into each), and in about ten weeks identified almost 18 work-months of net savings to the users through the use of ADRS rather than manual report preparation. In both cases, the real savings and the productivity improvement factors (2:1 and 3+:1) were used to convince management that an IC can have a significant favorable impact on the user community and, more importantly, that those benefits can be projected, tracked, and realized. These savings came about because report preparation was more timely using ADRS than with manual methods. The reports could be produced with fewer man hours and were more complete and accurate than was possible with manual methods.

A final example is that of a development organization that examined the development backlog and identified projects that were suitable for doing in an IC environment. The IS cost estimates and user benefits were available. The organization estimated the cost to do them using the IC and compared that to the IS estimates. Savings on the order of 3 to 5:1 were identified. A pilot effort covering 15 to 20 of the projects selected was set up as a validation test. When they met, and in some cases exceeded, their projections, full and permanent approval to continue operation of the IC was given.

Once initial justification has been accomplished and the IC begins formal operation, the IC manager, working with the users of the center, must begin to build the continuing business case to demonstrate the IC's contribution to the business. Occasionally some IC work yields a very large return. One such project occurred in the purchasing office of a firm that buys and distributes large quantities of materials. Through the use of the IC to control and manage their purchase orders, they were able to reduce the cost of each unit ordered by a fraction of a cent. The total savings turned out to be in excess of 12 million dollars per year.

Formalizing and solidifying the IC as a permanent part of the IS organization will require some careful planning. Before starting the first "opportunity," a sort of score card or evaluation document must be developed to record the actual expenses of the IC and user effort, an estimate of the cost to do it in a traditional IS fashion, and the user's estimate of the value of the task accomplished. This data is collected (along with user testimonials) for each project done during the start-up period and used to solidify the stronger business case. Some examples of the benefits that this process has provided are presented in the following paragraphs.

A service organization used APL/DI and ADRS to manage and track their service contracts and work performed against them. They can do the work in about three hours per week rather than the two days per week it took, and they receive a dollar savings of almost $15,000 per year. It took two days to develop the application initially. Another organization, a manufacturing location, spent ten hours per month manually selecting and manipulating information from several sources to generate a report. Using SAS, they invested three days of effort and implemented that report plus five more they needed. These reports now run with minimal intervention, whereas they would have required 60 hours per month to do without the IC support. Both sites illustrate a performance ratio of about 6:1, which they attribute to the IC environment.

In another situation, a department needed 17 reports to track work through a system. The estimate of IS to develop them in PL/I was one week each. After being taught GIS, the users produced the reports in about three to four hours each using the IC environment. This is a 10:1 ratio. Another location with GIS installed began to offer consulting and education to users. In a year, the number of jobs increased by 25 percent, but the system resources consumed dropped by 26 percent, which the location attributes directly to IC support.

Literally hundreds of these projects are being done by users of ICs each year, so the total savings mount up to substantial sums. The key is to identify them early, and then have the financial organization track the projects and recover the benefit when appropriate, either through workload increase or budget resource reductions.

Overall, there are several sites that have had an IC installed for at least two years and have produced a continuing record of two dollars returned for every one dollar invested in an IC. One of the newer sites, perhaps benefiting from the experience of those that came first, is showing about $3.50 returned for each dollar invested.

As the justification builds, another aspect begins to emerge as a significant factor. Users begin to cite the intangible benefits they receive from the IC approach. The following are some typical comments that reflect these benefits: the information was timely for the decision or problem solution, the number of factors considered per trial was much higher than ever before, the number of alternatives evaluated was higher than possible prior to the IC approach, and the "comfort level" with the selected alternative was much greater than under the "traditional" method.

The point they are making is that the quality of the solution has improved significantly as a result of the IC. In some projects the qualitative benefits could be more significant than the quantitative ones. The difference in investing a few million dollars in opportunities with different rates of return is computable, but measuring the return on the investment of helping to decide the direction of the business or where the product line must be in the future in order to keep the organization in existence is difficult to quantify. After the start-up period, the data on each task should continue to be collected to build stronger and stronger justification, not only for existence of the IC but for growth and expansion.

Cost allocation is the final component of the justification process. The simplest way to provide cost allocation data is to use a charge-back system for the resources consumed by the IC in the same way that project development costs are accounted for in the traditional development environment. The people costs for an IC staff can be fairly and legitimately incorporated into the overall IS rate for project people since their efforts will help the entire organization and will only be a tiny percentage of the total personnel costs. The charges to users of the IC can then be based on hardware costs (such as for terminals or direct access storage devices), line and connect charges (for on-line access), and CPU cycles used. Some organizations also include charges for hard-copy output by the page or line and special software costs if the package cannot be shared by other users. Some of the benefits of having such a charge-back system include the following:

- Usage can be monitored and, therefore, controlled.
- Users can gauge the value of the IC to their own environment.
- The concept that the IC is not a free resource is established.
- The expenses for both current operation and future growth can be supported with real information.

Staffing is another important aspect of justification. Typically the concern is how much extra headcount will be needed to support an IC. Although it is assumed that such support is not currently available, often individuals within an IS organization supply this support on an informal basis. It is possible for this informal support to negatively impact the due dates of major projects along with their associated costs. If this informal support is recognized and taken into account, the simple exercise of measuring its volume for a short period should provide enough data to support the claim that a redistribution of existing workloads will more than cover the initial staff of three to four people.

In summary, normal justification and/or business case procedures can be used to justify an IC. Several examples of techniques have been provided to suggest approaches to be used. Experience of the centers in operation suggests that a 2:1 return on investment is not uncommon. Continuing analysis of the IC is needed to be able to portray its contribution to the business. This contribution will be the aggregate of many efforts. Their assessment of the benefits must be matched with cost data to provide the real net contribution. Specific improvement factors normally run from 2:1 to 10:1

with some exceeding that figure in special situations. Intangible benefits will also be supportive of the IC. It will take more effort, but some of these can be quantified.

Finally, there is an ongoing responsibility to monitor and control utilization so that the IC retains its useful characteristic of timely support to users. With the right working relationship between IS and the users comes a sharing of the justification for growth.

ORGANIZATION

There are two structures for ICs which are emerging as successful, working organizations.

First Structure

The first, and most popular, is based on a structure set up by IBM Canada. It is an organization that has a manager responsible for the direction and health of the IC and a staff of people who work with the users to perform such tasks as:

☐ Analyzing user support requests
☐ Assisting with the development of business cases
☐ Guiding the users to the appropriate source for the solution to their problem including non-IC approaches as the situation indicates
☐ Training and guiding the users as they develop the solution
☐ Helping users evaluate benefits
☐ Identifying and introducing new users to the IC
☐ Identifying and introducing new packages into the IC

There are variations on how the above functions are implemented. One variant has individuals working with users from start to finish, meaning that the IC staff person must be able to analyze the requirements, select the appropriate packages, train the user if needed, and support the user in developing the solution. This variant has the advantages of a single user interface and a better understanding of what the users do within the IC. Drawbacks are the lack of enough people with all the skills needed to staff the center this way and the loss of exposure to other applications of the packages they support.

Another variation is to have people fill specific roles within the IC. This structure is the most popular today. These organizations have analysts who perform the initial consultation with the user and assist with requirement analysis and business case preparation. They pass the user to the appropriate product support specialists who help the user develop specific solutions.

In the course of this activity, some other specialist may be involved to do such things as education/training, data base creation, and technical support of other packages.

Both these variations need administration support, which is another role to be filled in the center.

Second Structure

The other organization is a distributed one which does not have a single manager for the IC. The commitment to provide users with IC support is formally recognized within the organization, and individuals are identified to provide it. A part of their work time is scheduled for this type of support. Usually, they reside in a development group that supports a specific user function. Their role is to develop an end user support interface within the users' organization and act as the window into the available IS resources to support them in IC activities. There will generally be some organization-wide support for some specific areas that require a high level of expertise, but this support will usually be a staff function to a technical support or operations group. This organization may be good where one or more of the following occur:

☐   Not enough usage to justify full time support
☐   Small development staff
☐   Highly diversified user groups with little overlap between the packages they use
☐   Highly specialized user functions with good skill levels within their own organizations
☐   Geographic separation of user functions

The distributed IC can still be supported on a centrally located machine complex if desired.

IC Placement

The placement of the IC within the organization is also important to its success. When placed too high, say as staff to the IS site manager, it is often viewed (and used) as a tool of IS and not the users. This placement limits the ability of the IC to develop a close partnership with the users. When it is placed too low, say reporting to a functional area AD/M manager, it is viewed as belonging to that manager and functional area and not to the organization as a whole, again limiting its effectiveness. The most satisfactory placement is at a level equivalent with the development managers so that it is available to everyone and has equal status with the project-oriented work within IS. Some organizations have placed the IC in a position within the organization similar to Data Base Administration and Data Management Departments. As the utilization of the IC grows and users start to request new packages (or the IC introduces them), the staff can be enlarged and support incorporated with minimal disruption to the existing structure.

STAFFING

Initially, a manager plus two or three IC consultants are satisfactory as a start-up staff. This size is about right to start and carry through IC operations for the first eight to twelve months and is sufficient to support one or two packages over a user population of three to five for the pilot period. As competence grows, this staff can support, depending on the packages selected, a user population of 60 to 80. As the staff and users gain more expertise, this staff could support two or three new packages, again depending on the packages selected. Support for more users and/or packages will most likely require an increase in staff size.

After the initial offerings have been available for about six months, additional staff can be added to support the next set of packages. Their first assignments should consist of

- Getting trained on the new package
- Installing the new package
- Creation of good dialogues to make access to the packages really "user friendly"
- Developing their own level of expertise on the package
- Developing user guides for each package
- Developing education materials to support the package
- Running two or three pilot tests with users
- "Going public" with the offering

This process could take two to four months and is repeated each time a new package is introduced. Of course, you may modify the steps as dictated by your situation (i.e., you may already have the package, you may choose to support it without new staff, education may already exist, etc.). Experience has shown that it is better to start slowly and stay under control with a limited set of packages and then add a package at a time to keep growth controlled rather than open the IC to any and all users at once or try to support a large set of packages right from the start.

The definition of the roles and responsibilities should be well thought out and documented prior to interviewing and hiring staff. You should interview prospective IC staff with one or two roles in mind that you think they could fill. The roles and responsibilities should be thoroughly reviewed with candidates since they represent a work environment the people are often not familiar with. For some, the unstructured nature of work and/or the education aspects are enough to terminate their interest. Prospects must want to be part of the IC environment. The main roles IC staff personnel would perform are those of consulting, teaching, and assisting users at the terminal. Their main responsibilities would most certainly include (1) the direct support of their assigned packages, (2) development of training modules on the packages and presentation of them to users, (3) evaluation of user requests and suggestions of possible approaches to solve the problems, and (4) the activities necessary to bring new users of the IC into the environment and get them comfortable enough to begin to do things on their own.

Consultant

The role of consultant involves the review of information presented by the users and a synthesis of it into a request for support. The request should identify the best package and approach to solve it. The role of users in this effort is to bring their application knowledge to bear on the problem and understand where the effort might lead from a "next business question" perspective. The role of consultant also involves screening requests to make sure the users understand and abide by the guidelines for use of the IC and to pass to the project development backlog those requests that belong there.

Product Specialist

The role of product specialists is to support users of the packages for which they are responsible. They must be "experts" in the uses and functions of the packages. The product specialists should have a general knowledge of the other packages so that they can direct users to them if the need arises. This knowledge is also useful in the development of solutions that may use multiple packages. It is also valuable when interfaces between packages must be structured so that a clean and workable interface can be developed.

A new product specialist can usually support about 20 users and be responsible for two to four packages, depending on experience, relationships between the packages, complexity of the package, and other similar factors. For example, a single person could be expected to support APL/DI and APL/ADRS because these packages have a common base and are so often used together. Some sites have linked another APL-based package called Financial Planning System (FPS) with ADRS and that could be added to the group. If the person had the facility for it, he/she could perhaps support native APL if that was an offering of the IC. Other areas which lend themselves to grouping are graphics and text processing. If the usage of query products such as QBE, GIS/VS, IQRP is high, you might consider assigning a single person to support each package. If the usage is not very high, the support responsibility could be combined.

The key point is to provide an adequate level of support to the users of the packages. Because of the nature of the area the package supports and the richness of its facilities, support for SAS, used for statistical analysis and output display, is often given as a singular support assignment. In all cases, however, adequate cross training should exist to provide for backup when the primary contact is unavailable and to ensure that staff will be available to be considered for new positions without unduly affecting the level of support of the IC to its users. Nothing is more frustrating to a user who has entrusted himself to the IC than not finding help available when it is needed. Cross training also helps when one consultant needs to "talk out" a problem or idea with someone reasonably familiar with the topic.

Teacher

The role of teacher is a multi-faceted one. Initially and intuitively, it addresses the basic training needed to teach users how to gain access to the packages and how to use them to solve their problems. In a more subtle vein, the role is to teach users the skill of solving problems and evaluating alternative solutions. It also involves teaching users how to use features of the packages past the basic level and how to do some debugging of their own work. Another key responsibility is to teach users how to articulate their future needs so the IC can position itself to satisfy their needs when appropriate. Another subtle teacher responsibility is to get users to respect the intent and capability of the IC and not abuse it. Such respect teaches them to look at the value of the environment and, necessarily, brings them to the position of standing with IS when justification and support are examined by top management within the organization. Obviously, all IC personnel are teachers, not just those providing formal education.

Terminal Assistance

The terminal-assistance role is every bit as important as the other two. All personnel in the IC should be able to provide some level of terminal assistance. Questions about package usage will most likely be answered by specialists or consultants, but sign-on and general terminal usage should be familiar to everyone. The whole purpose is to make the users' first few contacts with the IC as painless as possible, thus minimizing the impact of the new environment and concentrating their efforts on solving their problems. This support will typically continue only through the first few sessions until a user has developed enough confidence to take control. The assistance role is usually re-established when the first serious problem is encountered or the user wants to move past the basic stage. It is appropriate to accept the assistance role again at this time to keep the users' confidence level high and impress upon them that the IC is an environment that is both sensitive and helpful toward aiding them in solving their problems.

Other Responsibilities

Other responsibilities which IC staff will be expected to assume include developing personal expertise in the packages supported to the point of:

- Initiating creative uses for them
- Doing work for a user area (*but only when absolutely necessary!*)
- Evaluating new areas of support
- Training new IC staff

The IC should also work with and support the project teams in the IS organization. The purpose of this support is twofold: to help project teams work more productively and to educate them about the IC so that they consider it as an element of their design and development efforts.

When the IC is understood and appreciated by the project teams, there is the potential for a lot of cooperative effort. A way in which this potential can be tapped is to design systems without hard-coded reports whenever possible. In lieu of these reports, the project team will deliver a data base (or set of data bases) with the report information in them. This data will be made available through the IC. The users will work through the IC to develop their own reports from the data. The advantage for users is that they can define the format and frequency of the reports at will and add and delete reports as required; all they have to do is make sure the data will be in the report data base. The advantage for the project team is a cleaner interface between processing and reporting and a reduction in the maintenance and enhancement workload for the system. They will usually get a cleaner systems design since they can concentrate more on the processing logic with only a little consideration given to the reports. All they have to consider with respect to reports is whether to put an element into the report data base.

Personnel Characteristics

As you may well have guessed by now, there are some special characteristics IC personnel must possess to be effective and develop the proper attitudes about the IC among the user community. When you interview and select IC staff, consider such factors as

- Interpersonal communications skills
- Ability as a self-starter
- Teaching ability
- Problem-solving skills
- Patience and persistence
- Relationship to potential users
- Application expertise
- Package knowledge
- Salesmanship talents

While no universally agreed upon priority for these characteristics exists, general agreement is that the application and package skills can be taught and belong lower on the list than the "personality" type skills.

In conclusion, since this will be the first point of contact with IS for many users and in some cases the only contact they will ever have, you must staff the IC with quality personnel. They will project the image of IS to the user community, so be sure they create the image you want.

Physical facilities

There are only a few, but nonetheless important, considerations concerning physical facilities for an IC. First, the manager and staff should be located together where they are easily accessible to the users. Individual work cubicles or offices are recommended for each person to facilitate an undisturbed environment when working with users. There should be one or two unassigned areas where users can work when they come to the center, and a group of terminals should be available for their use. Three or four terminals should be in this group, and each staff person and work area should have one. Proximity to an instructional facility is also important, since there should be considerable activity in this area. The instructional area could be shared with another group which also needs education facilities, or it could be dedicated space used by the IC for demonstrations and formal presentations in addition to its use as a classroom. This area should have a terminal or the ability to install one when required. A nice addition for groups in excess of five or six is a large-screen display or two TV-type screen extenders. One IC has set up a training facility that can accommodate about a half dozen students, each one having an individual terminal. This setup is very helpful in giving a real feeling of "hands-on" experience to the training exercise. It is not recommended that the common terminal area be used as the instruction area because of the conflict of purpose and impact each activity has on the ability to do the other.

Lack of these facilities is not a reason to delay starting an IC. As long as terminals and workspace are available somewhere, you should begin to offer the service. The support you generate will help justify the proper physical facilities.

Some final observations on physical facilities concern terminals in user areas and physical security. Data security is discussed in the next section. As users build their competence, they will want terminals in their own areas and can point to productivity gains by not having to go somewhere else to work but rather having terminals immediately available when "the inspiration" hits. It is proper to support them so that they justify and acquire the terminal equipment; the IC must make sure they will be usable when installed. The IC maintains control over hook-ups and thereby controls access to the system which helps contain usage of the system. With regard to security, consider appropriate levels depending on the potential for abuse. You can put terminals in user areas out of general view, have the key lock feature installed, and/or put them in a locked area. It is possible to provide limited, controlled access to the power supply for the terminals, giving the ability to completely sever the connection between the terminals and CPU when the terminals are left unattended. In any event, let the level of security fit the requirement.

DATA SECURITY

The considerations surrounding data security are certainly among the most important relative to starting and operating an IC. If your corporation has a data security function, involve those people in the planning, implementation, and monitoring activities. If such a function exists at your site, solicit its involvement in the IC data security plans. Make sure that guidance and requirements set down in your site standards and procedures manual are included also.

Based on a composite of data security procedures available, two facts emerge: (1) all data security procedures depend for their success on the integrity of the people using the system and (2) it is possible to provide adequate data security in an IC environment.

There are several ways to provide data security. Packages and techniques used include the Resource Access Control Facility (RACF), data set password protection, encryption, sign-on profiles and passwords, and use of security provisions built into most of the packages you would offer through the IC.

The standards manual should address the security considerations for data, sign-ons, and passwords. Aspects typically addressed include

- Responsibility for confidentiality of passwords and sign-ons
- Frequency of password changes and by whom
- Classification criteria for data security levels
- How long a sign-on can exist without rejustification
- Access to production data bases
- Sharing of data between functions

Some organizations make it a standard practice to require users to change their own passwords every month. If this is not done (a 10-day grace period is usually allowed), the user is locked out of the system and must be reinstated by someone authorized to do so. Your organization may choose to implement a semi-annual or annual process in which user management must approve continuation of the sign-on. You may even consider sign-ons that are revoked at completion of the project. This type of sign-on means that if a project developed in an IC is going to be run as a production job, it must be validated and controlled under the security guidelines for production systems. The advantage of this mode of operation is that you can gain a better understanding of how and for what the IC is used since each project must be justified in order to get a sign-on.

Some auxiliary data security support is gained by restricting the access to live data bases to read-only and then only when it is the only reasonable way to provide access to the data. More support comes through *identifying* an owner for each group of data and requiring people to gain permission to use the data from its owner. The IC could accept the role of providing all data needed through extract programs which only take the elements requested, thereby not making extraneous, yet associated, data elements available just because they are in the same segment or record with the needed data. Still more support comes from having someone review a log (created by the security system) of all accesses to confidential and critical data and assessing any unusual situations identified.

When users ask to have the results of their IC efforts replace their current production files (and sooner or later they will), make sure there is a distinct procedure to be followed with multiple verifications and approvals of responsible personnel at each critical step to protect both the users and operations from "a simple *misteak*." The request is not uncommon in the areas of planning (financial and product), and people working with models or simulations. Special care must be exercised in taking backup copies of existing files to be used in recovery procedures. It is desirable to have a program you can run before and after the change which in some way would validate the success of the operation. The validation criteria would have to be determined based on the situation.

To make security work, personal involvement includes the protection of critical information such as passwords and generated reports, the observance of all security procedures, and the nonmisuse of data provided for legitimate purposes. Periodic changes of passwords with distribution based on a current need to know and periodic reviews of approvals to access data granted by owners of the data help enforce the security procedures.

Again, the key points in this area are (1) adequate security can be established; (2) it takes study, planning, and work to implement the appropriate controls for your IC; and (3) your corporate and/or local site guidelines for security are the ultimate authority for resolving questions concerning security.

INITIAL EFFORTS

Now that the "preliminary" work is out of the way, the focus turns to what, specifically, the IC will make as its initial offerings. The considerations cover the following areas:

☐ Package selection
☐ Pilot effort selection
☐ Training
☐ Execution
☐ Measurement/tracking/evaluation
☐ Reporting

Most ICs begin by selecting a package that is already installed and being used and then selecting two or three users who need that package to satisfy a current business need. The IC works with the users in a pilot project environment to accomplish the training and use of the package to resolve the requirement. The results are evaluated and a preliminary justification developed for the service the IC wants to offer. The user experiences are abstracted and published to indicate to others what potential uses of the packages might include. This pilot stage may last two months.

Pilot Group Characteristics

Some of the characteristics you should look for in your pilot user groups include

☐   Existing or imminent need for IS to help solve a business problem
☐   Willingness to develop skills to use packages within their own area
☐   Ability to quantify results of their efforts
☐   High level of "special report" type work in the development backlog
☐   Need for quick responses to their business issues
☐   Willingness to share their experiences with others
☐   Willingness to stand with IS to justify the IC concept

In general, users who speak negatively about the service they get from IS on small job requests are candidates to whom you could present the IC opportunity. Users with a history of good participation with IS are another obvious target population for the IC. After these groups, you must do some creative searching for candidates. Look for groups who would be strong supporters of the concept. A survey of top management levels may uncover some tasks they feel are not being adequately addressed. You may also uncover activities no one ever considered doing with IS participation that are now feasible to attempt. Small, low-visibility functions usually have IC-type work being done manually because of perceived high overhead cost to get IS service. Still another way to identify candidates is to hold an "open house" and show off your support. This method may attract people with problems you could solve right there. That would get a lot of publicity throughout the organization.

Application Criteria

Applications for the pilot efforts should be selected to fulfill a few basic criteria:

☐   They should be valuable to the users.
☐   The type of request should be typical of many organizations (e.g., extract,

sort, and list; query existing data; build and analyze small function-oriented data bases).

- The application must be able to be satisfied within the constraints of the selected packages.

Unless you cannot avoid it, do not make a new package the pilot offering. Look at the usage the packages are getting and at their users with respect to the level of expertise they possess relative to the packages. You want a package set your staff can support and with which the users are somewhat familiar but not one the users are already expert at using (save those for the second cycle of adding packages to your supported set); you must be able to provide something to the users that they cannot do for themselves and that they consider valuable to their function. You also want to select software packages that have a potentially broad user population to assist you in building a solid user community. Pick a package that someone can use to solve an existing or imminent problem.

The pilot efforts you select may come from any business area or function within your organization. First and foremost, pick a pilot that can be done within the limits of the package. Other key points to look for are a high chance of success, the good visibility that a success will provide, the need of the user, and the level of user participation you may expect. As you make the survey of package and users, have the staff look for potential pilot projects. Try to select a pilot project you could do yourself (in case the user support is not adequate) to prevent a negative exposure. Another key factor is data availability. Try to pick a project that will utilize existing data which is stable and accurate. Since these are to be your springboards into continuing IC operation, pick a project that has quantifiable results and a user who will quantify and support them. Last, in order to remove some of the bias, select users who would not give IS a very high rating as well as users who would react favorably towards IS. Hearing a positive story from a traditionally negative user is worth every second of effort to the success of the IC.

Prior Activities

Prior to starting the pilot IC project, a number of activities must take place. A user's guide must be developed for the use of the IC itself. It should include how to make the initial contact, the forms which may be required, a step-by-step procedure for filling them out, how to acquire a sign-on, and how to sign onto the system. It must include how to gain access to the education and support materials available and how to report problems with the system. In short, it must try to anticipate every user's need and provide the necessary guidance to walk him/her through it. In a similar fashion, guides for each of the packages must be prepared. Finally, education materials must be developed to train the initial set of users.

Also, user training must be done prior to starting the pilot to make users familiar with the packages' capabilities and limitations. In addition to the training modules you will develop for each package, consider the self-study courses now available for them. You should probably start with them as a base from which or around which you develop your courses. The quality of the recent course materials is really quite high. This training will also tend to shape the nature of their requests into things that are realistic to attempt. Be sure to spend extra time during training gathering comments on the training module and exercises. Plan to have another critique after the pilot offering to see what else users would say about the adequacy of the training. As part of the training, work through the general IC user's guide and the specific user guide for the package they will be using. Modify the guides to reflect the comments and experiences of those using them to do the pilot project.

During execution of the pilot efforts, keep careful, detailed notes on everything that happens. These notes can prove useful in preparing the success stories, business cases, and follow-on activities. Prior to starting to do the work, get agreement on what the completion criteria are for the project, and measure and evaluate results against them. The users will probably identify more things they want to include as they get into the pilot project, so use change control procedures to amend the criteria or identify them as new tasks outside the original scope. Measure and evaluate them apart from the original project. If at all possible, do the things that arise this way to impress upon the users the power and sensitivity of the IC as it aids them in meeting business needs. Try to limit the time to three to five days to actually learn the tool, state the problem, and solve it. Data availability could impact this significantly, and that is why you should work with data that is already well known, stable, and accurate.

It is very important to perform accurate and complete measurements on the projects. Because these are pilots, you may not wish to charge for any IC service and usage, but you should still gather the data and calculate the charges as a portion of your evaluation effort. The form you ask the user to fill out should be simple and capture relevant business case information. It should include space for qualitative comments and the users' appraisal of the value of those benefits. Perform the cost/benefit analysis with the users and get their concurrence with the results; if possible, get them ready to present it to top management as you do the last step in the initial cycle, which is to report the results to top management.

Finally, tell your success stories (better yet, have the users tell them for you) in order to gain the support needed to make the IC a permanent part of the IS organization. A side benefit of the success stories is that as management hears them, they picture ways to use the IC to help solve problems they face. When you give them the ability to solve those problems, they become a stronger set of supportive users. A very fundamental principle in the entire endeavor is that if someone once has successful experiences and appreciates the value, it is a major effort to get him/her to give it up. They will dare you to make it work, then dare someone to try to take it away from them.

GROWTH AND EXPANSION

With the initial success comes the opportunity for growth of the center and expansion of the offerings. There is a risk of failure if you attempt either or both of these on too large a scale. The best advice is to start slowly, gain control, then go fast. Success is an opportunity to gain control and to strengthen your base of user support, not to go fast. This stage occurs about two months after the startup of the center. The pilot projects have been done and the results presented; the experience and user comments have been incorporated into the training modules and package user guides; there has most likely been another round of projects done to validate the changes; and the users are asking for more access to the environment. It is really too soon to consider expanding the staff and offering more packages. You should use the next few months to work with the original set of users to do more projects and solidify their competence, to introduce new users to the IC and provide their initial training, and to start to identify the next area of support the IC will provide. Once this has been done, you can add staff and the packages selected to be offered next and open the initial packages to any users who want to use them. At this time you will probably be involved with justifying terminals in users' areas if you have not already encountered that question. With more users and more projects, the data security and data availability issues should be reviewed and revised as appropriate, for what was working on a small scale may now be insufficient on a large scale. As you can see, this is really a time to get control and not advance too fast.

It has been suggested by some existing ICs that each user get a "free" encounter with each new package he/she uses. It has also been suggested that each new package be introduced into the environment as if it were the first one, thus repeating the ideas expressed in the previous section. Both of these ideas have merit and should be considered at this time. Another problem you will be facing at this time is that of cost accounting/charge back and capacity projections. It is time to thoroughly review procedures in these areas.

Restaffing

Shortly, you will begin to face the problem of staff attrition and where to find replacements. In the case of attrition, planned cross-training is the key to having backup personnel available when the right opportunity to promote someone arises. A solution for replacements can be harder to obtain because, in addition to the logical sources of IS development people, personnel in user areas who have used the IC may want to compete for those positions. There are several good reasons to consider them: (1) they probably have excellent product knowledge; (2) they understand how user areas function; (3) they know the IC environment; and (4) they are probably among the user's top people. Several negative factors are also to be considered: (1) they are probably among the user area's top people; (2) they may tend to support only their former business area; (3) they may lack the IS background to enable them to make the proper trade-offs between the IC and project-oriented development; and (4) they may forget they are no longer "users."

Most of the negative aspects can be remedied with education and management control, but the item that appears on both lists cannot. When it comes to top performers moving between functions, there is usually a lot of emotion and finger waving and charges of raiding. The only way to handle this situation is head-on and above board with all appropriate levels of management (IS and user area) involved in an assessment of the impact of such a move and the alternatives available to provide proper coverage, should it occur. It is true that user managers should be providing the same type of cross-training and backup for their people to provide the mobility to make moves, but this situation is not usually met with logic and reason; it is an emotional and political one and must be dealt with as such. If logic prevails, fortune has smiled on you.

Service Evaluation

Some sites have implemented a user report card to gather service evaluation information. Some have printed forms they send to users at the conclusion of a project, and some have cards with every terminal so the user can send in any reactions after a session. A few sites have reported that they have, or are installing, a report card, presented as part of the log-off procedure, to capture user satisfaction opinions and comments while they are fresh in their minds. Regardless of how the data is collected, it is an important task. It supports your business case, monitors your service level performance, and provides guidance in determining future needs. The user report card should be easy to use and provide information you really need and will use. To keep usage of the data collection system at a high level and ensure the accuracy of the data, make certain there is a feedback loop that shows users that the data is important and is used as the basis for decisions affecting them. IC management has a responsibility to pay attention to the information and use it, and to modify the data requested as the environment changes. This information, used in conjunction with charge-back and benefit follow-up analysis, provides a strong base for justification of growth and expansion.

New equipment justification is actually a divided responsibility. Terminal justification is largely the responsibility of the users with assistance from the IC; CPU and DASD justification is largely the responsibility of the IC with support from the users. The final justification process and presentations should be made as a joint effort between users and the IC. Make every effort possible to have users provide the quantified benefit value based on their experience, and match that with the IC cost data. Make sure, however, that the data will stand up to some level of testing and that the users will defend the nonquantified part of the justification presentation which, by the way, may be more significant than the hard dollar figures. Prior to presenting the justification for equipment, spend time educating the people to whom you will make the presentation about the importance of the qualitative aspects of justification and how to appraise it. This effort will prepare them to accept this portion of the justification and treat it with some significance.

Finally, considerations for maintaining an adequate hardware configuration must be addressed. It is very important to maintain an adequate level of service and responsiveness to encourage users of the system to continue to use it. It has a companion responsibility, which is to support the dependency that develops so that increased utilization is not at the expense of performance. The information you capture from user "report cards," charge-back system, and project justifications must be used to plan and justify hardware to meet the projected needs of the user organization. Lead times for equipment may dictate an oversupply for a short time in order to ensure that the IC can meet its responsiveness commitments during periods of growth or transition. If service levels become too unpredictable or nonresponsive, users will not support the IC and the IC's value to the organization will be lost.

SUMMARY

The Information Center establishes a new user-IS partnership which will benefit the entire organization. Users benefit because their short-term, often one-shot, IS-related business needs can be addressed immediately. IS benefits because it can satisfy the short-term, one-shot user needs in a more efficient manner, thus being able to devote more of its resources to new project-oriented development necessary for the long-range success of the business. The total organization benefits because a scarce and valuable resource is used in a more effective and cost-efficient manner.

The possibilities for implementing an IC exist in almost every type of data processing situation. The need for an IC is accentuated by today's business dynamics. The decreasing cost of data processing systems makes it easier to justify the resources to implement an IC. The rise in the level of expectations of users of IS services creates a larger backlog of work for IS organizations. The difficulty of most IS organizations in acquiring and maintaining an adequate staff contributes to the inability of IS organizations to allocate sufficient resources to solve the problem within the traditional environment.

The realization that both users and IS have a role to play in resolving this situation is the key to its success. The basic concept of an IC environment is that users, provided with the tools, data, training, and consultation, are capable of and willing to generate their own queries to solve spontaneous business needs. This environment is usually established by allocating a few people from the IS organization to provide the proper support. The IC staff must possess a high degree of interpersonal skill as well as technical expertise in support of the set of tools the environment offers. The users' view of such an environment is that it is very valuable to them in helping to structure the business requirement into something that can be solved using the IC approach and assisting them as they actually develop the solution. It is perceived as a responsive organization interested in meeting the needs of the business in a timely and cost-effective manner. The development of the business case (cost/benefit analysis) is usually a shared responsibility between users and IS and helps to build the justification for an IC. The IC should not be considered a "free resource" since that can lead to misuse and decay of the IC.

The three key areas which must be addressed when initiating an IC are (1) the mission statement, (2) organization and position, and (3) staffing.

The mission statement must be a clear statement of the function of the IC and the roles and responsibilities of both users and IC staff. In addition, the relationship between the IC and project-oriented development activities must be a part of the document. A more detailed attachment to the mission statement should contain information on how the IC will meet its mission, the criteria for work appropriate to the environment, and specific sections covering such topics as roles and responsibilities, tools and data available, consultation and education, and accountability and charge-back considerations.

The organization of a typical IC is oriented around package support and functional roles rather than application areas. In cases where the application data is so complex that this is not practical, a few ICs have allowed someone to specialize in that area with the understanding that the user will develop data expertise as quickly as possible. Placement of an IC relative to other IS functions is also a key to its success. The best placement seems to be as an equal with both project-oriented development and operations, giving the IC the proper level of support and exposure to all potential users.

Staffing is the third key issue to be addressed. Staff personnel must be able to support their functional assignment (consultant, product specialist, educator, etc.) technically, but this is not the most important consideration in selecting staff. The ability to establish good harmonious relationships with prospective users and good problem-solving capability is more important. The impressions that this "first contact" of a user with IS (of which the IC is a part) will generate are a significant part of how successful that specific effort and the total IC effort will be and how it will be perceived by the organization.

The question of adequate physical facilities can be addressed at any time in the life of an IC. Initially, all that should be necessary is to make the IC staff accessible to the potential users and to make the packages and data available to the users through a terminal system. Data availability raises the question of *data security*. Most ICs have found that adequate data security (i.e., consistent with current data security practices) can be implemented using existing methods and packages. In addition, an owner of the data is identified and must give formal permission for someone else to use his/her data.

Getting started covers selection of initial packages and pilot users, training, and measurement/tracking/evaluating/reporting.

Most ICs will start with a query package that is already installed and supported by existing educational materials. A few users who have requests that might be satisfied by the package are selected and trained to be the initial users. Detailed records of the effort expended and benefits obtained are kept for each use of the package. At the end of the pilot phase, the results are evaluated and a recommendation for the future of the IC is made to top-level management by both users and the IC manager. Growth and expansion can be accomplished by adding new users to those already using the initial set of supported packages and by adding new packages to meet new business needs.

For further reading

1. R. M. Alloway, *User Manager's System Needs*, Center for Information Systems Research, No. 56, Alfred P. Sloan School of Management, Massachusetts Institute of Technology, Cambridge, MA (May 1980).

2. "Center serves walk-in clients," *IBM Data Processor* (May/June 1981).

3. W. Frank, "Prospects brightening for DP productivity," *Computerworld* (April 27, 1981).

4. *The Information Center—A Management Review*, Share 55 Session Report, Session No. M354.

5. *Information Center Implementation Guide*, Document No. GH09-0187, IBM Canada (March 1981).

6. *The Information Center Slide Presentation*, IBM Application Development Center, Rockville, MD (1980).

7. P.G.W. Keen, *Value Analysis: Justifying Decision Support Systems*, Center for Information Systems Research, Alfred P. Sloan School of Management, Massachusetts Institute of Technology, Cambridge, MA (September 1980).

8. P.G.W. Keen and T. J. Gambino, *Building a Decision Support System: The Mythical Man-Month Revisited*, Center for Information Systems Research, No. 57, Alfred P. Sloan School of Management, Massachusetts Institute of Technology, Cambridge, MA (May 1980).

9. D.C. Mollen and Van Bakshi, "How to support company end users," *IBM Data Processor* (May/June 1981).

10. J.F. Rockart and M. Treacy, *Executive Information Support Systems*, Center for Information Systems Research, No. 65, Alfred P. Sloan School of Management, Massachusetts Institute of Technology, Cambridge, MA (November 1980).

11. J.F. Rockart and M. Treacy, *The CEO Goes On-Line*, Center for Information Systems

Research, No. 67, Alfred P. Sloan School of Management, Massachusetts Institute of Technology, Cambridge, MA (April 1981).

12. J. Stone, "Users question computer center support," *Computerworld* (April 6, 1981).

QUESTIONS

1. Describe the Information Center (IC) concept.
2. What kind of work is the IC *not* intended for?
3. What are the staffing requirements for an IC? Do these requirements change over time?
4. What actions are necessary to establish the proper attitude within the user community toward the use of the IC?
5. Describe both (a) the necessity for, and (b) the contents of a mission statement for the IC.
6. Discuss the initial and ongoing justification of an IC.
7. Discuss various ways to organize and place an IC within the organization.
8. How might a stage theory be applied to the life of an IC?

Information Centers: the IBM Model vs. Practice

Houston H. Carr

Introduction

The information center is a place, a concept, a method of supporting users in achieving their own solutions to business problems that require computer resources and data. End-user computing (EUC) is an environment in which the user with a problem requiring computer resources addresses those resources directly. Rockart and Flannery defined a variety of end users, each group having a different need for support (see Table 6.1). The end users of primary concern to the information center and to this study are those that create applications for personal and departmental use. These are the end-user programmers and functional support personnel.

End-user computing developed in response to several conditions; long backlogs of requests for DP/MIS services; impatience on the part of users to wait for formal development; a better educated and more computer-literate user community; the advent of user-friendly software; and, ultimately, the development of the microcomputer. In 1974, IBM-Canada addressed the need for an alternative to formal development of computer-based systems. They accepted the fact that the DP/MIS organization was unable to respond to the large number of requests for new systems and established a support group (category 5 of Table 6.1) to help users (categories 3 and 4) satisfy their information needs directly. Eventually, the support group came to be called

Reprinted by special permission of the MIS Quarterly, *Volume 11, Number 3, September, 1987. Copyright 1987 by the Society for Information Management and the Management Information Systems Research Center at the University of Minnesota.*

TABLE 6.1
CATEGORIES OF END USERS

1. **Non-Programming End Users** whose only access to computer-stored data is through sofware provided by others.

2. **Command Level Users** who have a need to access data on their own terms. They perform simple inquiries, often with a few simple calculations such as summation, and generate unique reports for their own purposes.

3. **End-User Programmers** who utilize both command and procedural languages directly for their own personal information needs.

4. **Functional Support Personnel** who are sophisticated programmers supporting other end users within their particular functional areas.

5. **End-User Computing Support Personnel** who are most often located in a central support organization such as an information center.

6. **DP Programmers** who are similar to the traditional COBOL shop programmers except that they program in end-user languages.

Adapted from information found in Rockart and Flannery, "The Management of End-User Computing," Communications of the ACM, *Volume 26, Number 10, October 1983.*[26]

the 'information center'. Other firms have followed suit and the information center approach to supporting end-user computing is now well accepted.[1-6] This paper is the result of a field study to determine the nature of existing information centers.

THE IBM MODEL OF THE INFORMATION CENTER

L. W. Hammond described the IBM concept of the information center in a 1982 article in the *IBM Systems Journal*.[7] The description was, apparently, based both on personal experience and a conceptual model. The model and concept are widely referenced in the literature, and accepted by industry.[8-13] This paper compares the findings of empirical research to the model presented in the Hammond article in order to determine the extent of agreement between the two and to discuss the significance of their differences.

The IBM/Hammond information center (IC) model originated about 1974 to internally address the industry-wide problem of the information systems development backlog. Alloway and Quillard described the backlog as consisting of the official, visible backlog plus an invisible demand. The former was the official queue and was between two and three years in length in many companies. The invisible demand was not formally recognized and was estimated to be 535% greater than the known backlog.[14] As an alternative to formal IS development and uncontrolled user development, IBM-Canada established the end-user computing support concept that evolved into the information center. After internal success with the concept, IBM presented the idea to its customers in 1979. During the short time since its intro-

duction, the literature has reported the establishment of hundreds of information centers.[2-4,15,16] Specifically, Rifkin states that more than 400 companies opened IC's in the time period of 1981–1983,[4] and CRWTH estimates
that 2,100 IC's had been installed as of the end of 1984.[17]

Hammond describes the information center concept as:

"... a portion of the Information Systems (IS) development resource organized
and dedicated to support the users of IS services in activities such as report generation and modification, data manipulation and analysis, spontaneous inquires,
etc. The fundamental premise underlying an IC is that if provided proper education, technical support, usable tools, data availability, and convenient access to the
system, users may directly and rapidly... and willingly... satisfy a part of their
business area requirements that depend on an IS environment (p. 131).

The objective of an IC is to provide users access to data on their own terms so
that they can solve their own business problems (p. 133).

Both sides must provide people who bring with them an appropriate set of skills
to apply to the task. The IC staff provides the technical support and consulting
services; the users provide the application knowledge, task requirements, and
people to do the work (p. 132).

The type of work the IC is intended to support is the short job, the one-time
query, the simple report, the minor change, etc., and not the work that requires
the discipline of formal project development procedures. It is not a replacement
for or a way around the longer schedules usually required to develop a system (p.
134).

The typical characteristics of this (IC) kind of request are that: the time frame to
respond is short (hours or days); the request is not unreasonable; the data does
exist to satisfy the request, but no single existing report contains all the data.[7]

Figure 6.1 illustrates the Hammond concept of the information center,
including the specific areas of **support premises, DP options, management issues,**
and **benefits**.

THE CURRENT STUDY

To determine the validity of the assumptions made in the literature and
the practical nature of the information center concept, the author created
a structured, open-ended interview questionnaire based on a review of the
literature, including Hammond's article. After pretest, the questionnaire was
used to guide personal interviews with twenty information center managers of
companies having information centers in the Dallas-Fort Worth, Texas area.
The interviews were each two hours in length and covered a wide variety of
subjects dealing with the information center concept. Figure 6.1 provided an

FIGURE 6.1
IBM/HAMMOND MODEL OF THE INFORMATION CENTER

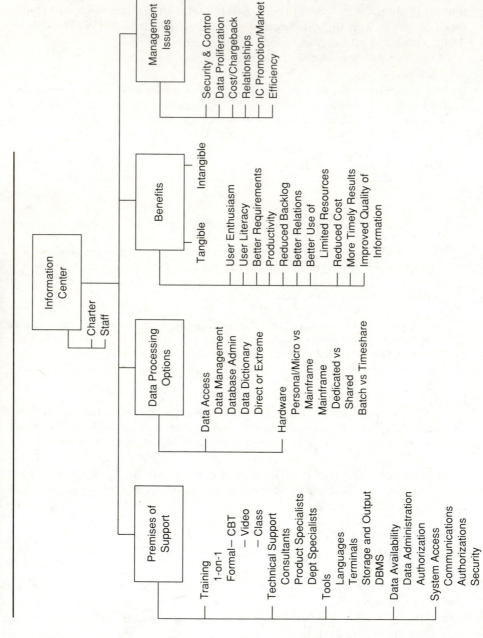

overall framework for the interviews. Table 6.2 shows the demographics of the companies interviewed and some of the characteristics of the IC's.

Methodology

The companies interviewed were a heterogeneous sample of firms in the Dallas-Fort Worth area. A list of companies with ongoing IC's was compiled. From the original list, plus additions that were suggested by other IC managers, a final group of 25 companies surfaced. These firms had established information centers in the June 1979 to June 1984 time frame. Sources from twenty information centers were interviewed. As noted in Table 6.2, the companies selected from this reasonably inclusive list were quite varied as to demographic features. Company size ranged from 400 to over 80,000 employees and sales varied from $160 million to over $10 billion. DP departments ranged from 40 to over 1,000 employees and the community of IC users numbered from 25 to 3,000. Over 8,700 users were supported by 169 staff members in the IC's in the study.

At the time of the research, the true nature of installed IC's was not known. Thus, an open-ended interview technique was utilized. The interviews were taped as well as recorded on a 17–page format. The data was then transferred to a tabular format (see Table 6.3). The results of these interviews are used as the basis for the research findings.

Findings

The following discussion directly addresses contentions made by Hammond.[7] Many individual IC issues and concerns have been addressed in the literature. However, this is one of the first attempts at exploratory field research to address a significant number of these issues in a comprehensive manner. The propositions are arranged according to the general areas provided in the Hammond model (See Figure 6.1).

Premises of Support

Hammond indicated that an IC is a function of the information systems (DP) organization and a way that users may satisfy a portion of their business information needs. While Hammond indicated that information centers could be created and administered by other than the DP/MIS department, all 20 IC's were created by and under the direct control of DP/MIS management. There was no indication by the respondents that it should be any other way. Remember, however, that the respondents were all from the DP/MIS department. Also, the information centers were created for a variety of reasons, but the resulting IC's always allowed the users to satisfy a portion of their business information and computer-related needs.

Hammond believed IC's should be established with a dedicated manager and a staff with special characteristics. Fifteen centers had managers with

TABLE 6.2
DESCRIPTIVE STATISTICS OF INTERVIEWED FIRMS

Company #	IC Date Install	Sales $000	Number of Employees	IC Users	IC Staff	Staff Ratio	Total DP Staff
1 Machinery	Jan 83	3,500	40,000	3,000	40	75:1	Unknown
2 Electronics	Feb 83	4,580	80,696	1,000	33	30:1	2,500
3 Bank	Dec 81	1,141	1,350	325	10	33:1	150
4 Airline	May 81	4,763	36,000	700	9	78:1	1,500
5 Electronics	Dec 79	500	5,000	750	8	94:1	100
6 Computer Services	Jul 82	651	13,000	225	7	32:1	5,000
7 Food Products	Sep 82	2,430	28,000	600	9.5	31:1	270
8 Oil Field Services	Mar 83	540	4,500	50	3.5	14:1	80
9 Defense Contractor	Feb 80	1,800	16,000	1,300	22	59:1	1,000

10	Construction Materials	Mar 81	392	3,600	40	2	20:1	60
11	Oil Field Services	May 83	800	5,000	75	4	19:1	110
12	Elec. Utility	Feb 83	1,200	2,360	100	3	33:1	120
13	Oil Field Services	Mar 82	500	4,000	170	3	57:1	100
14	Oil Field Services	Jun 82	315	4,700	70	3	23:1	100
15	Insurance	Apr 82	306	400	160	3	53:1	80
16	City Government	Jan 82	834	17,000	25	2	13:1	140
17	Convenience Stores	Jun 79	12,000	50,000	75	4	19:1	375
18	Retail Jewelry	Jan 83	940	13,455	50	1	50:1	350
19	Oil Exploration	Jun 83	321	500	30	1	30:1	55
20	Retail Sales	Jul 82	160	3,000	35	1	35:1	40
	Total or Average				8,780	169	52 (avg)	

Source: Houston H. Carr, "An Empirical Investigation of the Formal Support for End-User Computing Derived from the Information Center Concept," Unpublished Ph.D. Dissertation, University of Texas at Arlington (1984).

TABLE 6.3
NATURE OF IC STAFF DUTIES

Duties	Sample Company #	Number of Responses	Percentage Companies
User Support	1, 2, 3, 4, 5 6, 8, 10, 12, 13 15, 16, 17, 19, 20	16	.80
Training and Education	3, 4, 5, 6, 7 9, 14, 15, 16, 20	10	.50
Consultation	1, 3, 4, 5, 8 9, 10, 15, 18	9	.45
Product Evaluation and Planning	2, 5, 6, 9, 17 18	6	.30
Troubleshooting and Problem Resolution	3, 5, 11, 16	4	.20
Technical Interface with DP	4, 9, 11	3	.15
Assistance on PC's	5, 14	2	.10
		50	

Houston H. Carr, "An Empirical Investigation of the Formal Support for End-User Computing Derived from the Information Center Concept," Unpublished Ph.D. Dissertation, University of Texas at Arlington, (1984).

only IC responsibilities, two IC managers had additional major duties, and three of the IC's had no IC manager. The presence of alternate duties diluted the attention paid to the user population and tended to have a limiting effect on IC expansion. The researcher later concluded that the presence of a dedicated and enthusiastic IC manager was the most important factor in determining the success of an information center. As for IC staff personnel, the IC managers indicated many staff characteristics that were important to the success of an IC. Sixty percent of the managers indicated that a user orientation and an understanding of the user's problems and needs were the most important traits, followed by a reasonable technical background but possessing the view of a generalist, and the personal characteristics of patience, flexibility, and creativity. The respondents indicated that these traits were not generally found in IS staff groups.

Hammond expected the staff to provide a variety of services, including consultation, equipment and software evaluation, and classroom training. Eighty percent of surveyed managers indicated user support was a prime duty, 50% indicated training and education, and 45% listed consultation. Other duties specifically mentioned were product evaluation, problem resolution, technical interface with DP, and assistance on PC's. From the informal comments, it was obvious that training has an important and consuming role in support of the end user.

As to the nature of personal user support, Hammond indicated that the IC staff would perform the functions of analysis, consultation, and product specialization. Of the total staff population considered, IC managers indicated that 37% concentrated on analysis and consultation, 12% were product specialists, and 47% performed both functions. The remaining 4% provided administrative support. To compliment the staff, all IC's relied on departmental specialists—experienced users who helped other users in their own departments (category 4 of Table 6.1).

Two of Hammond's premises were not supported by this research. The first was the use of a user's guide in the IC. Only eight of the 20 IC's had user guides. Most IC's relied on the IC staff or departmental specialists to guide users in the use of IC capabilities.

The second proposition was the extent to which an IC performs data access assistance. Neither the IC staff nor any other specific group were indicated to be unique in assisting users in gaining permission to use data or in accessing data. In 45% of the firms, the users themselves accessed the data without help, in 20% of the firms the IC staff assisted the users, in another 20% other DP personnel assisted the user, and in the remaining 15% support was provided by a combination of IC and other DP staff members. Data administration organizations existed in only 50% of the firms, and informal comments indicated that the data management function was not strong.

Data Processing Options

Hammond described the IC as a place, having physical IC facilities. Sixty-five percent of the installations had one or more dedicated facilities for public use. These physical IC's ranged from a single cubicle with a PC to a well decorated area with terminals, consultation booths, and multiple training rooms. The existence of physical facilities was not critical to IC success but seemed to reinforce the level of management support.

Hammond believed that an IC should restrict access to live databases to the read-only mode. All but two of the firms restricted data access to a read-only mode or the use of extracted copies of files. As for the specific mode, 30% of the firms had direct access to live databases as the primary or exclusive method of data access, 45% used extracted copies exclusively, and 25% allowed both methods. In several of these firms, the IC staff created the access program and the user initiated it as required. All firms were sensitive to protecting the data.

In keeping with his idea of data security, Hammond believed an IC would have the user gain permission to access data and then would provide data extraction assistance as required. Only four of the 20 firms had data openly available for access by the end-user public. In the other 16 companies, the user had to gain access permission from the owner, the IC staff, or DP security personnel. The receipt of permission usually resulted in writing a rule in the computer-based security system that allowed the data to be accessed. The extraction of data was performed by the IC staff in over one half of the firms. The use of extracted data allowed users to directly access the copied data without assistance in many cases.

Hammond believed that an IC would be used to prototype medium and large systems. This was not found to be true for the IC's interviewed. When the IC managers were asked to state the major uses of the IC, none indicated that prototyping was a major use. This finding could be explained by either (a) the users doing the total job, as opposed just to prototyping for later development, (b) prototyping was used, but considered a minor use, or (c) that the method was not understood as an alternative by end users.

Benefits

In determining the nature of benefits achieved by installing an information center, the first consideration was how the benefits were recorded. Hammond believed that the process should be formal (i.e., the use of measured and recorded indicators). However, he also felt that there could be valid support by use of anecdotal evidence, success stories, and intangible benefits. Contrary to the IBM/Hammond model, 70% of the firms did not quantify and record IC benefits in any way. Several IC managers commented on the future value of recording IC benefits but the practice was not in wide use. While all IC managers could readily state benefits of the IC, only six indicated that they had any method of measuring them. The most used method of gaining feedback was a survey of users. This approach was used in 45% of the firms. Most indicated that formal recording of benefits was desirable but knew it was difficult to do. As an alternative to formal methods, they used anecdotal evidence that the IC was working to the company's benefit.

After asking if formal measurements were used to assess IC benefits, the question was posed as to non-measured indications of benefits. Only two IC managers could not give stated, or anecdotal evidence of IC success, and the remaining 18 managers provided a total of 28 stories without hesitation. When asked to indicate benefits (different from successes), all IC managers responded, with a total of 44 responses. The primary benefits were stated to be **enhanced (more competent or literate) users, improved productivity, better information,** and **an enhanced view of DP**.

As noted in Table 6.4, the most stated benefit of having an information center was users who had an enhanced perspective of data processing. This was followed by improved user productivity. Hammond expected this benefit. While one IC manager believed that he had seen financial managers spending too much time programming spreadsheets, the consensus was that end-user computing and the information center were effective and productive uses of users' time and talent.

Hammond indicated that an IC resulted in improved access to information in general, and on the users' terms, in particular. The third most stated IC benefit was greater access to information and, subsequently, the use

TABLE 6.4
STATED PRIMARY BENEFITS OF THE IC

Stated Benefits	Sample Company #	Number of Responses	Percentage Companies
Enhanced Users	3, 5, 7, 8 11, 14, 15, 16 20	11	.45
Productivity	1, 2, 8, 9 10, 15, 18	11	.35
Better Information	1, 4, 6, 13 14, 17, 19	8	.35
Enhanced View of DP	2, 5, 11, 18	4	.20
DP Enhancement	10, 13, 14, 20	6	.20
Enhanced Computer Literacy	11, 14, 15	4	.15
		44	

Houston H. Carr, "An Empirical Investigation of the Formal Support for End-User Computing Derived from the Information Center Concept," Unpublished Ph.D. Dissertation, University of Texas at Arlington, (1984).

of more suitable information in the decision-making process. IC managers believed that the users were more effective in their decision-making processes due to enhanced access to data and its resultant display as information. As for access to data on the user's own terms, 45% of the organizations allowed or required the users to access the data directly and all organizations assisted the user in data access. Although data management was not a highly developed process in many of the firms, the IC was instrumental in supporting user access to data.

Hammond indicated that an IC results in more harmonious relationships between users and the information systems department. The IC managers saw this in action. The indicated score on a 1–to–7 (1 = very poor and 7 = very good) scale for the IS staff/user relationship was a median of 4.0, while the median score for the IC staff/user relationship was 6.0. And although IS user relations were still in need of improvement, these managers believed that the IC/user relationship had been responsible for improving the user view of and relationships with all of the DP/MIS organization. The IC managers indicated that the IC staff performed a user interaction function often ignored by the IS staff.

Hammond indicated that the IC directly supported the short job, one-time query. The highest uses of the IC's were indicated to be reports (75%), queries (35%), and analysis (25%), all on an *ad hoc* basis. It was this need for quick response on short job, data query tasks that had prompted the creation of IC's in many firms.

Hammond believed that an IC resulted in lower cost and shorter development time than the use of formal development and IS personnel. Though not answered as a direct response, support for this concept was provided in two areas: (1) dollar savings was the most mentioned benefit in the few firms measuring benefits (30%), and (2) of the stated benefits, productivity was second only to enhanced users. These figures, and the informal comments of the IC managers, indicated that the IC provides a lower cost, shorter time alternative to IS development for many projects.

In addition to reducing the time and cost of development through use of end-user computing supported by an IC, Hammond saw another benefit. IS would have more time to work on large projects. Several IC managers used the IC staff as a way to insulate the IS staff from user requests so that the programmers and analysts could have more time for formal projects. Many managers indicated a desire to have the IC staff as the prime user interface and further separate the formal development staff from interruptions.

Finally, Hammond believed that an IC would result in a reduced application backlog. When asked to give measured or stated benefits of the information centers, no IC manager indicated a reduction in the application backlog. Several managers said that the IC did not address backlog items and that no reduction of the backlog was expected. This would seem to support a view that the IC addresses only the invisible backlog.

Management Issues

Management issues are probably the most important area, and the one area where the research failed to support a number of Hammond's propositions. One view of the information center is that it is a management response to an undesirable situation and a new way of providing information services. The initial discussion in this section supports Hammond's propositions. However, later discussion takes issue with aspects of the IBM/Hammond model and supports alternative views.

Marketing.   Hammond realized early that the potential for disaster existed when IC's promoted their capabilities too eagerly. He recommended that the IC market cautiously to insure that the services advertised could be delivered. Many of the IC managers interviewed began operation with no formal or public announcement and no marketing efforts. With the limited staffs available, a cautious beginning was vital. Only five of the 20 IC's employed active marketing at the time of the research. These tended to be larger firms with stable information centers and mature user populations. Nine of the IC managers had policies of no marketing in order to control the request for IC services. The remaining six had a low level of marketing. One point on which consensus was evident was that too high a level of promotion can create severe problems when the IC cannot deliver what was advertised.

Competition. Some authors have speculated that the IC would compete with other parts of IS due to the similarity in the nature of their respective jobs.[18,19] Hammond indicated that this would not be a problem and the IC managers agreed. Nineteen of the 20 information center managers interviewed reported to either the Director of DP/MIS or the Manager of Application Programming. There was no indication of competition between the IC staff and the rest of DP/MIS, nor was the IC viewed as offering competitive services.

Security. Many authors saw a significant threat to security with the advent of untrained end users accessing computer data.[8,20–24] Hammond believed that security was based on the integrity of people and that the user's lack of specific DP training would not be a problem. He further believed that adequate security was possible in the IC environment with existing security practices. The question of security was addressed via several avenues. The IC managers were asked about problems that were raised by the existence of an IC and 35% responded with a concern for security. All mainframe computer systems in question used some sort of data protection software, with 30% using ACF2 and 20% using TOP SECRET. Fifty percent of the IC managers indicated that downloading of data posed a problem, but all followed with a belief that the problems could be contained. All-in-all, the IC managers indicated high reliance on the users to insure data security and integrity. It was the informal consensus that adequate security was being maintained in the IC environment and that the standards of the formal DP environment were not being sacrificed with high user involvement.

Manager and Staff. Hammond believed that IC managers would perform both short term planning and strategic planning for the information center. The median planning horizon of the IC managers interviewed was six months, while 30% worked within a time span of three months or less. Ninety percent indicated that planning covered no more than a one-year span. The consensus was that the IC manager's job is operational in nature, not tactical, and certainly not strategic.

Hammond further indicated that administrative support would be required in an IC. Only 25% of the IC's had personnel for administrative support, and these IC's were in the larger companies having the larger IC staffs. Specifically, 4% of the total IC staff count was indicated to have administrative jobs.

The IBM/Hammond model indicated that initial staff would be 2 or 3 consultants and that it would evolve to support one consultant for every 20 users. Neither was the case. The median composition of the IC staff at initiation was the IC manager and one staff member. Thirty-five percent had only the IC manager or coordinator. The staff-to-user ratios at the time of the research ranged from 1-to-10 to over 1-to-100, with a mean of 1-to-51 and a median of 1-to-33.

The IC model also indicated that there would be specific roles for the IC staff, supported by job descriptions. Sixty percent of the IC's either had no job descriptions for the IC staff or described their job as no different than other jobs within DP/MIS. This was believed to be a problem in that the IC staff members were well received by the user community, were viewed as highly competent, but had neither a special job description nor a defined career path.

Hammond also saw user areas as a source of IC staff. In reality, the user area appears to be more of a potential source than an exploited source of IC staff members. Of the total number of IC staff members, only one-third had non-DP backgrounds. While not relying heavily on users as a source of IC staff, IC managers acknowledged the non-DP individual as a viable staff candidate. In most cases, the non-DP individual was hired into the firm as opposed to transferring to the IC from another department. Many of these newly hired staff had just finished bachelor degrees in business administration.

Charging for the IC.   Hammond strongly recommended a charging system for IC services in order to insure that it was not considered a free good. Part of the charging followed the normal DP chargeback for use of the computer, part was to support the fixed resources of the IC, including personnel. He did allow for reduced or no-cost access for pilot projects or new users.

All firms supported the cost of the IC staff and public facilities via overhead accounts. Some firms absorbed the costs in the firm's general and administrative account while many others included it as part of computer use overhead. A special problem not addressed by Hammond was the allocation of IC costs to users of personal computers. This was a subject of concern, but no firm had a method of allocating IC costs to PC's.

While 75% (15 of 20) of the firms had some form of chargeback for computer services, only eight of the 15 (40% total) held the users accountable for budgets or expenditures. A surprising outcome of this research was the lack of accountability in charging for computer services. Some IC managers indicated that the use of the computer in general, and the IC in particular, were of such great value that the tendency of chargeback to inhibit usage was avoided. As for no-cost access, only three of the 20 firms provided 'free' account numbers to users for pilot projects or to induce new users to avail themselves of the services. Considering that only eight of the 20 firms held the user departments accountable for charges, the provision of free accounts is a moot point.

IC Implemented as a Business Decision.   Hammond believed that this new form of providing data services would be viewed, planned, justified, and continuously supported as a business decision. The research did not support this part of the model. The evidence of this condition should appear as (a) the use of justification for the IC, (b) an indication as to the cost and benefit of the IC, and (c) use of follow-up analyses. Seventy-five percent of the firms used no justification for the creation of the IC and 65% had no cost document at the time that the IC was initiated. No IC manager indicated that a cost-benefit analysis was completed after the installation or after a period of use.

IC Mission.   Following the business decision view of an IC, Hammond believed such an organization should have a formal mission, stated in a mission statement or charter, setting out objectives, values, and appropriate tasks. Only seven of the 20 IC's had formally developed and issued mission statements. Five others used mission statements informally but did not pub-lish them. The remaining eight did not create or issue mission statements. Even though 60% had some form of mission statements, the majority did not publicize the mission. As for guidelines, only five of the 20 IC's had formal, published guidelines indicating appropriate use of IC capabilities. Some of the firms did have guidelines that they used *informally*, and 75% of the IC's indicated that users themselves identified, qualified, or justified projects, to some extent.

Hammond believed that the IC would act as a focal point for the users, supporting projects suitable for user development and forwarding those requiring formal development to the IS department. To support the proper use of the IC, he believed users should have training prior to IC access. The information centers in only five of the 20 firms acted as clearinghouses or integration points for formal and user developed projects. It was more usual for the MIS review committee to direct the lower priority and IC-oriented tasks back to the user. Additionally, only six of the 20 firms had any form of required training before the user accessed IC capabilities. Generally, only computer access authorization was required prior to gaining access to IC capabilities. No firm had an IC certification program.

IC Performing User's Work.   Hammond was concerned that the IC staff would perform work (such as programming) for the users, thereby developing their own backlog. This question was not directly addressed, but informal responses indicated that most (though not all) IC managers were against the practice of staff actually doing programming and other tasks that the end users could do themselves. Most believed that the IC staff could be more effective by getting the user started and being supportive of the task at hand.

End User Development Problems.   Hammond cautioned about problems attendant to end-user developed applications, particularly insufficient testing and poor documentation. This question was not addressed directly, but infor-mal comments by some IC managers indicated a belief that there was a lack of documentation on user developed programs. This concern was significant when the project was long lived and maintenance was required. In the area of development, only a few managers commented and those stated that program testing by the users was adequate.

Level to Which IC Reports. Hammond was somewhat concerned about the IC reporting to too low a level of management, therefore not being visible to the total user community. The IC managers interviewed reported to DP/MIS directors and application programming managers, at the vice-president, director, and manager levels. There was no evidence of problems associated with the organization level to whom the IC reported. This statistic may be an artifact of the research (i.e., only ongoing IC's were selected).

A Way around Formal Development. Hammond was very concerned about the IC being utilized to bypass formal development and its long schedules. Hammond's point was that the IC should not replace IS application development. However, eleven of the twenty IC managers reported that the IC was used to circumvent formal development delays. All but one of these managers indicated that the users had their managements' support in this effort. Their informal comments indicated that professionals and management alike would use whatever method was available to achieve their objectives and that the IC was providing a way for motivated personnel to get the job done, often in spite of the backlog and other MIS roadblocks.

Summary

Of the many attributes and practices concerning the information center that Hammond addressed, 46 specifics have been presented here. This research supported one-half of the items and failed to find support for the remainder. These are the issues for further discussion.

Surprisingly, charging for computer and IC services was not as widespread as was indicated by Hammond and the literature. It is refreshing to see companies addressing the use of the computer for business purposes, especially in end-user computing, as a business necessity and not a cost center. It is apparent that the IC was often started as a solution to a problem that could not be solved by other time-honored DP methods and that the IC was created by edict as opposed to being studied and justified. . . to death. It is viewed as a way around problems of formal MIS development and utilized as such. User and MIS management view the IC and end-user computing as an effective and productive method of solving computer-related problems, which is a revelation when one considers past attitudes concerning the use of the computer. It may well be that the advent of the IC is a major instance of organizational change. The computer has often been utilized to introduce change in an organization.

Because many IC's were started to solve a specific problem, as opposed to providing wide-spread support, they often had small staffs. A major problem of an IC, especially in the early days, is to keep a low profile in order to avoid too much success. This is a conflict situation (i.e., the users readily accepting support and management's hesitation to commit resources to this area). The users are able and willing to do their own work when supported. The support of 33 users via a single IC staff member may be the most cost-beneficial support method that MIS can provide. This is especially true when it relieves the MIS staff of day-to-day firefighting and allows them to address larger development opportunities.

Hammond saw the IC as another formal unit within DP/MIS, with its own physical and human resources. He recommended special people and a formal charter. However, it is possible to establish an IC with extensive centralized physical facilities or with only user-owned PC's and a telephone line for support by a remote IC staff. Though mission statements are usually created, they are seldom used formally.

A specific aspect of the formal nature of the IC group that has not materialized is the specification of the IC staff job and, thus, the rewards to the staff for meeting that challenge. IC staff members are viewed as highly qualified but they are often not recognized by the formal DP/MIS personnel system. They appear to be without a career path other than "back to MIS". Hammond apparently saw the IC staff position as an alternate career for DP professionals. However, this has not materialized. This will be an important area to watch in the future.

Training is one of the most important features of the IC and consumes a significant part of the staff's time. However, training or certification prior to IC use is not considered necessary, even as a way to constrain IC utilization. Companies have found that users can be trusted in the use of computer services and data access and that they will request personal training faster than the IC can respond.

Hammond says the IC is a way to direct projects to the proper development group. He indicates that the IC staff should be a clearinghouse for all projects, assist users with projects they can handle, and direct the larger ones to formal development. In reality, the IC staff does not need to do this as users appear qualified to make this distinction. Often the review committees redirect tasks back to the users for development, possibly as a way to recognize the backlog and its cost and time problems.

When Hammond presented the IC model he did so with only the mainframe environment in mind. The IBM personal computer had only recently been introduced when his article was published. Therefore, Hammond did not address many of the microcomputer issues that seem so prevalent today. It is important to realize that the IC concept is appropriate in environments that use PC-only, mainframe-only, or a combination of these resources. When the PC is dominant, there is no computer use overhead to support the IC facilities and personnel. This implies a different method of financial support than that used in a mainframe environment. The consideration of data proliferation in a PC environment is more acute and security takes on a different meaning. The information centers in the firms interviewed were aware of the problems and believed that solutions were available. In reality, the PC is just a slightly different instance of providing resources to the users.

The IBM/Hammond model of the information center appears to be basically valid when compared to operational IC's except in the area of management issues. It would seem that the IC varies from historical views and requires a different management perspective.

CONCLUSION

During its short, three-quarters of a decade existence, the information center concept has demonstrated a new way to provide data services and overcome problems associated with formal MIS development. This research shows differences between practice and the IBM/Hammond model. Hammond and this research agree that the information center is a successful concept, one that can be very effective in supporting end-user computing. And, as noted by Edelman, "End-user programming is 'inevitable' and will bring with it the need to change the data processing organization, if not the profession itself. End-user programming is coming, because it offers just too many benefits to end users."[25]

Change has been a way of life for organizations for many decades. The DP/MIS organization has been the harbinger of change but seems to have been somewhat static in and of itself. Along with less expensive and more powerful computer hardware and software, a more literate and less patient user community, and a constant demand for higher productivity, has come a force on the DP/MIS organization to support more of the organization's efforts with less cost. Formal development has been the prime methodology for creating maintainable applications, but is based on the availability of trained analysts and programmers. These talented personnel continue to be in short supply as the demand for applications, especially *ad hoc*, short time frame, decision-oriented applications increases. This has created a need for changes in the way data services are provided. The organization now has a need for personnel with interpersonal skills to support the users as they address the power of the computer themselves. This has two outcomes: (1) the need for an organizational structure within the DP/MIS organization to interact with the user community, and (2) a source of staff members with characteristics different than those of the traditional DP/MIS staff member.

This paper discusses the nature of the staff members of the end-user computing support group. It addresses the type of work performed, the nature of the management of the information center, and possible sources of staff personnel. The paper also shows advantages of having an IC, such as improving the relations between the users and the DP/MIS organization and insulating the programmers and analysts for uninterrupted work on formal development projects. This research is the beginning of the thought process by which management addresses the role of the DP/MIS organization and how that role will be implemented. Change is in order and this study shows the beginning of change for DP/MIS. The installation of an information center is the beginning of a new management style and thrust for the DP/MIS organization. The speed of evolution will depend on that organization's view of its role within the parent organization's goals and objectives.

REFERENCES

1. Clarke, W. "It's A Jungle Out There," *Computerworld*, Volume 17, Number 8A, 23 February 1983. pp. OA/31–33.

2. "DPMA Members Feel the Sudden Impact of Info Centers," *Data Management*, Volume 22, Number 2, February 1984, p. 22

3. McCartney, L. "The New Info Centers," *Datamation*, Volume 29, Number 7, July 1983, pp. 30–46.

4. Rifkin, G. "The Information Center: Oasis or Mirage?" *Computerworld*, Volume 17, Number 24A, 15 June 1983, pp. OA/13–16.

5. *The 1985 AMA Report on Information Centers*, American Management Association, New York, New York, 1985.

6. *The 1986 AMA Report on Information Centers*, American Management Association, New York, New York, 1986.

7. Hammond, L. W. "Management Considerations for an Information Center," *IBM Systems Journal*, Volume 21, Number 2, 1982, pp. 131–161.

8. Brya, J. "Information Center—A Management View," *SHARE Session 55*, Atlanta, Georgia, Report M354, August 17, 1980, pp. 241–252.

9. Harrar, G. "Information Center, The User's Report," *Computerworld*, Volume 17, Number 52, 26 December 1983–1984, pp. 70–74.

10. Rhodes, W. L. Jr. "The Information Center Lends a Helping Hand," *Infosystems*, Volume 30, Number 1, January 1983, pp. 26–30.

11. Smith, A. E. "A Concept Comes of Age," *Business Computer Systems*, Volume 2, Number 11, November 1983, p. 173–184.

12. Summer, M. "Organization and Management of the Information Center," *Journal of System Management*, Volume 36, Number 11, November 1985, pp. 10–15.

13. Torgler, R. H. "The Information Center—A Review of the Concept," *Proceedings of the Eight Annual SAS Users Group International Conference*, January 16–19, 1983, San Francisco, California, pp. 427–433.

14. Alloway, R. M. and Quillard, J. A. "User Managers' Systems Needs," *MIS Quarterly*, Volume 7, Number 2, June 1983, pp. 27–41.

15. Paul, L. "Study Predicts Growing Usage of Info Centers," *Computerworld*, Volume 17, Number 28, 11 July 1983, p. 28.

16. Seidman, M. "Coming of Age—The Information Center Grows Up," *Data Training*, Volume 3, Number 2, January 1984.

17. "The CRWTH Information Center Survey," *CRWTHnews for Better Training*, Volume 2, Number 1, 1984, pp. 3–8.

18. Carr, H. H. "An Empirical Investigation of the Formal Support for End–User Computer Derived from the Information Center Concept," Unpublished Ph. D. Dissertation, University of Texas at Arlington, Arlington, Texas, 1984.

19. Johnson, R. T. "The Infocenter Experience," *Datamation*, Volume 30, Number 1, January 1984, pp. 137–142.

20. Benson, D. H. "A Field Study of End User Computing—Findings and Issues," *MIS Quarterly*, Volume 7, Number 4, December 1983, pp. 33–45.

21. Egan, M. "Study: Micro Privacy a Worry," *MIS Week*, Volume 5, Number 14, 18 April 1984, p. 14.

22. Gillin, P. "DP Groups Warned to Prepare for Advance of Information Center," *Computerworld*, Volume 18, Number 21, 21 May 1984, pp. 19, 22.

23. "GSA Study Outlines Initiatives to Handle End User Computing," *Computerworld*, Volume 17, Number 43, 24 October 1983, p. 28.

24. O' Connel, D. J. "The Information Resource Center: Why so Popular?" *Computerworld*, Volume 16, Number 39A, 29 September, 1982, pp. OA/35–37.

25. "Supporting End User Programming," *EDP Analyzer*, Volume 19, Number 6, June 1981, pp. 1–12.

26. Rockart, J. F. and Flannery, L. S. "The Management of End User Computing," *Communications of the ACM*, Volume 26, Number 10, October 1983, pp. 776–784.

FOR FURTHER READING

1. "Change Can Bring Conflict", *Infosystems*, Volume 30, Number 1, January 1983, p. 30.

QUESTIONS

1. When, where, why and how did the information center (IC) concept originate?

2. Based on the findings of this study, categorize the nature of IC staff duties within the areas of direction, control, and support. What are the implications of these findings?

3. What is, and/or should be, the role of the IC in database access and administration?

4. What are the possible benefits from an IC? Are these benefits easy to measure? Can these benefits be quantified in a "bottom line" figure?

5. Which of Hammond's propositions concerning "management issues" were not supported by the findings of this study? Why do you think this was so?

6. Why, when, and how should a charge-back mechanism for IC services be instituted within an organization?

7

Training End Users: An Exploratory Study

■

R. Ryan Nelson
Paul H. Cheney

INTRODUCTION

A recent study conducted by the Society for Information Management (SIM) and the MIS Research Center at the University of Minnesota identified the ten most important information systems (IS) management issues.[1] Third on the list was "the facilitation of organizational learning and the usage of information systems technologies." Implicitly stated in their findings is that IS-related education/training begets the acceptance and usage of IS technologies throughout the organization.

Research suggests that most IS failures stem from a lack of user acceptance rather than poor technical quality. Why don't managers make better use of the computer? An early hypothesis blamed a lack of education on the part of many top and middle managers concerning how best to use computers and computer-generated information in decision making.[2] The same study concluded that the computer can have a significant positive impact on the organization if the firm provides adequate computer training for both middle and top management. Despite the obvious importance of IS training, there has been little previous empirical research in this area.

The research described in this article is intended to (a) offer a conceptual model (Figure 7.1) of how training can impact IS acceptance, and (b) present the results of an attempt to validate (empirically) the relationships set forth

FIGURE 7.1
**A DESCRIPTIVE MODEL FOR ORGANIZATIONAL LEARNING AND
ACCEPTANCE OF IS TECHNOLOGIES**

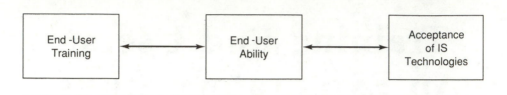

in the conceptual model. Specifically, the training of end users—the people who ultimately use the computer's output—is explored via an extensive field study of 100 middle- and upper-level managers from 20 companies.

THE RESEARCH

Model and Variables

The model for this research, presented in Figure 7.1, describes the components of the educational process within the context of an organizational IS environment. In the process of constructing this relatively specific representation of the impact of training on the end-user community, we were able to draw from a number of IS research frameworks that cite training, either directly or indirectly, in their general description of the IS environment.

As depicted in Figure 7.1, three variables (training, ability and acceptance) form the foundation for this research. A brief description of each variable follows.

Training

The terms *education* and/or *training* are used in this study to refer to formal efforts to transfer required IS knowledge. The topics include IS concepts, technical skills, organizational skills, and knowledge about specific IS products. Whereas education involves an understanding of abstract theory, training is involved in gaining the skills necessary to accomplish a task. While both terms are relevant to this research, training will be the primary focus.

The process of organizational learning is closely related to the problems of organizational change identified by Lewin[3] and described in action form by Schien[4] as an unfreezing, moving and refreezing process. Unfreezing is necessary because the end user comes already replete with ingrained habits of feeling, thought and action. To change an end user through training, his/her normal habits first have to be questioned and disturbed, or *unfrozen*. Training can do this by focusing attention on needs that end users cannot satisfy by habitual behavior. The trainer then introduces other methods which allow participants to try new ways of behaving, that is, *moving*. If they find the new behavior more useful in meeting their "new" needs, the individual will establish personal continuity by *freezing* the new behavior. Miles[5] conceptualizes this process as a "change-inducing temporary system."

The guiding principles for training strategies lie in the dynamics of the development process and in the minimum critical concentration of effort required during each stage of it. This basic process can be shown as an evolutionary model. (See Figure 7.2).

As Culnan[6] points out, when an IS is first introduced, end users will require a large amount of training and support in order to become comfortable with the system's command language. The design of systems with on-line help and menus to facilitate initial learning may promote the initial use and acceptance of an IS. This set of relationships, which extends throughout the useful life of a system, can be traced through our conceptual model (Figure 7.1). Essentially, through its impact on end-user ability, training serves to enhance acceptance by impacting the perceived accessibility of the system.[6,7]

Recent literature on the subject of end-user computing (EUC) has devoted a fair amount of attention to the development of IS training programs. In a survey of 67 end users, Benson[8] identified where end users tend to receive their training (e.g., vendor, college, company, and/or self) and noted that "a significant number of them expressed interest in further training for themselves. " Based on a separate survey, Rockart and Flannery[9] made five recommendations for the development of a substantial end-user education program. Within their program, the "type" of computer-related education varied depending on the "type" of end user(s).

In seeking to operationalize training in the present study, we first identified potential sources and instructional formats frequently encountered by end users. We then attempted to define an appropriate measure for each. Benson's four training sources (listed above) and a total of seven instructional formats (techniques) were selected (six of which were originally identified by Sprague and Carlson;[10] see Table 7.1). Measurement of training received was

FIGURE 7.2
EVOLUTIONARY MODEL OF TRAINING

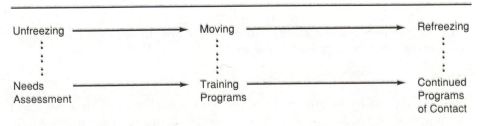

TABLE 7.1
TRAINING TECHNIQUES

1. Tutorial	Each user is individually taught by an instructor or colleague. There are usually few instructional materials, and the material is covered in an order determined by the interests of the student (i.e., user).
2. Courses, Lectures or Seminars	The instructor is an internal or external "expert" in IS. There are instructional materials, and the instructor determines course content. The course is conducted inside the organization.
3. Computer-Aided Instruction (CAI)	The original term for on-line use of a computer to administer instruction directly to one or more people. In many areas CAI has come to mean computer-based drill and practice; in other areas any computer-based tutorial, particularly one aimed at teaching the use of a particular technology, is referred to as CAI.
4. Interactive Training Manual (ITM)	A combination of tutorial and CAI. This is an application-oriented IS and a guidebook which are used together. The guidebook contains lessons and the application system provides the examples and exercises. ITM is reported to be effective in DSS settings. [15]
5. Resident Expert	This is a passive version of the tutorial technique in that training is user initiated. It takes advantage of the fact that users are more likely to ask when they need to know rather than to attend a course or consult a book or the system itself.
6. Help Component	Most IS contain at least primitive "help" components which give error messages when the user makes mistakes. In some cases short explanations of commands are also provided. "Layered" help components let the user proceed through successive layers of instructional materials, each involving more detail. The "bottom" level may be a CAI system.
7. External	This includes relevant college courses such as those present in an MBA program, vendor sponsored seminars and independently sponsored seminars. The courses are conducted at sites away from the organization.

done via a self-report of quantity within (a) each of the four sources, and (b) each of the seven instructional formats.

Ability

The variable ability in this study refers to the quality of having sufficient computer-related skill to accomplish an objective. An organization's desire to improve white collar productivity through more effective IS utilization is the primary motivation for the measurement and analysis of end-user abilities. Productivity benefits from IS result from both efficiently supplied and effectively utilized IS outputs. In addition, the rampant decentralization of computer usage via EUC has prompted arguments that utilization is directly related to the user community's computer- and system-related skills.

This connection, however obvious it may seem, can only be traced indirectly through prior studies and research frameworks in the IS literature. The organizational behavior literature, on the other hand, has consistently recognized performance as a function of ability and motivation. Ability moderates the effect of motivation on performance (i.e., at a given level of motivation, performance can increase with increased ability[11]). At high levels of ability, however, motivation can cause even higher performance levels to be obtained.[12]

In order to measure end-user abilities, the authors developed an instrument by which end users could report (1) the perceived importance of the ability as it affected an end user's propensity to use IS products and technologies, and (2) the current skill level the end user felt he/she possessed in each ability area. Initially, a list of fifteen abilities was created from the literature, personal experience, and discussions with information center personnel and end users. A group of four information systems faculty reviewed the list and made individual recommendations for the addition, deletion and/or modification of these ability factors. During several iterations they recommended the deletion of six factors, the addition of two factors, and the modification of four others. Twelve information systems professionals were then asked to comment on the revised list. The practitioners recommended no additions or deletions, but they did request a further explanation and definition of each factor.

Acceptance

Acceptance is the degree of willingness of an individual or group to utilize information systems.[7] As Bair[13] observes, system acceptance involves changes in the most basic habits embedded in one's daily activities: how one thinks, composes materials, and communicates. End-user acceptance of an IS involves not only learning new skills and habits, but extinguishing old habits as well. The successful introduction of an IS thus requires not only good system design,[14] documentation,[15] and workstation availability[6], but also the enhancement of a user's abilities via a computer-related training program[16] (unfreezing, moving, and refreezing).

Acceptance is a subjective factor and not easily measured. "Ideally, one would supplement the amount of use as an indicator with subjective ratings of a system's acceptability and potential benefits (satisfaction)."[7] In this study, we attempted to measure both factors. Since our study involved middle- and

upper-level managers, we decided to employ the same technique utilized by
Brady[2] two decades ago, when he sought to evaluate the role that the computer plays in an individual manager's decision-making process. Therefore,
as a surrogate measure for IS usage, we asked the question: To what extent
is the computer utilized in each of the six phases of decision making (from
identification of a problem/opportunity through the actual implementation
of a selected course of action)?

It should be noted that all of the managers interviewed were voluntary
users in the sense that their employing organization did not require them to
use the computer in their decision-making processes. In such instances Hiltz
and Turoff[17] point out, use of IS products and technologies can be considered
a valid measure of their acceptance, but nonuse does not necessarily imply
rejection.

Satisfaction was also addressed through a surrogate measure: The Ives,
Olson, and Baroudi[18] short-form questionnaire on user satisfaction. This
instrument was chosen for several reasons: brevity (an important consideration when dealing with managers), the inclusion of questions on both
IS product and service, and validity and reliability, as tested by its developers.

Research Questions

Based on the relationships presented in Figure 7.1, two primary research
questions were derived:

Q1.   What is the relationship between the computer-related training an indi-
      vidual receives and his/her computer-related ability?
Q2.   What is the relationship between the computer-related ability of an
      end user and his/her acceptance of information systems products and
      technologies?

In order to approach acceptance from the dimensions of use and satisfaction, two secondary questions were proposed:

Q2.1 What is the relationship between an end user's computer-related abil-
      ities and his/her utilization of IS products and technologies?
Q2.2 What is the relationship between an end user's computer-related abil-
      ities and his/her satisfaction with IS products and technologies?

Given the exploratory nature of this study, we chose the above research
questions in lieu of formal hypotheses.

Procedures

McFarlan and McKenney[19] note that for some organizations, IS activities represent an area of great strategic importance. In other organizations they play only a supportive role. It can be argued that organizations of the latter type will devote a smaller amount of organizational resources to IS training programs. To eliminate possible confounding effects from the standpoint of strategic relevance, this research chose only firms that have a high strategic dependence on existing operating systems, determined using the Operational Dependency Questionnaire developed by McFarlan and McKenney. Theoretically, these firms will be more likely to place a high emphasis on training.

Five managerial users were selected from each of 20 firms located throughout the Southeastern United States. The interviewees were selected at random from a list of managerial users provided by each company's information systems director. The unit analysis constituted all systems that were currently in use and being supported by the IS department, as well as any EUC technologies being employed by the end user.

A structured, taped interview with the director of IS ascertained *facts* concerning company sales, number of employees, IS budget, IS staff, hardware and software, and IS training program characteristics. Training personnel were also interviewed to gain further information about the IS training program. Follow-up telephone interviews gathered additional information when necessary. Prior to undertaking the research project, pretesting of all data-gathering instruments occurred at two sites.

Each user was (a) questioned via a 30-minute structured interview on IS training and use, (b) given the Ives, Olson, and Baroudi[18] short-form questionnaire on user information satisfaction (UIS), and (c) given an eleven-item Abilities Questionnaire.

Following the collection of data, an attempt was made to assess both the reliability and validity of the Abilities Questionnaire. The degree of reliability, defined as the absence of measurement error, was determined using the Cronbach alpha test applied to inter-item scores. The resulting reliability coefficient was .803. The acceptability of this score led us to assume the reliability of the instrument.

As part of a construct validation process, the factorial validity of the instrument was investigated. The varimax-rotated principal components solution is depicted in Table 7.2. The items loaded on three factors (labeled technical, modeling and application abilities) and together accounted for 54 percent of the variation in the data. We believe that this analysis suggests two potential improvements to the ability questionnaire. First, we need to clarify two items: "understanding and interpreting output" (this item loaded on two factors) and "handling data communications" (presumed to be more technical than applications-oriented). The second improvement is that these three factors can be used in future analysis rather than the eleven independent

TABLE 7.2
PRINCIPAL COMPONENTS ANALYSIS ON
THE USER ABILITIES INSTRUMENT

Ability to:	Factor 1 (Technical Abilities)	Factor 2 (Modeling Abilities)	Factor 3 (Application Abilities)
1. Program	0.75512	0.10443	−0.05770
2. Use Application Development Software	−0.03460	0.74111	0.11260
3. Use Packaged Application Software	0.07564	0.17113	0.67623
4. Use Office Automation Software	0.07880	0.18046	0.62318
5. Build Models	0.16182	0.77829	0.08843
6. Access Data	0.12187	0.03361	0.73006
7. Handle Data Communications	−0.03698	0.07054	0.60740
8. Use Hardware	0.78635	−0.08444	0.32528
9. Utilize Graphics Techniques	0.23144	0.74739	0.29788
10. Use Operating System	0.57578	0.17294	0.01513
11. Understand and Interpret Output	0.44927	0.16305	0.48869

Note: Underlining indicates that the item loads onto a particular factor (greater than .50).

questions separately or the sum of the eleven questions as a single overall ability measure.

Presentation of Findings

Profile of Training Programs

The IS directors at the 20 survey companies were asked to describe their computer training programs in terms of:

1. percentage of IS budget devoted to training,
2. number of employees devoted to computer-related training, and
3. current use of seven different training techniques. (See Table 7.1)

Most (80%) of the survey companies reported training budgets between 0 and 2 percent of the IS budget, with anywhere from zero to five people assigned to their training staffs.

Each of the seven training techniques was well represented in the survey companies. A minimum of 11 companies used each technique; all 20 companies used the resident expert technique.

Profile of Subjects

The 100 respondents include 34 top-level managers (e.g., chief executive officer (CEO), vice president, or corporate controller) and 66 middle-level managers (e.g., senior analyst, assistant vice president, assistant director, or manager of compensation). A large majority (61%) used both mainframe and microcomputer facilities, while 4% used only microcomputers and 35% used only mainframes.

Benson indicates that managers generally become direct users of computer technology either because of: (1) their need to retrieve specific kinds of information relating to their jobs, or (2) their need to analyze data and develop projections, models, and various kinds of "what if" procedures. Other complementary uses of both mainframe and microcomputer facilities, such as word processing, graphics, and electronic mail, have also evolved. Within this study, the largest percentage (45%) of use was for data retrieval and analysis, substantiating the results of Benson's study.

Mainframe products such as EASYTRIEVE, RPG, FOCUS, and RAMIS found frequent use for applications such as financial reports for board meetings, tracking mortgages, and tracking specific insurance claims. The microcomputer products most frequently used were LOTUS 1-2-3 (65%), Wordstar (35%), dBase II and III (30%), and Symphony (20%).

When managers categorized the source(s) of their computer-related training, the results substantiated earlier findings[2,8] which found "self-training" to be the dominant source of computer-related training. Interestingly, most respondents described the quantity of their computer-related training as being only slight to moderate. More specifically, 80% of those interviewed rated the four sources of training—(self-training, college training, company training, and vendor training)—as being none, slight or moderate. The five users from each of the companies were asked to describe all seven training techniques in reference to both the quantity and quality of training received. (See Table 7.3). Average quantity (hours/technique) represents the total number of hours of training the interviewees had received since joining their present employer, whereas average quantity (contacts/technique) represents

TABLE 7.3
QUANTITY AND QUALITY OF TRAINING EXPERIENCED (N = 100)

Technique	Average Quantity (Hours/Technique)	Average Quantity (Contacts)	Quality (Mean Rating*)
Tutorial	14.78	3.01	3.33
Course/Seminar	44.11	4.49	3.32
CAI	18.43	5.43	2.86
ITM	7.82	2.20	3.42
Resident Expert	104.82	23.32	3.96
Help Component	9.41	4.63	2.73
External	35.63	2.26	3.07

*Means are based on a 5-point Likert scale (1 = Very Low, 5 = Very High) and do not include those subjects who have not experienced the training technique.

the subject's estimate of the total number of times they experience each technique. Finally, the last column of Table 7.3 summarizes quality ratings for each of the training techniques (i.e., via a 5-point Likert scale). The Interactive Training Manual, a combination of an applications-oriented tutorial and guidebook, and the "help" component scored significantly lower than the other techniques in terms of quantity. The resident-expert technique ranked superior in both quantity and quality, while CAI and the "help" component had the lowest quality scores.

When separated by organizational level, middle-level managers reported having had a total of 258 hours of training, significantly more than the 190 hours reported by upper-level managers.

Finally, each manager described the eleven computer-related abilities in terms of (1) their importance to his/her job performance, and (2) the current level of ability he/she felt they possessed. Table 7.4 ranks, in ascending order, the eleven abilities by both perceived importance and current ability level. These levels were rated on a 5-point scale, with mean ratings also being presented. Understanding and interpreting output, accessing data and utilizing hardware ranked consistently high among the eleven abilities, while programming, model building and graphics scored among the lowest.

For ten of eleven computer-related abilities (all except programming) managers rated their perceived current level of ability significantly lower than the perceived level of importance attributed to each ability. (See Table 7.5.) In addition, when separated by organizational level, it is interesting, but not surprising to note that upper-level managers rated their computer-related abilities significantly lower than did middle-level managers ($p < .01$).

TABLE 7.4
RANKING AND RATINGS OF COMPUTER-RELATED ABILITIES
(RATING ON 5-POINT SCALE: 1 = VERY LOW, 5 = VERY HIGH)

Ability to:	Perceived Importance		Current Ability Level	
	Rank	Mean Rating	Rank	Mean Rating
Understand/Interpret Output	1	4.41	1	3.86
Access Data	2	3.46	2	3.00
Use Hardware	3	3.30	3	2.79
Use Pkg. Appl. Software	4	3.20	4	2.63
Use Appl. Dev. Software	5	3.10	6	2.14
Use Operating Systems	6	2.58	5	2.40
Handle Data Communications	7	2.48	8	2.03
Utilize Graphics Techniques	8	2.45	11	1.95
Use Office Automation Systems	9	2.40	7	2.06
Build Models	10	2.34	10	1.96
Program	11	2.12	9	1.97

TABLE 7.5
DIFFERENCE BETWEEN PERCEIVED ABILITY IMPORTANCE
AND PERCEIVED ABILITY LEVEL (RATING ON 5-POINT SCALE:
1 = VERY LOW, 5 = VERY HIGH)

Ability to:	Difference Between Importance and Ability	T
Program	.15	1.18
Use Application Development Software	.96	7.91**
Use Packaged Application Software	.57	4.85**
Use Office Automation Systems	.34	2.99**
Build Models	.38	2.84**
Access Data	.46	3.70**
Handle Data Communications	.45	4.07**
Use Hardware	.51	4.13**
Utilize Graphics Techniques	.50	3.92**
Use Operating Systems	.18	1.97*
Understand and Interpret Output	.55	5.94**
Total Ability Importance — Level	5.05	8.01**

*$p < .05$

**$p < .01$

DATA ANALYSIS AND RESULTS

To restate, the general objective of this study was to develop a better understanding of end-user training within the organization. In particular, its goal
was to develop a better understanding of the impact that computer-related
training has on management via an investigation of the use of existing IS
products and technologies, the satisfaction of the end-user community, and
the abilities of end users to employ computers in their work environment.
Therefore, relationships representing three different variable classes (training, ability and acceptance) were investigated. Due to the varying metrics of
the questions contained within the research instruments the data were stan-
dardized (Mean = 0, Std. Dev. = 1) prior to analysis.

Research Question 1 (Q1)

**What is the relationship between the computer-related training an individ-
ual receives and his/her computer-related abilities?**

In general, managers rated their current level of ability significantly lower
than the corresponding level of importance they attached to each item. (See
Table 7.5.) This evidence underscores the significance of examining the
relationship stated in Q1.

To examine the relationship described in each of the research questions,
correlation coefficients were generated. (See Table 7.6.) As depicted, statis-

TABLE 7.6
CORRELATIONS BETWEEN VARIABLES IN RESEARCH QUESTIONS

	Training 1	Training 2	Ability	Use	Satisfaction
Training 1	–				
Training 2	.33**	–			
Ability	.53**	.22*	–		
Use	.02	.07	.22	–	
Satisfaction	.04	.10	.06	.20*	–

Note: Training 1 = Quantity of training as measured by all *sources*.
         Training 2 = Quantity of training as measured by all *techniques*.
*p < .05
**p < .01

tically significant correlations exist between training source and ability
(r = .53; p < .01), as well as between training hours/technique and ability
(r = .22; p < .05). In this case, statistical analysis led us to conclude that there
is a relationship between the computer-related training that a user receives
and his/her ability to use the computer resource.

In addition, the relationship between each of the four individual sources
of computer-related training and the eleven individual ability levels was examined via the analysis of zero order correlations (r). (See Table 7.7.) Over 50%
of these pairings (33/60) represented significant relationships at the .05 level
or better. Some significant correlations are:

1. Computer-related training received in college seemed to support pro-
    gramming, modeling and graphing abilities, as well as the ability to use
    application development software (e.g., LOTUS 1-2-3) and operating
    systems. It also better enabled users to understand computer-generated
    output.
2. Computer-related training received from the company tended to support
    the handling of data communications, hardware, graphics and operating
    systems.
3. Vendor training was significantly correlated with the ability to use pack-
    aged application software, as well as other proprietary-oriented abilities
    such as hardware manipulation and data communications.

Research Question 2 (Q2)

**What is the relationship between the computer-related abilities of an end
user and his/her acceptance of information systems products and technologies?**

To facilitate operationalization of the variable acceptance, Q2 was further
subdivided into two secondary questions.

TABLE 7.7
CORRELATIONS BETWEEN SOURCE OF TRAINING
AND COMPUTER-RELATED ABILITIES (N = 100)

Ability to:	Self-Trained	College	Company	Vendor	Source Overall
Program	.18	.49**	.10	.02	.31**
Use Application Development Software	.32**	.26**	.07	.09	.35**
Use Packaged Application Software	.26**	.11	.17	.44**	.46**
Use OAS	.14	.15	.30	.06	.19**
Build Models	.07	.22*	.02	.14	.05
Access Data	.32**	.17	.09	.22*	.36**
Handle Data Communications	.28**	.09	.32**	.06	.34**
Use Hardware	.32**	.10	.27**	.21*	.39**
Utilize Graphics Techniques	.27**	.33**	.24*	.05	.35**
Use Operating Systems	.31**	.21*	.25**	.02	.32**
Understand and Interpret Output	.11	.21	.02	.10	.11
Overall Ability	.42**	.36**	.26**	.14	.53**

*p < .05

**p < .01

Q2.1: What is the relationship between an end user's abilities and his/her utilization of IS products and technologies?

As displayed in Table 7.6, a correlation of .22 between ability and the use of an IS in the decision-making process was statistically significant at the .05 level. This led us to conclude that there may be a relationship between an end user's abilities and his/her utilization of information systems.

Q2.2: What is the relationship between an end user's abilities and his/her satisfaction with IS products and technologies?

Based upon our examination of the correlation between ability and satisfaction, we are unable to conclude that there is statistically significant relationship between these variables at the .05 level. (See Table 7.6.)

DISCUSSION

Research efforts have done little for the educational development of the IS user community. Indeed, our literature review, as well as what is actually being done in a number of organizations, indicates a lack of consensus that training is the critical link in getting managers to use computer-based information systems. Education/training seems to be taken for granted—an occurrence often mentioned, yet seldom acted upon.

This study of the current training practices in a number of different companies largely echoed our findings from the literature review. In each case, interviewees stated, time and time again, how important they felt training was to the successful integration of systems. Yet the resources formally committed to training remained relatively low across the 20 survey companies. In general, companies were found to be "spending" less than 2% of their IS resources (human and financial) on training end users.

Statistical examination of the two primary relationships described within our research model yielded these significant correlations:

1. Computer-related training is positively related to computer-related ability (Q1).
2. Computer-related ability is positively related to use of computer resources (Q2.1).

Apart from the testing of the research questions and the validation of the model itself, several other interesting relationships were statistically examined. For example, in general, managers rated their current level of ability lower than the corresponding level of importance they attached to each item. In addition, the relationship between the "sources of training" and the eleven variables describing ability levels for the 100 managers contained a number of interesting implications concerning where users seem to be developing various abilities.

First, the finding that programming, modeling, graphing, and the use of software such as LOTUS 1-2-3 are skills that are more apt to be learned in college is a logical expectation. However, the additional knowledge that managers rated their programming, modeling, and graphics skill levels to be among their lowest could be a cause for concern. (See Table 7.4) Perhaps both colleges and companies alike need to become more cognizant of educational results.

Secondly, company training seemed to support the more "technically-oriented" abilities: use of data communications, hardware, and operating systems. Here, the question that comes to mind is "what are the company's training programs in LOTUS 1-2-3 accomplishing?"

Third, vendor training/support in the use of particular products has obviously been an important consideration in the purchasing decision for good reason. What the IS professional also needs to consider is "when is it cost effective to bring this training in-house?"

The findings suggest that the most successful computer-based information systems, from the standpoint of increased use, will be those in which users are able to utilize the computer resource for a variety of different purposes (e.g., modeling, accessing data, and/or interpreting output). Computer-related ability, therefore, joins other important factors such as the user-friendliness of a particular IS, the location of an access unit (terminal or stand-alone computer), and required use by a supervisor in determining the degree of utilization of an IS. All of these points are important to the practitioner, based on the premise that the more a system is used, the more potential that system has for success.

Given that ability enhances a manager's use of a system, the question now becomes "how can we enhance a manager's ability?" Research Question 1 examined this point via computer-related training.

IS practitioners and top management should be interested in the fact that managers do not feel they possess the necessary computer skills to do their jobs effectively (Table 7.5.) Managers perceive a greater need for training in ten of the eleven ability areas—every area except programming.

FUTURE RESEARCH

Both researchers and practitioners are encouraged to incorporate and build upon the research presented in this study. Further examination of this study's implications is required to gain a true understanding of the user-training problem.

In reference to the study's limitations, the companies and subjects included within the sample are not representative of all operational environments. We chose to examine (1) companies in which IS has a high strategic impact on existing operations, and (2) only top- and middle-level end users. Furthermore, the operationalization of the variables contained within the research model deserves close scrutiny. There is a myriad of ways to describe a research topic as new as this one.

We and other researchers are challenged to find new ways of testing educational relationships in the IS environment. The weak relationship described in Q2.2 calls for the design of new studies that incorporate different, perhaps more homogenous research instruments. For example, the development of a questionnaire specifically designed to measure end-user satisfaction is strongly encouraged. While the UIS questionnaire[18] remains one of the only validated instruments in the field, based on our experience it seems unlikely that it is appropriate for measuring satisfaction with end-user computing. In addition, future researchers might attempt to measure training in terms of *content* (e.g., training received for programming, use of LOTUS 1-2-3, or data communication), much along the same lines as the ability questionnaire attempted to measure the ability to program, to use LOTUS 1-2-3, etc.

This exploratory study has indicated several specific areas requiring more explicit and extensive research in order to help the organization operate as an effective change agent in the integration of IS technologies:

1.   It would be interesting to view the effects of computer-related training on ability and acceptance within a field or laboratory experiment, in which the variables are under some degree of control.

2.   Somewhat related to 1 above would be research of a controlled nature on the effectiveness of various instructional techniques within different educational scenarios. For example, it would be helpful to know under what circumstances the tutorial technique is most effective. Also, it would be interesting to note what combinations of techniques are effective, and under what circumstances.

3.   More in-depth case research on a smaller number of companies would also be a productive research effort. Companies within similar industries, yet found to approach user education differently, could be compared and contrasted in terms of successful/unsuccessful experiences. Here, one might seek to include companies operating at different stages of technological development.

4.   Related to 2 above would be research on the influence of a stage model (e.g., Nolan's Stage Hypothesis[20]) on the development of organizational education strategies[21]. Determination of a logical progression and time frame for a company's educational development would be very helpful to the practitioner.

5.   There is also a process of "evolution" in user behavior[17,22], and that in itself should provide an interesting backdrop for future studies on the impact of training on acceptance over time. Indeed, the relationship between training and a user's behavioral evolution is certainly an appropriate application of the S-shaped learning curve phenomenon. Perhaps a series of phases or stages can be identified under which a user progresses from a state of uncertainty, during which the user must overcome feelings of anxiety, to a point of integration, where the technology has been effectively integrated into a user's work environment.

Most of the above areas of research are broad and interrelated. However, if the present research has brought these issues into clearer focus, an important objective has been achieved.

REFERENCES

1. Brancheau, J. and Wetherbe, J. C. "Key Issues in Information Systems," *MIS Quarterly*, Volume 11, Number 1, March 1987, pp. 23–45

2. Brady, R. H. "Computers in Top-Level Decision Making," *Harvard Business Review*, Volume 45, Number 4, July–August 1967, pp. 67–76.

3. Lewin, K. "Group Decision and Social Change," in *Readings in Social Psychology*, G. E. Swanson, T. M. Newcomb, E. L. Hartley (eds.), Holt, Rinehart and Winston, New York, New York, 1952.

4. Schein, E. "Management Development as a Process of Influence," *Industrial Management Review*, Volume 2, May 1961, pp. 59–77.

5. Miles, M. B. "Temporary Systems," in *Innovation in Education*, M. B. Miles (ed.), Teachers College, Columbia University, New York, New York, 1964, Chapter 19.

6. Culnan, M. J. "The Dimensions of Perceived Accessibility to Information: Implications for the Delivery of Information Systems and Services," *Journal of American Society for Information Science*, Volume 36, Number 5, September 1985, pp. 302–308.

7. Kerr, E. B. and Hiltz, S. R. *Computer Mediated Communication Systems: Status and Evaluation*, Academic Press, New York, New York, 1982, p. 58.

8. Benson, D. H. "A Field Study of End-User Computing: Findings and Issues," *MIS Quarterly*, Volume 7, Number 4, December 1983, pp. 35–45.

9. Rockart, J. F. and Flannery, L. S. "The Management of End-User Computing," *Communications of the ACM*, Volume 26, Number 10, October 1983, pp. 776–784.

10. Sprague, R. H. , Jr. and Carlson, E. D. *Building Effective Decision Support Systems*, Prentice-Hall, Inc., Englewood Cliffs, New Jersey, 1982.

11. Chung, K. H. and Megginson, L. C. *Organizational Behaviors: Developing Managerial Skills*, Harper and Row, New York, New York, 1981, pp. 145–147.

12. Lawler, E. "Ability as a Moderator of the Relationship Between Job Attitudes and Job Performance," *Personnel Psychology*, Volume 19, Number 2, Summer 1966, pp. 153–164.

13. Bair, J. H. "Evaluation and Analysis of an Augmented Knowledge Workshop: Final Report for Phase I," Rome Air Development Center, RADC-TR-74, 79, Griffiss Air Force Base, New York, 1974, pp. 28–31.

14. Ginzberg, M. A. "Key Recurrent Issues in the MIS Implementation Process," *MIS Quarterly*, Volume 5, Number 2, June 1981, pp. 47–60.

15. Grace, B. F. "Training Users of a Decision Support System," *Data Base*, Volume 8, Number 3, Winter 1977, pp. 30–36.

16. Heany, D. E. "Education: The Critical Link in Getting Managers to Use Management Systems," *Interfaces*, Volume 2, Number 3, May 1972, pp. 1–7.

17. Hiltz, S. R. and Turoff, M. "The Evolution of User Behavior in a Computerized Conferencing System," *Communications of the ACM*, Volume 24, Number 11, November 1981, pp. 739–751.

18. Ives, B., Olson, M. H. and Baroudi, J. J. "The Measurement of User Information Satisfaction," *Communications of the ACM*, Volume 26, Number 10, October 1983, pp. 785–793.

19. McFarlan, F. W. and McKenney, J. L. *Corporate Information Systems Management*, Richard D. Irwin, Inc., Homewood, Illinois, 1983.

20. Gibson, C. F. and Nolan, R. L. "Managing the Four Stages of EDP Growth," *Harvard Business Review*, Volume 52, Number 1, January–February 1974, pp. 76–88.

21. Alavi, M., Nelson, R. R. and Weiss, I. R. "Strategies for End-User Computing: An Integrative Framework," *Journal of Management Information Systems*, (Volume IV, Number 3, Winter 1987-88, pp. 28–49).

22. Hiltz, S. R. *Online Communities: A Case Study of the Office of the Future*, Ablex Publishing Corp., Norwood, New Jersey, 1984.

FOR FURTHER READING

1. Bronsema, G. S. and Keen, P. "Education Intervention and Implementation in MIS," *Sloan Management Review*, Volume 24, Number 4, Summer 1983, pp. 35–43.

2. Lucas, H. C. , Jr. and Nielson, N. R. "The Impact of the Mode of Information Presentation on Learning and Performance," *Management Science*, Volume 26, Number 10, October 1980, pp. 982–993.

3. Nelson, R. R. and Cheney, P. H. "Educating the CBIS User: A Case Analysis," *Data Base*, Volume 18, Number 2, Winter 1987, pp. 11–16.

4. Nelson, R. R. and Cheney, P. H. "Training Today's User," *Datamation*, Volume 33, Number 10, May 15, 1987, pp. 121–122.

QUESTIONS

1.   Describe the components of the educational process within the context of an EUC environment.

2.   Describe the difference between education and training using the analogy of sex education versus sex training.

3.   How is the process of organizational learning closely related to the problems of organizational change?

4.   What is the primary motivation for the measurement and analysis of end-user abilities? What abilities seem to be (a) needed, and (b) possessed, more than other abilities within the end-user community?

5.   Describe the various sources and methods of training end users. Why and how would one want to examine the relationship between training sources/methods and end-user abilities?

6.   What evidence seems to support the statement that "education/training seems to be taken for granted—a subject often mentioned, yet seldom acted upon. " What are the implications of such a statement?

8

Training End Users to Compute: Cognitive, Motivational and Social Issues

■

Maung K. Sein
Robert P. Bostrom
Lorne Olfman

INTRODUCTION

The practice of end-users developing, maintaining, and using their own information systems is referred to as end user computing (EUC). One critical factor that can affect the success or failure of EUC within an organization is training.[1] Training for EUC involves several dimensions. End-users need to be instructed on system development techniques, database modelling, performing backup and recovery, systems security to name a few. Yet, the most crucial dimension is perhaps learning to use EUC software tools. This paper prescribes guidelines for training users in EUC software tools.

The success or failure of EUC within an organization will ultimately depend on whether end-users effectively use EUC software. The key question to be answered then is: What determines how an end-user behaves? Consider an example situation:

Reprinted by special permission of INFOR, *Volume 25, Number 3, August 1987, pp. 236–255.*

An investment manager is currently faced with deciding upon an investment decision from a set of very attractive alternatives. There are many involved, each varying in their degree of uncertainty. She needs to explore various scenarios to determine the best alternative. This manager has recently been trained in the spreadsheet/modelling language, Lotus 1-2-3. She thinks that Lotus 1-2-3 would help her make this decision. She defines a spreadsheet model using the Lotus software, and proceeds to check out various scenarios by changing appropriate investment values. However, while doing these "what ifs", she got frustrated when trying to examine scenarios that had already been processed. She did not know that she could save and reaccess the "what if" cases. Consequently, she did not fully compare all scenarios. Overall, this investment manager was very satisfied with her decision, and felt that Lotus 1-2-3 was very helpful in this situation, although she did not fully understand the capabilities of the software.

This example demonstrates the major determinants of end-user behavior. The user is engaged in goal-oriented tasks such as choosing between alternative investments. The user has a certain motivation to use available EUC software such as Lotus 1-2-3, and attempts to accomplish the goal as effortlessly as possible. There are certain constraints in this process imposed by the user-system interface, by what the user understands about the software, and by other individual characteristics such as previous experience with computers. These determinants for user behavior/performance can be stated in the following relationship:

User's task (e.g. problem to solve, decision to make)

+

User's motivation to use system

+

User's knowledge (understanding of EUC software)

+

User-system interface

+

User's other characteristics

⇓

User's behavior/performace

If we want to influence user behavior, we must change one of the determinants. The human factors literature emphasizes altering or improving the user-system (i.e. man-machine) interface. Alternatively, we can increase the user's knowledge through more efficient teaching methods, and increase the user's motivation by showing how the system can be used to accomplish various relevant tasks. The ultimate goal of those focusing on the user-system interface is to develop a system that is idiot-proof. Although we agree that better interfaces are badly needed, the objective of achieving error-free interfaces is being regarded as impractical by an increasing number of researchers and systems designers. For instance, Brown and Newman[2] emphasize this view when they called for "error management" rather than "error avoidance."

More importantly, waiting for an idiot-proof system sidesteps the difficult issue of the user's understanding of the system and the motivation to use it. We believe these issues cannot be avoided. They are central to developing a user's sense of control over the technology, which is in turn essential for effectively using it. We believe these issues cannot be avoided. They are central to developing a user's sense of control over the technology, which is in turn essential for effectively using it. Without understanding and motivation, users will not want to or be able to apply EUC software to new situations, or to deal with errors and systems malfunctions. We believe understanding and motivation can be achieved through good training.

IMPORTANCE OF TRAINING

Issues associated with EUC clearly demonstrate that it is critical for IS departments to implement training programs that enable end-users to use software tools effectively. The issues include the application development backlogs facing IS departments;[3] the growth in hardware and software available to end-users;[4] and the growing number of first-time software users.[5]

IS departments are not ignoring the need for EUC training. For example, there has been a substantial growth in the number of Information Centers (IC) in organizations.[6] In a survey of 21 organizations Zmud and Lind[7] found that training sessions for end-users were considered one of the most effective linking mechanisms in ensuring success of EUC. This awareness is emphasized by the critical importance that IS managers place on educational programs for end-users.[8,9] However, reports of unused personal computers (PCs) and software indicate that effective training programs are exceptions rather than the norm. Numerous documented cases of user developed systems generating erroneous results[10] further indicate the need for such programs.

Unfortunately, little guidance has been provided in research or practitioner literature for developing EUC training programs. Researchers have focused their attention almost entirely on the learning of procedure-oriented languages typically used by IS professionals. The nonprocedural/fourth generation languages (4GLs) utilized in EUC have been neglected. The reason for this neglect is perhaps attributable to the contentions by vendors of EUC tools that their products are easy to learn and use. These unsubstantiated claims have unfortunate implications.

Exploratory research regarding the learning of EUC software such as modelling languages,[11] and our experience as software trainers indicates that ease of learning and use for EUC tools cannot be taken for granted. As Mack *et al.*[12] demonstrated, even learning simple tools such as text editors is not easy. Learning difficulties for end-users can and should be expected. Moreover, without effective training programs, these difficulties will have a serious negative impact on organizations.

While some research has been directed toward how to make EUC tools easier to learn, the issue of motivating end users to continue to learn and use these tools has been virtually ignored. In EUC training, especially for novices, initially focusing on the development of appropriate motivational levels may be more important than knowledge acquisition. Research on learning to use computers seems to have lost sight of the research findings that indicate that learning is a function of ability and motivation (see Wlodkowski, 1985[13] for a review).

The training guidelines presented in this paper are based on an analysis of the training/learning process. The analysis is structured in an integrated framework developed by Bostrom *et al.*[14] that addresses both the cognitive and motivational dimensions inherent in training and learning. In the next section of this paper, the framework is introduced, and key variables are defined. Two key outcomes of training are identified:

1.   That the trainee acquire a useful mental model of the software tool, and
2.   That the trainee have a high motivation to use the software.

Based on available research findings, the third section describes the prescriptions for effective training, and guidelines for supporting continued learning. Each prescription is based on achieving the training outcomes, and is evaluated in terms of the key variables in the framework. Prescriptions are supported by examples. The conclusion outlines some research studies that would refine and enhance the guidelines presented in the paper.

END-USER TRAINING FRAMEWORK

The framework developed by Bostrom *et al.*[14] is illustrated in Figure 8.1 and Table 8.1. It presents a conceptualization of what occurs when someone learns to use a software tool. The first stage of the learning process is termed training. Training occurs prior to the time when an individual applies their new skills on the job. Second and subsequent steps of the learning process are called problem solving. Problem solving occurs when the trainee uses new software skills to complete tasks at work.

During any of the stages of learning, three general classes of inputs are involved: the characteristics of the trainee, the software system to be (being) learned, and the environment. The environment in the problem solving stages will be somewhat different than in the training stage, where instructional tools will be utilized. In each learning stage, the characteristics of the trainee will change, with the changes reflecting the main outcomes of the learning process. A related outcome in problem solving is the accomplishment of a particular task.

The guidelines presented in this paper pertain to the design of the training and task environments to support learning of an EUC software tool. This is not to say that one cannot define prescriptions applicable to the design

FIGURE 8.1
TRAINING/LEARNING PROCESS (FROM BOSTROM ET AL. 1987)

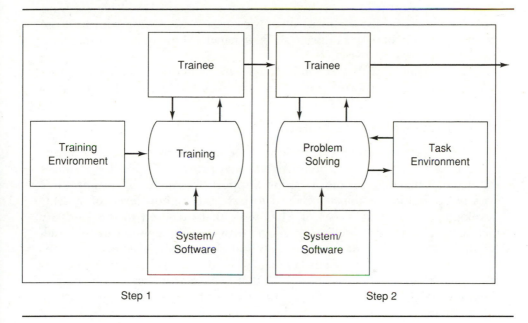

TABLE 8.1
VARIABLES IN THE FRAMEWORK

Trainee Characteristics	Training Environment	System Software
Mental Model of Systems	Methods	Ease of Use
Motivation to Learn/Use System	Conceptual Models	Type of Language
Task Importance	Motivation Planning/	(e.g. 4GL)
Ease of Use	Management	Type of Interface
Usefulness	Physical Aspects	Direct or Indirect
Enjoyment of Using		Manipulation
Cognitive Traits		
Learning Style		
Visual Ability		
Procedurality		
Motivational Traits		
Self-Concept		
Need for Achievement		
Attitude Toward Computers		
Task Domain Knowledge		
Other Factors		
Previous Computer		
Experience		

(From Bostrom et al. 1987)

of software to be learned, or to the type of skills that trainees can bring to training. Rather, in the paper we concentrate on the organizational situation where employees need to be trained to use a currently available software tool. More specifically, we focus on novice users—i.e. those who have no experience with the EUC software to be learned. They may, however, have previous computer experience.

The remainder of this section is devoted to the definition and description of the trainee and software/system components of the learning framework.

The Software/System to Be Learned

The training guidelines and definitions presented in this paper focus on the category of software used to build systems that provide support for managerial decision making. Termed Decision Support System (DSS) software, this class of application system is believed to have the highest levels of systems development backlog.[3] Types of EUC tools that are used in this category include database and modelling language software. These tools can be implemented on mainframe or PC machines, and each can be classified as either direct or indirect manipulation languages. In direct manipulation, the system provides representations of objects that behave as if they are the objects themselves.[15] Instead of describing the actions of interest through syntactical commands, the user performs those actions directly on the model world of objects presented to him/her. Spreadsheet programs on PCs incorporate many essential features of direct manipulation.

The type or category of software is important because the combination of language function, host system, and level of manipulation all have implications for the training process. A designer of training methods must take into account the contribution that a software tool will make to the learning process. For example, researchers believe that direct manipulation languages are easier to learn and use compared to indirect languages.[16] At the same time, the designer must be aware of how the EUC tool to be learned fits into the task domain of the trainee.

Novice trainees may also be overwhelmed by the numerous features available on the software for the same construct. For example, in a modelling language, there may be several ways of designating and computing a variable. There may be a need to tailor the software to suit the comfort level of the trainee. Carroll and Carrithers[17] employed the concept of "training wheels" to train novices. Training wheels imply restricting the number of features that are made available to new learners. The full system was presented to them only after they have gained confidence with the software.

Outcomes: What the Trainee Gains from Training

The crucial objective in training is to provide the trainee with the know how and desire to use EUC software on the job. This objective can be formalized into two specific and measurable outcomes termed *mental model* of the software and *motivation to use*. These outcomes are reflected in changes in trainee characteristics, and are carried on to future stages in the learning process.

Mental models are mental or internal conceptual representations of the software the user is learning. Various definitions include a set of basic concepts,[18] the user's belief about the system,[19] and an essential core of knowledge.[20] Mental models aid users in making inferences about the system,[21] reasoning about it,[18–20] and guiding actions.[22] To be effective, a training program should provide aids that will help users form initial mental models.[23] Conceptual models of the system/software serve as such aids. They will be discussed in detail later in this paper.

Merely learning how to use a software tool is an incomplete outcome of training. The trainee must leave with a high motivation to continue to use the software on-the-job. This is especially important in the EUC environment where the user has a choice of whether or not to use the software to support or enhance a task.[24] Dimensions that are important in motivating use include usefulness, ease of use, task importance, and enjoyment of using software.[25] Motivational planning and management of training should be applied to generate high levels of motivation.[13,26]

We view learning to be a constant ongoing process. A structured training program, by definition, has a fixed time span and must end when the specified time span elapses. But learning goes on. Therefore, the training outcomes—mental model of the system and motivation to use it—are not static objectives. A user will not have a complete mental model of the software, however well-designed the training program is. What he/she will have, however, is a cogent and accurate initial mental model encompassing certain vital and essential parts of the software. Mental models are constantly refined and perfected through the user's continuous interaction with the system.[20,27] Novice users need to experiment with the system to form and test hypotheses about it by using their mental models.[2] Each time they test the boundary condition of the mental model, their understanding of the system is extended, and a richer and more accurate mental model results. It is important to ensure that when trainees return to their jobs, the social environment is conducive to this learning process.

However, the user will use the system only if he/she is motivated to do so. Good mental models give the user a feeling of control over the system, which contributes to his/her perception of how easy the system is to use and to his/her enjoyment of using the software. As Davis[25] has shown, ease of use and enjoyment will lead to motivation to use the system. The two outcomes, motivation and mental models, are thus interrelated.

Trainee Characteristics

Each trainee brings a set of characteristics to the training. These include cognitive traits, motivational traits, task domain knowledge, and referent experiences. These characteristics will be defined in reference to the end-user, who is the trainee of interest in this paper.

Cognitive traits include basic aptitudes related to problem solving such as visual and spatial ability.[28] These traits also include individual preferences or learning styles.[29]

Motivational traits refer to individual differences regarding potential for being motivated to learn. Two broad dimensions for learning motivation are self-concept and need for achievement. Self-concept is the trainee's view of his/her ability to learn the target skills. Need for achievement is the trainee's desire to succeed at the learning task.[13,30]

Task domain knowledge is the expertise that manager's bring from their job. It will be this knowledge that end-users want to utilize in developing their own IS.

Referent experiences are the previous interactions that the end-user has had with computer systems and software. Trainees may be expected to have a wide range of such experience and will vary from raw novices to long-time users.

These characteristics need to be considered when designing training methods. Research findings indicate that learners benefit differently from the instructional method used depending on their individual characteristics.[31–34,35]

GUIDELINES FOR TRAINING PROGRAMS

The design of training and task environments to support end-user managers' learning of EUC software is addressed in this section. Training environments are made up of two main components, physical aspects and training methods. The guidelines provided here center around two specific training methods, namely conceptual models and motivational planning and management. Task environments are not directly designed by trainers. Yet, the trainee can benefit from the social environment of use, and so must be provided with support and encouragement to continuously reinforce the outcomes of the training stage.

As we have stated earlier, very little research has been conducted on EUC training. The practitioner literature is equally scanty in providing guidelines for effective training. This is unfortunate, because research findings in several disciplines are germane to training issues. This paper is an attempt at providing a systematic and integrated direction to EUC training. Our training guidelines are based on research findings in educational psychology, cognitive science, organizational behavior and information systems. It should be noted that, in developing our guidelines, we have extrapolated most of these findings to the EUC environment. Further research needs to be conducted in an EUC setting to determine if our extrapolations were valid and appropriate. Research studies carried out at IBM's Watson Research Center[36,37] are notable steps in this direction. The research program initiated by us is a further effort towards establishing an integrated multi-disciplinary tradition. Initial findings from these studies argue favorably for the efficacy of our prescriptions.[31,38]

Physical Aspects of Training Environments

These are structural factors such as the physical setting of the training, the ambiance of the setting, and the materials to support learning. The goal is to provide the trainee with a stimulating learning environment.

The training environment can be formal or self-instructional.[39] Formal environments are structured, and are typically conducted by an instructor in a classroom that affords hands-on use of the system. Users generally train in a group over a fixed period of time. The self-instructional environments, on the other hand, are most often unstructured and self-paced. These are typified by the absence of an instructor although someone may be designated to supervise the training.

Computer Aided Instruction (CAI) falls somewhere in between the two classes. It is usually structured and standard, but is also self-paced and conducted on a one-on-one basis. Garcia[6] claims that the best method for learning a software product is to "sit with a patient expert." CAI materials can be built to simulate experts.[40] They can be tailored to suit individual aptitudes and needs. CAI has the potential to be a cost-effective mode of training. Yet, very little is known about the efficiency and efficacy of using CAI. We will consider CAI as a special case of the self-instructional environment.

Although Bikson and Gutek[39] found that trainees favor formal settings over self-instructional, the latter setting is widely used in organizations. It is a very useful and practical method to employ when one or a few trainees are involved. We therefore present our training guidelines for both training environments.

Conceptual Models

A key problem that a learner faces in any new domain is lack of prior knowledge that can be transferred to the domain. This was dramatically illustrated when prominent non-scientists were taught concepts of physics at the University of Chicago.[41] To quote one learner: "... I lacked any framework of prior knowledge ... that could have helped me order the information I was receiving." (p. 13)

Conceptual models provide such frameworks by conveying basic concepts of the system to be learned to the learners. For example, in training naive users, an office filing cabinet is often used as an analogy for a computer filing system. The contention is that a filing cabinet is very much a part of the trainee's referent experience. He/she can transfer his/her knowledge about the filing cabinet to the computer filing system. This mapping of prior knowledge facilitates the learning of the new system. This analogy thus serves as a conceptual model of the system to be learned. Conceptual models provide anchoring structures for incoming knowledge and thus, a basis for forming mental models.

New learners of a system encounter an initial fear of the system; they do not feel that they are "in control" or feel that they are "lost."[2] Users make mistakes that are frequently aggravated by their erroneous efforts at extricating themselves.[12] This happens when they fail to develop an accurate mental model of the system. A good conceptual model that can be used to build mental models is essential to avoid these problems. Novice users must be provided with multiple conceptual models. Firstly, they need a conceptual model of the computer. Next, they must understand the basic concepts of the software architecture, and finally the software syntax.

Types of Conceptual Models:

Conceptual models can be classified as analogical and as abstract. Analogical models represent the to-be-learned system in terms of another system. For example, a spreadsheet is an analogy for a modelling language. Abstract models are synthetic representations of the system. For example, a system may be depicted as a mathematical model or in schematic diagrams.[19,42,43]

The most common form of conceptual models used, both in research and practice have been analogical.[21,44,45] The main advantage is that these are part of most learner's referent experiences. It also follows that analogies cannot be used if the learner has no prior experience with the analogy. In a formal setting, analogies can be used very gainfully. The instructor must, however, indicate the shortcomings of analogies. Analogical models can be misleading unless the boundary conditions of the analogical mapping are explicitly pointed out, i.e. trainees are told where the analogy fails. For example, the office file cabinet analogy for a computer file system holds until the issues of file-level security and hierarchical directory pop up.

In a self-instructional setting, analogies can be used only with extreme caution. An abstract model may prove to be better because it cannot be over-generalized, that is, an incorrect mapping is unlikely. The difficulty is that because abstract models are synthetic, users must first learn the model itself. This imposes an added burden on the learner.

Differences in a trainee's cognitive style and ability also must be considered before a conceptual model is provided. Sein[31] found that learners of low visual ability were hampered by abstract models; however, they learned as well as their high visual counterparts when provided with analogical models.

Evolution of Mental Models:

The success of an EUC training program will not be ensured by simply helping the trainees to build an initial accurate mental model through conceptual models. As we have stated earlier in the paper, mental models are continuously revised and enriched through interaction with the system. Trainees need to test and "stretch" their mental models in order to form a more accurate mental model.[2] They must be encouraged to experiment with the system. As mentioned earlier, there may also be a need to modify the system to facilitate this experimentation.

A caveat must be offered here. A key assumption behind this recommendation is that users have the prerequisite abilities necessary to benefit from a training program based on the experimental mode of learning. Chief among these skills is formulating and testing hypotheses. If this assumption is not met, then users must first acquire these basic abilities, possibly through training.[2] It is our belief that EUC managers have the necessary abilities to learn EUC tools.[11]

Motivational Planning and Management

A trainee's motivation must be managed before, during, and after the training process.[13] The following prescriptions will focus on the before and during phases. After training motivation management, that is, concern for motivation during the problem solving stages of learning, will be addressed in the section on the social environment of use.

Figure 8.2 shows how a high level of motivation could be instilled in a trainee during training. In this hypothetical example, prior to and at the outset of training, the trainee's negative feelings toward computers are balanced by the need to retain a job. In this example, no apparent motivational planning has been undertaken before training begins. During training, the level of motivation is increased by providing relevant problems and ample feedback.

An important consideration in motivational management is that the meth-

FIGURE 8.2
POSITIVE MOTIVATIONAL DYNAMIC

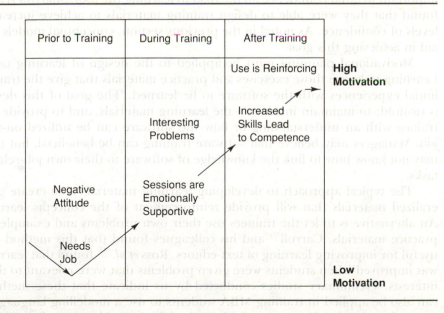

ods used must take account of the motivational traits of trainees. Keller[26] defines factors that tap into self-concept and need for achievement. These broad categories are termed expectancy (related to developing confidence in success), satisfaction (managing reinforcement), relevance (connecting instruction to important needs and motives), and interest (arousing and maintaining curiosity and attention).

Before Training Assessments: Before training planning should include an assessment of the goals, needs, aptitudes, cognitive styles and previous experiences of the trainee. This assessment will provide the trainer with the ability to direct specific information about the usefulness of the EUC tool to their job situation. It might also allow matching of trainees of equivalent aptitude, experience and domain knowledge in training sessions. Sharrow et al.[46] used this type of pretraining assessment successfully. Before training assessment may also help when trainees are sent to training without a high level of initial self-motivation.

When a manager begins to learn a software tool, it is important that there be a match between the level of motivation going in, and the training methods used. For example, managers may come to training believing that the software to be learned will be a panacea in their job. They will be highly motivated to learn, but unless the training method focuses on these motivations, the result could be disastrous.

Motivational Considerations during Training: Trainees may arrive with a genuine feeling of need, but an overall fear of computers. In these cases, it is important to build confidence on the road to learning the tool. Sharrow et al.[46] found that they were able to design training materials to achieve increased levels of confidence. As noted in the previous section, conceptual models can aid in achieving this goal.

Motivational planning must be applied to the design of learning tasks. Learning tasks are those exercises and practice materials that give the trainee initial experiences with the software to be learned. The goal of this design is twofold: to maintain interest in the learning materials, and to provide the trainee with an understanding of how the software can be utilized on-the-job. Managers may believe that software training can be beneficial, but they may not know how to link the knowledge of software to their own job-related tasks.

The typical approach to developing learning materials is to create generalized materials that will provide reinforcement of the concepts learned. An alternative is to let the trainees use their own problems and examples as practice materials. Carroll[36] and his colleagues found that this method was useful for improving learning of text-editors. Ross et al. [47] found that learning was improved when students were given problems that were relevant to their interests. Preliminary studies conducted by us indicate that these methods can also be applied in training MBA students to use a modelling language.[37] An explanation for the success of this method lies in Kublanow et al's [24] finding that the use of a software is related to the user's perception that it supports his/her job. Providing a link to job-related functions, through the use of relevant examples and problems, ensures that the manager can apply domain knowledge in support of the learning task.

Another benefit of having trainees bring their own problems to training is that they become aware of the process of applying EUC tools to their tasks. They will gain initial experience with formulating, developing and testing problems in their own domain. By contrast, generalized learning tasks may fail to address the application issue. Even when the training focuses on this dimension, it is difficult to design generalized problems that contain appropriate meaningfulness for all trainees.

In a formal setting, the trainer has the ability to tightly control motivational management. Given that learning tasks will be focused on trainees' own problems, the instructor can interact with individuals on a one-on-one basis to assist them in their learning. The difficulty in maintaining motivation in a self-instructional setting is that the trainee may get bogged down on some aspect of the instructional materials. However, at least for text editors, Carroll[36] indicates that self-training manuals that include having trainees try out their own problems can be successfully used during the learning process.

After Training Assessment: The focus of after training assessment is to ensure that the trainee (now a novice user) continues to be motivated to use the software on the job. Wexley and Baldwin[48] explored the effectiveness of several strategies to facilitate posttraining transfer and found that assigned and participative goal setting strategies were useful in inducing behavioral change positively towards using the software. Under both strategies, trainees set the learning points to achieve a specific behavioral goal. An example of a goal is ". . . use a daily planner and construct a daily to-do list" (p. 507). Wexley and Baldwin [48] found that these behavioral outcomes were evident two months after the training was over.

The importance of posttraining strategies cannot be understated. However, to foster the desired behavioral outcomes, it is essential to provide an appropriate social environment that will be conducive to such behavioral changes.

Social Environment of Use

Sociological variables are relevant mainly to the problem solving stages of the framework. Brown and Newman[2] advocate the use of the "larger social environment" to aid understanding of the system. The key goal is to foster a spirit of community support and sharing of information. Computer artifacts such as electronic mail and community knowledge bases in addition to newsletters can be used for this purpose.

The facilitation of continued learning of EUC software implies the need to manage hardware, software and human resources. Both technical and social networks must be made available to a wider and wider body of users.

Software that can foster inter-user communication and experimentation must be provided to users. Organizations such as Information Centers (IC) can help create links between designated experts and users. The onus of assuming these responsibilities rests on the MIS organization. Several of the linking mechanisms suggested by Zmud and Lind[7] for supporting EUC, such as IC, and approaches proposed by Leitheiser and Wetherbe[49] for regulating and clarifying roles for users and MIS organization can create an appropriate social environment.

An important source of support can be those colleagues of the user who themselves are heavy users of the system. Almost every organization has individuals who are known to be "experts or "lead users"[50] in a particular system. They serve as "informal consultants"[50] and can be approached for general information, and more importantly, when the trainee is in trouble. The informal grapevine route can be replaced by a formal process of designating these individuals. We know of one organization that focuses their training on developing such facilitators in different areas of the firm. There is however a danger of overdependence on such lead users on the part of novice users. This will indicate that either the training methods employed are ineffective or that the lead users are not versed in the training outcomes (i.e. they do not know how to help). We recommend that lead users be made aware of the training guidelines so that they can facilitate the attainment of the specific training outcomes of useful mental model and motivation to use on the part of the trainees.

We have emphasized the importance of experimentation in fostering a discovery mode of learning (which also continually motivates learners). A crucial concern in learning through experimentation and discovery is that errors should never lead to disaster (e.g. corrupted corporate database) or irrecoverable situations. The use of test systems with easy restart features, and systems with complete undo facilities to encourage productive guessing represent useful mechanisms to encourage a discovery mode of learning. ICs and lead users can provide trouble shooting and consultation help.

In a formal setting, social environment factors are relevant only to support continued learning after the training program is over. They assume an even greater role for trainees whose initial learning takes place in a self-instructional setting. Without a structure, the trainee is even more dependent on the community for effectively learning the software. The use of CAI for training could provide much of the one-on-one interaction. However, no system can foresee all possible difficulties that a trainee may encounter. The design of any self-instructional system (e.g. CAI) should focus on error management rather than error avoidance.[2] In an unstructured setting, error management cannot be adequately provided without invoking the support of organizational social forces.

The measures suggested here go beyond a commitment by top management to EUC training. Bikson and Gutek[38] found that users were expected to learn a software tool in addition to performing their normal routine responsibilities. In discussions with training specialists for large organizations we found that some training sessions for self-motivated trainees were held on weekends or on the trainees' own time. While this is less of a concern for the self-motivated trainee, those who have to attend such sessions as a job requirement may have their level of motivation reduced. A further implication will be that the trained users may be inhibited in providing help to learners. Such persons should be allowed to allocate a portion of their time to support new user's learning activities. Trainees should also be given time off for training.

CONCLUSION

In this paper we have proposed guidelines for designing training programs for EUC tools in both formal and self-instructional settings. Our prescriptions were framed around the factors proposed in the end-user training framework developed by Bostrom *et al.*[14] Three factors were identified as crucial components in end-user training: conceptual models of the system to be learned, motivation planning and management, and the social environment of use.

In summary, we wish to reiterate the crucial elements that must be included to design an effective end-user training program. Based on research findings in several related fields and our experiences, we believe that these elements apply across all training settings and environments. We will also present some directions for future research in this area.

Summary of Prescriptions

Table 8.2 presents a temporal view of a trainee's progress through the before, during and after phases of a training program. Elements relevant for each phase are shown. The following is a list of prescriptions based on these elements:

TABLE 8.2
SUMMARY OF PRESCRIPTIONS

Before	During		After	
Pre-training analysis	Physical environment	Learning materials	Learning tasks	Social environment of use
Assess fit with	*Provide*	*Provide*	*Provide*	*Ensure*
–needs	–ambiance	–conceptual models	–fit with domain knowledge	–more experimentation
–goals	–chance for immediate feedback	–manuals	–fit with motives	–support
–aptitude		–examples	–experimentation	–network
–experience	–one-on-one to extent possible		–self-direction	of users

1. Before the training:

☐ Demonstrate to the trainee the relevance of software to his/her goals, needs, and experiences.
☐ Assess their individual characteristics (e.g. learning style), prior computer and reference experiences.
☐ Select the training method that matches the trainee's individual characteristics.

2. During the training:

☐ Provide conceptual models to the trainees. Analogies may be used if the trainees have requisite referent experiences. The limitations of the analogies need to be explicitly stated. In a self-instructional setting abstract models may be used.
☐ Problems and exercises should emphasize "stretching" the boundary conditions of mental models.
☐ Problems and exercises should emphasize domain knowledge and relevant application, e.g. have trainees bring their own problems. Provide a stimulating physical environment.
☐ Provide immediate feedback.
☐ Allow and encourage free interaction between trainees. Encourage experimentation with the software/system.
☐ Inculcate self-directed learning.
☐ Warn trainees of likely errors and show them how to recover. Provide proper documentation for this purpose.

3. After the training:

☐ Provide opportunity for more experimentation.
☐ Provide a variety of information sources.
☐ Encourage formation of a network of users who can share ideas and support each other.
☐ Locate knowledgeable users and designate them as facilitators or lead users. Make sure that these lead users are aware of the training outcomes.

Future Research Directions

The recommendations and guidelines provided in this paper are based on the current state of knowledge. We acknowledge the lack of empirical support in an EUC environment to support our prescriptions. Much of the evidence we presented in the paper is extrapolated from research findings in other relevant fields such as educational psychology. We could present only a few findings, mostly of exploratory nature, from an EUC or an IS setting. A few of our guidelines were based on methods that were primarily devised and used by practitioners in the field of end-user training. The evidence for their effectiveness is anecdotal in nature. Further research needs to be carried out. Bostrom et al.[14] have identified key research issues in the crucial but sadly neglected area of end-user training. The following paragraphs briefly outline some of the important research questions.

The best form of conceptual model has remained a debatable issue with researchers in the field. While the most common and popular form has been analogical, several researchers have pointed out their shortcomings, and advocate the use of abstract models instead.[42] We are currently conducting research studies to examine this question.

It is also not clear just how the use of motivationally planned learning materials will influence the outcomes of training. It has been suggested that training that focuses on a narrow aspect of the software tool through the use of specific applications-oriented learning may be detrimental to gaining an extended knowledge of the system.[38] Most software training programs follow a method of using standard and generalized learning tasks. Research studies are currently being conducted that compare these conventional methods with those that require trainees to bring their own problems to the training session. These studies are designed to determine if there is indeed a trade-off between knowledge gained from training and subsequent motivation to use the software.

The Aptitude Training Interaction (ATI) paradigm in educational psychology stresses the need to tailor instructional methods to suit individual traits.[34] Pintrich et al.[30] summed up the rationale for this approach in these terms: ". . . what the learner brings to the instruction situation in prior knowledge and cognitive skills is of crucial importance" (p. 613). We have emphasized the need to take into account the trainee's motivational traits in managing his/her motivation before and during a training program. Individuals differ along this dimension. The degree to which these differences affect the training outcomes is an important area of research. A related issue is whether individual differences such as visual ability, learning style and previous experience with computers have an impact on the suitability of the type of conceptual model that should be used.

The answers to these research questions will provide further insight into the complex cognitive, motivational, behavioral and social issues that influence end-user training. The results will furnish additional support for many of the prescriptions stated in this paper and will provide a better foundation for developing truly effective training designs. The achievement of the stated training outcomes—understanding of the system (accurate mental model) and motivation to use the system—is directly dependent on the efficacy of training methods. For end-user computing to be successful, end-users must use systems, and successfully apply the software learned on the job. To accomplish this outcome, we must first learn how to train them to compute.

REFERENCES

1. Cheney, P. H., Mann, R. I. and Amoroso, D. L. (1986). Organizational factors affecting the success of end-user computing. *Journal of MIS*, 3, 65–80.

2. Brown, J. S. and Newman., S. E. (1985). Issues in cognitive and social ergonomics: From our house to Bauhaus, *Human Computer Interaction*, 1, 359–91.

3. Alloway, R. M. and Quillard, J. A. (1983). User managers' systems needs. *MIS Quarterly*, 7, 2 (June), 27–41.

4. Benjamin, R. I. (1982). Information technology in the 1990's: Long range planning scenario. *MIS Quarterly*, 6, 2 (June), 11–32.

5. Rockart, J. F. and Flannery, L. S. (1983). The management of end user computing. *Communications of the ACM*, 26, 10, 776–84.

6. Garcia, B. (1985). The second CRWTH information center survey. *CRWTH News for Better Training*, 3, 2.

7. Zmud, R. W. and Lind, M. R. (1985). Linking mechanisms supporting end-user computing. *Proceedings of the 12th Annual Conference of ACM SIGCPR/SIGBDP*, Minneapolis, 74–80.

8. Hartog, C. and Herbert, M. (1986). Opinion survey of MIS managers: Key issues. *MIS Quarterly*, 10, 351–361.

9. Dickson, G., Leitheiser, R. L., Wetherbe, J. C., and Nechis, M. (1984). Key information systems issues for the 1980's. *MIS Quarterly*, 8, 3, 135-159.

10. Davis, G. B. (1984). Caution: User-developed systems can be dangerous to your organization. MISRC-WP-84-04, MIS Research Center, School of Management, University of Minnesota.

11. Olfman, L., Sein, M. and Bostrom, R. P. (1986). Training for end-user computing: Are basic abilities enough for learning? *Proceedings of the Twenty-Second Annual Computer Personnel Research Conference*, Calgary, AB.

12. Mack, R. L., Lewis, C. L., and Carroll, J. M. (1983). Learning to use word processors: Problems and prospects. *ACM Transactions on Office Information Systems*, 1, 3, 254–271.

13. Wlodkowski, R. J. (1985). *Enhancing Adult Motivation to Learn*. San Francisco, Jossey-Bass Publishers.

14. Bostrom, R. P., Olfman, L. and Sein, M. K. (1987). End-User Computing: A research framework for investigating the training/learning process. Forthcoming in a book on Human Factors in Computing, ABLEX Human Factors Series.

15. Hutchins, E. L., Hollan, J. D. and Norman, D. A. (1985). Direct manipulation interfaces. *Human Computer Interaction*, 1, 311–338.

16. Shneiderman, B. (1983). Direct manipulation: A step beyond programming languages. *IEEE Computer*, 16, 57–69.

17. Carroll, J. M. and Carrithers, C. (1984). Training wheels in a user interface. *Communications of the ACM*, 27, 800–806.

18. Foley, J. D. (1980). Methodology of interaction. In R. A. Guedj *et al.*(Eds). *Methodology of Interaction*, North Holland.

19. Bennett, K. B. (1984). *The Effect of Display Design on the User's Mental Model of a Perceptual Database System*. Unpublished doctoral dissertation, The Catholic University of America.

20. Owen, D. (1986). Naive theories of computation. In D. A. Norman and S. W. Draper (Eds), *User Centered System Design*; Hillsdale, NJ, Lawrence Erlbaum Associates.

21. Borgman, C. L. (1984). *The user's Mental Model of an Information Retrieval System: Effect on Performance*. Unpublished doctoral dissertation, Stanford University.

22. Young, R. M. (1983). Surrogates and mappings: Two kinds of conceptual models for

interactive devices. In D. Gentner and A. L. Stevens (Eds), *Mental Models*, Hillsdale, NJ, Lawrence Erlbaum Associates.

23. Bayman, P. and Mayer, R. E. (1984). Instructional manipulation of user's mental models of electronic calculators. *International Journal of Man-Machine Studies*, 20, 189–199.

24. Kublanow, S. M., Durand, D. E., and Floyd, S. W. (1985). Measurement of office system use. IBM-University of Colorado Joint Study.

25. Davis, F. D., Jr. (1985). *A Technology Acceptance Model for Empirically Testing New End-User Information Systems: Theory and Results*. Unpublished doctoral dissertation, MIT.

26. Keller, J. M. (1983). Motivational design of instruction. In Reigeluth, C. M. (Ed.) *Instructional Design Theories and Models: An Overview of their Current Status*, Hillsdale, NJ, Lawrence Erlbaum Associates, Publishers, 386–434.

27. Norman, D. A. (1983). Some observations on mental models. In A. L. Stevens and D. Gentner (Eds), *Mental Models*, Hillsdale, NJ, Lawrence Erlbaum Associates.

28. Pellegrino, J. W. (1985). Anatomy of analogy. *Psychology Today*, October, 49–54.

29. Kolb, D. A., (1983). *Experimental Learning: Experience as the Source of Learning and Development*. Englewood Cliffs, NJ, Prentice-Hall.

30. Pintrich, P. R., Cross, D. R., Kozma, R. B. and McKeachie, W. J. (1986). Instructional psychology. *Annual Review of Psychology*, 32, 611–651.

31. Sein, M. K. (1987). *Conceptual Models in Training Novice Users of Computer Systems: Effectiveness of Analogical vs. Abstract Models and Influence of Individual Differences*. Unpublished doctoral dissertation, Indiana University.

32. Butcher, D. F. and Muth, W. A. (1985). Predicting performance in an introductory computer science course. *Communications of the ACM*, 28, 263–68.

33. Rosson, M. B. (1984). The role of experience in editing. In B. Shackel (Ed). *Human–Computer Interaction—Interact*, 84 Amsterdam, North–Holland, 45–50.

34. Cronbach, L. J., and Snow, R. E. (1977). *Aptitudes and Instructional Methods: A Handbook for Research on Interactions*. New York, Irvington.

35. Green, G. I. and Hughes, C. T. (1986). Effects of DSS Training and Cognitive Style on Decision Process. *Journal of MIS*, III, 2, 83–93.

36. Carroll, J. M. and Mazur, S. A. (1986). Lisalearning. *IEEE Computer*, November, 35–49.

37. Carroll, J. M. (1984). Minimalist training. *Datamation*, 30, 18 (Nov. 1), 125–136.

38. Olfman, L. (1987). *A Comparison of Construct-Based and Applications-Based Training Methods for DSS Generator Software*. Unpublished doctoral dissertation, Indiana University.

39. Bikson, T. K. and Gutek, B. A. (1983). Training in automated offices: An empirical study of design and methods. In J. I. Rijnsdorp and Tj. Plomp, *Training for Tomorrow*, Proceedings of IFAC/IFIP 1983 Symposium, 129–143.

40. Anderson, J. R., Boyle, C. F., and Reiser, B. J. (1985). Intelligent tutoring systems. *Science*, 228 (April 26), 456–462.

41. Blakesee, S. (1986). Colleges ask, what makes science hard? *New York Times*, May 13.

42. Halasz, F. (1985). *Mental Models and Problem Solving in Using Calculators*. Unpublished doctoral dissertation, Stanford University.

43. Halasz, F. and Moran, T. P. (1982). Analogy considered harmful. *Conference Proceedings: Human Factors in Computer Systems*, Gaithersburg, Maryland, 383–386.

44. Galletta, D. (1984). *A Learner Model of Information Systems: The Effects of Orientating Materials, Ability, Expectations and Experience on Performance, Usage and Attitude*. Unpublished doctoral dissertation, University of Minnesota.

45. Mayer, R. E. (1981). The psychology of how novices learn computer programming. *Computing Surveys*, 13, 121–141.

46. Sharrow, J., Weaver, V., and Kilduff, K. (1985). Appreciation and confidence: A study in micro training. *Information Center* (December), 44-47.

47. Ross, S. M., McCormick, D. and Krisak, N. (1986). Adapting the thematic context of mathematical problems to student interests: Individualized versus group-based strategies. *Journal of Educational Research*, 79, 245–252.

48. Wexley, K. N. and Baldwin, T. T. (1986). Posttraining strategies for facilitating positive transfer: An empirical exploration. *Academy of Management Journal*, 29, 3, 503–520.

49. Leitheiser, R. L. and Wetherbe, J. C. (1986). Service support levels: An organized approach to end-user computing. *MIS Quarterly 10*, 12, 337–349.

50. Lee, D. M. S. (1986). Usage pattern and sources of assistance for personal computer users. *MIS Quarterly*, 10, 12, 313–325.

FOR FURTHER READING

1. Gilfoil, D. (1982). Warming up to computers: A study of cognitive and affective interaction over time. *Conference Proceedings: Human Factors in Computer Systems*, Gaithersburg, Maryland, 245–250.

2. Jagodzinski, A. P. (1983). A theoretical basis for the representation of on-line computer systems to naive users. *International Journal of Man-Machine Studies*, 18, 215–252.

3. Snow, R. E. (1980). Aptitude process. In R. E. Snow, P. A. Federico and W. E. Montagne (Eds). *Aptitude Learning and Instruction: Cognitive Process—Analyses of Aptitude*, Hillsdale, NJ, Lawrence Erlbaum Associates.

QUESTIONS

1. What determinants are thought to influence user behavior/performance?
2. Evaluate the end-user training framework presented in this reading. Is this framework considered to be static or dynamic in nature?
3. Define the following terms within the context of end-user training: (a) mental models. (b) motivation. Are these terms considered to be static or dynamic in nature?
4. What types of trainee characteristics need to be considered when designing training methods?
5. How might training and task environments be better designed to support end-user managers' learning of EUC software?
6. How do training, motivation, and time interact to form the "positive motivational dynamic"?

PART

III

THE DEVELOPMENT OF USER-CENTERED SYSTEMS

■

End-user computing in an organization can begin in a variety of ways. At one extreme, an individual may develop a system on an entrepreneurial basis, whereas at the other extreme, the organization may commit itself to directing, supporting, and controlling EUC as part of its corporate strategy. Whatever approach is taken, there are a number of developmental issues that need to be addressed, such as timing, methodology, risks, roles, and responsibilities.

This section of the book contains four readings on the development of user-centered systems. It ranges from broad selections on developmental methodologies to narrower ones such as how to select software for EUC applications. It includes both conceptual ideas and illustrations of how user-centered systems are actually being developed. The end result should be an enhanced understanding of how to develop effective systems from an end user's perspective.

It is widely believed that user-centered systems require a unique development approach. The names *prototyping, iterative, evolutionary,* and *adaptive design* are all used to describe this approach, which combines requirements analysis, design, development, and implementation into a single phase, which is reiterated in a short period of time. James Kraushaar and Larry Shirland, in "A Prototyping Method for Applications Development by End Users and Information Systems Specialists" (Reading 9), describe how the prototyping development method can be applied to EUC.

The "right software" can do much to facilitate the building of user-centered systems. Lawrence Meador and Richard Mezger, in "Selecting an End User Programming Language for DSS Development" (Reading 10), discuss how to evaluate and select software for end-user applications. They recommend that a multidisciplinary task force follow a seven-step process.

The success of user-developed applications (UDA) can be evaluated from multiple points of view (e.g., those of the user(s), management, and the IS department). The UDA literature suggests that IS departments can expect to receive two major types of benefits: decreases in both the backlog of IS application development projects and the proportion of IS resources spent on applications maintenance. Suzanne Rivard and Sid Huff, in "User-Developed Applications: Evaluation of Success from the DP Department Perspective" (Reading 11), examine the legitimacy of these and other suggested benefits of UDA.

It must also be recognized that user-developed systems have inherent short- and long-term dangers that seem to be overlooked in the enthusiasm to implement the user-development capabilities. Gordon Davis, in his article, "Caution: User-Developed Systems May Be Hazardous to Your Organization" (Reading 12), explores the dangers and risks in user-developed IS applications and suggests organizational procedures and system design features to reduce the risks to a tolerable level.

9

A Prototyping Method for Applications Development by End Users and Information Systems Specialists

James M. Kraushaar
Larry E. Shirland

INTRODUCTION

Many information systems (IS) managers face the challenge of reducing a rapidly growing and seriously underestimated applications development backlog. One strategy for doing this would be to reduce the demand for application systems by raising the price of development. This might be accomplished by developing realistic chargeback systems and/or by creating bureaucratic hurdles. Obviously, this latter approach contains significant risk that the users will satisfy their demand without utilizing the IS department. The potential problems with systems developed without the assistance of the IS department are numerous.[1,2]

Another approach would be to increase the IS department's ability to supply applications development by improving productivity with respect to

Reprinted by special permission of the MIS Quarterly, *Volume 9, Number 3, September, 1985. Copyright 1985 by the Society for Information Management and the Management Information Systems Research Center at the University of Minnesota.*

159

systems development. This can be accomplished by either developing systems more quickly, or by providing proper development guidelines and assistance so that functional areas can develop their own application systems with minimal IS department resources.

Several methods have been suggested to improve the productivity of the IS department's applications development effort. For example, Martin[3] suggests that the information center approach to IS department organization encourages the supply of proper development guidance and assistance so that functional areas can develop some of their own systems. According to Howdon,[4] automated systems development also shows promise in reducing the application backlog; however, it currently requires resources and expertise that many IS departments may not have available.

Prototyping is another approach that can be used to reduce the applications backlog by producing new systems more quickly and effectively than the traditional approach. Unlike automated systems development, prototyping is not sophisticated or expensive. Canning[5] suggests it can be used by both IS department development personnel and end-user groups, and Jenkins[6] indicates it is applicable to a wide variety of system development projects.

Our experience, and that of others,[7–10] support these claims. In addition, research findings of Katz[11] in job redesign and Behrens[12] in project development productivity measurement indicate that a prototyping process can encourage the efficient development of application systems by breaking a complex, and often ill-defined problem into several comprehensive, yet smaller and simpler parts.

The purpose of this article is to propose a specific prototyping method. In order to clarify the relationship between this method and alternative application development methods, we present a state-transition model of the IS development process. Following this, we describe a two-prototype process and our experience with applying it to two IS projects.

A STATE-TRANSITION MODEL

Application development and prototyping can be viewed as state-transition processes as shown in Figure 9.1. In this model each state represents a system, and efforts to change the system are transitions. From a systems life cycle perspective, state #0 might represent the initial system, state #1 through state #N–1 might represent enhancements and modifications to the initial system, and state #N might represent a mature system. The transitions might be accomplished by various development methods. For example, state #1 might be achieved after a systems development project that resulted in the purchase and installation of a packaged application system. States #2 through #N might result from IS department efforts to expand the packaged system to make it more effective and efficient. Transition #N + 1 could represent efforts to replace an undesirable mature system.

FIGURE 9.1
**A STATE-TRANSITION MODEL FOR APPLICATION
DEVELOPMENT AND PROTOTYPING**

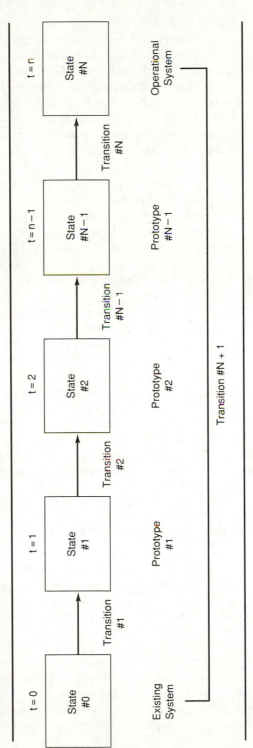

The prototyping approach views the final operational system as the desired state that is achieved by passing through earlier, less desirable states. The transition from one state to the next can be accomplished by the traditional development process of analysis, design, and implementation, or by other appropriate methods. Naumann and Jenkins[13] have described a prototyping model as a four-step process which is repeated until a satisfactory operational system evolves. But this does not clearly show the potential relationship between prototyping and alternative development approaches within the same project. The state-transition model shows that each transition requires a development approach, but not all transitions need to use the same approach.

Another view of the prototyping process might emphasize the states rather than the transitions. An initial working model (state #1) of the target system is first developed. This initial state, or prototype, might represent an incomplete and much simplified model of a dimly perceived operational system. Based on the experience of the users and designers with the initial prototype, a second and more complex prototype (state #2) can be developed. The process continues in an iterative and adaptive fashion until an operational system (state #N) evolves.

The traditional life cycle and heuristic development methods can be viewed as special cases of the general state-transition application process model. As seen in Figure 9.2, they have only two states, the current system and the desired operational system. In the life cycle approach as described by McKeen[14] and Zelkovitz,[15] a linear sequence of steps is followed to make the single transition. A variation of this method described by Bally, Brittain and Wagner[16] uses a loopy linear sequence to make the transition. Berrisford and Wetherbe[17] have suggested a modification to the traditional life cycle process called heuristic development. They propose the use of prototypes in the design step of the traditional development cycle, however, it should be clear from Figure 9.2 that the application of prototypes need not be limited to the design step.

A TWO-PROTOTYPE DEVELOPMENT PROCESS

While the literature describes prototyping in general terms, it does not provide operational recommendations for building application systems. In this section we present detailed guidelines for a two-prototype development method by describing our experience with two system projects.

Two different application system development efforts used a two prototype development process. One project developed a large application system for a state child nutrition and development agency. This agency had a budget in excess of $600 million per year with several hundred full-time employees. The project required $250,000 and three years to complete. It used a large IBM mainframe computer and the RAMIS II language.

A second project developed an application system for a small community

FIGURE 9.2
STATE TRANSITIONAL VIEW OF THE TRADITIONAL AND
HEURISTIC APPLICATION DEVELOPMENT PROCESSES

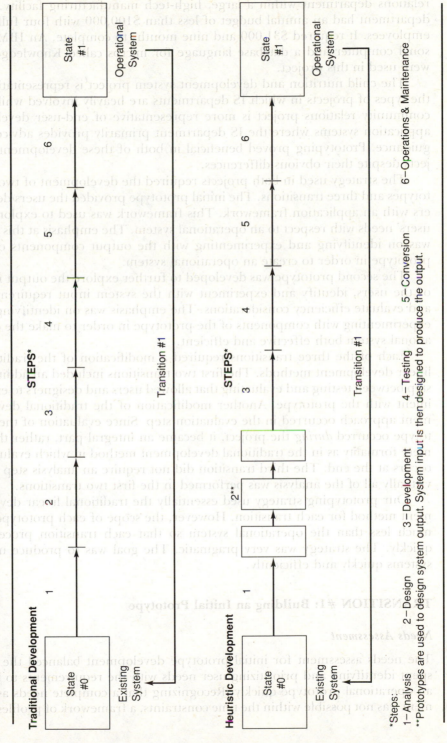

Traditional Development

Heuristic Development

STEPS*

Transition #1

State #0   Existing System   State #1   Operational System

*Steps:
1—Analysis   2—Design   3—Development   4—Testing   5—Conversion   6—Operations & Maintenance
**Prototypes are used to design system output. System input is then designed to produce the output.

relations department within a large, high-tech manufacturing facility. This department had an annual budget of less than $100,000 with four full-time employees. It required $31,000 and nine months to complete. An IBM personal computer and a database language for micros called Knowledgeman were used in this project.

The child nutrition and development system project is representative of the types of projects in which IS departments are heavily involved while the community relations project is more representative of end-user developed application systems where the IS department primarily provides advice and guidance. Prototyping proved beneficial in both of these development projects despite their obvious differences.

The strategy used in both projects required the development of two prototypes and three transitions. The initial prototype provided the users/designers with an application framework. This framework was used to explore the users' needs with respect to an operational system. The emphasis at this point was on identifying and experimenting with the output components of the prototype in order to create an operational system.

The second prototype was developed to further explore the output needs of the users, identify and experiment with the system input requirements, and evaluate efficiency considerations. The emphasis was on identifying and experimenting with components of the prototype in order to make the operational system both effective and efficient.

Each of the three transitions required a modification of the traditional linear development methods. The first two transitions included an additional step between testing and evaluating that allowed users and designers to experiment with the prototype. Another modification of the traditional development approach occurred in the evaluation step. Since evaluation of the prototype occurred *during* the project, it became an integral part, rather than a mere formality as in the traditional development method in which evaluation occurs at the end. The third transition did not require an analysis step since virtually all of the analysis was performed in the first two transitions.

Our prototyping strategy used essentially the traditional linear development method for each transition. However, the scope of each prototype was much less than the operational system so that each transition proceeded quickly. The strategy was very pragmatic. The goal was to produce useful systems quickly and efficiently.

TRANSITION #1: Building an Initial Prototype

Needs Assessment

The needs assessment for initial prototype development balanced the time spent identifying and prioritizing user needs with the requirements to build an operational prototype quickly. Recognizing that a complete needs assessment was not possible within the time constraints, a framework of profiles and reports was identified. A profile is basically a snapshot of a single occurrence of an entity at one point in time while a report describes a collection of occurrences for one or more entities, either at one point in time or longitudinally. In a later step, changes to the contents of these initial profiles and reports, along with the development of additional ones, were a means for communicating the prototyping philosophy of adaptation based on experimentation.

Design of the Initial Prototype

Our experience and previous research findings indicate that users relate quickly and easily to systems composed of a series of linked screen menus.[18,19] These menus provide a logical framework for profiles and reports that comprise the system. A simple illustration of these linked menus is provided in Figure 9.3.

A sample of data items (fields) was selected for each of the profiles and reports that were chosen for prototype development in step 1. The data items were representative of the type of information users expected and had values that were easily obtained.

After defining the prototype output, the database was designed. There were several acceptable models for the logical design of the prototype database. A semantic database model could provide a tool for expressing the meaning and structure of data. An entity-relationship model could be used to emphasize entities and relationships between entities. A relational model would use tables or flat files to represent relations. Common attributes would relate the tables and allow for much flexibility as relationships need not be predefined. We chose the relational data model for the design of the logical database because its flexibility allowed us to make changes quickly.

The physical design was different for each project as they used two quite different DBMSs. In both projects, attempts were made to normalize the logical relations before the tables were defined in the DBMS. This normalization process is extremely important as it provides the prototypes with the flexibility necessary for rapid change.

A data sample was collected from users and loaded directly into the database via a utility provided by the DBMS. Efforts were made to collect "real" data that represented what the users considered to be typical values. A recent attempt in another prototyping project to use data "created" by the designers was not successful as users spent more time and effort trying to relate to the data than in evaluating the prototype. The sample of data was small with 1-5 occurrences for each data item.

Implementing the Initial Prototype

Using the screen formatting and report writing features of the DBMS, the prototype application program was created. The process of creating the initial program could be accomplished quickly since the language was already known.

FIGURE 9.3
AN ILLUSTRATION OF LINKED MENUS FOR INITIAL PROTOTYPE

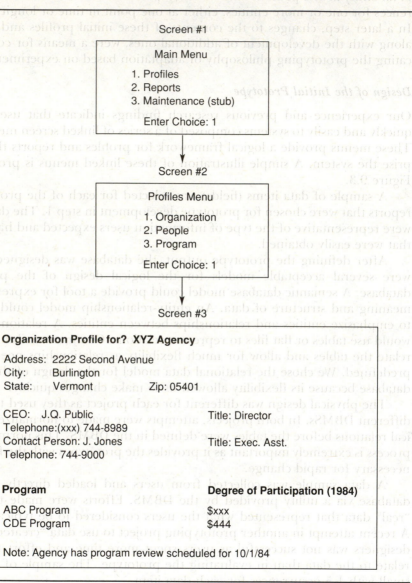

Screen #1

Main Menu

1. Profiles
2. Reports
3. Maintenance (stub)

Enter Choice: 1

Screen #2

Profiles Menu

1. Organization
2. People
3. Program

Enter Choice: 1

Screen #3

Organization Profile for? XYZ Agency

Address: 2222 Second Avenue
City: Burlington
State: Vermont   Zip: 05401

CEO: J.Q. Public   Title: Director
Telephone:(xxx) 744-8989
Contact Person: J. Jones   Title: Exec. Asst.
Telephone: 744-9000

Program   **Degree of Participation (1984)**
ABC Program $xxx
CDE Program $444

Note: Agency has program review scheduled for 10/1/84

Testing the Initial Prototype

The correctness of the application program was determined by adequate testing with the designers and a single representative user. This was a relatively easy task because of the simplicity of the initial prototype and the use of the DBMS screen formatting and report writing features.

Experimenting with the Initial Prototype

After a short presentation on the project and the prototyping process and philosophy, the prototype was demonstrated to small groups of 1 to 4 users. The purposes of this demonstration was to set the "experimental" tones and to give the users an understanding of the prototype's general framework.

After the short demonstration, users were encouraged to suggest changes and additions to the system with respect to menu organization, menu contents, and profile and report contents. Those suggestions that seemed representative and simple were made immediately utilizing the power of the DBMS system. These "on-the-fly" changes further encouraged the experimental tone and user involvement. Representative changes requiring more substantial effort were proposed for inclusion in the next prototype. This step was designed to utilize the prototype as a vehicle to bring users into the development effort, revise the users previous needs assessment, and communicate project purpose and goals.

Evaluating Initial Prototype and Project

Based on the experience obtained from building and exercising the initial prototype, a proposal for a second prototype was developed. Management evaluated this proposal as if it were an entirely new project. The cost of developing the next prototype was weighed against the potential benefits of an operational system. Keen[20] presents a method for determining if the cost of a project is justified when benefits are qualitative.

Transition #2: Building the Second Prototype

A design process similar to the design of the initial prototype was followed. However, the design extended and/or modified the initial prototype to develop a more realistic model of the desired operational system with respect to both effectiveness and efficiency factors. The second prototype included the following:

- ☐ illustrative database loading and maintenance routines for users,
- ☐ novice (linked menus) and expert (function keys) usage modes,
- ☐ software monitors for recording prototype usage,
- ☐ more and expanded reports and profiles, and
- ☐ a more efficient database.

The same sample of user groups that experimented with the first prototype continued to experiment with the second. However, whereas the designers operated the initial prototype, the users operated the second prototype after a short demonstration of novice and expert usage modes.

The initial sample of users was expanded to include users with responsibility for the loading and updating of the data, and representatives of the IS department management, if they were not already part of the project team. This insured that groups having an interest in the project were exposed to the prototype during at least one of the first two transitions. For example, with the community relations project representatives (management and development staff) of the IS department were shown a demonstration of the second prototype so that they would be in a position to provide input at the project evaluation step. In the child nutrition and development project, managers and staff representing organizational levels above those directly involved in the project, were shown the second prototype. The purpose was to demonstrate: (1) what had been accomplished quickly with limited resources, (2) the potential of the application system if and when it was operational, and (3) the prototyping process and its advantages and disadvantages.

The usage of the prototype was recorded by the users and the software monitors. Prototype system problems and user/designer suggestions were documented. However, unlike the initial prototype, suggested changes were not implemented unless they were critical to continued successful experimentation of the prototype. Designers also experimented with the prototype to collect operating data. Utilizing this data, design criteria values for an operational prototype were developed for inclusion in the proposal for an operational system. For example, the anticipated number of concurrent users, records, and record accesses were estimated from the prototype experiments. The adequacy of the system users manual was also determined.

The project team prepared a report that included user/designer experience with the prototype and a proposal for an operational system. The proposal included an estimate of the amount of modification of the prototype necessary and/or desirable for an operational system, a revised list of cost/benefits, and a budget and schedule for transition #3. A presentation to management included the proposal and a demonstration of the prototype.

Transition #3: Building the Operational System

The effort required for this transition is proportional to the degree of modification required of the second prototype. In some cases the second prototype is very close to an operational system. In others, a relatively full-scale application development project may be required. In either case, the prototyping experience is used to build the operational system.

Many components of the second prototype were transferred to the operational system making the development effort much shorter. For example, some data, software, and data structures were transferred. At the very least, users and designers had a much better understanding of what the operational system should do and how it would operate. Under these conditions the traditional approach was the most appropriate for quickly building the operational system.

SUMMARY AND DISCUSSION

In this article we have presented a general state-transition model of the application development process that clearly shows the large number of potential application development strategies. We have shown that application development methods such as prototyping and heuristic development can be viewed as transitions between system states. Also we have shown how the traditional life cycle development method can be represented by this model.

The prototype development process appears to be a useful strategy for efficiently delivering effective application systems. In our study, the initial prototype encouraged the development of an effective system by emphasizing the building of a user needs framework. Users were involved in the design phase and were encouraged to experiment with the system in order to define their needs. This led to reasonable system expectations, fewer surprises, and user ownership of the final operational system. The process also accommodated the changes typically experienced in the user's dynamic world and allowed the projects to focus on building and expanding rather than limiting and controlling. The second prototype was used to further explore and develop the system definition while processing efficiency considerations were examined. It gave the users and designers a realistic view of the potential effort required to operationalize and maintain the system and helped insure an efficient operational system.

It would appear that the prototype process would not be appropriate when user needs are static or well-defined, or when development experience with similar applications has been extensive. Of course, more research and experimentation is needed to determine which applications are not well suited to prototyping. However, our experience indicates that prototyping can provide ontime and within-budget systems for both large and small application projects that are typically developed by information systems specialists and/or end users. The prototyping methodology clearly has the potential to improve productivity over a wide range of applications.

REFERENCES

1. Benson, D. H. "A Field Study of End User Computing: Findings and Issues," *MIS Quarterly,* Volume 7, Number 4, December 1983, pp. 35–45.
2. Rockart, J. F. and Flannery, L. S. "The Management of End User Computing," *Communications of the ACM,* Volume 26, Number 10, October 1983, pp. 776–784.
3. Martin, J. *Applications Development Without Programmers,* Prentice-Hall, Englewood Cliffs, New Jersey, 1982.
4. Howden, W. E. "Contemporary Software Development Environments," *Communications of the ACM,* Volume 25, Number 5, May 1982, pp. 318–329.
5. Canning, R. G. "Where Will Applications Be Developed," *EDP Analyzer,* Volume 21, Number 12, December 1983, pp. 1–12.

6. Jenkins, A. M. "Prototyping: A Methodology for the Design and Development of Application Systems," *Discussion Paper #227,* School of Business, Indiana University, Bloomington, Indiana, April 1983.

7. Canning, R. G. "Developing Systems by Prototyping," *EDP Analyzer,* Volume 19, Number 9, September 1981, pp. 1–12.

8. Gill, H., Lindvall, R., Rosin, O., Sandewall, E., Sorensen, H. and Wigertz, O. "Experience from Computer Supported Prototyping for Information Flow in Hospitals," *ACM SIGSOFT Software Engineering Notes,* Volume 7, Number 5, December 1982, pp. 67–70.

9. Scott, J. "The Management Science Opportunity: A Systems Development Management Viewpoint," *MIS Quarterly,* Volume 2, Number 4, December 1978, pp. 59–61.

10. Young, T. R. "Superior Prototypes," *Datamation,* Volume 30, Number 7, May 1984, pp. 152–158.

11. Katz, D. and Kahn, R. *The Social Psychology of Organizations,* (2nd Ed.), John Wiley and Sons, New York, New York, 1978.

12. Behrens, C. "Measuring the Productivity of Computer Systems Development Activities with Function Points," *IEEE Transactions on Software Engineering,* SE-9, Number 6, November 1983, pp. 648–652.

13. Naumann, J. D., and Jenkins, A. M. "Prototyping: The New Paradigm for Systems Development," *MIS Quarterly,* Volume 6, Number 3, September 1982, pp 29–43.

14. McKeen, J. D. "Successful Development Strategies for Business Applications Systems," *MIS Quarterly,* Volume 7, Number 3, September 1983, pp. 47–65.

15. Zelkowitz, M. V. "Perspectives on Software Engineering," *ACM Computing Surveys,* Volume 10, Number 2, June 1978, pp. 197–216.

16. Bally, L., Brittan, J., and Wagner, K.H. "A Prototype Approach to Information System Design and Development," *Information and Management,* Volume 1, Number 1, November 1977, pp. 21–26.

17. Berrisford, T., and Wetherbe, J. "Heuristic Development: A Redesign of Systems Design," *MIS Quarterly,* Volume 3, Number 1, March 1979, pp. 11–19.

18. Brown, J. W. "Controlling the Complexity of Menu Networks," *Communications of the ACM,* Volume 25, Number 7, July 1982, pp. 412–418.

19. Mason, R. E. A., and Carey, T. T. "Prototyping Interactive Information Systems," *Communications of the ACM,* Volume 26, Number 5, May 1983, pp. 347–354.

20. Keen, P. G. W. "Value Analysis: Justifying Decision Support Systems," *MIS Quarterly,* Volume 5, Number 1, March 1981, pp. 1–16.

Questions

1. Describe the prototyping method for applications development.

2. How does prototyping differ from more traditional methods? Be sure to include both the advantages and disadvantages of prototyping vs. traditional methods in your discussion (e.g., when would one approach be preferred over another?).

3. How did prototyping prove to be beneficial in the two projects described within this reading?

10

Selecting an End-User Programming Language for DSS Development

■

C. Lawrence Meador
Richard A. Mezger

Decision support systems (DSS) represent a relatively new way of thinking about managerial use of computers. A decision support system is a computer-based information system that is designed to help managers in private corporations and policymakers in public sector organizations solve problems in relatively unstructured decision-making environments. Long-range and strategic planning, merger and acquisition analysis, policy formulation, policy evaluation, new product development, marketing mix planning, research and development, and portfolio management are a few areas where the DSS concept has been successfully applied.[1-4]

Unstructured decision-making environments are those where the global problem is not well enough understood for a complete analytical description. A DSS is a system which provides computational and analytical support in situations where it is necessary to integrate judgement, experience, and insight of managerial or policy decision makers along with computer-supported modeling and presentation facilities. DSS focuses on achieving productivity improvements from managers and policymakers, rather than from the reduction of clerical and administrative costs.

As used in this article, a DSS language is one very important example of

Reprinted by special permission of the MIS Quarterly, *Volume 8, Number 4, December, 1984. Copyright 1984 by the Society for Information Management and the Management Information Systems Research Center at the University of Minnesota.*

the generic set of computer application development tools generally known as end user programming languages (or in some cases, fourth generation languages). Other examples include relational database facilities with powerful report generation and ad hoc inquiry facilities; general purpose statistical data analysis languages; and broad based graphics generation languages. While each of these four types of languages usually address different user needs, they often share some subset of similar capabilities and characteristics such as:

- Integrated database management (sometimes relational)
- User friendliness to nontechnicians
- Both procedural and nonprocedural command structures
- Interactive on-line utilization
- Support of prototyping and adaptive development
- Modest training requirements for end users
- Easy debugging and intelligent default assumptions
- Quantity of code required only a fraction of Cobol, Fortran, etc.
- Internal documentation generation support
- Understandable code for non-developers.[5]

The methodology presented here has been developed and used in software selection projects in a wide range of fourth generation software—including software for the emerging microcomputer marketplace. The DSS languages have been chosen as an example to illustrate the language selection methodology. This article deals with the process by which an organization acquires a DSS language (i.e., a tool to be used by end users and/or by analysts to develop DSS applications).

INTRODUCTION

Today's managers and policymakers are confronted with an overwhelming range of choices of computer software to develop decision support systems for many of the important corporate applications referred to previously. Making the right choice of software for a particular organizational context can have a profound impact on the success of a DSS. A new, more powerful, cost-effective, productive, and flexible generation of software has now been developed and made commercially available for DSS applications. These so-called fourth generation languages are so much better than prior languages (such as Fortran, Cobol, Basic PL/I, etc.) that we believe DSS developers should only consider utilizing the prior generation of software tools in very unusual circumstances.

The purpose of this article is to address significant managerial issues in the evaluation and selection of a DSS language. Attention is focused on the critical areas of DSS end user characterization, problem diagnosis, and needs assessment along with their implications for the software evaluation and selection process. The role of top-level managers as well as data processing staff in the evaluation and selection process is also considered. (Some of these topics are also discussed in Meador and Mezger, "Decision Support Systems for Minis and Micros,"[6] and in Meador, Rosenfeld and Guyote, "Decision Support Planning and Analysis: The Problem of Getting Large-Scale DSS Started".[7]

The selection and acquisition of a decision support language is too complex and important to exclude end users from the evaluation process. Top-level managers and their analytical support staff, who will be in the DSS user community, must participate in the evaluation and selection process in order to ensure that their needs are adequately addressed by the language selected. This discussion presents a range of methodologies and criteria which should be carefully considered by every organization embarking on a serious DSS development process.

A MULTI-STEP PROCESS

The selection of an appropriate DSS language is an important and challenging undertaking. The necessity of matching the range of language capabilities to the range of organizational needs is crucial in light of the cost of computer and professional resources required to develop and effectively utilize the language. In addition, a formal process for DSS language evaluation and selection is an educational process. In the end the organization has a much better appreciation of what it needs, what it is buying, and the costs and benefits of accomplishing the planned improvement in managerial decision support. This education process not only improves the odds that the organization is making a good choice, it also provides a broad base of knowledge and appreciation of the facility being acquired and the process of deploying it. Thus, the educational component enhances the probability of successfully using DSS.

A multi-step process of DSS language evaluation and selection is needed. The individual steps within the process are shown in Table 10.1 and discussed

TABLE 10.1
STEPS IN DSS LANGUAGE EVALUATION

- End user needs assessment and problem diagnosis (decision support analysis)
- Critical success factor identification
- Feature analysis and capability review
- Demonstration prototype development
- External user surveys
- Benchmark and simulation tests
- Programmer productivity and end user orientation analysis

in the remainder of this article. It may not be necessary to perform each step in order to complete an effective evaluation process. However, it is important to note that each step addresses different aspects of the planned use of the DSS language. Thus, each step provides additional knowledge that improves the chances of success (also see Keen[5]).

Organizing for DSS Language Evaluation and Selection

It is often useful to establish a multi-disciplinary task force to accomplish the DSS language evaluation and selection process. Our experience has shown that such a task force can accomplish its work in six to twelve weeks if the application domain is not extremely broad and if the number of people on the task force is kept small. We have observed such evaluation projects taking considerably more time in some organizations. We recommend that the group of individuals involved in the process include at least one senior manager and at least one representative of each of the major functional user areas which are designated to be DSS application areas (e.g., finance, marketing, research, sales, and so forth). There also needs to be representation from the data processing community so that all issues and consequences of hosting a responsive DSS environment can be adequately considered. In many cases, substantial computer systems resources are required for model utilization, date storage, and output display in a timely and responsive manner. Finally, the task force needs to include the individual(s) who will form the nucleus of the DSS support group (see Figure 10.1). This multi-disciplinary task force may be comprised of six to ten individuals who will play important roles in the evaluation and selection process.[8] In most situations a core group of three, at most four, members of the task force should be charged with the primary responsibility for data gathering and analysis.

End User Needs Assessment and Problem Diagnosis

It is important to involve the DSS user community in the language evaluation and selection process. While the "user requirements" phase of a traditional data processing project is always critical to success, the involvement of the intended DSS end users in this process is ever more important. This is because many DSS languages are directly used by the decision makers or their immediate staff, individuals who are not computer systems analysts. Thus, in the context of trends toward more emphasis on end user computing, involving the end users in the early stages of analysis of requirements is crucial.

End user needs assessment and problem diagnosis is a systematic, organized, and structured procedure for identifying and evaluating features necessary for the DSS language. It involves direct contact with the intended users to understand the general nature of the business decisions which they are making and to identify the modeling, analytic, data manipulation, and display functions needed to support the business decision processes. Information is

FIGURE 10.1
ORGANIZING TO EVALUATE DSS LANGUAGES

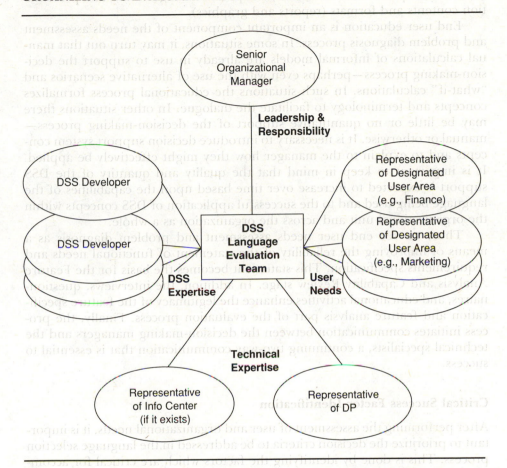

gathered by interviews and questionnaires: mechanisms that permit an experienced DSS analyst to understand the users' needs and to place these needs in the context of the facilities and features of DSS languages. (Research on DSS end user needs assessment is described in Meador, Guyote and Keen[9] and a structure for the process is recommended in Keen.[5])

The end user needs assessment and problem diagnosis activity of the language evaluation process is similar to, but less detailed or intensive than the planning and analysis phase of the development life cycle. Both processes involve a DSS analyst exploring the nature of planned applications with its user community. For language selection, the objective is to determine the general nature and extent of the language functions and features which will be required to build the applications. Language functions and features which are not required are also identified. For actual DSS application development, the more detailed end user needs assessment and problem diagnosis is concerned with specific data structures, computational algorithms, and presentation contents and formats (reports and graphics).

End user education is an important component of the needs assessment and problem diagnosis process. In some situations, it may turn out that manual calculations of informal models are already in use to support the decision-making process—perhaps even with the use of alternative scenarios and "what-if" calculations. In such situations the educational process formalizes concepts and terminology to facilitate the dialogue. In other situations there may be little or no quantitative support of the decision-making process— manual or otherwise. It is necessary to introduce decision support system concepts and to explain to the manager how they might effectively be applied. It is important to keep in mind that the quality and quantity of the DSS support is expected to increase over time based upon the capabilities of the language being used and to the successful application of DSS concepts within the organizational unit and across the organization as a whole.

Thus, we see end user needs assessment and problem diagnosis as a means of improving the reliability of the statement of functional needs and requirements specification. This statement becomes the basis for the Feature Analysis and Capability Review stage. In addition, the interviews, questionnaires, and educational activities enhance the legitimacy of the feature specification and feature analysis part of the evaluation process. Finally, the process initiates communication between the decision-making managers and the technical specialists, a continuing two-way communication that is essential to success.

Critical Success Factor Identification

After performing the assessment of user and organizational needs, it is important to prioritize the decision criteria to be addressed in the language selection process. This is done by identifying the factors which are critical for accomplishing the objectives of the DSS applications (and thus, by implication, the objectives of the key managers). These factors are referred to as Critical Success Factors (CSF), a concept introduced by John Rockart.[10] Critical Success Factors help to determine the key language features for which satisfactory performance will ensure overall project success.

Critical Success Factors for the DSS language selection process should reflect information gained in the interviews with users, executives, and technical personnel within the organization. By incorporating the input of personnel at all levels of DSS involvement, the CSF's address user needs in addition to economic factors such as budgets and projected growth, and technological factors such as system capacities and trends in hardware and software.

For each of the Critical Success Factors, a minimum level of performance is established and adequacy of each alternative language environment should be evaluated with respect to these criteria.

Feature Analysis and Capability Review

General Features

The purpose of the DSS language feature analysis is to match the capabilities of the candidate DSS languages with the requirements determined in the user needs assessment and problem diagnosis activity. To do this, it is first necessary to select a number of candidate DSS languages for the evaluation. This process is a difficult one because of the large number of choices available. One of two situations is likely to exist. The first is that the host computer systems hardware has been selected—and in fact is installed and operational. In this situation it is necessary to determine the spectrum of DSS languages that are available to run on the selected computer systems hardware and within the operating system of that computer environment. In some cases, this process substantially narrows the choices of available DSS languages. The other situation is where the hardware selection is to be made upon the completion of the software selection. The latter situation presents substantially more language choices and also provides more latitude and flexibility for the language to quite closely meet the requirements of the organization.

In both cases there are a number of general considerations relative to language features which are important to the evaluation and selection process. These are listed in Table 10.2. These general considerations cover a broad range of areas of interest and are introduced briefly here. *Compatibility* deals with the manner in which the DSS language fits into the ongoing corporate computer systems environment, and whether it meets hardware, operating system, and data structure specifications. *Availability* issues are concerned with whether the language can be accessed on more than one hardware configuration and whether it can be used via remote computing services, and service bureau facilities as well as in-house. Frequently, the ability to begin DSS development out-of-house and then bring it in-house when usage increases and economics dictate can be very valuable. *Maintainability* considerations are concerned with how much effort is required to support ongoing use of the language. *Reliability* issues have to do with failure rates and recovery characteristcs, and of the software's ability to perform all variations of its functions

TABLE 10.2
LANGUAGE FEATURES:
GENERAL CONSIDERATIONS

Compatibility
Availability
Maintainability
Reliability
End user orientation
Programmer productivity

and to do so through the series of upgrades of the language which occur over time.

Two related topics are *end user orientation* and *programmer productivity*. They both involve the ease-of-use of the language and the amount of systems orientation, design, and programming skill required to use the language. Important issues here include whether the language has a procedural or non-procedural orientation. Some "languages" are essentially two-dimensional spreadsheet calculators with relatively restricted notations to refer to the rows and columns of the "model;" other DSS languages have comprehensive relational data management capabilities and substantially more powerful conventions and mechanisms for addressing data. Non-procedural languages with easy symbolic references to data and goal-oriented control conventions represent more of an end user orientation. Similarly, these features, representing more powerful and logically concise functions, are expected to improve programmer productivity during the initial development of a model and during the ensuing maintenance and modification cycle.

Specific Language Features

There are a number of technical considerations relative to evaluating DSS language features which are briefly summarized in Table 10.3 (a more detailed list is given in Appendix 10.1). One of these deals with the design of the interface between the machine and the user, and the abilities of the language to provide a friendly and supportive environment for both novice and experienced users. In this regard, one needs to consciously distinguish between various "levels" of users as to how efficient they wish the system to be. (For a discussion of the user/system interface, see Sterling.[11])

Multidimensional data management is often considered an important requirement of the DSS language. While there exists a substantial class of decision support problems involving only a two-dimensional analysis, it is more and more common to see three-dimensional and more than three-dimensional problems being modeled to support important organizational decisions. When the activities of a company are viewed by product line and geographic area, as well as by time and specific business variables

TABLE 10.3
LANGUAGE FEATURES: TECHNICAL CONSIDERATIONS

Interface design
Data management — external, internal
Data analysis
Modeling
Data display — reports, graphics
Hardware/operating software environment
Multi-user interaction/sharing
Security and integrity protection

(sales, depreciation, etc.), a four-dimensional problem exists. DSS languages approach the multidimensional manipulation of data in different ways, which is sometimes reflected in the level of complexity of the language code when developing a model to access the data. In other words, if multidimensional data models are to be constructed, the multidimensional data manipulation features of the DSS language should be powerful and easy to use.

Access to *external data* may also be an important requirement for a DSS language. External data for a model may come from other transaction processing or management information databases within the organization, on the same computer system, or on another one. Alternatively, it may be economic and demographic databases which are external to the organization and available on a subscription basis. The ability and ease with which a DSS facility can access these databases can be an important element in its successful use. The system-to-system interface to support this access needs to be "black boxed" because the day-to-day user of the application is often not a systems specialist.

Data analysis is the collective term applied to statistical and forecasting applications and requirements. There are numerous standard statistical and forecasting functions, many of which may need to be available for frequent use. Checklists for these statistical and forecasting functions generally exist in DSS literature or can be provided by the vendor of a DSS language. One should be modestly cautious here. User needs assessment activity may mistakenly identify requirements for more complex and sophisticated statistical and forecasting algorithms than are really needed. The issue here is to avoid selecting (or rejecting) a DSS language on the basis of the presence (or absence) of an advanced feature which, in reality, is likely never to be used. Alternatively, when such a sophisticated feature is required, but on an extremely infrequent basis, it may be appropriate to access that feature from a statistics language within a remote computing services (RCS) environment.

The *modeling* function is generally acknowledged to be the heart of a DSS application. Modeling is a process of representing, through mathematical equations and logical expressions, aspects of the organization's business activities. By representing important parts of the organization and/or the competitive and external environments in which it operates, the model is able to support a careful study and analysis of alternative courses of action and outcomes. Such models often require complex sets of simultaneous equations where automatic equation reordering and simultaneous solution functions of a modeling facility are needed. "What-if" analysis evaluates the effect of changes in critical parameters. "Goalseeking" provides a backwards calculation capability which, in essence, determines the parameters of the problem given the parameters of the solution. Hierarchical processing and consolidation across products, regions, and geographical entities frequently must be modeled. On occasion, multidimensional equations permit solution of highly complex models representing diverse and numerous parts of an organization. In some cases mathematical optimization routines (linear, nonlinear, integer, mixed integer, and goal programming, for instance) may be useful components of the language.

Data display of the results of analysis and modeling activity is, of course, essential. Results are usually printed in hardcopy or as video display outputs. Printed output is frequently needed in a rough format which permits the examination of intermediate values. When the analysis is complete, presentation-quality reports may be needed with appropriate formatting, labeling, and text. In graphics, features generally offered are line charts, scatter plots, bar charts (or histograms) and pie charts with options for multiple charts per page and various color, display, sizing, and labeling options.[12,13]

In a production environment, providing for access by more than one user at a time may be important. Options should exist to allow *multiple users* to execute the same model (program) to access different personal databases as well as for multiple users to access parts of a common historical database by the same or different programs at the same time. An important capability relating to simultaneous access is the ability to prevent simultaneous attempts to modify a database's contents. In general, a user community should have broad flexibility in terms of sharing models (programs) and databases.[14]

Database security and integrity protection features are important to the successful use of a DSS language. It is common for many users to share the same computing system environment. Password control at the model and database levels is needed to protect the privacy of users, models, and data.

Vendor Support Considerations

In evaluating a DSS language, it is also necessary to consider the capabilities of the vendor who supports the language. Table 10.4 represents a number of vendor capability and support issues which need to be considered. All of the vendor capabilities shown are quite important; substantial deficiencies in any one of them could produce a painful and non-productive experience. *Training* and *documentation* are related capabilities which directly address the process of learning how to effectively use the DSS language. Training and documentation need to be available for a variety of levels and types of users so that first-time and infrequent users obtain adequate training in the basic of using the language while more sophisticated users are able to receive

TABLE 10.4
VENDOR CAPABILITIES

Training
   vendor facilities
   in-house
Application systems development
Consultation
Crisis reaction
Error/bug correction
Documentation

advanced training and have access to detailed reference documentation. In order to minimize the computer resources consumed, the efficient use of a DSS language becomes very important for large and/or multi-user models.

Two other related capabilities are *crisis reaction and error/bug correction*. There will be occasions, without doubt, when the application written in the DSS language does not work. The error diagnostics produced under such circumstances may be mysterious, or they may point to the DSS language itself as the source of the problem. In either case, there may indeed be a fault in the DSS language, or the model may have exceeded the capabilities of the language in some ill-defined manner. Crisis reaction or hot-line support means that the vendor has qualified systems personnel available on a standby basis to respond rapidly to such problems and to research and correct the difficulty. It may call for a suggestion as to how to program around the error or it may be a high priority activity to correct the problem and to provide updated software so that development and operation of the model can continue.

Finally, there are situations where it may be appropriate to look to the vendor for assistance in the design and programming of a DSS application. After all, the vendor is likely to be (and in fact should be) highly qualified and thoroughly experienced in designing and building applications using the language. *Consultation* involves relatively small amounts of support, more likely in the areas of design review or of designing and/or programming particularly difficult model segments. Application systems development support, unlike consultation, usually involves the full spectrum of development activities from design through deployment and is typically performed on a contractual basis. As to costs, application systems development support is almost always performed under contract and for a fee. Consultation may be for a fee or without fee—some vendors have limits below which the consultation is free and above which a fee is assessed. However, one should reasonably expect that brief periods of consultation via the hot-line support mechanism will be provided without fee. In this regard, there is typically an annual maintenance fee for ongoing support of a DSS language. In addition to providing updates to the DSS language and its documentation, the fee should include access to new language features and to training opportunites.

Acquisition Cost Considerations

One of the important features of a DSS language is its direct acquisition and utilization cost. Usually the cost factor which is given the most consideration is the initial acquisition cost. Important considerations when comparing the costs of DSS languages include the features of the language that are included, or not included, in the basic license cost. Some languages come in a totally bundled format while others are available in major functional segments (unbundled). Also, vendor support capabilities may or may not be bundled into the license fee; thus, there may or may not be a training allowance, a complement of technical documentation, and access to the hot-line. Even where there is an initial allowance, the cost evaluation should consider the costs of additional training, documentation, and start-up consultation support.

Other cost factors need to be considered. The cost of additional licenses for second and subsequent CPU systems are typically considerably less than for the first. The availability of the DSS language in a time-sharing or remote computing services environment, where it can be used and paid for on a fee-for-use basis, is often attractive. This is especially the case if models and databases can be moved from the remote environment to an in-house environment without costly conversion activities.

Another extremely important cost factor is that of the ongoing maintenance fee which frequently runs in the range of 1% of the license fee per month (e.g., a $75,000 license fee for a DSS language might well have a monthly maintenance cost of $750). The maintenance fee often guarantees receipt of the latest versions of the software and documentation. Further, it may very well provide for receipt of new and expanded features of the DSS language as they become available through the vendor's continued program of support and enhancement.

Two related cost considerations are worthy of discussion. The first is the cost of the computer systems hardware required to operate the organization's models when developed in the selected language. On the surface, the host computer environment may seem to be an almost limitless resource relative to the anticipated usage by the DSS community, although such a view is often deceiving. Experience shows that the use of a facility expands to meet the resources available. Models and databases grow in size, complexity, and frequency of use. In general, a DSS language which will permit twenty busy users to obtain good throughput and response time in the host environment is substantially more desirable than one which only supports ten users with the same quality and range of performance capabilities.

The other cost consideration concerns the personnel costs needed to develop and maintain models written in the selected language. As will be seen, different levels of programmer productivity are possible when the same quality of individual uses different DSS languages. Consider that it might be substantially less expensive overall to invest funds in a more powerful host computer environment to permit the use of an inefficient DSS language (in terms of computer resources consumed) if the language is very efficient in programmer productivity.

Demonstration Prototype Development

Experience has shown that there can be significant value from using a language on a trial basis to develop a meaningful application before a decision is made to select the language for a major application or for corporate-wide deployment.[15-17] This approach involves the development and operation of a demonstration prototype. This prototype model should be based on a real need and should accomplish the major objectives of some planned DSS application.

There are several reasons why the development of a prototype application has significant value in the DSS language evaluation and selection process. It serves to:

- ☐ Verify the size and complexity of a meaningful DSS application as programmed in the target language.
- ☐ Quantify and measure the computer systems resources needed to develop and operate the application.
- ☐ Determine the characteristics and qualifications of the personnel needed to develop the application.
- ☐ Understand the training requirements for the use of the language.
- ☐ Test the vendors technical documentation and hot-line support necessary for effective model development and utilization.
- ☐ Determine estimates of programmer productivity with a given language.
- ☐ Demonstrate the feasibility of the DSS application and obtain operational experience in the application area.
- ☐ Experience the entire DSS application development process from an educational perspective in what is clearly a realistic setting for future uses of the DSS language.
- ☐ Obtain at least some real decision support value in a limited timeframe, i.e., actually build, deploy, and use a DSS application which has immediate value to corporate management.

It is often true that in-house professional staff will be used to design, develop, and deploy the prototype DSS application with support from the vendor. It is possible that support from outside consultants specializing in DSS software evaluation, selection, and application implementation would provide assistance on a cost effective basis in the prototype development as well.

External User Survey

An external user survey is an evaluation of the experience of other organizations using the DSS languages being considered. The user survey is of particular value in an important business undertaking such as DSS development since it provides insights into key considerations and potential problems. Specifically, the objectives of conducting an external user survey are to:

- ☐ Obtain independent and unbiased information on the performance of the DSS language and of the vendor.
- ☐ Identify potential problems as well as sources of strength and weakness of candidate DSS languages and of their operation in particular host hardware environments.

☐ Verify computer systems hardware and support software requirements across a range of DSS applications.

☐ Develop realistic implementation planning information including an understanding of training requirements and implementation productivity considerations.

☐ Assess the end user managerial and technical staff satisfaction with the candidate DSS language.

This process of performing an intensive reference check can be done in stages as the DSS languages move closer to final selection and as some candidates are eliminated. Initially, an informal, but organized, one-half to one hour telephone conversation with the DSS coordinator of an organization using the candidate DSS language will suffice to obtain a useful impression. As the finalists emerge from the selection process, more in-depth interaction with heavy users of the language, including an on-site visit, can be quite valuable and is definitely encouraged. The vendor can be helpful in providing names of candidate organizations to choose from, as can be a user's group. Picking a reference organization with similar applications and/or in the same industry is especially worthwhile.

A major objective of the external user survey is to determine overall satisfaction with the DSS language. Dimensions of "satisfaction" include ease of learning and use, quality of documentation, programmer productivity, and efficiency of performance. Table 10.5 presents an overview of the information which is sought in the external user survey process.

TABLE 10.5
EXTERNAL USER SURVEY

HIGH PRIORITY INFORMATION REQUIREMENTS OF:	
DP	USERS
Programmer Satisfaction	Management Satisfaction
Installation Impacts of Language	User Orientation of Language
Hardware/Software Implications	Functional Analysis Implications
Memory	Graphics
Disks	Modeling
CPU	Report generation
Operating systems	Data analysis
Lines of execution code	Data access/manipulation
Programmmer Characteristics	Direct User Characteristics
Background in DP	Range of potential users
Training required in language	Ease of learning
Organization location (DP?)	Ease of use
Cost	Cost/Effectiveness

Vendor performance is to be examined in two areas: 1) the timing and smoothness of the initial installation and any modifications and upgrades subsequently provided; and 2) the overall quality and quantity of ongoing vendor assistance. Aspects of vendor assitance to be examined include: initial installation, user support, product maintenance and upgrades, technical competence in providing support, reliability of product, cooperativeness and availability of support, and availability and timing of training. The analysis of vendor assistance should be summarized by determining and understanding both the strongest and the weakest points, as the organization will seek to maximize the vendor strengths and to minimize or bypass vendor weaknesses.

Experience has shown that many corporate users of DSS languages are quite receptive to participating in such an extensive reference check. They have an opportunity to demonstrate their success as well as to discuss potential DSS applications and how the applications provide decision support assistance to their management. A well-organized approach with specific information-gathering objectives is likely to be most successful in developing a receptive and cooperative relationship and in obtaining the desired information.

Benchmark and Simulation Tests

At first glance it might appear that benchmarks and simulation tests are similar to, or even redundant with, a demonstration prototype project. While there is a general similarity in the objectives, the two activities are quite different in an important and meaningful way. A benchmark is a series of simulated tests of a comprehensive set of the features of the DSS language. It seeks to determine the level of computer systems resources utilized by the various capabilities of the DSS language (see Table 10.6). With these objectives, the programs or models which comprise the benchmark do not, in general, solve real DSS applications problems; rather, they are specially constructed to exercise various features or capabilities of the DSS language in a known manner.

For example, a benchmark program may seek to shed light on the amount of computer main memory consumed by a typical model and the way in which

TABLE 10.6
BENCHMARK EVALUATION

Measure Computer Systems Resources Consumed by DSS
  Software in Typical User Operations
CPU Cycles
Main Memory—including virtual memory paging load
Large-Volume Disk Input/Output
Input/Output Activity
Response Time

the memory is managed by the support software. This benchmark program is constructed to consume a predetermined amount of memory, although the way in which it uses the memory only approximates the manner in which a real model uses memory. All of this contrasts with the demonstration proto-type approach where the emphasis on solving a real DSS application problem may very well require only a small subset of the total DSS language features and capabilities to be exercised.

The objectives of a benchmark evaluation are to:

1. Measure computer systems resources consumed by the DSS language in typical user operation (see Table 10.6 for resources to be measured).
2. Determine cost of computer resources consumed (where costs are under-stood to be determined to be a usage algorithm intended to simulate the utilization of specific computer resources).
3. Learn about programming with the DSS language.
4. Check and verify the operation of a number of important language fea-tures and capabilities.
5. Evaluate the user friendly or English-like features of the DSS language.
6. Improve confidence in the DSS language's features and capabilities to meet the needs of the organization's DSS applications.
7. Improve confidence in feasibility of DSS application development.
8. Develop a series of sample programs for analysis of programmer produc-tivity and user orientation.

In essence, the benchmark activity enhances the user needs assessment activity by forcing the analyst and the user to think through in more detail the specifics of the needs. It permits exploration of important systems fea-tures and often exposes multiple ways of meeting a user requirement. It also requires the use of the DSS language's technical documentation and pro-vides an opportunity to test the vendor's technical support. Finally, when the benchmark is run on an in-house computer, it allows for an observation of the installation process, and, quite likely provides experience in moving DSS models and their data from one computer system environment to another. In summary, Table 10.7 presents one possible set of benchmark components for consideration.

Programmer Productivity and End User Orientation Analysis

Two additional issues of importance in the selection of computer software for DSS development, maintenance, and enhancement include the extent of programming development effort that must be expended to achieve a given set of objectives (a function of programming language productivity), and the range of types of individuals who directly use the language who

TABLE 10.7
BENCHMARK COMPONENTS

Databases: Statistical and Financial

Benchmarks:
  Data entry
  Financial model calculations
  Goalseeking (backwards iteration)
  Aggregation
  Data communications
  Large-model startup
  Linear regression
  Basic descriptive statistics
  T Test
  Matrix correlation
  Exponential smoothing and moving averages
  Growth rates
  Volume data transfer
  Report output
  User interface

may reasonably access the software (a function of simplicity and end user orientation of the language). These are the issues which, among others, tend to differentiate fourth generation languages and distinguish them from third generation languages.

Unfortunately, no set of agreed-upon criteria exists which allows an absolute comparison of the relative productivity and degree of end user orientation of various computer languages. However, several useful measures have been constructed and tested which lead to insights on these issues for specific instances of utilization of different languages.

In general, it can be stated that "more productive languages" support the achievement of end user application goals with less total program development effort (and thus cost) than would be expected of less productive languages. More end user oriented languages are accessible by a wider range of users (because the languages are more like the "natural" language of the users and thus are more "user friendly".[18]

More productive languages tend to require less specification of the detailed procedures by which desired goals are achieved. These highly productive languages are often referred to as goal-oriented or non-procedural languages for this reason. They tend to require the specification of fewer lines of executable code and fewer lexical items (shorter and simpler lines of code) to accomplish a given purpose. User-oriented languages tend to emphasize logical names of entities such as variables, commands, labels, locations, logic, and dimensions, rather than numeric codes or highly constrained acronyms.

Some fundamental criteria related to productivity and end user orientation which can be applied to DSS applications are:

- Executable lines of source code in an application program—excluding program comments.
- Lexical entities in the programs—excluding program comments, where a lexical entity is any continuous character string of one or more characters with meaningful definition such as a variable name, command, label, data item, logical or arithmetic operator, etc.
- Average number of lexical entities per line of code in each program.
- Numeric string ratio in each program—defined as the total number of numeric strings divided by the total number of lexical entities.

The number of executable lines of source code and the number of lexical entities are taken to be measures of the quantity of code that has to be produced to achieve the application objective (with programmer productivity implications). The average number of lexical entities per line of code is a conservative measure of statement complexity (with both productivity and end user orientation implications). The numeric string ratio is an approximation of the relative use of numeric codes rather than logical names of variables, labels, locations, etc., (with end user orientation implications for nonprogrammers).

Programmer productivity analysis is an important part of the language evaluation process that can reveal potentially large hidden costs in language acquisition. Dunsmore and Gannon,[19] for example, show that significantly different levels of programming effort can exist between almost-identical languages. However, it should also be noted that much disagreement exists among both academics and practitioners on the proper metrics for measuring programmer productivity and end user orientation characteristics of different languages.

Multicriteria Assessment

It would seem that much of the language evaluation process could be facilitated by some sort of multicriteria scoring or weighting scheme. We have observed, and sometimes used, schemes which assigned weights and point scores to different functions of the language and to outcomes of other aspects of the evaluation process. The merit of such an approach is that it collapses results and evaluations among several dimensionally incompatible criteria into a single metric, and produces a simple scalar comparison to rank candidate languages. But in presenting recommendations to user management, we think that relevant summarized raw data in its native dimensions should still be presented. User managers may have differing weights which will change over the evaluation timeframes as they learn more and more about the issues that count.

Conclusion

The selection of an appropriate DSS language is a challenging and important task for organizations that are starting to focus on information technologies to improve the effectiveness and productivity of managers and policymakers.

Both the process and the structure of the language evaluation activity are likely to impact its effectivenes and its success. The software technology for decision support is changing rapidly and substantial variance exists in the quality and relevance of the hundreds of products designed for potential decision support applications. Investment in a careful, well thought out and credible user-driven evaluation process is likely to be worthwhile but care should be taken to avoid studying the alternatives so long that the decision support opportunity evaporates.

References

1. Keen, P.G.W. and Scott Morton, M.S. *Decision Support Systems: An Organizational Perspective*, Addison-Wesley, Reading, Massachusetts, 1978.

2. Little, J.D.C. "Brandaid, an On-Line Marketing Mix Model, Part 2: Implementation, Calibration, and Case Study," *Operations Research*, Volume 23, Number 4, 1975, pp. 656–673.

3. Meador, C.L., and Ness, D.N. "Decision Support Systems: An Application to Corporate Planning," *Sloan Management Review*, Volume 15, Number 2, Winter 1974, pp. 51–68.

4. Urban, G.L., and Karash, R. "Evolutionary Model Building," *Journal of Marketing Research*, Volume 8, 1971, pp. 62–66.

5. Keen, P.G.W. "Computer-Based Decision Aids: The Evaluation Problem," *Sloan Management Review*, Volume 16, Number 3, Spring 1975, pp. 17–29.

6. Meador, C.L. and Mezger, R.A. "Decision Support Systems for Minis and Micros," *Small Systems World*, Volume 11, Number 3, March 1983, pp. 27–31.

7. Meador, C.L., Rosenfeld, W.L. and Guyote, M.J. "Decision Support Planning and Analysis: The Problem of Getting Large-Scale DSS Started," MIT Working Paper MERG-6, Cambridge, Massachusetts, October 1983, pp. 1–35.

8. Alter, S.L. *Decision Support Systems: Current Practice and Continuing Challenge*, Addison-Wesley, Reading, Massachusetts, 1980, pp. 38, 149–153, 173–174.

9. Meador, C.L., Guyote, M.J. and Keen, P.G.W. "Setting Priorities for DSS Development," *MIS Quarterly*, Volume 8, Number 2, June 1984, pp. 117–129.

10. Rockart, J.F. "Chief Executives Define Their Own Data Needs," *Harvard Business Review*, Volume 57, Number 2, March-April 1979, pp. 82–88.

11. Sterling, T.D. "Humanized Computer Systems," *Science*, Volume 190, Number 4220, December 19, 1975, pp. 1168–1172.

12. Remus, W. "An Empirical Investigation of the Impact of Graphical and Tabular Data Presentations on Decision Making," *Management Science*, Volume 30, Number 5, May 1984, pp. 533–542.

13. VanDam, A. "Computer Graphics Comes of Age," *Communications of the ACM*, Volume 27, Number 7, July 1984, pp. 638–648.

14. Meador, C.L., Keen, P.G.W., and Guyote, M.J. "Personal Computers and Distributed Decision Support," *Computerworld in Depth*, Volume XVIII, Number 19, May 7, 1984, pp. ID/7-ID/16.

15. Alavi, M. "An Assessment of the Prototyping Approach to Informative Systems Development," *Communications of the ACM*, Volume 27, Number 6, June 1984, pp. 556–563.
16. Keen, P.G.W. "Adaptive Design for Decision Support Systems," *Database*, Volume 12, Number 132, 1980, pp. 15–25.
17. Keen, P.G.W. "Value Analysis: Justifying Decision Support Systems," *MIS Quarterly*, Volume 5, Number 2, 1981, pp. 1–15.
18. Harris, L.R. "Natural Language Front Ends," in *The AI Business*, P.H. Winston, and K.A. Prendergast, (eds.), MIS Press, Cambridge, Massachusetts, 1984, pp. 149–162.
19. Dunsmore, H.G. and Gannon, J.D. "Analysis of the Effects of the Programming Factors on Programming Effort," *Journal of Systems and Software*, Volume 1, Number 2, February, 1980, pp. 141–154.

For Further Reading

1. Martin, J. *An Information Systems Manifesto*, Prentice-Hall, Inc. Englewood Cliffs, New Jersey, 1984, pp. 19–38.

Questions

1. Describe the capabilities and characteristics common to most end user programming languages.
2. What are the recommended steps in an end-user language evaluation?
3. Who should participate in an end-user language evaluation? Why?
4. Once an end-user language evaluation has been completed, how can and should the findings be presented to user management?

APPENDIX 10.1
SAMPLE CRITERIA FOR EVALUATING DSS TOOLS

A. Functions and Features
  1. Modeling—able to calculate with the information in the system, do optimization, "what-if" analysis
  2. Procedurability—ability to solve equations independent of their ordering, symbolic reference of data
  3. Data Management—number of dimensions, handling of sparse data, ad hoc inquiry
  4. Report Generator—ability to produce high quality formal reports quickly and easily
  5. Graphics—line, pie, bar, quality of output
  6. Statistics & Analysis—descriptive statistics, regression, significance tests
  7. Project Management—PERT/CPM, multi-level work breakdown structure
  8. Operations Research—linear, integer, dynamic programming
  9. Forecasting & Econometrics—time series analysis, seasonalization, smoothing

    10. External Databases & Interfaces

    11. Security—database, file, model, class of user

B. Ease of Use

    1. End User—analysis performed directly by person who needs the information

    2. Programmer/Analyst—interested in the quality of the editor, data management, report writer, etc.

    3. Ad Hoc Inquiry—end user answering questions for which no standard report is available

C. Facilities

    1. Documentation—for user, programmer, operations

    2. Training—novice/advanced, systems/user

    3. Support—consultant, hot line

    4. Host Hardware—computers supported

    5. Operating Environment—operating systems, disk requirements, etc.

    6. Availability—in-House & on Timeshare

D. Market Posture

    1. Pricing—lease, rent, purchase

    2. Installations—number of users, length of use

    3. Target Market—type of business actively pursued by the vendor

    4. Plans—commitment to DSS as a business area, amount of R & D

    5. User Perceptions—degree of use and support, functions used

    6. Vendor Viability—size of company, revenues, etc.

11

User-Developed Applications: Evaluation of Success from the DP Department Perspective

■

Suzanne Rivard
Sid L. Huff

INTRODUCTION

User development of computer-based applications (UDA) is a relatively new phenomenon that is occurring in many organizations today. Two major factors have contributed to the rapid growth of UDA. First, the extensive and ongoing decrease in computer hardware prices has made it possible for organizations of all sizes to place serious computing facilities in the hands of numerous non-data processing staff. The second factor has been the advent of "user-friendly" software, that is, software packages intended for the use of individuals with little or no knowledge of computing or data processing techniques. Much of this software consists of general-purpose tools that let users create their own applications.[1] This combination of inexpensive hardware and easy-to-use software has led to a rapid increase in the number of

personal computers installed in firms,[2] and in the number of data processing departments which have chosen to provide their users with mainframe
access.[3]

The "conventional wisdom," as reported in the UDA literature, suggests
that the two primary benefits of UDA for DP departments are reduction of the
application project backlogs, and reduction of the application maintenance
load. However, the results of the research reported here show that these are
not, in fact, the benefits of importance to the organizations studied.

This article will provide some background on the UDA phenomenon,
including the "conventional wisdom" regarding UDA success from the DP
management perspective. The research methodology used is presented, followed by a discussion of the study's major findings. A framework for UDA
evaluation is proposed and illustrated in the contexts of the firms studied and
the role of the DP department in the UDA evaluation process is discussed.

BACKGROUND

There are two key "players" in the UDA movement: (1) the user community,
which wants access to computing resources in order to carry out certain
application development activities; and (2) DP management, which usually
wants to facilitate and yet maintain control over UDA activities. To each
player, UDA offers certain advantages.

To users, most of the advantages of UDA are related to the ultimate
involvement of the user in the development process. Since users do not
have to translate and communicate their information needs to outsiders, the
problems inherent in determining information requirements are reduced or
eliminated. UDA also has the potential of making application development a
more flexible process, so users can readily adapt their applications when the
need arises. These and other advantages, such as improved timeliness with
which applications are developed and greater independence of users from
the DP department, have been suggested in the UDA literature.[1,4,5]

It has been argued that users cannot reap these benefits without active,
ongoing support from the DP department in the form of user-oriented software tools, access to computing facilities, access to data, and training and
support.[1,5] Such DP contributions serve a control, as well as a facilitating
function. In companies where DP units have attempted to inhibit UDA, user
departments have often turned to locally purchased microcomputers or outside timesharing services. In such situations, dysfunctional effects are likely to
follow, such as "fragmented departmental data, poorly written user programs,
and hardware that cannot be connected to a company's data network."[6] Moreover, the DP group's loss of control may lead to higher company data processing costs.[7]

DP departments have taken a variety of approaches to support and control UDA. Some firms have designated "product coordinators"—individuals

usually reporting to the DP unit who monitor and support end users in their use of a particular software tool. Another popular approach is the Information Center. In 1975, IBM established a user support group, and physically situated them in a central location together with open terminals, manuals, training aids, etc., in their Canadian headquarters. This group/location was referred to as the Information Center. IBM Canada experimented extensively with the Information Center concept and developed guides and other documentation based on their findings.[8] IBM and other companies are continuing to strongly market the Information Center concept to their customers.[3] Recent surveys indicated that over 40 major IBM customers have an Information Center underway,[9] and a considerably larger number of companies expect to implement one or more in the future.[10]

A third form of DP support has entailed providing advice and assistance to users in the acquisition of microcomputers. This type of support is becoming increasingly important as more and more companies decide to incorporate microcomputers into their MIS strategy.[11]

The implementation of DP department support for UDA involves substantial investment in software, computing capacity, terminals support staff, and so on. Much of this investment must be borne and administered by the DP department. An important question then, concerns the benefits that the DP unit might expect for its efforts. The UDA literature suggests that DP departments can expect to receive two types of benefits: a decrease in the backlog of application development projects and a reduction of DP resources spent on application maintenance.[1,5,7,8]

RESEARCH APPROACH

At the time this study was conducted very little empirical research had been done on UDA. The authors of the existing UDA literature mainly reported opinions and beliefs based on their own or other's direct experience with UDA,[7,12] or based on their knowledge of the broader MIS field.[4,5] An exception to this is Rockart and Flannery's case study of end user computing in a large company.[13]

A clinical research approach was adopted in this study to investigate the UDA phenomenon and UDA success from the perspective of the DP department. The study was conducted in 10 of the 100 largest Canadian business firms. Table 11.1 provides some background information on the participating firms. The main criterion for choosing these organizations was the number of years experience they had had with UDA. Four firms (A, B, D, I) had substantial experience with UDA (two to three years) using the Information Center approach. Three companies (C, E, J) had extensive experience with UDA itself (six to twelve years), but did not have an Information Center. The remaining three organizations (F, G, H) were in an intermediate situation: UDA had existed in those three firms for several years, but an Information Center type of user support group was just being implemented.

The research findings presented here are primarily based on in-depth interviews, conducted with DP executives and other DP professionals responsible for providing end user support services (Information Center managers, Information Center staff, product coordinators, etc.). Secondary sources of data used in the study include: (1) a DP profile questionnaire,[14] (2) internal documents made available by DP departments, and (3) direct observation.[15]

INITIAL DEFINITION OF UDA SUCCESS

Drawing on the available literature, UDA success from the DP perspective consisted of two components:

1. decrease in the DP application project backlog; and
2. decrease in the DP maintenance load.

Difficulties in measuring these constructs were recognized at the start. Two specific problems with respect to measuring the application project backlog were foreseen. First, most organizations develop a number of different types of applications, and UDA would not reduce the backlog of all types equally. McLean, for example, has suggested that computer applications can be categorized as three types: personal applications, departmental applications, and corporate applications.[5] Personal applications are designed to serve the needs of an individual. "They draw upon capabilities, facilities and data that are already in place."[5] Departmental applications "provide the reports, both routine and special, the queries, the analyses, and the many other items of computer-based data that form the backbone of a department's management information system."[5] Corporate applications involve data from several departments and are generally large systems ". . . designed to meet external, as well as internal requirements."[5]

The literature suggests that applications developed by users will usually be of the personal or departmental type.[5,8] Consequently, what is important in studying the impact of UDA on the DP applications backlog is not so much the absolute backlog, but rather the *composition* of the backlog. Rosenberger, for instance, suggests that UDA would tend to "skim off the top" of the DP backlog those ill-defined, "one-shot" types of applications (usually of the personal and departmental type), while leaving the larger "production" projects untouched.[7]

The second problem in measuring the change in the backlog is that other events, apart from UDA, may have taken place in an organization during the period in which change is measured. For instance, the DP department may have hired more programmers or analysts, or may have implemented some

TABLE 11.1
SOME CHARACTERISTICS OF THE TEN FIRMS STUDIED

	A	B	C	D	E
Industry	Financial	Insurance	Utility	Manufacturing	Forestry
Assets	> $50 Billion	> $4 Billion	$1.3 Billion	$2.8 Billion	$1.05 Billion
Sales	Not Applicable	> $4 Billion	$1.1 Billion	> $8 Billion	Not Provided
Number of Employees	23,000	4,500	2,700	39,000	7,000
Monthly Hardware & Communications Rental Equivalent	> $2.5 Million	> $200,000	$225,000	$800,000	$32,000
How is UDA Facilitated?	Information Center	Information Center	Product Coordinators	Information Center	Product Coordinators
Length of Time that UDA Has Been Facilitated as at Present	3 1/2 Years	1 1/2 Years	8 Years	2 Years	10 Years

	F	G	H	I	J
Industry	Utility	Financial	Manufacturing	Communications	Manufacturing
Assets	$1 Billion	> $60 Billion	$1.7 Billion	$2.3 Billion	$900 Million
Sales	$800 Million	Not Applicable	$1.4 Billion	$900 Million	$800 Million
Number of Employees	2,400	28,000	11,500	14,400	5,000
Monthly Hardware & Communications Rental Equivalent	$200,000	$5 Million	$250,000	$460,000	$200,000
How is UDA Facilitated	Information Center	User Computing Facilities	Timesharing Support Group	Information Center	Product Coordinators
Length of Time that UDA Has Been Facilitated as at Present	9 Months	2 Years	11 Months	4 Years	10 Years

"modern programming techniques"[16] in order to increase the DP professionals' productivity. The backlog may also have appeared to decrease because users became so dissatisfied with the service provided by DP that they gave up requesting applications.[17] Consequently, when measuring change in backlog, it is necessary to take such factors into account.

Problems in measuring the decrease in the DP maintenance load were also foreseen. As in the case of application backlogs, attention must be paid to the *type* of maintenance being examined. Leintz, *et al.*,[18] defined three types of maintenance: (1) corrective maintenance, which consists of emergency fixes and routine debugging, (2) adaptive maintenance, which pertains to "the accommodation of changes to data inputs and files and to hardware and system software,"[18] and (3) perfective maintenance, which encompasses changes due to user requests for enhancements, improved documentation, and recoding for computational efficiency. The literature suggests that UDA is most likely to impact perfective maintenance.[5] Thus, as with the impact of UDA on the DP application backlog, the key variable would be the *composition* of the maintenance load, rather than the overall load.

RESEARCH FINDINGS REGARDING UDA SUCCESS

As noted above, the initial definition of UDA success from the DP departments' perspective centered on the decrease in the application backlog plus the decrease in the maintenance load. As the field investigation progressed, this definition of success changed dramatically.

In none of the ten firms studied was the decrease of application backlogs or maintenance load identified as being a primary aspect of success. Table 11.2 lists the primary and secondary definitions of UDA success for these 10 organizations, as provided by the DP managers. "User satisfaction" is identified by three of the ten DP managers interviewed as the primary indicator of UDA success. "User satisfaction" was taken by the DP managers to mean satisfaction with the services provided by the DP department, as evidenced by "no complaints." In the other seven firms, the DP managers indicated that "tangible benefits to the user community" were the primary measures of UDA success. Tangible benefits include such factors as improved user productivity, assurance that users apply the computing resources in a manner that is profitable to the firm, and decreased outside timesharing usage. Table 11.3 summarizes the results regarding UDA success, as viewed by the DP departments in the firms studied.

With regard to the original success indicators, "decrease in application backlog" and "decrease in maintenance load," the DP executives interviewed were asked to what extent they believed UDA would impact these factors. In most cases, these managers felt that UDA might have some effect on the amount of DP resources devoted to perfective maintenance or on the portion

TABLE 11.2
DP DEFINITION OF UDA SUCCESS

Company	Primary Definition	Secondary Definition
A	Assurance that users use computer resources in a manner which is profitable to the firm	User satisfaction with IC services
B	Improvement in user productivity and in decision making outcomes due to UDA	User satisfaction with IC services
C	User satisfaction	—
D	User satisfaction	Assurance that users use computer resources in a manner which is profitable to the firm
E	Improved user productivity	—
F	Improved user productivity	—
G	User satisfaction	Decreased outside timesharing usage
		Assurance that users use computer resources in a manner which is profitable to the firm
H	Decreased outside timesharing usage	User satisfaction
		Assurance that users use the computer in a manner which is profitable to the firm
I	Assurance that users use the computer resources in a manner which is profitable to the firm	Decreased outside timesharing usage
J	UDA should be profitable for the firm (low cost, high user benefits)	Reduction of the number of small one-shot requests

of the backlog which consists of smaller, "one-shot" applications. However, in *no* instances had the DP managers attempted to measure these factors. More importantly, the decrease of the applications backlog and the decrease of the maintenance load were *not* perceived by the DP executives as being important components of UDA success. Thus, the initial definition of UDA success as derived from the UDA literature was found to be inappropriate.

TABLE 11.3
SUMMARY OF DP DEPARTMENTS'
DEFINITIONS OF UDA SUCCESS

	Tangible Benefits to User Community	User Satisfaction
Primary Definition	7	3
Secondary Definition	2	3
TOTAL	9	6

The authors began to focus on the broader issue of overall *evaluation* of the UDA effort in an organization. In the next section, this issue is elaborated further, and a framework is proposed.

THE EVALUATION ISSUE

While the change that took place in the definition of UDA success from the DP department point of view is an important finding of the study, the research results suggest that the related evaluation issue is more critical. That is, in most cases DP executives accompanied their definition of UDA success with statements indicating that the DP department was responsible for demonstrating to top management that users indeed derived tangible benefits from the applications they developed. Furthermore, it appears that the DP executives were not always successful in demonstrating this. The following quotes from DP managers illustrate these points.

> "Unless we can demonstrate that the applications users develop are profitable to the company, we won't be able to assert that UDA is successful. And for the time being, we cannot perform such a demonstration."

> "The president comes from Finance. What he wants to see as a result of our efforts (to facilitate UDA) is a good ROI."

> "How do I define success? User satisfaction . . . However, we have to have "hard" numbers in order to assure top management that UDA is cost effective. It would be most embarassing for us to go to the steering committee with a demand for a $6 million increase (in computer capacity) to accommodate UDA if we cannot demonstrate that what users do is profitable for the company."

As indicated in Table 11.4 in seven of the participating firms, DP was responsible for demonstrating to top management that there were tangible benefits provided by the applications users developed. Interestingly, those seven firms were also the ones where an Information Center support group

TABLE 11.4
DP DEPARTMENTS' ROLES IN UDA EVALUATION

	A	B	C	D	E	F	G	H	I	J
Are users charged for UDA?	No	Yes	Yes	Yes	Yes	No	Yes	No	No	Yes
Is DP responsible for evaluation?	Yes	Yes	No	Yes	No	Yes	Yes	Yes	Yes	No
How is UDA supported?	Information Center	IC	Product Coordinator	IC	PC	IC	IC	IC	IC	PC

had been implemented. Although the available data do not allow conclusive testing of the question, this observation can perhaps be explained by the fact that establishment of an Information Center (IC) or similar group usually entails a significant expenditure for facilities and staff. Management perceives the IC as a type of data processing capital investment, and thus holds the DP department responsible for return on that investment.

Considering the experiences of DP departments that were successful in demonstrating the tangible benefits achieved through the applications users developed, and of departments which were less successful, the following views of evaluation seem to be most relevant to UDA:

> Evaluation is a set of planned . . . activities undertaken to provide those responsible for the management of the change with a satisfactory assessment of the effects and/or progress of the change effort . . . (one) key word in this definition is planned. Evaluation is often glossed over and viewed as an add-on or extracurricular activity of a change effort.[19]

> Evaluation is part of the wider process of implementation and begins before the system is designed.[20]

In his discussion of the implementation of decision support systems, Keen stresses the importance of a negotiated contract between the consultant (system designer) and client (user, top management). Also important is the fact that this negotiation should occur "well before the system is even designed."[20] Keen suggests the following as an "ideal agenda for negotiation":

1. define "success";
2. allocate resources and responsibilities;
3. develop methods and criteria for evaluation, including a consensus as to what "key indicator" may be used to test the status or accomplishment of the aim of the system.[20]

The experiences of the firms studied, taken in light of Keen's arguments, suggest that the evaluation process must begin before UDA is introduced. Moreover, it is critical that DP and top management negotiate a "contract," and that they both respect the terms of this contract. The following section proposes a framework for evaluation of UDA, which borrows heavily from Keen's "ideal agenda for negotiation."

A UDA Evaluation Framework

The UDA evaluation framework illustrated in Figure 11.1 indicates that successful management of the UDA evaluation process should include four critical steps. While those steps are presented here in a linear fashion, it is likely that they overlap and that iterations will take place. The four steps are to;

FIGURE 11.1
A UDA EVALUATION FRAMEWORK

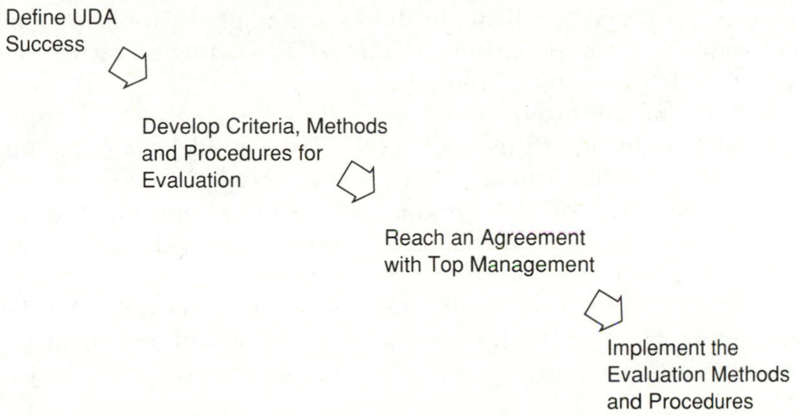

Define UDA
Success

Develop Criteria, Methods
and Procedures for
Evaluation

Reach an Agreement
with Top Management

Implement the
Evaluation Methods
and Procedures

(1) define UDA success, (2) develop criteria methods, and procedures for evaluation, (3) reach an agreement with top management with regard to (1), (2) and (3), and (4) implement the evaluation methods and procedures. In the discussion which follows, experiences of companies B and H are used to illustrate situations where the DP group successfully managed the UDA evaluation process. The experiences of companies A and D are presented to illustrate a case where the evaluation process was not as successfully managed.

Define UDA Success

From the DP department perspective, the definition of UDA success is closely related to the types of pressures for introduction of UDA being exerted upon it. In the cases of firms B and H, these pressures were clearly identified, and UDA success was readily defined. At H, the costs of outside timesharing had been doubling every year for a number of years. Both top management and DP management were concerned with the increasing costs. The DP department decided to introduce an in-house Timesharing Service, and defined UDA success as the "slow-down of the growth of outside timesharing, and eventual 'repatriation' of all outside timesharing usage."

At firm B, the DP group had received a mandate from top management to participate fully in the corporate effort to increase productivity. Providing users with UDA tools and support was identified by the DP manager as an appropriate way of increasing user productivity. The DP department defined UDA success as "the increase in user productivity and improvement in decision making outcomes."

Develop Criteria, Methods, and Procedures for Evaluation

For the DP unit at firm H, the procedures for evaluation of UDA success were rather straightforward. The outside timesharing expenses of user departments were monitored, particularly the expenses of two or three "heavy" outside timesharing user departments. The DP department directed much of its effort toward "repatriating" those heavy users.

At firm B, the DP group developed a document entitled "Information Center Guidelines for User Business Cases." Those guidelines, based on pilot studies conducted in the firm and on the experiences of other firms, assisted users in calculating the value of productivity improvements and the value of improved decision making capabilities that result from the applications they developed. Moreover, users were charged for the services they received from the Information Center, as well as for their use of computer resources. Finally, the manager in charge of the Information Center met with user management on a regular basis in order to assess, in "hard numbers," the cost effectiveness of UDA.

Reach an Agreement with Top Management

For both firms B and H, a consensus was reached with top management on the definition of UDA success and on the methods and procedures of evaluation. However, reaching such a consensus required strong arguments on the part of DP management. At firm B for instance, DP staff conducted pilot studies in order to demonstrate productivity improvements which could be obtained from the introduction of UDA. At company H, DP staff made several presentations to the firm's DP steering committee in order to make clear how the in-house Timesharing Service would "attack" the problem of outside timesharing use.

Implement the Evaluation Methods and Procedures

This step of the evaluation process comes after the UDA tools and support have been introduced. The responsibility of the DP group at this stage is to ensure that the evaluation procedures are appropriate and that they work well. In the case of firm B, for instance, the task of assessing the cost effectiveness of UDA required the manager in charge of the Information Center to obtain the collaboration of users. While this seemed to work well at company B, it was found to be more difficult to achieve in some of the other firms (company D for instance).

In contrast to these examples of successful management of the UDA evaluation process, two firms experienced significant difficulties. At company A, DP management defined UDA success as the assurance that the applications users developed were profitable for the firm. However, evaluation methods and procedures were not well developed. When the Information Center was introduced at firm A, it was decided that users should not be charged so that they would be encouraged to use the Information Center services and tools. Since they did not have to pay for the services, users were not motivated to determine the cost effectiveness of the applications they developed, and no mechanism existed to formally require users to assess the cost effectiveness of their applications.

The latter is a difficulty that company D also had to face. While users at D were charged for their use of the computer resources, there was no formal mechanism requiring them to assess the "profitability" of the applications they developed. In this case, DP management, together with the Information Center staff, bore the burden of proof but lacked the authority to require users to assess the value of their applications.

The Proper Role of the DP Department in UDA Evaluation

The foregoing framework is useful in examining why some DP departments are more successful than others in demonstrating to top management that tangible benefits are derived from the applications users develop. However, the framework takes for granted that DP will play a central role in the evaluation process. Whether, in fact, a DP department *ought* to play such a central role in UDA evaluation is a separate question.

Imagine a case wherein the DP group fails at its job of convincing top management that user developed applications are cost effective (assuming, in fact, they are). In such a situation, senior management would be likely to register concern at the money being spent on UDA, and would decide to restrict the Information Center budget (as happened at firm D). This provoked negative user reaction against the DP department and the IC staff, as users perceived themselves as being poorly serviced in their UDA activities. Thus, the DP group was "caught in the middle," and was seen as a poor performer by both users and top management.

The solution to this problem seems clear. Users themselves should be held directly responsible for demonstrating that the applications they develop are cost effective for the firm. In order to make this feasible, a chargeback scheme would have to be implemented so as to provide a cost calculation mechanism for users' cost benefit analyses.

It might appear that users in organizations with no central DP chargeback scheme would not undertake UDA activities at all, since central DP services were "free," and they would be charged for UDA service. However, most users interviewed in this study indicated that such would not be the case: users *are* willing to pay (via their operating budget) for UDA support. Rockart and Flannery[13] drew a similar conclusion from the data they collected in one large company. They stated that "users are willing to pay significant hardware running cost premiums to get systems up and running quickly under their control."[13]

This is not to imply that the DP group would not have a role in the evaluation process. However, this role would be one of advisor; that is, DP staff might assist users in their cost benefit analysis, but the final responsibility for demonstrating cost effectiveness would reside where it belongs—in the hands of the users.

The advantages of this approach to UDA evaluation are:

1. It properly couples the authority and responsibility associated with undertaking UDA activities.
2. It is more efficient since users better understand the situation surrounding their application. They are in a better position to advocate the benefits (and delineate the costs).
3. It serves a purpose similar to UDA itself, that is, it distributes the evaluation activity "out to the users," thereby reducing the potential bottleneck that would be caused by limited central DP manpower resources.
4. Finally, it helps to make the end user better aware of the true costs and benefits of computer-based systems, by forcing him or her to think through carefully—and be prepared to defend—the benefits and costs of specific applications.

There are two major areas of difficulty posed by the approaches advocated above. The first involves the use of a chargeback scheme; the second concerns the non-tangible benefits that might be derived from the applications developed.

Effective use of chargeback as an information systems measurement and control mechanism is difficult.[21] If charges are not well understood by users, dysfunctional effects may occur. Criteria for effective chargeback systems are well known, but designing and implementing them is still a challenge.[22]

Perhaps more problematic still is the use of intangible benefits.[23] While evaluation of the full spectrum benefits provided by information systems has been discussed in some depth in the literature,[24,25] the present study and other field studies suggest that most organizations still concern themselves only with measurable monetary benefits.[26] However, many of the computer applications which are developed by users themselves address decision support needs or similar requirements for which assessment of tangible benefits is difficult or impossible. The issue of intangible benefits is also of concern at the level of overall evaluation of UDA in an organization.

The value of reducing user frustration stemming from long waiting periods for new computer applications to be developed by the DP department does not lend itself to simple cost benefit analysis.

SUMMARY

There is a growing literature addressing the concept of end users developing their own computer applications. These studies focus mainly on the advantages of UDA to users, although advantages to DP departments are also frequently discussed. Such investigations tend to emphasize reductions in the DP application development backlog and application maintenance load as being the primary advantages of UDA to DP departments.

The results of this study indicate that, rather than being concerned about impacts on either backlog or maintenance load, DP managers are primarily interested in being able to demonstrate that the applications developed by users are of demonstrable, tangible benefit to the organization, and that the users themselves are satisfied with the UDA services made available to them via the DP department. Moreover, it was found that the evaluation of such tangible benefits is a critical issue for DP managers. This article proposes a simple evaluation framework, based on an earlier model by Keen, to help explain why some DP departments are successful in their evaluation while others are not. Finally, this article argues that the responsibility of the evaluation should belong to users rather than to the DP department.

REFERENCES

1. Martin, J. *Application Development Without Programmers*, Prentice-Hall, Englewood Cliffs, New Jersey, 1982.
2. Wohl, A.D. and Carey, K. "We're Not Really Sure How Many We Have...", *Datamation*, Volume 28, Number 12, November 1982, pp. 106–109.
3. Targler, R. "Information Centers," *Information Processing*, Volume 2, Number 1, March 1983, pp. 12–13.
4. Davis, G.B. "Caution: User-Developed Decision Support Systems Can Be Dangerous to Your Organization," Working Paper No. MISRC-WP-82-04, Management Information Systems Research Center, School of Management, University of Minnesota, 1981.
5. McLean, E.R. "End Users as Application Developers," *MIS Quarterly*, Volume 3, Number 3, December 1979, pp. 37–46.
6. McNurlin, B.C. "Supporting End User Programming," *EDP Analyzer*, Volume 19, Number 6, June 1981.
7. Rosenberger, R.B. "The Productivity Impact of an Information Center on Application Development," *Proceedings GUIDE 53*, Dallas, Texas, November 1981, pp. 918–932.
8. Hammond, L.W. "Management Considerations for an Information Center," *IBM Systems Journal*, Volume 21, Number 2, 1982, pp. 131–161.
9. Rhodes, W.L. "The Information Center Extends a Helping Hand," *Infosystems*, Volume 30, Number 1, January 1983, pp. 26–30.
10. McCartney, L. "The New Info Centers," *Datamation*, Volume 29, Number 7, July 1983, pp. 30–46.
11. Hesprich, S.F. "Corporate Brainchild — Microcomputers," *Journal of Systems Management*, Volume 33, Number 9, September 1982, pp. 6–9.
12. Bradish, J.R. "Administration of an Information Center: User's Experience," *Proceedings GUIDE 52*, Atlanta, Georgia, 1981, pp. 656–662.
13. Rockart, J.F. and Flannery, L.S. "The Management of End User Computing," *Proceedings of the Second International Conference on Information Systems*, Cambridge, Massachusetts, December 1981, pp. 351–363.

14. Goldstein, R.C. and McCririck, I.B. "The Stage Hypothesis and Data Administration: Some Contradictory Evidence," *Proceedings, Second International Conference on Information Systems*, Cambridge, Massachusetts, 1981, pp. 309–324.

15. Rivard, S. and Huff, S. "User Developed Computer- Based Applications: Analysis of Survey Results," Working Paper No. 83–04, School of Business Administration, The University of Western Ontario, February 1983.

16. Jensen, R.W. and Tonies, C.C. *Software Engineering*, Prentice-Hall, Englewood Cliffs, New Jersey, 1979.

17. Alloway, R.M. and Quillard, J. "User Managers' Systems Needs," *MIS Quarterly*, Volume 7, Number 2, June 1983, pp. 27–42.

18. Lientz, B.P., Swanson, E.B. and Tompkins, G.E. "Characteristics of Application Software Maintenance," *Communications of the ACM*, Volume 21, Number 6, June 1978, pp. 466–471.

19. Beckhard, R. and Harris, R.T. *Organizational Transitions: Managing Complex Change*, Addison-Wesley, Reading, Massachusetts, 1977.

20. Keen, P.G.W. "Computer-Based Decision Aids: The Evaluation Problem," *Sloan Management Review*, Volume 16, Number 3, Spring 1975, pp. 17–23.

21. Nolan, R.L. "Controlling the Costs of Data Services," *Harvard Business Review*, Volume 55, Number 4, July-August 1977, pp. 114–124.

22. Benard, D., Zmery, J., Nolan, R. and Scott, R. *Charging for Computer Services: Principles and Guidelines*, Petrocelli Inc., New York, New York, 1977.

23. Hamilton, S. and Chervany, N. "Evaluating MIS Effectiveness—Part 1: Comparing Evaluation Approaches," *MIS Quarterly*, Volume 5, Number 3, September 1981, pp. 55–69.

24. Keen, P.G.W. and Scott Morton, M. *Decision Support Systems: An Organizational Perspective*, Addison-Wesley, Reading, Massachusetts, 1979.

25. Kleijnen, J. *Computers and Profits*, Addison-Wesley, Reading, Massachusetts, 1980.

26. Huff, S., Grindlay, A. and Suttie, P. "Current Issues in Managing Information Systems: The Systems and Data Processing Manager's Viewpoint," Working Paper No. 317, School of Business Administration, The University of Western Ontario, June 1982.

QUESTIONS

1. What benefits do users stand to gain from the development of their own applications?

2. Based on the results of this study, how do DP departments *define* UDA success? How did these findings differ from expectations? Why?

3. Discuss the issues surrounding the *evaluation* of UDA success within an organization.

4. Describe the four steps of the UDA evaluation process. What role should the DP department play in the evaluation process?

12

CAUTION:
User-Developed Systems
Can Be Dangerous
To Your Organization

■

Gordon B. Davis

There is an enthusiasm about users doing their own information system applications. Along with the "good news" in this development, there is potential "bad news". The purpose of this paper is to identify possible dangers in user-developed systems. An awareness of these dangers may allow organizations to avoid them.

Three scenarios involving user-developed systems illustrate possible unintended, unfavourable consequences of encouraging or allowing user-developed information applications.

EXAMPLE 1: A FAULTY MODEL

The rapid decline and sudden collapse of the XY Corporation has had financial analysts puzzled. In reconstructing the events that led to the bankruptcy, a reporter was able to identify some key decisions and actions that precipitated the rapid decline.

1. The XY Corporation was in negotiations to acquire the Kando Company. Thomas Lonnasen, Financial VP, was in charge of the proposal. Using a personal computer in his office, he constructed a model of the XY

Reprinted by special permission of Professor Gordon B. Davis, University of Minnesota.

Corporation before and after the acquisition. Based on his model, he arrived at a purchase offer using stock in XY. Unfortunately, the acquisition model was faulty, so that the offer was excessive by 150 per cent.

2.   The owners of Kando Company immediately accepted the offer with the provision of that there be no restrictions on their sale of the XY stock received.

3.   The Kando holders of XY stock sold out immediately depressing the price of XY stock by 40 per cent.

4.   XY delayed a large planned stock offering and added to its bank borrowing but was unable to borrow enough to carry out the integration of Kando. Planned savings were not achieved.

5.   Due to a drop in profits, the bank demanded immediate payment of loans. The result was involuntary bankruptcy.

EXAMPLE 2: ERRORS IN DATA RETRIEVAL AND ANALYSIS

The board of Directors of the Zeta Company met Tuesday and appointed a new president to replace Inge Ting who resigned last Friday at the request of the Board. The cause of the Board's dissatisfaction centered on recent labour troubles. Inside sources identified the sequence of events that led to the trouble.

1.   Last May, Ms. Ting began to consider a college aid plan for children of employees. She felt this would be an attractive incentive for obtaining and retaining employees. The high technology company has a high percentage of professional employees.

2.   Before deciding on the college aid plan, the president assigned a staff analyst to make cost projections. The analyst developed an analysis using ANALYSIS, a user-friendly package that accessed employee data stored in the company employee/payroll database. The analysis was defective because it examined only 30 per cent of the employees. There were no controls in the analysis that disclosed this undercounting. The problem was that four different data names were assigned to four different types of employees, and only one name was used in the analysis. Also, cost estimation for each recipient was defective. It assumed an average (nation-wide) per cent for students attending college; the high professional orientation of Zeta employees caused a 2.4 times greater rate for their children.

3.   A college aid policy was announced. The funds disbursed in September for the first semester were eight times greater than projected.

4.   In November, the aid policy was rescinded. This led to several key resignations by employees with college-age children who were angry at the apparently arbitrary reduction in benefits.

5. In January, the professional employees' union demanded that the college aid policy be restored as part of the new contract.
6. In February, there was a strike. The college aid policy was only one of the issues but it was a very emotional component.
7. The professional employees' union settlement included a college aid provision less than the prior policy but it still represented a significant cost factor. It was estimated that it would reduce future profits by 13 per cent.
8. The Board requested the resignation of the president.

EXAMPLE 3: LACK OF DOCUMENTATION

The YZED Company dropped a lawsuit against Harry Jenkins, former financial VP of the company. The company had sued for return of computer programs and data files used in the management of cash funds and to enjoin Jenkins' use of them. Mr. Jenkins had taken the programs and data with him when he left to form a consulting firm. He claimed they were similar to private papers and documents that traditionally executives have been allowed to take. The company claimed they were developed on company time using company resources, and they belonged to the company. The out of court settlement stipulated that Jenkins would document the system, so it could be used by his successor, but he could also use the system in his consulting business. The agreement reflected the fact that the system, if returned without additional documentation, would have been worthless to anyone except its developer, Jenkins.

END-USER COMPUTING AND USER-DEVELOPED SYSTEMS

User-developed systems is one part of the larger trend to end-user computing. End-user computing will be described briefly as the framework in which user-developed systems are occurring.

End-user computing is the organization of computing resources and design of information system applications such that:

- Application systems provide direct, immediate support for user activities.
- Information requirements are specified by the user and may be changed by the user as the system is used.
- The development use of the system is under user control.

The importance of end-user computing is apparent from rapid development of information centres to support it and the forecasts of experts who have studied it. For example, Bob Benjamin of Xerox[1] estimates that by 1990, end-user computing will take 75 per cent of corporate computer resources. Rockart and Flannery estimate a growth rate of 50 to 90 per cent per year in companies promoting end-user computing; this is contrasted with a growth of 5 to 15 per cent in traditional data processing.

The computing resources that support end-user computing include hardware, software, and organization:

☐ The hardware support can vary depending on the organization. The following may be used individually or in combination:
– Terminals to external time-sharing system
– Terminals to mainframe
– Stand alone microcomputers
– Microcomputers in network

☐ The software support for end-user computing will generally include the following:
– Planning languages and spread sheet processors (examples are IFPS, EXPRESS, VISICALC, etc.)
– Procedural languages such as BASIC and APL
– Very high level languages for programming and query. Examples are NOMAD, FOCUS and RAMIS
– Statistical analysis software. Examples are SAS and SPSS
– Database management system

☐ The organization for end-user computing may use one or more of the following options:
– Information centre with analysts who program to user specifications
– Information centre with analysts who assist users to utilize the facilities and provide training and consultation
– Analysts assigned to user areas who assist users by doing the work or by aiding users with the facilities
– A policy supporting end-user computing, but no direct support organization
– No policy or support
– Policy that there will be no end-user computing

The last item in the organizational options makes clear that some organizations are not happy with the idea of end-user computing and especially user-developed systems. Some of the reasons for the resistance will be explained later.

There are some interesting statistics on end-user computing in a survey by Rockart and Flannery of *timesharing* users (see Table 12.1).[2]

The Rockart and Flannery survey also found that 37 per cent of the applications used data from productions systems, but 31 per cent keyed in data from reports (indicating a lack of facilities, ability, or knowledge to obtain the data from the computer files), and users generated and keyed the data in 17 per cent of the applications. The survey excludes many other forms of end-user computing, but it does describe part of the phenomenon.

The use of personal microcomputers is indicated by an Infosystems Magazine survey of use of personal computer software (see Table 12.2).[3]

TABLE 12.1

Type of User	Per cent of Application Systems	
	Developer of System	User of System
Non-programming end user	0	55
Command-level end user	13	17
End-user programmers	22	21
Functional support personnel	48	5
End-user computing support personnel	3	1
Data processing programmer	10	1
Outside consultant	4	—

User-developed systems is that part of end-user computing in which applications are developed and implemented without the use of an analyst (or with minimal interaction with an analyst). User-developed systems may occur in a variety of ways:

☐ The user-developed systems data files may be completely outside the regular information systems or the systems may access datafiles maintained by the regular information systems.
☐ The user may operate with independent equipment or may utilize equipment that is under the control of the computing facility.
☐ The user may operate without assistance or the computing centre may provide various levels of support.
☐ The user may operate with independent software or the software may be obtained and maintained by the computer centre.

TABLE 12.2

Personal Computer Software	Percentage Who Use
Spread sheet processors	76
Word processors	30
Languages	26
Planning languages	20
Graphics	16
Office support	11
Database management systems	8
Communications	2
Other	6

This survey highlights the importance of end-user computing and explains how user-developed systems fit into it. The question to be explored is the organizational benefits and risks with user-developed systems and how the benefits can be achieved and the risks can be managed and minimized.

THE INFORMATION SYSTEM ADVANTAGES OF USER-DEVELOPED SYSTEMS

A user-developed system differs from the traditional development procedure in eliminating the central role of the analyst as the elicitor of requirements, analyzer of needs, supervisor for development and enforcer of organizational standards (Figure 12.1). The tools of user-development are designed for non-technical personnel, whereas analyst development tools may require technical expertise.

In practice, there is not a dichotomy of user-developed and analyst-developed systems. Rather, there is a continuum in which at one end analysts have little or no involvement and at the other extreme the analyst takes most of the development responsibility. The domain of this paper is the user-developed system with no (or very little) analyst participation.

There are three advantages to the information system area in having users develop their own decision support systems:

1. Relieves shortage of system development personnel.
2. Eliminates the problem of information requirements determination by information system personnel.
3. Transfers the information system implementation process to users.

Relieves Shortage of System Development Personnel

A common complaint by users is that they cannot get systems implemented. There are simply not enough analysts and programmers to keep up with the demand. There are several alternatives to this problem:

☐ Make analysts more productive
☐ Use more package software
☐ Transfer development functions to users

The last alternative is very appropriate when users can do the task satisfactorily. This usually requires user development tools such as modelling languages database query language, etc. The question remains whether or not providing such tools to users will ensure that they can develop satisfactory systems.

One caution to note is that user-developed systems may actually increase

FIGURE 12.1
COMPARISON OF TRADITIONAL AND USER-DEVELOPED
SYSTEM APPROACHES

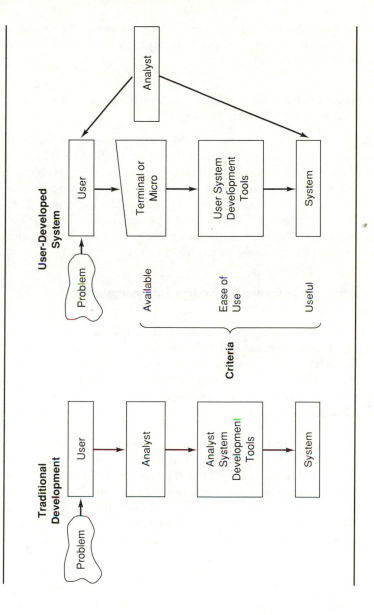

the demand for analyst services, data availability, and regular applications. In other words, user-developed systems may increase the overall demand for information services.

Eliminates the Problem of Information Requirements Determination by System Personnel

One of the major problems in information systems is the eliciting of a complete and correct set of requirements. Various methodologies have been proposed but it still remains a difficult process. The problem is made more difficult because the analyst is an outsider who must be able to communicate with a user in eliciting the requirements. Having users develop their own system eliminates the problems of the analyst at the interface. It does not eliminate the problem of obtaining requirements; but it places an "insider" in the role of requirements problem solver.

Transfers the Information System Implementation Process to Users

Implementation is a key process. Poor implementation is one of the major reasons systems are not utilized. There are difficulties from the interaction of the "expert" analysts and the non-technical users who are providing requirements for the system. There is a direct analogy for analyst involvement in decision support system design and implementation and operations research models and their implementation.

☐ Operations researchers have been observed as desiring to elicit requirements from user personnel but not to confide in user personnel during the evaluation of the elicited requirements and the development of a system. The result has been resistance to the use of the system.
☐ Operations research personnel have designed sophisticated systems beyond the understanding of the users, but user personnel will not use systems they do not understand.

The effect of transferring development and implementation to users is to eliminate the potential conflict from technical system experts and non-technical users. Users may develop less sophisticated systems when they do the design and development, but they will use them.

Systems get implemented and used. These advantages of user-developed systems are impressive. However, there are serious risks in the elimination of the analyst role as a developer. Some major dangers and risks are a result of:

1. The elimination of separation of the functions of user and analyst.
2. The limits on user ability to identify correct and complete requirements for a DSS application.

3. The lack of user knowledge and acceptance of application quality assurance procedures for development and operations.

4. Unstable user systems in organizational situations requiring stable systems.

5. Encouraging of private information systems in an organization.

6. Permitting undesirable information behavior.

THE RISK FROM ELIMINATION OF THE FUNCTIONS OF USER AND ANALYST

It is not sufficient to merely build and use information systems; they must meet organizational objectives and meet a level of quality and completeness that is appropriate to the organizational unit and the decision activity. The analyst serves three purposes.

1. A technical expert in system design and development.

2. An independent reviewer of requirements.

3. An enforcer of acceptable standards and practices.

Technical expertise has been important with traditional development techniques. There is less need for technical expertise when development is performed with user friendly development facilities. The first technical role for the analyst is therefore decreasing in importance; but not meeting the second and third purposes poses significant risk.

The analyst, in eliciting requirements and analyzing needs, provides an "outside" review. Users needs are questioned and alternatives suggested and discussed. System documentation is improved because two different functions use the documentation. Of course, the review can be performed by another person in the user area, but organizational experience with independent review suggests the analyst as outside reviewer is an important function.

The use of an analyst in the development process provides an organizational mechanism for enforcing appropriate standards and practices. The users may not perceive the need for the standards; the analyst can better understand their value and is therefore an appropriate person to be given the role of system standards enforcer. Standards and practices include documentation, controls, testing, interfaces with other systems, etc.

THE RISK FROM LIMITS ON USER ABILITY TO IDENTIFY CORRECT AND COMPLETE REQUIREMENTS FOR A DSS APPLICATION

Data processing personnel have long recognized the difference in risk from master file errors and input data errors. A master file error affects processing for period after period while a transaction input error affects only a single transaction. By analogy, the decisions in designing an application system are more crucial than the making of a single decision using the system because the design decisions will influence many decisions over a period of time.

The frequently observed difficulty of users to identify a correct and complete set of requirements stem from:

1. Human cognitive limits as reflected in decision making affecting requirements.
2. Errors in decision making affecting requirements determination.

Basic Human Cognitive Limits in Decision Making Affecting Requirements

A user in a user-design situation has several strategies for determining the requirements for the decision support system:

1. Rely upon current understanding of needs.
2. Obtain requirements from some existing system the user has seen or can examine.
3. Obtain requirements from analysis of the characteristics of the decision system or other utilizing system.
4. Obtain requirements through trial and error incremental changes in an evolving application.

Selection of a strategy should probably be based on the underlying uncertainty of being able to obtain a complete and correct set of requirements. For example, a relying-on-current-understanding strategy is suitable for low uncertainty and trial and error incremental development is suitable for high uncertainty.

Performance of a user in following one of these strategies for deciding on system requirements is affected by human information handling and problem solving procedures. Some examples of human information processing behaviour that are significant to information requirements determination are described in Table 12.3.

The net effect of these human information processing behaviours on the determination of information requirements is a significant bias toward requirements based on current procedures, currently available information, recent events, and inferences from small samples of events.

Requirements determination is also affected by human problem solving behaviour. In this connection, two problem-solving concepts from Newell and Simon, task environment and problem space,[1] are relevant. The task environment is the problem as its exists; the problem space is the way a particular decision maker represents the task to work on it. The information require-

TABLE 12.3

Human Behaviour	Explanation and Effect on Information Requirements Determination
Anchoring and adjustment	Humans tend to make judgments by establishing an anchor point and making adjustments from this point. When asked for information requirements, humans will therefore have a tendency to respond by an adjustment from an anchor of requirements representing the information currently available to them.
Concreteness	Decision makers tend to use only the available information in the form it is displayed. They tend not to search for data or transform or manipulate data that is presented. For information requirements determination, this means that user specification of requirements will be biased by the information they have and the form of this information.
Recency	Humans are influenced more by recent events than by events of the past. In defining information requirements, users will be biased by those events that happened recently. An information need that was experienced recently will be given greater weight than a need based on a less recent event.
Intuitive statistical analysis	Humans are not good as intuitive statisticians. For example, humans do not usually understand the effect of sample size on variance and therefore draw unwarranted conclusions from small samples or a small number of occurences. There is overemphasis on easily imagined unfavourable consequences. This is an important limitation because many organizational phenomena occur at a fairly low rate. There is a tendency to instinctive-ly identify causality with joint occurrence and assign cause where none exists. These limits of humans in processing low-occurence data and in identifying causality mean users may misjudge the need for information.

ments task environment is the determination of information requirements for an application. The problem space in this case is how a particular user formulates a representation to use in working on the problem of requirements.

A characteristic of proficient systems analysts is that they have learned to use a general model of requirements to bound the problem space and aid in an efficient search for specific requirements; poorly rated analysts have a poorly developed model and therefore a poorly developed search procedure in the problem space.[5] Also, the highly rated analysts consider organizational and policy issues in establishing requirements; the low rated analysts do not include these in their problem space. Presumably, the same results apply to users doing their own requirements. Although many users will have a good general model, many will fit the poorly rated analyst behaviour. The completeness and correctness of the requirements obtained is limited not only by the model but also by the training, prejudice, custom, and attitude of the users.

In an analyst/user development, the analyst generally provides structure to the problem space as a part of eliciting requirements. The interaction between analyst and user helps to provide some assurance the problem space is correctly defined. In user-developed systems, there is an assumption that the user can structure the problem space unaided except by the development software facilities.

Errors in Decision Making Affecting Requirements Determination

Users may not adequately perform the application system requirements task. There may be several possible errors in the process and outcome.

1. Over analysis and inefficient search.
2. Solving the wrong problem.
3. Applying the wrong analysis or the wrong model.

Over Analysis and Inefficient Search

Over analysis and inefficient search in the problem space may be due to the desire for an optimal solution and uncertainty reduction. The decision maker performs additional analysis that adds very little information.

The over analysis and inefficient search may also be due to the lack of a model for problem solving in the task environment. Vitalari found that a differentiating characteristic of high rated analysts was their use of a model of the problem. The model allowed them to react to clues and quickly eliminate many alternatives. The poorly rated analysts had no search strategy or overall model and they performed much more undirected or poorly directed analysis. Without training or experience in analysis, many users are likely to perform like the poorly rated analysts.

Solving the Wrong Problem

This is not unique to information applications. However, the dynamics of user-developed applications increase the probability that the user will solve the wrong problem. The reason is that providing users with extensive analytical and modelling capabilities encourages them to perform solution procedures without adequate problem analysis and problem formulation. If solution procedures are fairly difficult to implement, problem solvers are more likely to spend time making sure the right problem is being solved. Interaction with analysts and problem documentation also help to avoid solving the wrong problem.

An example of solving a problem in response to the availability of computational procedures is an organization that had developed a rather complex profit sharing arrangement. The provisions of the profit sharing became so complex that it was not possible to compute the profit sharing using ordinary arithmetic. The user consultant assigned to the problem applied simultaneous linear equations to solve the profit shares. In other words, the problem solver viewed the problem as applying a computational procedure. The problem solving anchored on the existing solution and sought an adjustment. However, the real problem in this case was to have a profit sharing agreement that would provide incentive. Any agreement that must be solved using simultaneous linear equations cannot have any incentive value because an employee does not know the impact of a decision on profit share. To solve the right problem required an analysis of the objectives of the utilizing system. The real solution was to revise the profit sharing agreement.

Applying the Wrong Analysis or the Wrong Model

This again is not unique to decision support systems. However, the results of a computer model seem to receive added credibility. Therefore, the output of a model may be accepted without adequate skepticism, testing, and evaluation of assumptions and methods. Given a readily available repertoire of methods, it is easy to apply the wrong analytical procedure. An example that illustrates the problem involved manual computation, but the situation is analogous. A manufacturer of heavy equipment used in the construction and mining industries needed to forecast future demand. A staff person did a least squares regression on the logs of historical sales. There was an almost perfect constant percentage increase in sales. This was extrapolated forward and showed the need for a new plant which was built. Sales dropped and immediately after opening the plant was sold at a heavy loss. The company almost failed. The problem was that the regression (even though it apparently fitted historical data) was an inappropriate technique for such a forecast. User-developed systems, without the interaction of an analyst, are more susceptible to such errors of applying the wrong analysis. (Of course, analyst developed systems without user interaction and review have the same danger.)

THE RISK FROM LACK OF USER KNOWLEDGE AND ACCEPTANCE OF APPLICATION QUALITY ASSURANCE PROCEDURES FOR DEVELOPMENT AND OPERATIONS

There are risks from user-developed systems caused by a lack of user knowledge and acceptance of organizational quality assurance procedures. These risks occur from a reluctance to apply adequate procedures for:

1. Testing
2. Documentation
3. Validation and other programmed assurance processes
4. Audit trails
5. Operating controls

There is an interesting phenomenon very observable in students. They believe their programs to be relatively error free. "All I have to do is correct one error" is a common comment. This perhaps relates to the humans as information processors research by Langer[6] in which she found subjects had an illusion of control leading to over-optimistic estimates of chance-based outcomes. Based on this research plus my observation of my own behaviour, the behaviour of students, and the behaviour of people in organizations, it appears that users developing their own systems will significantly underestimate the probability of errors and discount the need for and value of quality assurance and testing procedures.

Reluctance To Test

Testing is a difficult and time consuming process. Users are likely to ignore the range of testing that is desirable because of their confidence in the system and their confidence in simple, cursory testing. They are likely to resist procedures such as walkthrough.

Reluctance To Document

Documentation is important in quality assurance procedures such as reviews. It is also important to future modification. Yet, the tendency is to avoid documentation. User development software should enforce necessary documentation, but user languages such as BASIC do not.

Reluctance To Include Validation

Certain quality assurance procedures need to be built into programs. All input data should be validated and echoed back to the person doing the input. There should be record counts, control counts, crossfooting tests, tests for reasonableness, etc. User-oriented procedural languages such as FORTRAN and BASIC are typically taught without incorporating this discipline.

Reluctance To Include Audit Trails

Users will frequently omit audit trails because they do not appreciate the need for them. The concept of an audit trail sounds as if it is needed for an auditor (and so it is unnecessary for user systems). Very wrong. The concept is a processing reference trail. Any resulting figure should be traceable back to its constituent data items or any data item should be traceable forward to its impact on results and its inclusion in result figures. The output from a model should provide tracing pointers and immediate outputs, so that any recipient can evaluate the assumptions of the model and the processing flow.

Reluctance To Have Operating Controls

Using a model should include quality assurance procedures to make sure:

- All input data have been entered.
- All input data are valid.
- All records are processed.
- Results are compared to independent control figures (example: an analysis of receivables should provide a control total that is compared to the general ledger total).

Users without data processing experience may not understand the need for and value of these controls.

THE RISK FROM UNSTABLE USER SYSTEMS

Most organizational processes depend on stable systems. Communication among subsystems will increase dramatically without interfaces such as stable procedures and stable decision rules. There are, of course, rigidities from stable systems. Instability may not be entirely bad, but it does present considerable risk of overall organizational instability with accompanying high expenditure for communications. Some areas in which instability may appear as a result of user developed systems are depicted in Table 12.4.

It has been suggested by Hackathorn and Keen[7] that task interdependency is a key variable in deciding on the appropriateness of personal computing. Independent tasks in which the manager reaches a decision through private analysis are appropriate; pooled or sequential interdependent tasks are not suitable because of the need for stable interfaces.

THE RISK FROM ENCOURAGING PRIVATE INFORMATION SYSTEMS

The complete information system of an organization is composed of systems that are formal or informal and public or private (see Table 12.5).

TABLE 12.4

Area of Instability	Comments
Changes in inputs and outputs	A user-developed system is almost, by definition, easy to change. But a change may afflict the inputs required from other systems and the outputs that will be available to other systems. These changes make it difficult to track overall performance of the system.
Changes in processes	The user who develops a system may wish to make frequent changes in the processes and logic. A change in the logic applied to a problem may be desirable, but it introduces the possibility of the errors described earlier. It also reduces comparability from period to period, so it is difficult to make comparative evaluations.
Changes in use of system	User-developed systems may become very personal. They are identified with a person holding a position rather than the functional characteristics of the duties of the position. This leads to additional instability when personnel are changed.

TABLE 12.5

System Characteristic	Description
Formal	Documented and institutionalized in procedures, forms, documents. Fairly stable.
Informal	Ad hoc, changeable, dependent on individual.
Public	Information is available to all who are authorized to receive, i.e., access is based on position or function.
Private	Information is available to the person (not the position).

From these two sets of characteristics, there are four subsystems in the complete information system (see Table 12.6).

One objective of computer-based information systems is to expand the scope of the formal public system to include information otherwise contained only in private formal systems. The reasons for this objective are:

1. Private systems frequently contain information that should be available in the public system.

TABLE 12.6

	Public	Private
Formal	Formal information system	Little black book Individual files and records
Informal	Bulletin boards Memoranda	Professional contacts "Golf" discussions

2. A private system depends on an individual and if that individual leaves the organization, the private information system leaves. Even though the system may have been formalized by the individual, it is not institutionalized by formal documentation, recorded procedures, etc.

   User-developed systems will tend to expand the scope of private formal systems. In fact, by definition, a user-developed system is a formal private system unless it is institutionalized and made a public system (available to the function or position) through public documentation and organizational quality assurance. The user-developed system, by encouraging private (formal) systems, encourages information hiding by individuals. It also makes it difficult to transfer systems to new persons taking over a position.

THE RISK FROM PERMITTING UNDESIRABLE INFORMATION BEHAVIOUR

There are psychological and organizational behaviour reasons for individuals in organizations to accumulate information (even if not needed). These reasons include:

☐ Psychological value of unused information. Knowing it is there if needed or "just in case" seems to give information accumulation a positive value.

☐ Information is often gathered and communicated to persuade (and even to misrepresent).

☐ Information use is a symbol of commitment to rational choice. Having information resources thus represents user competence.

Traditional development provides countervailing pressures to these reasons. User-development systems may provide a way for users to avoid countervailing pressures and meet these psychological/behavioural needs for information.

SOME METHODS FOR MINIMIZING RISKS FROM USER-DEVELOPED SYSTEMS

This paper does not deal with all decision support systems, only those that are user developed. The following suggestions for methods to minimize risk should not inhibit experimentation with user-developed systems. Rather, they provide mechanisms for organizational controls to assure user developed systems will be appropriate for incorporation into the organization system.

1. Provide analysts as advisors and reviewers.
2. Have organizational policy that user-developed systems must be reviewed and documented (or that an analyst must participate during development).
3. Provide user training in problem finding, problem formulation, and requirements analysis.
4. Provide ongoing training feedback through review (by analysts, auditors, and others) for design, requirements, quality, controls, stability.
5. Include automatic documentation procedures and quality assurance procedures in the development system.
6. Provide user training in application quality assurance and controls. Provide analyst walkthrough.
7. Provide user motivation for and training in stable systems.

The seven methods for minimizing risks from user-developed systems are organized by risk causes in Table 12.7.

One major factor in training is that unless there is substantial use of facilities, their use will not be habitual. This suggests the need for consultants who can refresh abilities. Users should be assisted to form reasonable expectations about what they can accomplish and the need for frequent refreshing.

SUMMARY

End-user computing is a significant development in organizational use of information resources; user-developed systems represent an important subset. There are a number of significant advantages to user-developed information system applications:

1. Relieves shortage for development personnel.
2. Eliminates the problem of information requirements determination by information systems personnel.
3. Transfers the use of information system implementation process to users.

There are serious risks in the elimination of the analyst role as a developer. These are a result of:

TABLE 12.7
TABLE OF DANGERS AND RISK CAUSES
AND METHODS FOR MINIMIZING RISKS

Cause of Danger and Risk	Method for Minimizing Risks
Elimination of separation of the functions of user and analyst.	Provide analysts as advisers and reviewers. Have organizational policy that user-developed systems must be reviewed and documented (or that an analyst must participate during development).
Limits on user ability to identify correct and complete requirements for an application.	Provide user training in problem finding, problem formulation, and requirements analysis. Provide ongoing training feedback through review by analysts and other reviewers such as auditors.
Lack of user knowledge and acceptance of application quality assurance procedures for development and operation.	Provide user training in application quality assurance and controls. Include quality assurance and control in development system procedures. Provide analyst walkthrough for development. Provide ongoing training feedback through analyst and auditor review.
Unstable systems in organizations that need stable systems.	Provide user motivation for and training in stable systems. Analyst/audit review of user systems affecting organizational stability.
Encouraging private information systems in an organization.	Have an enforced organizational policy on review and documentation to allow system transfer to new user. Include documentation in development system.
Permitting undesirable information behaviour.	Provide user training in requirements analysis.

1. The elimination of separation of the functions of user and analyst.
2. Limits on user ability to identify correct and complete requirements for a DSS application.
3. The lack of user knowledge and acceptance of application quality assurance procedures for development and operations.
4. Unstable user systems in organizational situations requiring stable systems.
5. Encouragement of private information systems.
6. Permitting undesirable information behaviour.

The risk from limits on user ability to identify requirements arises from human cognitive limits and errors in decision making relative to requirements. The cognitive limits stem from behaviour based on anchoring and adjustment, concreteness, recency, intuitive statistical analysis, and the structure of the problem space. Errors in decision making relative to requirements result from over analysis and inefficient search, solving the wrong problem and applying a wrong analysis or model.

The risk from lack of application quality assurance procedures is evidenced in testing, documentation, validation procedures, audit trails, and operating controls. The risk from unstable systems arises from the instability plus increase in communication when an organizational system is unstable and rapidly changing.

The risk from encouraging private information systems is that information will not be available to other parts of the organization and the system will not be transferred to the new person in a position when there is a change.

The risks from permitting undesirable information behaviour arise from psychological and behavioural pressure to accumulate information. User-developed systems remove some restraints.

These risks can be minimized by various procedures for documentation and quality assurance, training providing review support, and enforcement of an organizational policy. These mechanisms allow user experimentation with user-developed applications but enforce reasonable quality in the results.

REFERENCES

1. R.I. Benjamin, "Information Technology in the 1990s: A Long Range Planning Scenario," *MIS Quarterly,* 6:2 (June 1982), pp. 11–31.
2. J. Rockart and L. Flannery, "The Management of End User Computing," *Communications of the ACM,* 26:10 (October 1983), pp. 776–784.
3. *Infosystems,* April, 1983.
4. Allen Newell and Herbert A. Simon, *Human Problem Solving,* Englewood Cliffs, NJ: Prentice-Hall, Inc., 1972).
5. Nicholas P. Vitalari, "An Investigation of the Problem Solving Behavior of Systems Analysts," Unpublished Ph.D. Dissertation, University of Minnesota (1981).
6. Ellen J. Langer, "The Illusion of Control," *Journal of Personality and Social Psychology,* 32:2 (1975), pp. 311–328.
7. Richard D. Hackathorn and Peter G.W. Keen, "Organizational Strategies for Personal Computing in Decision Support Systems," *MIS Quarterly,* 5:3 (September 1981), pp. 21–33.

QUESTIONS

1. Compare and contrast traditional versus user-developed system approaches.
2. Describe several short- and long-term dangers/risks associated with user-developed systems. Why are these dangers/risks often overlooked?
3. Describe six potential *causes* of dangers and risks often associated with user-developed systems.
4. What organizational procedures and system design features can be implemented to reduce the dangers/risks to a tolerable level?

THE MANAGEMENT
OF EUC

∎

As suggested in the previous section, many of the user-developed and -operated applications are not personal or private in nature. That is, they are not merely used by a single individual to support his/her activities. In some cases, real-time access to user-developed systems is essential for the efficient performance of one or multiple departments and functions. The breadth of impact of these end-user systems necessitates comprehensive and extensive management attention.

Indeed, the need for the management of EUC seems to be well recognized. However, comprehensive and well-defined procedures do not exist in many organizations. The objective of this section is to provide some insights into EUC management via four articles on the subject.

Maryam Alavi and Ira Weiss, in "Managing the Risks Associated with End-User Computing" (Reading 13), address many of the concerns identified in the article by Gordon Davis (Reading 12). The authors associate EUC risks with different stages of the end-user applications life cycle. Generic controls are then introduced in a manner that allows EUC management to select those most appropriate to their EUC environment.

Reading 14, "The Management of End-User Computing," by John Rockart and Lauren Flannery, is well regarded as a "classic" in the field. Based on interviews with 200 end users and 50 members of IS staffs responsible for EUC support, the authors set forth a number of managerial recommendations for EUC.

As Rockart and Flannery conclude in their article, "Developing the appropriate strategy, support processes, and control processes for EUC is a stag-

geringly large job." Maryam Alavi, Ryan Nelson, and Ira Weiss address this
concern in the next reading, "End-User Computing Strategies: An Integrative
Framework" (Reading 15), by developing a framework consisting of five core
strategies, or organizational postures, vis-a-vis EUC. Following a description
of each of the strategies, the authors employ a two-step process to represent
(1) **how** to effectively implement a particular EUC strategy, and (2) **when** to
adopt a particular EUC strategy.

The increasing proliferation of EUC is obvious from the evidence presented in previous readings. However, if the concomitant problems in
the areas of security, integrity, documentation, and accountability are not
addressed, management may be forced to impose drastic cutbacks on the
organizational use of EUC. For this reason, the identification of variables that
may affect the success of EUC facilities within an organization is extremely
important. Paul Cheney, Robert Mann, and Donald Amoroso, in their article, "Organizational Factors Affecting the Success of End-User Computing"
(Reading 16), identify success/failure variables based on a three-part classification scheme: controllable, partially controllable, or uncontrollable.

13

Managing the Risks Associated with End-User Computing

■

Maryam Alavi
Ira R. Weiss

INTRODUCTION

End-user computing (EUC) is a rapidly growing and irreversible phenomenon. It is estimated[1] that the share of computer capacity employed by EUC activities in large corporations will grow from 10% in 1981 to 70% of an expanded capacity by 1990. The major advantages attributed to EUC include: enhanced productivity of professional and white-collar workers, overcoming the shortage of DP professionals, provision of user-friendly and responsive systems, and overcoming the implementation problems by transferring this process to the user.[2,3] In the enthusiasm to benefit from EUC activities, corporations are overlooking the potential risks of these activities. Organizational exposure to EUC risks is costly. In order to minimize the cost, the potential risks of EUC should be identified and managed.

Many of the end-user developed and operated applications are not personal or private in nature. That is, they are not merely used by a single individual to support his/her activities. In a recent study[1] more than half of the systems surveyed concerned applications relevant to the operations of an entire department. Seventeen percent of the systems involved multiple departments and multiple functions. In some cases, moment-to-moment

Reprinted by special permission of the Journal of MIS, *Volume 2, Number 3, Winter 1985–86, pp.* 5–20.

access to the user-developed systems was essential for the efficient performance of one or multiple major departments.[1] The breadth of impact of
these end-user systems necessitates comprehensive and extensive management review and control procedures. The term "control" employed throughout the paper does not imply impeding or discouraging EUC, but guiding,
directing, and encouraging its effective use. There is a growing concern that
EUC activities are poorly managed and are getting "out of control." Control
procedures adapted to the idiosyncrasies and special circumstances of EUC
are needed to ensure that EUC activities produce complete, accurate, authorized, and consistent information.

The need for management and control of EUC seems to be well
recognized. However, comprehensive and well-defined procedures do not
exist. The objective of this article is to provide some insights into the EUC
risks and suggest a comprehensive and specific framework in which EUC can
be effectively employed and controlled.

ORGANIZATIONAL RISKS ASSOCIATED WITH END-USER COMPUTING

The first step toward establishing EUC control and review procedures is
to identify potential risks associated with the different facets of EUC. The
control and review procedures are then developed in order to minimize or
eliminate the risks. EUC risks associated with the different stages of the end
user applications life cycle are displayed in Table 13.1 and discussed below.
Table 13.1 has been divided into the three traditional stages of the systems
development life cycle: analysis, design, and implementation. This allows
specific categorization of risks and a hierarchical framework in which to view
them. The risks displayed in Table 13.1 are most common to those end
users that design, program, and operate their own applications. According to
Rockart and Flannery[1] end users can be classified into six distinct categories.
Of the six categories defined it appears the risks relate the most to command
level users, end-user programmers, and functional support personnel because
they are all heavily involved in the design, programming, and operation of
their applications.

Risks Associated with Analysis of End-User Tools

Management of the acquisition of end-user software and hardware tools is
important in guiding EUC toward achievement of organizational goals. An
indicator of eventual success or failure of EUC seems to be whether users
are engaging in end-user activities with a clear idea of what they want to
accomplish. End-user tools may be adopted as a response to the "technological
push" and not because of meeting specific organizational needs. The sum
of false or abandoned starts on EUC may collectively be a considerable

TABLE 13.1
ORGANIZATIONAL RISKS ASSOCIATED WITH DIFFERENT
STAGES OF END-USER APPLICATION LIFE CYCLE

	End-user applications life cycle stages	Organizational risks
Analysis	Analysis of end-user tools	Ineffective use of monetary resources Incompatible end-user tools Threats to data security and integrity
	Analysis of end-user applications	Overanalysis and inefficient search in the problem space Solving the wrong problem
Design	Conceptual design of end-user applications	Applying the wrong model Mismatch between the tools and applications Little or no documentation Lack of extensive testing
	Development of end-user applications	Lack of validation and quality assurance checks Inefficient expenditure of non-DP personnel time Redundant development effort
Implementation	Operations of end-user applications	Threats to data integrity Threats to security Taxing the mainframe computer resources
	Maintenance of end-user applications	Failure to document and test the modifications Failure to upgrade the applications

misconceived investment of organizational resources. Other risks associated with uncontrolled acquisition of EUC tools include incompatibility of software and hardware devices, threats to integrity and security of organizational data resources, and ineffective or inappropriate use of EUC tools.

Some see device incompatibility as a minor risk because they believe a "black box" technological solution to the incompatibility problem can be developed. But the unchecked proliferation of end-user devices (specifically micros) can turn a simple problem into a much more complicated one. For example, end-user training and support requirements may increase sharply under these circumstances.

Uncontrolled acquisition of end-user tools presents threats to data integrity and security. Duplication of applications and data, although not always avoidable, increases risk of errors, inconsistency, and inefficiency. The impact of EUC (particularly when micros are used) on security of organizational data is a growing concern. User-friendliness and easy access provided through end-user tools increase the risk of unauthorized access to data.

Risks Associated with Analysis of End-User Applications

The analysis of end-user applications involves diagnosis and definition of the problem and identification of systems requirements by the end user. Often the end user has not been formally trained in applying the systems analysis techniques needed to adequately perform these activities. Davis[2] identifies two risks associated with this phase:

1. overanalysis and inefficient search for the solution.
2. solving the wrong problem.

Overanalysis and inefficient search may result from the desire to find "the best" answer or the desire to reduce the uncertainty inherent in the decision process. Research[4] has shown that good analysts use models and heuristics to guide search and analysis processes. In the absence of heuristics and models, analysis and search processes tend to be indirect and inefficient.[4] Due to lack of training and experience in analysis and modeling, end users are likely to undertake inefficient search and analysis approaches.

Under the pressures of daily activities, the end users may not spend sufficient time on problem definition and diagnosis. End users are likely to proceed with solving the problem (using the readily available end-user tools) without adequate problem specifications. They are, hence, more likely to solve the wrong problem. Furthermore, due to the availability of the end-user computing tools, work with the computer may become a substitute for hard and good thinking about the problem.

Conceptual Design Risks of the End-User Applications

Mistakes in the conceptual design of end-user applications can be very costly in that the application may affect decisions and activities over a period of time. Design risks also exist for the analyst-developed systems. But due to the special circumstances of EUC, the risks increase with end-user design of complex models and decision support systems.

User designed systems seem to be more susceptible to modeling errors because users typically lack specialized training and relevant experience. For example, least squares regression analysis is a forecasting technique which is not applicable to all forecasting situations. An end user, unfamiliar with the underlying assumptions of the technique, may inappropriately apply it to a forecasting problem.

End users may also select an inappropriate software tool during the conceptual design phase of their applications. Different end-user computing activities such as word processing, modeling, information storage and retrieval, and so on cannot currently be effectively and efficiently supported within the structure of a single software tool. Hence, there is the risk of selecting the wrong software tool and stretching it to perform jobs in a way far less efficient than could be done with the appropriate tool. The mismatch between the software tool and the application may be due to the reluctance of users who have become proficient with one tool to begin learning another. The higher the user's success with a software package, the greater the tendency to apply it to other, possibly inappropriate tasks. Selection of EUC software tools should be monitored to ensure that the right tool for the job at hand is obtained.

Development Risks of End-User Applications

End-user applications are developed with little or no analyst involvement. The development process is best characterized as incremental and evolutionary. The development process usually does not include documentation, formal validation procedures, and extensive testing.

End users avoid documentation because they typically view it as a waste of time and an unnecessary activity. Documentation is important to reviews and future modifications. In a survey[5] of end-user developed systems, several users admitted that if they left the firm their applications would go with them since no one else could understand or maintain them. The development process employed by the end users typically does not enforce necessary documentation.

User-developed applications do not typically include validation and other quality assurance checks and procedures. These procedures are needed in order to ensure that the output of the user-developed systems is accurate, complete, valid, and credible. Users usually do not include these procedures because they do not appreciate their importance.

End users are also reluctant to extensively test the applications that they develop because testing is time consuming. Testing of user-developed applications at best is limited to simple and superficial procedures. The majority of users are unaware of many possibilities for programming errors. They seem to significantly underestimate the possibilities of errors and hence discount the need for and value of extensive testing.[2]

Some end users are becoming highly computer literate, supporting other end users within their particular functional areas. These end users spend a large percentage of their time (estimated up to 80%) developing applications for other users.[1] They are not data processing professionals or programmers. Rather, they are corporate planners, financial analysts, or market researchers. There is a potential risk and cost that, by getting too involved in application development, these end users are becoming sidetracked from their primary organizational responsibilities.

The end-user development effort may also be redundant and inefficient for two primary reasons. First, different users in different organizational locations may be "reinventing the wheel" and developing similar applications (e.g., cash flow analysis models) for similar organizational activities. Second, due to lack of specialized training and experience, a single user may redevelop the same application for use in different contexts and with different problems.

This may be due to the end-user tendency to develop inflexible, too specific, and situation-dependent models versus generic and parameter driven models. For example, a single generalized cash flow model may be used in analysis of multiple projects by single or multiple end users. This may be accomplished by employing variables versus constants in the model and hence allowing different input values. A user, on the other hand, may develop multiple but similar cash flow models for use in different projects. Such redundancy may lead to analysis and data inconsistency in addition to inefficient expenditure of user time and effort.

Operation Risks of End-User Applications

The major risks associated with operation and utilization of end-user applications involve data integrity and security issues. These are perhaps the biggest risks associated with EUC activities. Organizations have managed to establish procedural, physical, and technological controls over their large databases and large "production" systems. For the most part, these control structures are nonexistent in the area of EUC. Users create, update, and eliminate applications and data files without observing any well-defined and standard procedures for quality assurance and creation of audit trails.

In a study of 271 end-user developed and operated systems, it was indicated that up to 70% of the systems used data generated by the large "production" systems.[1] The study indicated that, in about half of the cases, there was a "data extraction gap." That is, there were no automated data extraction links between the user-operated application and the organization "production" files. The data were laboriously keyed in from previously prepared reports. This situation increases the likelihood of introducing input data errors in the user-operated applications. Threats to data integrity also stem from the lack of quality assurance procedures and inadequate testing as discussed in the previous section.

User-operated applications typically lack well-defined and documented operating procedures for updating, back-up, and access control. Poor operating procedures and control coupled with user friendliness and easy access to some of the end-user tools such as microcomputers and diskettes make end-user operated applications particularly vulnerable to security threats.

Uncontrolled growth in EUC activities may place an increasing demand on the organizational mainframe computing resources. Unplanned and unanticipated end-user computing activities in some large organizations may soon create mainframe capacity constraints unless considerable investments in expansion of the capacity are made.

Maintenance Risks Associated with End-User Applications

An inherent characteristic of end-user developed applications is that they are easy to change. User-developed applications tend to be unstable because changes made to these applications are frequent, undocumented, and not thoroughly tested. Frequent changes in the user applications increase the likelihood of introducing errors and may affect the inputs required and the outputs generated by the system. These changes make it difficult to ensure performance integrity of the system. Lack of documentation and piecemeal and incremental development of the applications also contribute to their maintenance difficulty.

User-developed and operated applications may not be adequately maintained because end users do not usually have an organizational responsibility for maintenance of these applications. Also, organizational and environmental changes requiring a change in the end-user application may go unnoticed by the end user.

A FRAMEWORK FOR CONTROL

Organizations presently find themselves in a paradoxical position. To try to rigidly control the extent and types of uses of micros and other EUC tools will be viewed as a frontal attack on employee/professional productivity. To open the gates and allow and encourage EUC experimentation at all organizational levels has the potential of leading to all or many of the risks outlined previously. Therefore, a well-thought-out corporate control philosophy/policy is needed. Even more important is the way this policy is introduced and implemented within organizations.

Prior to developing a control policy and implementation plan it becomes important to understand why controls are critically important to consider. Without controls the probability of financial losses occurring is heightened. A micro or terminal sitting in the middle of an unlocked office has a greater probability of being misused or taken than one that has been carefully placed in a secured area. Risks may be thought of as merely the probability that a financial loss may occur. Controls address those probabilities by reducing them and therefore reducing the expected loss. Corporate management would be negligent if they did not consider and implement appropriate controls for the organization since they directly address corporate assets.

Considering the above it becomes clear that management has the responsibility to control the EUC environment. By control we do not mean to impede but rather to carefully plan for the expanded, productive use of EUC. To do this management needs to understand that control is not a unidimensional process. When controls are referred to, it is generally understood that there are three distinct control types each addressing the "timing" of risks.

Preventive controls are those policies, procedures, and authorization structures that are put into place to minimize the possibility of a risk occurring. Preventive controls are passive in their nature and relate to such things as:

- acquisition policies,
- training,

☐   job descriptions,
☐   diskette handling and back-up procedures.

Detective controls may be considered second lines of defense and are much more action oriented. Detective controls attempt to enforce the policies that have been defined in the preventive area. They relate to such activities as:

☐   access to databases,
☐   edit and validation checks,
☐   supervisory review of logs and performance reports.

Corrective controls provide the mechanisms to correct violations that have been detected. Corrective controls include:

☐   password changes,
☐   data re-entry procedures,
☐   discharging personnel.

In the EUC area, management's greatest opportunities lie within the preventive control framework. Within this area management has the opportunity to set "guidelines" within the following areas:

☐   acquisition of hardware and software,
☐   involvement of the MIS group within the EUC process,
☐   accessibility of corporate databases,
☐   local versus shared EUC results,
☐   types of applications that "fit" within the organization EUC scope,
☐   long term opportunities for "blending" EUC within the corporate information network,
☐   EUC support concept such as an Information Center,
☐   creation of an environment where EUC productivity gains are rewarded within a budgetary framework,
☐   creation of the operational environment under which EUC will operate (libraries, documentation, security, backups).

In reviewing the above "opportunities" for management it can be seen that the terms "management involvement" can be easily substituted for the terms preventive controls. Given the potential resistance to the term control this substitution may be appropriate. Figure 13.1 outlines a control framework that formalizes the interdependencies within EUC. Paramount within this framework is the management control or management involvement process. As may be intimated all other control elements are subordinate to it. A brief review of each of the elements is appropriate.

As mentioned previously, management control is primarily preventive in nature. Within its scope reside all policies and procedures regarding the

FIGURE 13.1
AN EUC CONTROL FRAMEWORK

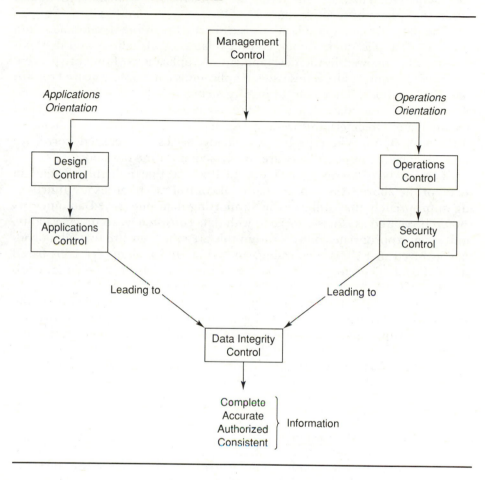

acquisition, strategies, and use of EUC within the organization. Management control may be viewed as the strategic plan for EUC with the subordinate elements developing the tactical and operational plans.

Below management control reside two diverse paths: operations and applications. The operations side is needed to develop a framework in which EUC can function in a compatible and complementary fashion with traditional computing functions. Within this path a further division is made between operations and security, operations being primarily responsible for overseeing EUC tools within libraries, documentation for tools, and the management of the support environment for successful EUC (e.g., Information Centers, MIS SUPPORT, etc.). Generally the types of controls needed within this sphere would be preventive in nature. The detective and corrective controls for ensuring that only authorized individuals gain access to libraries, documentation, databases, and terminals or micros are predominantly found within the sphere of security control.

The path defined as applications is associated with the development and use of EUC applications. Design control relates to procedures and methodologies to be followed in the development of applications. Primarily preventive controls would address this issue. Applications controls are geared toward detection methods. They tend to involve stringent edit tests for valid, complete, and accurate data. They also are associated with the examination of documentation to determine overall adequacy as it applies to the maintenance of the application. Where problems or inadequacies are detected, corrective methods must be in place to assure timely action on the deviations.

The last box described in Figure 13.1 is one that is highly dependent on all of the above. It is implied that if all control mechanisms are functioning appropriately they will assist in supporting data integrity. Data integrity should be viewed as issues associated with data consistency, accuracy, validity, and so on. Appropriate controls within this area must ensure that all individuals involved in EUC are accessing, analyzing, and making decisions based on valid data. Therefore appropriate detection controls must be designed to identify and extract data that may contaminate the database.

As packaged together, all of the above types of controls should lead to the organization accomplishing its EUC goals by ensuring that the effectiveness of EUC is supported by accurate, complete, authorized, timely, and valid information.

The next section will attempt to identify specific types of controls that may be employed within each of the areas defined.

CONTROL MECHANISMS

It becomes necessary to identify those controls that need to be considered in the EUC environment. In order to avoid the "control overkill" syndrome the approach taken within this section will be the following:

1. Specific controls will be identified that address each of the organizational risks enumerated in section 2 and depicted in Table 13.1.
2. Each of the risks and associated controls will be classified according to the control framework previously outlined.

Controls Associated with Analysis of End-User Tools

A. Ineffective Use of Monetary Resources. The issue of ineffective use of monetary resources was defined as potentially the uncontrolled growth of

EUC devices within the organization. The most effective control method for this issue is ensuring that all acquisitions are preceded by formal requests and appropriate justifications including some form of cost/benefit analysis. This forces the user to enumerate exactly the purposes for purchase and the expected benefits to be gained. The value of this exercise cannot be adequately stressed. Users must have a plan prior to receipt of these tools and a cost/benefit analysis forces upon them the development of that plan.

B. Incompatible End-User Tools/Devices. The issue of incompatibility not only reinforces the issue of ineffective monetary uses but also addresses the potential inability to get optimum uses out of EUC tools. The most effective method to ensure compatibility is to have the organization create standards for both hardware and software. Requests to violate standards would have to be accompanied by salient arguments (e.g., software needed runs only on specific machines).

C. Threats to Data Security and Integrity. Data security threats range from disclosure, destruction, and modification of corporate data to incorrect data entering and being used within the database. Also possible are potential inconsistencies between corporate data and EUC data leading to erroneous decisions. Policies relating to downloading and uploading within the corporate database need to be addressed. Issues relating to access from remote locations (e.g., home) must be resolved. Technical methods need to be developed which indicate to an end user that data being used within an EUC model have recently been modified through normal corporate data processing functions and therefore need to be modified for the EUC model being employed.

Within the control framework defined, all of the above control issues addressed may be classified as management, design, and operational control. Issues related to monetary resources and incompatibility are preventive in nature and are predominantly policy oriented. Data integrity issues should fall under operations control.

Controls Associated with Analysis of End-User Applications

A. Overanalysis and Inefficient Search for the Solution. To address the issue of overanalysis and inefficient search the organization needs to develop comprehensive training programs for users. These programs must be multi-dimensional in nature, addressing both operations and the process of decision making within an EUC environment.

B. Solving the Wrong Problem and Incorrectly Solving the Problem. Inexperienced computer users often accept computer results as being the correct answer. Unfortunately, errors in developing the algorithm or sloppiness in coding the solution can lead to the outcomes of either solving the wrong problem or incorrectly solving the problem. An environment must be created within the organization that is so accommodating to the user that proceeding to use the result of a tool without first getting a "second opinion" would be considered out of the norm. Developing this accommodating environment (e.g., Information Center) is a major undertaking to which the organization must have committed resources. To invoke the desired behavior the organization must provide the talents needed to administer the environment and highly encourage its use.

In classifying the controls addressed to support this life cycle stage it becomes apparent that they are a combination of management, operation, and design controls. Management must design a training strategy for EUC but generally that strategy needs to be implemented within the operations area. Management must design a strategy for supporting the EUC functions but operations again would be responsible for managing the daily operations of the Information Center or whatever method is devised. Design Control would provide the talent, resources, and/or methodologies in order for the Information Center to effectively operate.

Controls Associated with the Conceptual Design of End-User Applications

A. Mismatch between the Tools and Application.   The potential mismatch problem highlights the problems that many new computer users find themselves in. Once a tool is mastered it potentially may be used indiscriminantly for all problems. Outcomes of this process could be significant inefficiencies or incorrect outcomes. An effective method for addressing this type of problem is the use of technical review teams for all new EUC applications. This has a dual benefit in that the mismatch is addressed as well as an inventory of applications being developed. This inventory also is an effective method of reducing duplication of efforts. These technical reviews *must* be operationalized such that they are responsive to the user in a timely fashion. The emphasis must be on both accommodating the user and ensuring that appropriate tools are used.

B. Applying the Wrong Model.   The risk of using the wrong model is probably not significantly different from manually-based systems except for the potential ease of access and use of the model. User training combined with technical assistance and review would also adequately address this risk.

The use of technical review teams and adequate training may be classified as management, design, and operational control. Management must support both activities but the design and operational areas must insure that technical review teams and user training are provided during the design, installation, and implementation of the applications.

Controls Associated with the Development of End-User Applications

A. Little/No Documentation.   The lack of documentation issue is not strictly an EUC issue. Documentation gains made over time within traditional MIS applications must be transferred to EUC. To accomplish this there must be explicit documentation standards in place which describe documentation deliverables at each stage of development and implementation. There must be means developed to enforce documentation standards. For example, methods such as the Information Center/technical assistance will be made available only if appropriate documentation is displayed upon requesting assistance. Other methods would include the inability to download or access corporate data without the appropriate documentation for the application.

B. Lack of Extensive Testing.   Serious problems can occur when the user assumes, after limited tests, that the application is ready for implementation. Testing and validation standards must be enumerated and testing methods must be taught to the users. The firm can experiment with using EUC quality assurance groups while using this group to teach valid testing methods to end users.

C. Lack of Validation and Quality Assurance.   This risk is similar to the above mentioned one. The major difference resides within the question of who does the validation and testing. The use of quality assurance groups and information systems auditors would be appropriate to give the organization the assurance they are looking for as to the validity of the EUC application. This may be especially critical when the application falls into the category of affecting more than the end user.

D. Redundant Development Efforts.   Redundant development risks basically fall into two categories:

1.   users not knowing what other users have developed.
2.   development of application specific rather than generic models.

The development of an EUC library and a document describing the contents of the library would address the first risk. The second needs to be addressed through training. Users may initially see each problem as being different when in fact the parameters are the only factors that are changing. Effective training can go a long way toward resolving this problem.

E. Inefficient Expenditure of Non-DP Personnel Time.   To date no definitive studies have shown the level of productivity gains through EUC. It is just "assumed" that productivity is enhanced. Given this situation it becomes necessary to question the value of highly paid executives/professionals spending considerable amounts of time in developing EUC applications. Management must address this issue in a tactful but responsive manner. Support teams should be made available for this group of individuals, therefore accommodating their needs but ensuring that most of their time is spent doing their job.

In classifying the above controls outlined in this life cycle stage we find that they predominantly relate to design and application control. Documentation standards, testing methods, audit/quality assurance, and edits all relate to following the appropriate standards enumerated within the development process and assuring that they are working within the application process. The last risk addressed, inefficient expenditure of professional time, is a management issue.

Controls Associated with the Operation of End-User Applications

A. Threats to Data Integrity.   Data integrity relates to the accuracy, consistency, validity, and veracity of data. To address these issues two sets of controls must exist: edit and access controls. Within the edit area the user must define and implement appropriate checks to ensure that errors and omissions bypassing the user are caught by the application. Within the access control framework it must be determined that the user or the application has authorization to use certain data. Instead of authorizing users the possibility of controlling applications by "certifying" them as valid users of the system might be appropriate.

B. Taxing the Mainframe Computer Resources.   To truly estimate the cost of EUC the impact on the organizational mainframe cannot be ignored. Uncontrolled EUC users can cause significant efficiency problems and inhibit organizational data processing functions. Planning for EUC must be done in conjunction with DP management in order to understand the interdependencies and trade-offs. Budgets must be set and reviewed; meaningful charge-back schemes must be implemented. Methods must be imposed such that users become aware of the underlying operational costs as well as the hardware/software costs.

C. Threats to Security.   Security must be viewed as both physical and data/software security. EUC places significantly more moveable hardware resources within the organization. Individually each one of these devices might be relatively inexpensive; collectively they are not. Physical access/custodianship controls must be established. Access controls have already been mentioned. Depending upon the nature of the EUC applications backups and methods of re-creation must be considered.

Classifying controls within this life cycle stage results in the categories of security, application, management, and operations. Effective security controls are needed within the data integrity and physical/software security issues. Within the data integrity issue appropriate application controls are also vital. Management must be responsible for setting policy on the interaction with the mainframe resource but operations through budgets and charge-backs will be responsible for operationalizing the issue.

Controls Associated with Maintenance

A. Failure to Document and Test Modifications. The failure to document and test modifications of applications is no different from the initial issue discussed within the development of the application. Maintenance, though, becomes a more frequent and on-going process. Non-maintaining as well as inadequate maintenance are both critical issues. Standards must be imposed within the maintenance cycle. Those standards must address the modification and testing issues and explicitly identify the minimum "new deliverables" that are appropriate. Analyst or quality assurance review may be effective. Information systems audits should address this issue periodically by auditing the application, associated documentation, and change control documents.

B. Failure to Upgrade the Application. Failure to maintain may be caused by ignorance, oversight, or more critically a timeliness factor. Having limited time to maintain an application is an indication that the end user might be the wrong candidate for being responsible for the EUC application. Audits can assist here also by reviewing with users the last time changes were made and the currency of the application. Change control documents should be required. Therefore applications without any filed change control documents either are in violation of maintenance standards or are potentially "unmaintained" applications.

All of the above controls would fall into the classification of Application or Design Control.

Table 13.2 summarizes and classifies the discussions of this section. The figure may be used as a reference to understand the nature, extent, and organizational responsibility of controls that may be applied to EUC risks. It is incumbent upon EUC management to consider all controls for the specified environment and select those that effectively and efficiently accomplish stated objectives.

SUMMARY

The potential organizational risks of end-user computing activities which we have reviewed highlight the evident need for well-defined control processes in this area. Specific risks associated with the different stages of end-user applications life cycle and specific control mechanisms for reduction or elim-

TABLE 13.2
THE RELATIONSHIP BETWEEN THE CONTROL MECHANISMS
AND THE ORGANIZATIONAL RISKS ASSOCIATED WITH THE LIFE
CYCLE STAGES OF END-USER APPLICATIONS

	End-User Application Life Cycle Stages	Organizational Risks	Control Mechanisms
Analysis	Analysis of end-user tools	Ineffective use of monetary resources	Cost/benefit analysis
		Incompatible end-user tools	Hardware/software standards
		Threats to data security and integrity	Policy for end-user access to corporate data base
	Analysis of end-user application	Overanalysis and insufficient search for the solution	Provide user training in problem solving and modeling
		Solving the wrong problem	Involve analyst in the design process for review
Design	Conceptual design of end-user application	Applying the wrong model	Technical training Reviews Policy for Technical reviews
	Development of end-user application	Little or no documentation	Enforce documentation standards Include documentation in development process
		Lack of extensive testing	Testing/validation standards User training in application quality assurance
		Lack of validation and quality assurance	Analyst/auditor "walk-though" Auditor reviews
		Redundant development effect	End-user training in modeling application development Common application library
		Inefficient expenditure of non-DP personnel time	Management policy for limits on allocation of non-DP personnel time Support from analyst

	End-User Application Life Cycle Stages	Organizational Risks	Control Mechanisms
Implementation	Operation of end-user application	Threats to data integrity	Input data validation routines
			User training in data integrity issues
		Taxing the mainframe computer resources	Management policy on the role of end-user computing
			Integrating EUC and DP planning
			Control of EUC growth through budgets and charge-backs
		Threats to security	Access control via pass words
			Physical access control (restricted areas)
			Standards for backups
	Maintenance	Failure to document and test modifications	Maintenance Review by analyst
		Failure to upgrade the application	Periodic system review by user analyst

ination of the risks were identified and briefly discussed. The variety and scope of EUC controls, as evident in our argument, indicate that developing a comprehensive set of appropriate EUC controls is a staggeringly large job and requires significant managerial attention and involvement. It is important to point out here that establishing controls in themselves is not sufficient. Specific procedures for enforcing them and periodic compliance testing are also required. It is the belief of the authors that the introduction of an organizational EUC control process will have a much greater chance of being embraced if it is "marketed" appropriately within the organization. Top management is always being criticized within the information systems environment for noninvolvement. It is our belief that the control process can be marketed through management involvement.

REFERENCES

1. Rockart, John F., and Flannery, Lauren S. The Management of End-User Computing. *Communications of the ACM*, 26, 10 (October 1983), 776–784.

2. Davis, Gordon B. Caution: User-Developed Decision Support Systems Can Be Dangerous to Your Organization. Presentation at the Fifteenth Hawaii International Conference on System Sciences, Honolulu, Hawaii, January 6–8, 1982.

3. Keen, Peter G.W. A Policy Statement for Managing Microcomputers. *Computer World,* In Depth (June 1983), 35–39.

4. Vitalari, Nicholas P. An Investigation of the Problem Solving Behavior of Systems Analysts. Unpublished Ph.D. dissertation, University of Minnesota, 1981.

5. Benson, David H. A Field Study of End-User Computing: Findings and Issues. *MIS Quarterly,* 7, 4 (December 1983), 35–45.

QUESTIONS

1. What organizational risks are associated with different stages of the end-user application life cycle?

2. Identify and briefly discuss specific control mechanisms useful in the reduction or elimination of the risks associated with EUC.

3. Discuss the importance of "marketing" the EUC control process within the organization.

14

The Management of End-User Computing

■

John F. Rockart
Lauren S. Flannery

Today, interest in end-user computing (EUC) is booming. While most information systems departments are still heavily involved in processing paperwork, there are a host of signs which suggest that this traditional focus will soon become a junior partner to user-developed and -operated computing. End-user oriented languages are increasingly plentiful and better than ever. Improved man-machine interfaces are being developed;[1,2] users are becoming more aggressive and more knowledgeable.[3,4] Formerly the sole province of scientists and engineers, end-user computing is spreading throughout the entire organization. It is at the point where in some companies, EUC now utilizes 40–50 percent of the computing resource.[5] This has led to increased attention to appropriate organizational forms to support this growing phenomenon.[6-8]

Despite all this activity, "end-user computing" is still poorly understood. There has been a mass of exhortative literature and occasional single case-based discussion of end-user computing. But there has been a paucity of conscientious research into who the users are, what they are doing, what their needs are, and most significantly, how to manage this new phenomenon.

In order to shed more light on this, we interviewed 200 end users and 50 members of information systems staffs having the responsibility for supporting end-user computing in seven major organizations. The companies involved were three Fortune 50 manufacturing companies, two major insurance companies, and two sizable Canadian companies. Users interviewed were all making use of "time-sharing" of one sort or another. We are just nearing the end of a parallel study of personal computer users in ten major corporations. Preliminary data analysis suggests that although some details differ, managerial recommendations made at the end of this paper remain essentially the same.

Method

The interviews, which were confidential, began with an open-ended discussion of each participant's computing activities. The approach was aimed at surfacing key issues with regard to end user computing as perceived by the users themselves. The interview was guided by a structured questionnaire. Ultimately, after allowing the user to discuss all issues and aspects of EUC he or she believed to be important, each user was asked to comment on each of the questionnaire items upon which he had not touched. Quantitative data was not gathered in the early interviews, but as the issues became clear, such data was obtained from 140 of the users representing 271 different applications. Analysis of this data is noted.

In each company, interviewees were selected at random from a list of users designated by the company as "heavy and/or frequent users of time-sharing." It was felt that this procedure would provide a diverse, unbiased sample of the population of most interest—the major users: we believe it did. Our sample, however, is *not* representative in its proportions of the entire end-user community. We will return to a discussion of the evident, and interesting, results of this method of user selection.

Findings

We present both the *findings*, which were the facts observed during the study, and our *conclusions*, which are our interpretations of the findings. The findings of the research can be grouped into four major areas as follows: the significant growth evident in end-user computing, the nature of the user population, attributes of the applications being performed, and the managerial processes being employed with regard to end-user computing. Each of these are discussed in turn.

Growth

In each of the companies observed, end-user computing was growing at a rate of approximately 50%–90% per year. This was measured by either actual allocation of computer hardware power or external time-sharing budgets. The highest measured growth rate observed in the study companies was 89%. Later discussion, with a significantly larger sample of companies, strongly suggests that these figures generalize well. At the same time, traditional data processing oriented toward processing the paperwork of the company is growing at a far lesser rate. On the average, in both our sample companies and others, this growth rate appears to be only 5%–15%. These widely divergent growth rates have led some observers such as Robert I. Benjamin at Xerox to predict that by 1990, end-user computing will absorb 75% of the corporate computer resource.[9]

Users were asked to note the factors underlying their growing utilization of end-user computing. Four major clusters of reasons dominated their replies. The first of these is "a vastly increased awareness" of the potentials of EUC. A new generation of users has arrived which understands EUC and views it as a means of facilitating decision making and improving productivity. Most of these employees are recent graduates who have had experience with an end-user language in college. At the same time, more senior personnel have been introduced to EUC by colleagues who have made use of EUC's capabilities. A second route to top management awareness is through managerial journals such as *Business Week* and *Fortune*, which have increasingly been informing their readers both of the potentials of EUC and of the software products available. Finally, users noted, hardware and software salesmen are making calls directly on them in their "end-user" departments.

A second set of user-perceived reasons for the high growth rate of end-user computing centered around recent improvements in "technical" capabilities which make end-user computing increasingly more feasible and less costly. Vast improvements have been made in end-user software.[3,7,10] Today's languages, while not quite "user friendly," certainly are significantly easier to use than those even available 3 to 4 years ago. Decreasing hardware costs have made feasible the use of "cycle-eating" interpretative languages and relational databases. Users also refer to the increasing availability of both internally and externally purchasable databases, providing automated access to information previously unavailable, or which would have had to be painstakingly entered by hand.

The third set of reasons for the increase in EUC concerns the more difficult "business conditions" which prevail today. These conditions have intensified the need in all organizations for more effective analysis, planning, and control. High interest rates, inflation, and worldwide competitive pressures have made it increasingly important for both staff and line managers to have access to more, and often more detailed, information within a greatly decreased time frame.

Finally, and noted by almost all users, their needs cannot be satisfied through the traditional information systems organization. For a significant portion of their new applications, users find the tools, methods, and processes adhered to by the information systems organization as entirely inappropriate. Even for those applications where proven information systems (IS) methods would be appropriate, however, users have turned to available end-user languages since the waiting period to get the application up and running through the IS department—most often 2 to 3 years—is seen as intolerable.

The End Users

Clearly, if one is attempting to understand end-user computing, it is important to know *who* the users are, *where* they are located, and *what* they do. We developed a classification of end users and their locations within the organizations we studied. The tasks that are being carried out by these users through EUC will then be noted in the next major section of this paper entitled "the applications."

Who Are the Users?

The literature provides three recent classifications on end users. The simplest available categorization is that provided by the Codasyl*end-user facilities committee.[11] Their three-part breakdown includes "indirect" end users who use computers through other people (e.g., an airline passenger requesting a seat through his travel agent); "intermediate" end users who specify business information requirements for reports they ultimately receive (e.g., marketing personnel); and "direct" end users who actually use terminals. It is only the last category that is of interest to us here.

Two authors, Martin[7] and McLean,[4] recently further broke down the "direct" category. Their two classifications are almost exactly the same. McLean's classes are:

☐   DP professionals (who write code for others)
☐   DP amateurs (non-IS personnel who write code for their own use), and
☐   non-DP trained users (who use code written by others in the course of their work, but know nothing about programming)

In the companies we studied, we observed a finer-grained and, we believe, more useful classification of end users. Six distinct classes of end users who differed significantly from each other in computer skills; method of computer use; application focus; education and training requirements; support needed; and other variables emerged. Although all utilized end-user languages or the products of these languages, each user class is distinctly different from the others. They are:

Nonprogramming end users whose only access to computer-stored data is through software provided by others. They neither program nor use report generators. Access to computerized data is through a limited, menu-driven environment or a strictly followed set of procedures.

Command level users who have a need to access data on their own terms. They perform simple inquiries often with a few simple calculations such as summation, and generate unique reports for their own purposes. They understand the available database(s) and are able to specify, access, and manipulate information most often utilizing report generators and/or a limited set of commands from languages such as FOCUS, RAMIS II, EXPRESS, SQL, or SAS. Their approach to the computer is similar to that of an engineer to a slide rule in days past. They are willing to learn just enough about the database and the software to assist the performance of their day-to-day jobs in functions such as personnel, accounting, or market research.

End-user programmers who utilize both command and procedural languages directly for their own personal information needs. They develop their own applications, some of which are used by other end users. This latter use is an incidental by-product of what is essentially analytic programming performed on a "personal basis" by quantitatively oriented actuaries, planners, financial analysts, and engineers.

Functional support personnel who are sophisticated programmers supporting other end users within their particular functional areas. These are individuals who, by virtue of their prowess in end-user languages, have become informal centers of systems design and programming expertise within their functional areas. They exist today as "small pockets of programmers" in each functional organization of the companies we studied. They provide the majority of the code for the users in their functions. In spite of the large percentage of time that these individuals spend coding (several estimated over 80%), they do not view themselves as programmers or data processing (DP) professionals. Rather, they are market researchers, financial analysts, and so forth, whose primary current task is providing tools and processes to get at and analyze data.

End-user computing support personnel who are most often located in a central support organization such as an "Information Center." Their exact roles differ from company to company. Most, however, are reasonably fluent in end-user languages and, in addition to aiding end users, also develop either application of "support" software.

DP programmers who are similar to the traditional Cobol shop programmers except that they program in end user languages. Some corporations have developed a central pool of these programmers to provide service to end-user departments wishing to hire "contract programmers," to avoid high consultant/programmer fees, and to build a larger base of knowledge of end-user language computing within the corporation.

The distribution of the end users whom we interviewed is shown in Table 14.1. This distribution is *not* representative of the entire user population in

TABLE 14.1
DISTRIBUTION OF END USERS INTERVIEWED

User Class	Number	Percentage
Nonprogramming End User	13	9
Command-Level End User	22	16
End-User Programmers	30	21
Functional Support Personnel	53	38
End-User Computing Support Personnel	7	5
Data Processing Programmers	15	11
TOTAL	140	100

the companies we studied, but reflects the bias inherent in our selection of users who were the "major users of the computing resource." It is our belief, from discussion and observation in the companies studied, that with respect to the entire end-user population, the first two classes of users are seriously underrepresented in our sample, by perhaps an order of magnitude. (Upon reflection, however, we would not change our selection process. It led us to the most involved user population, and the one most capable of shedding light on the area.)

For managerial purposes, our user classification has four major "messages" which we discuss in a later section of the paper. These are:

- End users are a *diverse* set. There is no single, stereotyped "end user" with a single, defined set of characteristics. We have defined at least six major types—there may be more.
- Diversity in the end-user population and what they do leads to a need for *multiple software tools* in the end-user environment. Some sophisticated users need bit-level, procedural (e.g., BASIC, APL) languages to carry out their functions. For others, text processors, report generators, and simple command-level languages will suffice. Since no single end-user language can meet the range of function needed by these different users, a broad menu of end-user tools must be supplied.
- Diversity in the end-user population also surfaces an evident need for strongly *differentiated education*, training, and support for the quite different classes of users. Nonprogramming users desire only well written instruction sets. "Command-level" users want brief, limited training and education targeted to their specific interests. The more sophisticated "end-user programmers" need in-depth understanding of the one or two software products most relevant to the particular function they perform. Finally, the functional support personnel members and professional DP people desire and need more extensive training in a wider variety of software products. In all the companies studied, education, training, and support seem targeted at only a single segment of the end user population—usually the most sophisticated: this was a major source of user discontent.
- Finally and most significantly, the classification highlights the *existence and importance of functional support personnel*. These people are not only the key utilizers of end-user computing, but they are a source of significant opportunity *and* of potential problems for the IS function.

User Location

Table 14.2 shows the location, by function and role, of the users interviewed. The most significant point is that 81% of the users interviewed were in major, definable staff groups in their corporations: this is natural. Staff personnel, almost by definition in most major organizations, are those responsible for the gathering, manipulation, analysis, and reporting of information.

TABLE 14.2
USER FUNCTIONAL LOCATION

Staff	Number	Percentage	Cumulative Percentage
Corporate Strategy, Planning Forecasting	16.	11.4	11.4
Marketing—Research	8	5.7	17.1
Marketing—Planning	9	6.4	23.5
Finance—Accounting	10	7.2	30.7
Finance—Planning/Analysis	7	5.0	35.7
Purchasing, Scheduling, Distribution	9	6.4	42.1
Human Resources/Personnel/Industrial Relations	9	6.4	48.5
Actuarial	5	3.6	52.1
Operations Research	5	3.6	55.7
Engineering	12	8.6	64.3
IS–Developer/Support/User	20	14.3	78.6
Other—Special Projects, Legal	3	2.1	80.7
Line:			
Management	3	2.1	82.8
Marketing/Sales	9	6.4	89.2
Manufacturing	5	3.6	92.8
Claims/Rating	6	4.3	97.1
Other	4	2.9	100.0
TOTAL	140	100.0	

It is clear that staff groups represent major "clumps" of end-user computer activity. This is an important finding. It provides a positive response to the remarks of many interviewed IS managers best expressed by one who, despairing of his ability to bring end-user computing under control, noted that end-user computing is spread all over the company like grains of sand. "I don't know how I can possibly plan for it, support it or manage it, I can't get my hands around it." Our data, which generalizes both through the seven companies studied and others with whom we have discussed this issue, suggests that with a limited number of fact-finding missions into the major staff groups in his organization, this manager could gain a significant insight into the bulk of the end-user computing taking place in his organization. It appears that the 80/20 rule, once again, has validity.

The Applications

Of significant interest were the types of applications being performed by end users. Tables 14.3-14.9 record various aspects of these applications. Some 271 applications were discussed, on the average of about two per user, which was the design objective. Some users were involved with only one application. Up to four applications apiece were discussed with a few users.

Table 14.3 shows one classification of interest, the primary focus of the application. It shows a highly diverse range of systems which ran the gamut from traditional "paperwork processing" to the provision of complex analytical assistance. As shown, about 10% of the systems were "operational" paperwork processing systems such as inventory systems or commission check producing systems which might alternatively have been coded in Cobol. Most were programmed in an end-user language to "get them up quickly." Another 39 systems primarily served as "automated back ends" of Cobol-type systems. In most cases, these involved information databases taken from production systems (often with additional data keyed in) which turned out reports regularly or on demand. (We return to this class of system again during the discussion of Table 14.9.)

One fifth of the applications provided software to merely extract particular data items from a database or to do simple command-level manipulation of items in the database. Not surprisingly, however, one-half of the applications supported more complex analysis of data. Included in these systems were financial pro forma analysis, engineering calculations, operations research, optimization models, and simulations. Although the analytic techniques and software were complex (and usually developed by functional support personnel), many of these systems could be operated by a relatively naive user through the insertion of a few parameters–often in a menu-oriented way.

A second cut at understanding the applications used by end users is the "scope" of the system. Table 14.4 indicates that less than a third of the systems were "personal" in nature, being operated by a single person to carry out one of his or her tasks. More than half of the systems concern applications relevant to the operations of an entire department, with 17% of the systems being multidepartmental (most often multifunctional) in scope. In general, the scope of the data utilized followed quite precisely the functional scope of the system. The breadth of impact of these systems was surprising to us and to the management of the companies which we studied. We, and they, had

TABLE 14.3
APPLICATIONS (BY PRIMARY PURPOSE)

Purpose	Number	Percentage
1. Operational systems	24	9
2. Report generation	39	14
3. Inquiry/simple analysis	58	21
4. Complex analysis	135	50
5. Miscellaneous	15	6
TOTAL	271	100

TABLE 14.4
SYSTEM SCOPE

Scope	Number	Percentage
Multi-Departmental	45	17
Single Departmental	141	52
Personal	85	31
TOTAL	271	100

expected a much larger proportion of single person systems. On the contrary, we found in each company a large, and growing, number of very large information databases where moment-to-moment access was *absolutely* necessary for the efficient functioning of major staff departments or combinations of departments. The users were adamant in stressing the importance of these systems and the information systems management implications of them.

Table 14.5 shows the *primary* source of the data used for each application. In about a fifth of the systems, data came from two or more of these sources, but Table 14.5 shows only the primary source. The importance of the paper-work-processing "production" systems as a data generator for end user analysis is clearly evident. As their primary input, 190 of the 271 applications rely on such data. Interestingly, and very significantly, this data is transmitted directly from the production files in only slightly more than half of these cases. For the other 92 systems, the data is laboriously keyed in from previously prepared reports. This emphatically indicates a "data extraction gap"—an area in which end users feel strongly that IS is "dropping the ball." Unable to get the data directly, and needing it, users are resorting to keying it in themselves. The exhibit also illustrates the minimal interdependence from one end user system to another and a relatively limited use today of "externally purchased" data.

TABLE 14.5
PRIMARY SOURCE OF DATA

Primary Source	Number	Percentage
Extract from Production Files	98	36
Keyed in from Reports	92	34
Generated by User and Keyed In	45	17
Process Control	10	4
Extract from other end-user systems	9	3
From purchased database	6	2
Other (time clock, log punch, etc.)	11	4
TOTAL	271	100

Table 14.6 which shows the six categories of end users on each dimension as users and developers (to whom outside consultants are added), illustrated patterns that are not at all surprising. Although the figures cannot be relied upon too precisely, it does appear both quantitatively (and qualitatively from user comments to us) that the bulk of the systems (approximately 48%) being used by end users are being developed for them by local "functional support" personnel. Behaviorally, it makes extreme sense that users would tend to rely on people within their own function who speak their own language and with whom communication of their system needs is relatively straightforward. Certainly, this was stressed to us by users at all levels. The overwhelming primary use of these systems by nonprogrammers (55%) is also not surprising. A significant number of departmental and multidepartmental databases (discussed above) exist today which can be accessed on a menu basis by accounting, marketing, financial, and other staff personnel.

Looking at the data in the cells of the matrix (Table 14.6) showing "who develops systems for whose use," an expected pattern emerges. In the lower right quadrant of the matrix, we see a few systems developed by functional support personnel and IS professionals for their own use, but the bulk of the systems developed by them are for nonprogramming users. Almost all the systems developed by end-user programmers are for their own use. (From further analysis of the available data, we learned that 75% of the applications developed by this developer class are complex analytic programs. The remainder are divided almost equally between simple inquiry systems and report-generating programs.) Command level "amateur" programmers, as expected, develop application programs only for themselves. Almost all of these are sets of commands to access the database through a QBE entry, an ADRS routine, or other report generation or simple inquiry routine.

One of the greatest advantages of creating and controlling a program for oneself is to be able to run it whenever it is useful rather than being bound by formal scheduled "run" procedures. Table 14.7 illustrates that end users take advantage of this. Fully two-thirds of the applications are run only "as needed." Still, a significant portion of the applications are used on a regular weekly or monthly basis. As might be expected, these "regular" systems have a heavy population from the "operational" or "report generation" systems classified in Table 14.3.

Only 15% of all the systems, as seen in Table 14.8 utilize graphics. The most interesting finding, however, with regard to graphics is shown by the detail of this exhibit. Graphics systems use by the two least professional sections of the user population averages only 10%. On the other hand, systems developed for use by the four more professional segments show almost three times the frequency of graphics use. Since these systems, in almost all cases, are developed by each of these user classes for their *own* use, the perceived value of graphics by these user-developers is clear.

TABLE 14.6
DEVELOPERS AND USERS OF THE APPLICATIONS

	Application Users						
Application Developers	Nonprogramming End Users	Command End Users	End-user Programmers	Functional Support	Support Personnel	DP Programmers	Total (%)
Nonprogramming End Users	...	...	...	...	...	...	0 (0%)
Command Level End Users	...	34	...	...	...	...	34 (13%)
End-User Programmers	2	2	56	...	...	...	60 (22%)
Functional Support Personnel	112	6	1	12	...	...	131 (48%)
End-User Computer Support Personnel	6	...	...	1	2	...	9 (3%)
DP Programmer	21	3	...	...	...	3	27 (10%)
Consultants	9	1	...	...	...	...	10 (4%)
Totals (Percentages)	150 (55%)	46 (17%)	57 (21%)	13 (5%)	2 (1%)	3 (1%)	271 (100%)

259

TABLE 14.7
FREQUENCY OF USE

Frequency	Number	Percentage
Daily	16	6
Weekly	34	12
Monthly	27	10
As Needed	178	66
One-shot	16	6
TOTAL	271	100

Management of End-User Computing

A fourth level of facts we sought was data on the organizational structure and processes used to manage end-user computing. Two different structures were apparent. These can be termed "traditional time-sharing management" and "centralized end-user computing support."

Five of the seven organizations, including the three largest, were still primarily treating the surge in end-user computing as just an extension of in-house "time-sharing." Management practices put in place a decade earlier to support and control a then limited amount of "time-sharing" were still in effect. As a result, users were essentially given a hardware resource, one or few available software languages, and (sometimes) basic education classes on the most prominent software languages. In general, the information systems personnel managing these resources saw their major task as keeping the systems running and staying ahead, where possible, of the users and their demands for more capacity. A secondary task in several companies was the attempt to bring more expensive external time-sharing onto the in-house facility. The three largest companies all had multiple time-sharing hardware in diverse geographic sites with little coordination evident to us or the users in their software offerings or data extraction procedures. In all cases, users felt there was "no one in charge" and felt significantly frustrated at their inability to locate data they knew was stored somewhere in the corporation's files or to get extracts of that data once located.

The two other organizations did provide support to end users desiring it, but in both cases, this came only from a centralized group at corporate headquarters. In one case, this was called an "Information Center"; in the other, it was designated a "Decision Support Group." Both support groups were charged to find and bring up good software tools and to educate users in the use of these tools. In one of these companies, an "end-user language programming group" had been set up in the traditional Information Systems organization to assist users wishing to contract out programming in end-user languages.

In general, this latter, support-oriented approach to end-user computing produced a more satisfied user population. Still, the centralized nature of

TABLE 14.8
GRAPHICS – USER-BY-USER CATEGORY

	User Class						
Graphics	Nonprogram-ming End Users	Command End Users	End-User Programmers	Functional Support	Support Personnel	DP Programmers	Total
Yes	17 (11%)	4 (9%)	16 (28%)	4 (31%)	0 (0)	1 (33%)	42 (15%)
No	133	42	41	9	2	2	229
TOTAL	150	46	57	13	2	3	

261

the organization in both cases was troublesome to many end users. In both of these companies, we found users relying more heavily on the informal "functional support" personnel within their functions than on the central end-user group. In both companies, some users had rebelled against one or more of the corporation's "standard" software languages being supported by the centralized end-user computing group. They had chosen instead to use similar, but different, software which their functional support people felt to be more appropriate. As user populations grow in size, solely centralized approaches of any form appear inadequate.

What We Did Not See

Perhaps more significant than the structures and processes we saw with regard to the end-user computing were those that we did *not* see. Among the most important missing processes were:

A Strategy for End-User Computing.   Though all of these companies have well-documented, strategic, long-range plans for the "COBOL shop," there was, with one outstanding exception, little evidence of any strategic thinking with regard to end-user computing and the resource mix, tools, processes and structures which will be necessary for it over the next several years.

Development of End-User Computing Priorities.   Most of the companies were very proactive with regard to developing priorities for paperwork-processing applications (through the use of BSP or similar planning devices), but end-user computing was essentially in a "reactive" mode. No attempt had been made in any company to help users zero in on those end-user systems which might most significantly affect the profitability or productivity of their organizations in the future.

Policy Recommendations for Top Management.   There was an awareness in each organization that the information systems policies developed for the paperwork-processing eras of Information Systems would most probably not be appropriate in the end-user era. However, only in one case had significant thought been given to recommending a new policy set for top management concurrence.

Control Methods.   It was recognized in each company that the Information Systems department could *not* control the use of the end-user computing resource. Most probably because of this attitude, control policies for end-user computing were largely ignored. Those that existed were oriented around the decades-old, cost-benefit oriented procedures which had been developed to manage and control an entirely different type of computer usage.

In short, the Information Systems management attitude toward end-user computing in most of the companies was on the order of "this is the business of the users. We will give them the hardware, some software tools and perhaps some centralized support and let them do their thing. We really do not have the time to develop new procedures and policies. Even if we did, it's not clear that we are the appropriate people to do so."

Recommendations

It is impossible to talk to 250 people, both users and managers in the end-user area, without coming away with some strong personal conclusions concerning the management of end-user computing. Many of these are backed up by the data discussed in the previous section. Some, however, are based on a qualitative feel which is compounded through many hours of discussion. Our fourteen conclusions group into three major areas: end-user strategy, support of end users by the Information Systems organization, and control of end-user computing.

Strategy

With regard to the end-user computing arena, we reached six conclusions concerning strategy:

1. There Should Be an End-User Strategy. Little attention has been paid to the development of a strategy for end-user computing either in the organizations we studied or in the perhaps two dozen organizations with which we have discussed these findings since the study. Most of these same organizations have extensive information systems strategic plans dealing with conventional paperwork-oriented data processing. Yet, when it comes to end-user computing, they have, at best, put an information center or a "DSS group" in place with a relatively small budget and a cursory plan. If one believes: (1) that end-user computing will reach 50–75 percent of the MIPS in almost every corporation in the next several years; (2) that end-user oriented "information databases" have increasingly become an integral part of the working environment of major corporate staffs; and (3) that rapid change in the tools and techniques available in this area require guidance—then, the lack of a strategy and a clear long-range plan in this area is a serious mistake for the IS function.

2. The Marketplace for End-User Computing Can Be Defined. As noted earlier, the usual statement one hears from an information systems manager when it is suggested that there should be a strategy in the end-user computing area is "I can't develop a strategy in such a nebulous area. Conventional paperwork processing is centered in a few areas and a few systems and can be well-defined. To the contrary, end-user computing is 'everywhere'." Our data would suggest however, that by far, the bulk of the end-user computing is generated by a few major staff groups (marketing, finance, quality assurance, personnel, etc.) in each organization. In defining the marketplace, it is clear that significant help can be gained by contacting a small and well-defined set of functional support personnel in each staff group.

3. There Is a Need To Proactively Help End Users Develop Application Priorities.   To date, end user applications have been developed as the need has been perceived by each end user. On the contrary, for paperwork processing systems, IS has helped users through the utilization of planning processes, such as BSP, to zero in on those applications which are of high priority. Experience to date suggests that application planning processes, such as the Critical Success Factors method can be utilized in the same manner as BSP in the end-user environment to direct attention to "high payoff" end-user applications.[12,13] Much more effective use can be made of the financial and human resources currently expended on end-user computing.

4. Emphasis Should Be Placed on a Strategy Aimed at Developing and Managing the "Third Environment."   Two thirds of the applications we saw involved large departmental or multidepartmental information databases. This multiuser, shared database invironment is a vast, growing, and clearly significant part of the data processing scene. By far, the majority of the purchasing, personnel, financial, and market research staff systems we saw are of this type. Increasingly too, corporations are developing executive databases which involve multidepartmental bases.[14]

As Table 14.9 shows, IS in the past has supported two computing "environments," a *Cobol environment* and a timesharing environment. These have supplied vastly different facilities. In the Cobol environment, IS has taken total charge. It has provided a well-managed process in which it develops and programs the systems, operates them, and ensures that they are documented, well-controlled, and secure. The traditional timesharing environment, on the contrary, is only marginally served by IS. IS provides hardware in one or more languages. The user does the rest.

A "third" or *shared* environment is now necessary to effectively manage the growing number of departmental and multidepartmental end-user systems. As Table 14.9 notes, this environment demands that IS perform its "housekeeping" functions, such as data management, privacy, security, maintaining uptime, and so forth, while the users take responsibility for developing and operating their programs. Two of the companies in our study have recently placed major attention on this shared environment, having discovered that the majority of their key end-user systems demand this environment.

5. There Is a Need for New Corporate Policies.   It is clear that policies toward information systems which worked in the days of paperwork-processing, must be revised in an end-user era. These policies must fit with the end user strategy. New justification policies are required for systems which enhance analysis but do not replace clerical personnel. New pricing policies are required in an era when distributing the "cost" of computer cycles is less

TABLE 14.9

I. Cobol Environment	III. Third "Shared" Environment	II. Time-Sharing Environment
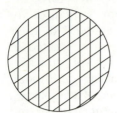		

<u>I/S Dominated</u>
I/S Programs
I/S Operates
 	
<u>I/S Provides:</u>
Data management
Privacy
Security
Restart, recovery
"Uptime" contact
etc.
	<u>Shared Responsibility</u>
	<u>I/S Provides:</u>
	Hardware
	Languages
	Data management
	Privacy
	Security
	Restart, recovery
	etc.
	
	<u>But Users:</u>
	Program
	May enter some data
	Operate
	Have responsibility
	  for systems
		<u>User Dominated</u>
		I/S Provides Only:
		Hardware
		Languages
		Users Programs
		Users enter data
		Users operate
		Users have responsibility
		  for systems

important than providing signals to users as to the relative desirability of using internal versus external timesharing, large machines versus personal computers, and "standard" software offerings versus user-unique systems. Several other new corporate IS policies in areas such as education and computer budgeting are also needed in the end-user area.

6. The Strategy Should Be Promulgated.   End users today in many corporations are confused about the actions being taken by the information systems organization with regard to end-user computing. They strongly (in many cases, vehemently) desire to know exactly what support and what future direction they can expect from information systems management. This knowledge is necessary so that they can make informed decisions on the increasing number of computing alternatives available to them.

Support

The second area with which information systems management must be concerned is that of *supporting* the end users. Although there are a multitude of areas which deserve attention in the support process, we believe through our data and our discussion with end users that four actions are most necessary.

7. The Development of a "Distributed" Organization Structure for Support.   At the present time, most formal end-user support structures are either located in a "time-sharing" office or an "information center." By their nature, these are primarily "centralized" organization structures located in offices, often near the hardware. Quite often the personnel are "product specialists" each knowing a different language or software package. Although the information center has proven very useful in a number of companies, in our view, it is only the first stage of end-user management. The second stage is "distributed" support. End users plead for two major things. The first of these is for a "focal point" person to whom they can go with *all* of their requests for assistance no matter which software language or product they are using. The second is that this "focal point" be as "local" as possible. In fact, for most major departments, the "functional support" personnel are serving exactly this function. Yet, they are unrecognized by the formal IS organization structure. If recognized as a resource and worked into the formal IS end user support structure, probably through the lightest of matrix operations, the functional support personnel could be of significant assistance to the IS organization in carrying out its strategic approach in end-user computing. They would also become of increased use to end users through improved, routine contacts with new systems, languages, and procedures being introduced by the information systems function. In short, a "distributed" end-user support organization could be developed to make more optimal use of both the technical expertise of the central IS people and the functional area knowledge of the functional support personnel. Allen's research,[15] which shows the importance of localness, is very relevant here.

8. The Provision of a Wide Spectrum of Products.   Today, there is no "all-singing, all-dancing" software product which an end user can use to effectively perform calculations, develop spread sheets, do text processing, and so forth, within the structure of a single software language or architecture. Each of these (despite recent efforts to combine them in some packages) is still essentially a specialized task. As a result, the end-user computing establishment should offer a spectrum of at least a half dozen different types of available software. Otherwise, as was quite clearly occurring in many of the organizations we studied, users will stretch the available end-user software products to do jobs in a manner far less efficient than could be done with the appropriate software.

9. The Development of a Substantial Education Program.   This is a critical area today. Different types of education are necessary for the end-user era. The first is the need to educate information systems personnel as to the capabilities and uses of end-user software. At the present time, according to an informal survey we made, less than 10% of the more than 500 information systems people responding feel that they have an adequate knowledge of even one end-user language. This leaves these information systems analysts in a very weak position when it comes to comprehending the end-user world. At the simplest level, they are unable to recommend to user managers which methodologies (Cobol-based or end-user language-based) they should be following for any particular system need.

Second, there is also a need for in-depth education in end-user languages and capabilities for the more "professional" end-user programmers (our Types 3 to 6). Third, there is a need for brief, "how-to," example-based education for the nonprogramming and command-level end users who desire to know only as much of an end-user language or user system as they need to perform a few tasks of importance to them. Fourth, there is a need to educate line management and key staff managers at all levels in the basics of end-user computing so that they can more effectively judge which systems they would like to have their people develop at what probable cost. As we will note below, information systems management *cannot* control all end-user computing. The most effective control is to have functional management knowlegeable in the basics of end-user computing. Finally, there is a need to educate top line management—or at the very least the steering committee members—as to the tools, techniques, and potential impacts of the end-user computing era, so that the need for effective policies (discussed in Point 6 above) can be understood.

This education load, it is true, is overwhelming. Certainly, the education of top management is the first priority. After that, each company must decide on the most effective allocation of a hopefully expanded, education budget.

10. The Development of Effective "Data Migration" Procedures. A major complaint of many of the end users we interviewed was their inability to either locate where data was stored in the corporation, or, once located, have the data extracted and forwarded to them. As noted in our findings above, many of the end users solved this problem by rekeying data which they obtained in the form of hard copy reports from production systems. Obviously, this is a waste of corporate resources. Not only is there the time and energy involved in rekeying, but there is also significant potential for data errors in manual processes. It is very evident that, despite a few available packages such as IBM's *XPRS*, existing approaches to extracting and migrating data for end users have not been given enough attention, either by computing vendors or, in most cases, by information systems management.

Control

In addition to the need for a *strategy* for end-user computing and significant steps to *support* end-user computing, there is also an evident need for well-defined *control* processes for each organization in the end-user area. Line and IS managements are concerned that end-user costs are rising too fast and are "out-of-control." They are concerned that little attention is being given to justification of these systems, that amateurish development processes are not well-managed, and that they are approaching Nolan's third stage in the end-user area.[16] We saw several aspects of this. A control policy adapted to the special circumstances of the end-user area is needed. The most important of the steps to be taken with regard to control are:

11. The Need to Flag "Critical" Applications.   As noted earlier, 29 of the applications which we studied were *operational* in nature. Some of these feed other operational paperwork processing systems in the Cobol-domain. The failure of any of these systems to run would, therefore, significantly impair the ability of each of the corporations to function efficiently on a day-to-day basis. In almost all cases, the necessary documentation and/or controls usually developed by IS professionals for operational systems were lacking in the end-user developed systems. In each organization, there should be a "control" process which identifies and highlights these systems for consideration of careful documentation, the incorporation of necessary edit and control features, and inspection by the corporation's auditors.

12. A Need to Exercise Control Primarily through Line Management—Not Information Systems Personnel.   It is impossible for information systems personnel to be totally in touch with all of end-user computing. Further, the valuation process for these systems is highly subjective. Only functional managers can perform this valuation. It is, therefore, necessary for line management to implement and monitor justification and control procedures for those systems being developed and used by their subordinates. (See Point 9 above.)

13. A Need for IS Expert Involvement in the Control Process.   Line management, however, cannot do it all. For large systems, at least, we believe there is a necessary procedure to ensure that professional information systems personnel assist line management in deciding whether the systems should be developed in an end-user mode, *which software should be used*, whether the system is essentially a timesharing environment or "third environment" system, and so forth. There is a clear role for a professional information systems consulting group to aid line management in this process.

14.   The Provision of IS "Environmental Control" Through Incentives.   One area in which the information systems organization can exert some "control" is in the development of the "environment" for end-user computing. Standards for end-user hardware and software should be developed and incentives (in terms of price and support processes should be offered) to motivate end users to adopt the organization standard relational database, word processing software, and so forth. The advantages of an IS-managed environment are in allowing IS professionals to better understand the software that is developed, to support users in questions they may have concerning the use of a limited set of software, and to keep critical systems running when the user or developer leaves the company. In one of the companies studied, several such incentives were being offered by IS. For example, standard user software packages were being made available to end users at no cost. A predominantly standard environment was being created.

Conclusion

Developing the appropriate strategy, support processes, and control processes for end-user computing is a staggeringly large job. The trends toward end-user computing, however, are irreversible. There is little doubt in our minds that end-user computing will be the dominant segment of information systems in most large companies by the end of this decade. It requires significant managerial attention.

References

1. Sondheimer, N. K., and Relles, N. Human Factors and User Assistance in Interactive Computing Systems: An Introduction. *IEEE Transactions on Systems, Man, and Cybernetics SMC-12*, 2. (March-April 1982) 102–107.

2. Yavelberg, I.S. Human Performance Engineering Considerations for Very Large Computer-Based Systems: The End User. *The Bell System Technical J. 61*, 5. (May/June 1982) 765–797.

3. Canning, R.G. "Programming" By End Users. *EDP Analyzer* 19, 5 (May 1981).

4. McLean, E.R. End Users as Application Developers. *Proc. Guide/Share Application Development Symposium* (October 1974).

5. Rockart, J.F., and Flannery, L.S. The Management of End User Computing. *Proc. Second Conference on Information Systems*, Boston, Massachusetts (December 1981), 351–364.

6. Canning, R.G. Supporting End User Programming. *EDP Analyzer* 19, 6 (June 1981).

7. Martin, J. *Application Development Without Programmers*. Prentice Hall, Inc., Englewood Cliffs, New Jersey, 1982, 102–106.

8. Rosenberger, R.B. The Productivity Impact of an Information Center on Application Development. *Guide 53 Proceedings*, Dallas, Texas, (November 1981).

9. Benjamin, R.I. Information Technology in the 1990's: A Long Range Planning Scenario. *MIS Quarterly 6*, 2 (June 1981), 11–31.

10. Sisson, R.L. Solution Systems and MIS. *Proc. Twelfth Annual SMIS Conference*, Philadelphia, Pennsylvania, September 1980.

11. Codasyl End-User Facilities Committee Status Report, North Holland Publishing Company, *Information and Management* Two (1979) 137–163.

12. David, G.B. Strategies for Information Requirements Determination. *IBM Syst. J.* 21, 1 (1982), 4–30.

13. Rockart, J.F., Chief Executives Define Their Own Data Needs. *Harvard Business Review* (March/April 1979), 81–93.

14. Rockart, J.F., and Treacy, M.E. The CEO Goes Online. *Harvard Business Review* (January/February 1982), 82–88.

15. Allen, T.J. *Managing The Flow of Technology*. MIT Press, Cambridge, Massachusetts, 1977.

16. Nolan, R., and Gibson, C.F. Managing the Four Stages of EDP Growth. *Harvard Business Review* (January/February 1974), 76–88.

QUESTIONS

1. Evaluate Rockart and Flannery's categorization of end users.
2. Based on the findings of this study, describe the applications associated with EUC in terms of focus, scope, primary source of data, and frequency of use.
3. Compare and contrast the following two EUC management structures: "traditional time-sharing management" vs. "centralized end-user computing support."
4. What issues surround the effective development of (a) appropriate strategy, (b) support processes, and (c) control processes for end-user computing?

15

Strategies for End-User Computing: An Integrative Framework

■

Maryam Alavi
R. Ryan Nelson
Ira R. Weiss

Introduction

As organizational computing enters its fourth decade, a number of structural changes appear to be taking place, leaving management information systems (MIS) strategy formulation in a state of transition. Once the sole domain of large, highly structured MIS groups, computers now seem to be permeating the entire organization via a process of decentralization. As a result of this decentralization, strategy formulation must go beyond the planning for mainframe acquisition to include end-user-based technologies, such as microcomputers, telecommunications, and office automation. In addition, by diffusing these technologies the organization should not only expect significant benefits in terms of competitive edge and return on investments, but must also realize it is creating cultural and socio-technical changes in its work force. If a shift is occurring which imposes significantly greater expectations on end users, then the organization must develop a strategy to ensure that these expectations are realized. This strategy must include a management framework for policy setting and planning, support, and control. The purpose of this paper is to (a) develop a set of end-user computing (EUC) strategies and (b) design an integrative framework for the adoption of those strategies within an organization.

Reprinted by special permission of the Journal of MIS, *Volume 4, Number 3, Winter 1987–88, pp. 28–49.*

An EUC strategy refers to the organizational posture vis-à-vis end-user computing. It consists of processes and approaches adopted by an organization for identification, assessment, and assimilation of end-user technologies in that organization. An end-user computing strategy directly affects the rate of diffusion of EUC technologies and the outcomes of EUC activities. For example, a strategy that seeks to firmly control EUC activities results in slow diffusion and limited application of end-user computing. On the other hand, a strategy that encourages organizational adoption of EUC technologies may lead to rapid growth and widespread EUC applications. Hence, EUC strategies have direct and important implications on the scope and resource requirements of EUC activities in organizations. In fact, development of an effective end-user computing strategy may be the most important short-term decision the organization can make if it hopes to benefit from its investments in end-user-based technologies.

The need for an explicit organizational strategy for the management of EUC is well established in the literature.[1-6] Both practitioners and academicians consider an EUC strategy to be an important and necessary prerequisite for successful and effective EUC. While no single "best" strategy can be identified, the literature identifies five major strategies:

1. laissez-faire
2. monopolist
3. acceleration
4. marketing, and
5. operations-based

Within this paper, each of these strategies will be discussed via:

(a) an overall description,
(b) a profile along three dimensions of EUC management: policy setting and planning, support, and control, based on some field observations, and
(c) a prescribed timing for the adoption of a particular strategy.

A DESCRIPTION OF EUC STRATEGIES

Laissez-Faire Strategy

A laissez-faires strategy[7] lacks organizational procedures for either promoting or containing EUC activities. It is a "do-nothing" approach and a "wait-and-see" attitude toward EUC. No or little explicit effort is made at encouraging the development of EUC. On the other hand, no organizational controls to limit EUC activities occur either. EUC activities are undertaken within existing organizational constraints or opportunities such as availability of monetary resources and user computing literacy and skills. This strategy allows a "free-market" access to computation, and end users, as long as they have their own budgets, can acquire whatever tools they please: time-sharing, microcomputers, and even minicomputers.[7] No central organizational policies and procedures for EUC exist, and a "hands-off" posture regarding EUC activities prevails. In other words, the laissez-faire approach is a "take-what-you-want" approach for which no central direction, guidelines, or control mechanisms are established. A laissez-faire strategy provides some degree of experimentation with EUC technologies and innovation, but the EUC growth is unanticipated and unplanned. This strategy tends to be an unstable strategy in that it may lead to uncontrolled growth and proliferation of incompatible EUC technologies and applications. As such, it eventually needs to be replaced with a more proactive EUC strategy.

Monopolist Strategy

A monopolist strategy[7,8] attempts to maintain firm control over all EUC activities. Specific control mechanisms (e.g., economic justifications and formal review and approvals) are enforced to slow the growth rate of EUC and confine it to prespecified boundaries. This strategy is based on the belief that a central organizational entity (typically the MIS/DP—management information systems/data processing—department) should control all information processing activities in order to ensure efficient use of information processing resources.[7] Hence, EUC activities are carried out within a limited range or options delineated by the control procedures.

A monopolist strategy controls EUC activities in an effort to lead to efficient and cost-justified applications of EUC technologies. On the other hand, it is a low-growth strategy and may result in the loss of opportunities for productivity enhancement and organizational innovation.

This strategy may be unstable if adopted too early in the evolution of EUC and seems to be breaking down in most of the companies that have adopted it in an effort to curtail EUC activities altogether. A number of reasons may be given, including the following:

1. An increasingly computer-literate end-user population is demanding the capabilities and resources to directly develop some of its own applications.
2. With the cost of microcomputer hardware and software declining constantly, many end users are acquiring these tools out of local budgets and as "office equipment" in defiance of the corporate strategy.

Acceleration Strategy

An acceleration strategy, also referred to as an expansionist[9] or implementation[10] approach, is almost the exact opposite of a monopolist strategy and has the objective of increased EUC activities and user satisfaction. This strategy attempts to build an enthusiasm toward the adoption of EUC tools through end-user education, support, and consulting, with no or little regard to the direction and the form that these activities may assume. This is typically accomplished through establishing central organizational structures (e.g., Information Centers) for the provision of support and training. A benefit of a central support group such as an Information Center is that it creates a center for EUC expertise in the corporation. Given the variety of hardware and software tools that exists today, much can be gained by having a center of expertise to continually evaluate the available tools and guide users to obtain the appropriate technology for their activities.[7] On the other hand, Information Centers react to the expressed user needs. As such, without backing and input from top management they often lack the overall perspective needed to undertake a proactive approach to EUC management and identification of high payoff EUC applications.

An acceleration strategy results in the rapid growth of EUC and encourages innovation and experimentation, which in turn may lead to user satisfaction and enhanced productivity. A successful acceleration strategy, however, leads to increased demand and high organizational investment in EUC technology and support. In fact, in a successful acceleration strategy, it may become increasingly difficult to adequately respond to the needs of the growing end-user population and meet the demands for support and training in a timely fashion.

Marketing Strategy

A marketing strategy is one of *directed* growth. End users are viewed as consumers whose demand for EUC tools and services may be influenced through effective product design, advertising, and distribution.[10] With use of this approach, EUC is developed at a high rate to conform to predetermined forms and characteristics. This is usually accomplished through provision of value-added products and services to end users. The value-added products and services differentiate themselves from the competition. For example, adoption and utilization of certain end-user tools may be accompanied by free training and product support. The EUC support structure in a marketing strategy involves centralized, as well as decentralized (departmental), support groups. The central group maintains a global perspective of the EUC activities in the organization and provides specialized services, training, and products to the "local" department groups, which in turn support the users. For example, software and procedures for providing end-user access to corporate databases may be developed by the central group and then "marketed" to end users through the department support groups. Furthermore, the central group can provide guidelines and direction to the end users as to what is feasible and desirable, as well as ensure that an appropriate framework for EUC policy and control is established. The localized support groups, on the other hand, are distributed throughout the organization to effectively meet the individual needs of users via a synthesis of technical knowledge with functional and application knowledge. The result should be a comprehensive and centrally coordinated distribution network. End-user education and training has the dual role of both developing skills and serving as a mechanism for influencing choice.[10] A potential disadvantage of this strategy is that it can easily revert to the acceleration strategy if the central drive for guiding EUC activities and manipulation of demand is weak and disorganized.

Operations-based Strategy

An operations-based strategy[10] focuses on the on-going management of equipment, software, personnel, and other EUC resources in an effort to maximize the efficient use of these resources. This is accomplished by utilizing control procedures (e.g., procedures developed for the identification and reduction of duplications in EUC applications), enforcing technological standards, and using formal EUC planning activities. Furthermore, EUC resources are integrated in an effort to enhance their efficient use. For example, microcomputers may be connected together through local area networks to promote data and software sharing. The support structure here is quite similar to that of a marketing strategy in that a centralized group is responsible for planning and developing standards and controls while the decentralized department staff provides local support to end users and implements the plans and controls. Under this approach, EUC applications are selected and prioritized based on traditional cost/benefit analysis.

As depicted in Table 15.1, these five strategies differ in terms of the objectives, emphasis, form and level of support, and formal controls. Thus, implementation of different strategies results in varying degrees of EUC growth and different end-user computing environments.

Furthermore, each of these strategies provides particular strengths at different times in the evolution of end-user computing. Hence, two important considerations with respect to EUC strategies are:

1. *how* to effectively implement a particular EUC strategy, and
2. *when* to adopt a particular strategy.

The first issue involves the need to identify specific attributes and processes associated with EUC strategies, while the second issue concerns the timing of a specific strategy with respect to the stages of evolution of EUC activities in organizations. These two important issues are addressed in the next two sections.

PROFILING THE EUC STRATEGIES

As Table 15.1 indicates, each strategy, to be successful, needs a different type of organizational structure and a different emphasis on organizational processes. In essence, each strategy must be supported by a management

TABLE 15.1
CHARACTERISTICS OF DIFFERENT END-USER COMPUTING (EUC) STRATEGIES

Characteristics	Strategies				
	Laissez-faire	Monopolist	Acceleration	Marketing	Operations
Objective	"Do nothing"	Contain and restrict EUC activities	Encourage and expand EUC activities	Expand EUC activities in certain form and directions	Obtain integration and efficiency in EUC activities
Emphasis	"Hands-off" approach to EUC	Implementation of explicit controls Formal approval procedures	Provide support and broad-based education Highly responsive to end-user needs	Provision of value added products and services Shaping the EUC demand	Standards Formal cost/benefit analysis
Organizational structure	No formal structure	Management information systems/data processing department active in EUC containment and control	Centralized general support facility (e.g. IC)	Centralized facility for planning and coordinating Departmental support	Centralized planning, prioritization, and monitoring Departmental support and enforcing standards and controls
Level of control	Very low	Very high	Relatively low	Relatively high	High

Note: IC = information center.

276

framework designed to ensure it accomplishes its objectives. Though management may be perceived as encompassing many different attributes, the three most critical attributes relating to EUC are the following:

Policy Setting and Planning. Policy setting identifies appropriate EUC practices and clarifies the acceptable form of outcomes concerning EUC activities,[4] whereas planning efforts are aimed at identifying goals/objectives and establishing the framework for coordination and allocation of resources to EUC activities.

Support. EUC support refers to activities such as provision of tools and training opportunities that enhance the development and growth of EUC in organizations.

Control. Control processes ensure that planned activities are performed effectively/efficiently and in compliance with policies and plans.

In order to identify the scope and type of activities involved in EUC policy setting and planning, support, and control, the authors conducted some preliminary field work. Five organizations were selected for in-depth interviews from the Information Systems Research Center (ISRC) at the University of Houston. All the organizations are listed on the New York Stock Exchange and may be categorized as follows:

(a) a utility company,
(b) a service organization,
(c) a bank, and
(d) two energy companies.

These five companies were selected for the study because they seemed to be highly successful in managing their EUC activities. Following interviews with top management, information center (IC) management, and end users from each of the five firms, the authors developed a list of activities within the three dimensions, policy setting and planning, support, and control. The following four paragraphs summarize the information ascertained.

During the interviewing process, it was determined that policy setting and planning attributes were viewed as being separate activities. While most of the issues involved in policy setting tend to be long term in nature, most of the managers interviewed had not been "formally" involved in EUC long enough to have developed long-term perspectives. This mismatch created a diverse set of critical issues addressed in this area. One of the energy companies took a very conservative posture toward EUC. This company identified five activities pertaining to policy setting which they viewed as being important to the long-term viability of EUC: acquisition of hardware and software, standards for EUC, management of data, setting the appropriate scope of EUC activities, and definition of DP versus departmental roles and responsibilities. Of the remaining four firms, three concurred that acquisition activities as well as standards relating to data and EUC were needed and should be in place. In addition, it was evident that the majority of the firms had given little thought as to how much could be accomplished through EUC within their organizations. As a result, role ambiguities existed between DP and non-DP personnel in these companies. Other than these five activities, the interviews did not reveal any additional issues categorized as policy setting.

Planning, for all five organizations, appeared to be the means under which they operationalized EUC activities. Clearly, all five organizations felt that planning for capacity issues relating to equipment and personnel resources was critical. For example, one overriding concern was the inability of DP to effectively manage and schedule mainframe utilization if the ability to tap into these resources by distributed micros or dependent end users was out of the control of the DP manager. Therefore, planning for the integration of EUC and DP was perceived as being as critical as resource planning itself. EUC within all the organizations appeared to be localized and departmental in nature and therefore little, if any, real coordination between departments had been planned for. Although priority setting was seen as an issue that needed to be addressed, because of the number of developing EUC applications, it too had received little attention within the planning agenda. In short, within the planning dimension the five companies demonstrated similar behavior in terms of identifying the critical planning variables and the importance of each.

Individually each organization voiced the opinion that support in the form of training/education was critical to the success of EUC within their respective organizations; yet only the utility company had an effective training program in place. Also worth mentioning was that one of the energy companies provided virtually no training to speak of. The same company provided no support for data access while recognizing that EUC is not a valuable activity in the long run without direct access to data. The remaining four companies were well versed on this point and unanimously supported this activity. Consistent with the above, those companies that were supportive of training and access to data also provided on-site consulting to enhance the effectiveness of EUC.

The message communicated by the companies in general is that control of EUC is important but is a function of the maturity of the activity within the organization. Chargebacks were mentioned the most often as effective means of accountability; yet only the utility company employed them uniformly. Those interviewed expressed concern about untrained DP professionals developing applications for departmental usage and about the ramifications of unchecked errors. Consistent with these views, each organization had put into place some form of development and operational controls. Though risk was obviously the reason for developmental controls, it was interesting that four of the organizations did not employ appropriate audit techniques. This too appeared to be tied to the maturity issue.

The insights gained within the interviewing process allowed the authors to identify the activities to be managed within the policy setting and planning, support, and control dimensions. Table 15.2 provides a summary of the EUC-

TABLE 15.2
END-USER COMPUTING (EUC) RELATED ACTIVITIES

Policy setting

1. Acquisition framework—addresses the procedures and requirements for formal approvals of, as well as economic justifications of, EUC tools and resources.
2. EUC standards—focuses on (a) hardware, software, and communications, as well as (b) EUC applications development and operations.
3. Data management—refers to procedures that make data accessible, reliable, consistent, and secure.[10]
4. Assignment of roles and responsibilities—reduces role ambiguities of management information systems/data processing (MIS/DP) staff and end users vis-à-vis EUC.
5. Scope of EUC activities—develops clear distinctions between the applications that can be developed by end users and those that should be developed by the MIS/DP group.

Planning

1. Setting priorities—focuses on those end-user applications which affect the productivity and profitability of the organization.[8,11]
2. Planning for equipment, capacity, and manpower—ensures that sufficient resources for EUC activities exist.
3. Coordination of EUC among departments—focuses on the management of EUC activities that cross functional lines.
4. Integration of DP/EUC—planning for and facilitation of the technological interdependence between DP and EUC.

Support

1. Training and education—develops an on-going, comprehensive training program that identifies and then addresses the needs of end users, management, and the MIS/DP professional.
2. Data access—enhances the end-user community's ability to obtain data needed for EUC applications.
3. Consulting—provides consultation services in the areas of EUC tool selection, cost justification of EUC applications, problem solving, modeling, and application development.

Control

1. Financial controls and chargeback systems—provides a mechanism (e.g. budgeting system) to appropriately allocate and then "fine tune" financial resources; may involve allocation (chargeback) of EUC costs to end-user groups.
2. Development and operational controls—develops procedures and methodologies to be followed in (a) the design and implementation of end-user systems, (b) the documentation of end-user developed systems, and (c) the on-going operation (i.e., input, processing, and output) of end-user systems.
3. Audits and reviews—provides a system of checks and balances to ensure that appropriate EUC controls and standards are both (a) developed and implemented and (b) adhered to by end users.

related activities identified within the five firms, categorized by dimension, as well as a brief description of each.

Having identified the specific management activities now allows for the profiling of the five EUC strategies (laissez-faire, monopolist, acceleration, marketing, and operations-based) along with the three management dimensions (policy setting and planning, support, and control). The profiles, as described herein, afford a potential value to the reader in that they can provide specific guidelines for implementation of the strategies.

Laissez-Faire Strategy Profile

Consistent with the "do-nothing" posture that characterizes the laissez-faire strategy, no formal and explicit EUC management processes exist. Likewise, no organizational policies regarding acquisition of EUC tools, standards, and data management are established. Acquisition procedures and justification are at best locally conducted and tend to be lax. Neither the users nor the MIS/DP staff have any well-defined organizational responsibilities concerning EUC activities. The scope of end-user-developed systems is not predetermined and tends to evolve in an ad hoc fashion. In short, EUC activities are unplanned and uncontrolled. Due to the lack of policies and planning, end-user activities among the departments are uncoordinated and the data processing and EUC activities are carried out independently. No explicit EUC support structure exists. End users are self-trained and consulting is provided by the self-made "local" experts. Corporate databases are inaccessible to end users and a large percentage of end-user data is entered manually. No control framework has been established; therefore, no financial controls or development and operations standards are in place for end-user applications.

Monopolist Strategy Profile

The policy setting and planning, support, and control dimensions in a monopolist strategy are geared to restricting EUC activities. Acquisition policies involve explicit procedures, economic justifications, formal reviews, and approval from the MIS/DP department. The MIS/DP department is responsible for monitoring EUC activities and usually has the authority to veto acquisition requests. Stringent EUC standards are established and enforced in an effort to contain EUC growth. Given the restricted and narrowly defined scope of EUC, these activities are minimally planned and are coordinated through the established standards.

Some training and consultation may be organizationally provided. However, these activities are ad hoc, have low frequency and availability, and are usually carried out within narrowly defined and predetermined areas. In this strategy, end users' access to corporate databases is restricted. In some cases, however, limited data support is provided. This may take the form of closely monitored read-only access to copies of corporate databases. Although the MIS/DP department is closely involved in controlling the EUC activities, these activities are not integrated with the traditional MIS/DP operations. Instead, MIS/DP and EUC area basically treated as independent areas in terms of planning, resource allocation, and management.

Control is very high in the monopolist strategy. A number of control mechanisms may be put into place, such as chargeback systems, development and operational controls, and/or audit and review teams. For example, acquisition, installation, and training costs may be charged back to the user departments, and end-user application development methods and operational procedures may be enforced through regular and unscheduled reviews by audit or quality control teams.

Acceleration Strategy Profile

Policy, planning, and support activities in an acceleration strategy are designed to promote the organizational growth of end-user computing. Acquisition policies are non-restrictive and encourage EUC. For example, the review of EUC acquisition requests is a mechanism for enhancing quality (e.g., ensuring that the right tool for the end-user application is obtained) rather than a mechanism for constraining EUC activities. Furthermore, detailed and elaborate economic justifications are not required for EUC tools. The acceleration strategy is based on a philosophy of "the user knows best." End users are typically allowed free rein to obtain whatever end-user tool is desired. Given this philosophy and approach, standards for hardware/software and data management are minimal. The primary role of the MIS/DP staff is that of EUC support and consulting. End users, on the other hand, play an active role in the selection, definition, development, and operation of the EUC applications. Unlike the case in a monopolist strategy, in an acceleration strategy the scope of EUC activities is not organizationally and narrowly predetermined but instead is determined by the users. EUC activities are managed in a reactive mode, and minimal plans for capacity, equipment, and manpower requirements are made. However, attempts are made to meet these requirements. Similar to the situation in laissez faire and the monopolist strategies, in an acceleration strategy EUC activities are independent of the traditional MIS/DP activities in the organization. As such, EUC activities among the departments are not well coordinated because of the unanticipated scope and form of the EUC applications. Also, little coordination between the MIS/DP and EUC operation exists.

A high degree of support for end-user training and consulting is provided. Formal training courses, computer-based training, hot lines, and newsletters are some common mechanisms for delivery of this support to the end users. Since support is the central theme of the acceleration strategy, formal organizational units (e.g., an information center) are developed and charged with providing EUC support. In addition, an effort is made to make corporate data available to end users.

Formal controls are kept to a minimum in this strategy. EUC costs are treated as corporate overhead and are not charged back to the users. One approach to establishing an awareness of EUC costs among the users may be to keep EUC as an unallocated cost center, and yet through memos keep the users informed of what their EUC costs would have been if a chargeout system had been in place. This approach gives the users a feel for the general magnitude of their EUC costs. End-user application development and operations guidelines are not strictly enforced. Review teams if present assume more of a support versus a monitoring role.

Marketing Strategy Profile

A marketing strategy is based on more formalized policies and planning procedures in an effort to direct EUC growth in some predetermined direction. Standards for the acquisition of hardware and software as well as for data management are established. The end users are led toward these standards through value-added products and services, advertising, and effective distribution. The role and responsibility of the MIS/DP staff is to increase market share (and hence achieve the objective of diffusing EUC technology throughout the organization) through the delivery of effective and timely products and services.[10] The end users are responsible for the selection, application, and operation of their EUC applications. In order to promote directed growth and to maximize product and service availability, planning for capacity, manpower training, and services are carried out by a central EUC support group. This group also coordinates EUC activities among departments in order to effectively guide these activities toward the established goals. However, EUC and MIS/DP activities are not highly integrated and are essentially treated as two independent activities.

In order to understand end-user demand and at the same time effectively manipulate it, the end-user support staff is departmentalized or functionalized.[9] The departmental support units provide consulting and training and are in turn supported and directed by the central support staff. Training is aimed at developing skills as well as educating the consumer (end user) as to the benefits of the value-added products. Support and services are provided in order to guide EUC activities in certain directions. In the acceleration strategy, support is provided in a reactive mode in that the EUC support staff attempts to satisfy whatever demands users have. On the other hand, in a marketing strategy, EUC support attempts to manipulate user demand through education and effective product design. For example, for certain types of software, training and consultation may be provided free of charge. Or, users may be supported in accessing corporate databases only when certain procedures and methodologies in end-user application development are followed. Or, assistance in application development is provided only if certain development methodologies and standards are followed by the end users.

Since EUC growth is the objective of a marketing strategy, control mechanisms are not very restrictive, with EUC costs not fully charged back to the end users. Development and operational controls are enforced through value-added products and services. Review teams, if present, play more of a marketing role for the value-added products than a monitoring and control role.

Operations-Based Strategy Profile

An operations-based strategy views information as an organizational resource that should be planned for, controlled, and efficiently allocated among the users. Explicit EUC policies that govern the acquisition of tools and hardware/software and data standards are established and enforced. Acquisition procedures are formally reviewed and based on economic justifications and cost/benefit analysis. Standards are developed to enhance the integration and sharing of EUC resources and in an effort to increase efficiency. In this strategy, the MIS/DP staff is responsible for the support, as well as the implementation, of plans, standards, and control. Specific guidelines and criteria specifying the scope of end-user-developed systems are established. Central planning provides a mechanism for integrating and prioritizing the EUC applications. Applications making high contributions to the organization or those with favorable cost/benefit ratios are selected for implementation and funding. In order to obtain more efficiencies, EUC activities among different departments are closely coordinated. For example, a central library of end-user applications can be maintained to promote the sharing of applications among the departments. Furthermore, since this strategy has the objective of maximizing the efficient use of information technology and resources, the EUC and traditional MIS/DP activities are integrated through high-level standards and policies.

The support activities in an operations-based strategy are primarily concerned with the provision of services in order to maximize the efficiency of EUC applications. Examples include automated data access tools such as software for up- or downloading data and automated end-user software libraries. Efficiency is also emphasized in the delivery of end-user support services. For example, computer-based training courses tend to increase the efficiency of end-user training.

An operations-based strategy is a high-control strategy. Financial controls are implemented through chargeback systems and budgets where costs are fully charged back to the end users. By allocating the costs to the user departments, a chargeback system brings the cost-effectiveness of EUC applications into focus and enforces efficient EUC applications. EUC plans and priorities are implemented through budgets. Budgets are allocated to ensure that only the planned activities and high-payoff EUC projects are carried out. Application development and operations control (e.g., development methodologies and documentation standards) ensure the quality, efficiency, coordination, and integration of EUC activities. These controls are enforced and maintained through scheduled and ad hoc audits and reviews. The audit and

TABLE 15.3
SUMMARY OF PROFILES

Management dimensions	Activities	Laissez-faire		Monopolist	
		Presence/ absence of activities	Notes	Presence/ absence of activities	Notes
Policy setting	Acquisition framework	○		●	
	EUC standards	○		●	
	Data management standards	○		●	
	Assignment of roles and responsibilities	○		◑	MIS/DP responsible for EUC control
	Scope of EUC activities	○		●	
Planning	Setting priorities	○		○	
	Planning for equipment capacity, and manpower	○		○	
	Coordination of EUC among departments	○		◑	Limited coordination through policies and standards
	Integration of DP/EUC	○		○	

Notes: ● indicates that the activity is performed; ◑ indicates that the activity is partially performed or is performed on a limited basis; ○ indicates that the activity is *not* performed.
MIS = management information systems; DP = data processing; EUC = end-user computing.

Acceleration		Marketing		Operations	
Presence/ absence of activities	Notes	Presence/ absence of activities	Notes	Presence/ absence of activities	Notes
◐	Acquisition guidelines are non-restrictive.	●	Steps toward development of standards through value-added products and services	●	
○		◐		●	
○		◐		●	
◐	MIS/DP personnel have the role of support and consultation.	◐		●	
○	End users determine the scope of their activities	◐	Guidelines for defining the scope are established	●	
○		○		●	
○		●	Conducted by a central group	●	
○		◐	Some coordination through central planning	●	
○		◐	Some coordination through central planning	●	

TABLE 15.3 continued

Management dimensions	Activities	Laissez-faire		Monopolist	
		Presence/ absence of activities	Notes	Presence/ absence of activities	Notes
Support	Training and education	◑	Self-training or training obtained outside the organization	◑	Limited in scope and availability
	Data access	○		◑	Limited in scope and availability
	Consulting	◑	Provided by "local" end-user experts	◑	Limited in scope and availability
Control	Financial controls and chargeback systems	○		●	
	Development and operational controls	○		●	
	Audits and reviews	○		●	

Notes: ● indicates that the activity is performed; ◑ indicates that the activity is partially performed or is performed on a limited basis; ○ indicates that the activity is *not* performed.
MIS = management information systems; DP = data processing; EUC = end-user computing.

Acceleration		Marketing		Operations	
Presence/ absence of activities	Notes	Presence/ absence of activities	Notes	Presence/ absence of activities	Notes
●		●	Also aims at educating the users on the value-added products	●	Support activities focus on maximizing efficiency of EUC
◐	Some limited data access support may be provided	◐	Some mechanisms for data access on a limited basis	●	
●		●		●	
○		◐	Some costs (e.g., training) may be charged back	●	
○		○		●	
○		○		●	

review teams stay abreast of EUC activities in the organization and ensure that the policies, plans, and standards are adapted and appropriately followed.

A summary of the five EUC strategies and their corresponding management profiles is contained in Table 15.3. Given this set of organizational postures vis-a-vis EUC, the emphasis now shifts to the development of an appropriate framework useful in the adoption of EUC strategies over time. The next section introduces one such framework by overlaying EUC strategy formulation onto an S-shaped learning curve.

PRESCRIPTION FOR ADOPTION OF EUC STRATEGIES

The objective of this section is to prescribe a framework for the timing and adoption of EUC strategies. This framework will be based on the premise that EUC technology adoption follows a learning-curve phenomenon, similar to that proposed by McFarlan and McKenney.[12] Table 15.4 displays McFarlan and McKenney's phases of technological assimilation in relation to the EUC strategies. Synthesis of the assimilation model and the specific strategies is a product of comparison, in particular, a comparison of EUC strategy objectives and policy and planning, control, and support characteristics with the assimilation requirements as described by McFarlan and McKenney. The objective of this section is to present such a synthesis as a tool useful to organizations in the management of EUC; for, given a set of EUC strategies (e.g., as described in the last two sections), the next logical step is to determine the appropriate timing for implementation.

Pre-Strategy Phase

Typically, prior to the time any formal/active approach is taken by management on the subject of EUC, an informal/inactive or simply "unconscious" attitude can be observed within organizations. This state of unawareness seems to have been a fairly common phenomenon over the past several years, as organizations have realized that a significant proportion of their non-information systems personnel have been doing a majority of their own computing. Following this realization, the organization can do one of two things, either remain formally detached from EUC development and let EUC evolve naturally without organizational intervention, or take some kind of formal action—perhaps in terms of a formal, corporate-wide framework for the phased adoption of EUC strategies.

Phase 0

One addition to McFarlan and McKenney's assimilation model, congruous to what we believe to be an accurate representation of formal EUC strategy formulation, is an initial *conscious* state of either (a) "doing nothing," termed laissez-faire, or (b) imposing a monopolist strategy upon the user community.

TABLE 15.4
SYNTHESIS OF MCFARLAN AND MCKENNEY'S[12] PHASES OF TECHNOLOGICAL ASSIMILATION AND END-USER COMPUTING (EUC) STRATEGIES

Phase	Phase Description	Management and Organizational Approaches	Prescribed EUC Strategy
I	Technology identification and investment	Expansion-oriented management	Acceleration
II	Technology learning and adaption	Sales-oriented management	Marketing
III	Rationalization/ management control	Control-oriented management	Containment*
IV	Maturity/widespread technology transfer	Resource-oriented planning and control	Operations-based

*This strategy will be introduced within the discussion of phase III.

During the laissez-faire phase, a hands-off posture is assumed via both (a) a very low level of control and (b) no formal EUC structure. This phase of passive behavior can be viewed as being a null phase, or phase 0, due to the relative inactivity along the dimensions of policy and planning, support, and control.

In phase 0, the role "technological pioneer" is taken on by a small subset of the user community at large. These individuals are typically self-starters or innovators who may become "resident experts" or "gurus" in a particular EUC technology.[13] Knowledge about the utilization of EUC technologies and/or applications takes a slow and uncertain path through the organization as these resident experts train colleagues via one-on-one encounters.

Some organizations may choose to formally put EUC development "on hold" by imposing a monopolist strategy upon the user community at large. There are a number of reasons why an organization may choose to assume a monopolist strategy at such an early stage, such as:

(a) a "wait and see" attitude toward EUC technology development within the marketplace,
(b) technological immaturity within the organization itself (e.g., poorly trained personnel), or
(c) lack of resources for EUC activities.

With the above descriptions in mind, phase 0 tends to be an unstable state in that it may lead to either (a) an uncontrolled growth and proliferation of incompatible EUC technologies and applications, or (b) a highly controlled, dissatisfied user community. As such, it eventually needs to be replaced with a more proactive EUC strategy, such as that found in phase I.

Phase I

Phase I is the result of an organization's recognition that specific benefits can be accomplished through an EUC environment. Here, EUC activities are encouraged and expanded via centralized support and education facilities (e.g., information centers) which are highly responsive to the needs of the end-user community. In phase I, an expansion-oriented management seeks to initiate and/or accelerate EUC by maintaining a relatively low level of control.

The strategy taken within phase I (acceleration) is an attempt to build an enthusiasm toward the adoption of EUC technology through end-user education, support, and consulting. An acceleration strategy taken at this stage in a company's development may lead to enhanced user satisfaction and productivity by encouraging innovation and experimentation. It should be noted that success via the acceleration strategy often leads to increased *demand* and high organizational *investment* in EUC technology and support. In fact, it may become increasingly difficult to adequately respond to the growing end-user population and meet the demands for support and training in a timely fashion. Therefore, it is recommended that management be on the lookout for signs of excessive demand and/or investment and be prepared to shift the organization into a period of directed growth. At this point in an organization's EUC development, management should begin to look upon the end-user population as a growing customer base and proceed to a phase II strategy.

Phase II

Phase II is geared toward a marketing strategy, highlighted by a sales-oriented management posture. However, the emphasis should be on shaping the EUC demand rather than letting it grow totally unchecked. In other words, the strategy taken within phase II is one of *directed growth* in which end users are viewed as consumers whose demand for EUC tools and services may be influence through effective marketing techniques, such as product design, advertising, and effective distribution.

In order to achieve the objective within phase II (i.e., expansion of EUC activities in a certain form and direction), the support structure is altered to provide both (a) a central facility for planning and coordinating and (b) distributed facilities in the local departments for functional application support. The central group is responsible for broad-based planning, development, and support (e.g., interdepartmental applications and database administration), while the "local" departmental groups directly support individual application development.

Two caveats concerning phase II are (1) if guiding activities are weak and unsuccessful the organization can easily revert to the unchecked path of acceleration found in phase I, and (2) even in those cases where EUC growth patterns have developed as planned, organizations run the risk of computer-related resource exploitation. In either case, an impetus is provided to *add* control activities (phase III) to the management framework established to date (phase II).

Phase III

During phase III the organization enters a period of digestion and reevaluation of direction via what can be termed a containment strategy. A containment strategy is a transition strategy. It may be viewed as entering a phase of technology absorption. It allows the organization to momentarily pause and apply the appropriate checks and balances to ensure organizational return on investment. Under a containment strategy, an organization seeks to *add* control activities (e.g., of a monopolist strategy) to the management activities established within earlier stages. In other words, a level of saturation has been reached and the primary objective now becomes one of control. Both budgeting and data administration controls are introduced while management pushes toward a portfolio of efficient and cost-justified applications.

Specific control mechanisms (e.g., economic justifications and formal review/approval) are enforced by a centralized group to curtail EUC growth. During phase III, management should be aware that a potential by-product of the containment strategy is a loss of opportunities for organizational innovation. In fact, this strategy is similar to the laissez-faire, or monopolist, strategies found in phase 0, in that it may become unstable. In other words, long periods of extensive control by management can potentially cause developmental breakdowns to occur due to the very *raison d'etre* of EUC—a shift of computational control to the hands of the end user.

Following an effective synthesis of management and control activities via phases II and III, an organization should be in a position to assume more of an "optimization strategy" (phase IV). By simultaneously maximizing the utilization of end-user products while minimizing the exploitation of resources, an organization progresses into a mature phase of widespread, yet efficient, integration.

Phase IV

An operations strategy emerges in phase IV with more of a resource-oriented management style. The focus is the on-going management of EUC resources in an effort to maximize the efficient integration and utilization of these resources. To paraphrase McFarlan and McKenney,[12] the objective within phase IV should be one of "managed evolution" by transferring EUC technology to a wider spectrum of systems applications within the organization than previously. In phase IV, with organizational learning essentially complete and a technology base installed with appropriate controls in place, it is appropriate to look more seriously into the future and plot longer-term trends (e.g., the sharing of EUC resources).

For example, a major objective within this phase is the sharing of both data and software through such mechanisms as local area networks (LANS) and software libraries. A high level of control is maintained throughout phase IV via centralized planning, prioritization, and monitoring. In addition, policies and procedures are enforced within existing application systems while formal cost/benefit analyses are imposed upon new application developments.

The support structure of phase IV is quite similar to that of phase II, in that a centralized group is responsible for planning and enforcing controls and standards while a decentralized departmental staff provides local support to end users and implements the plans and controls. However, a higher level of integration is reached within phase IV, highlighted by a "mature" structure and well-developed management and control techniques.

By drawing from McFarlan and McKenney's assimilation model and its implications for the business world, one can make certain assumptions about the growth dynamics of organizational movement through the phases of EUC development:

1. Movement through the individual phases is a function of organizational learning. For example, the limited experimentation of phases 0 and I forms the basis for the expansion of phases I and II, and the accelerated use allows diffusion of the technology before controls are applied.

2. Phases should not be skipped because experience is necessary before the organization is ready for the next phase. In other words, the bypassing of a particular phase, or phases, could very well disrupt the "natural" learning and maturation process attributed to the S-shaped theory of the stage/phase development.

3. Although there are certain "natural" growth processes involved, the five phases of EUC growth can be planned, coordinated, and managed to move the organization through the phases effectively and efficiently. Management styles and control mechanisms shift to meet the needs of each phase. The phases thus represent a sequence for planned and managed change.

SUMMARY

As discussed, the EUC strategies differ in terms of their objectives, form and level of support, and mechanisms for formal control. Thus, implementation of different strategies at various points in time results in varying degrees of EUC growth and different EUC environments.

Within this paper, a two-step process was employed to represent (1) *how* to effectively implement a particular EUC strategy, and (2) *when* to adopt a particular EUC strategy. The first issue involved a descriptive profiling of each of the EUC strategies via the management attributes of policy setting and planning, support, and control. The second issue provided the impetus

FIGURE 15.1
PHASES FOR ADOPTION OF END-USER COMPUTING STRATEGIES

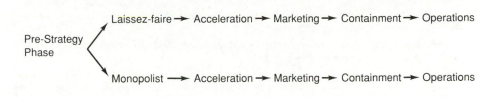

to develop a prescriptive timing with respect to the phases of EUC strategy evolution. The integrative framework that resulted from this two-step process was based on the premise that EUC technology adoption follows a learning curve phenomenon. Figure 15.1 illustrates the two possible paths an organization might traverse in its adoption of and maturity within EUC.

Basically, such a framework can be useful to organizations in evaluating actual versus desired phases of EUC development. Then, it becomes the responsibility of management to review and evaluate those factors that influence the choice of an EUC strategy in an organization and come up with (1) a strategic plan for EUC development within the organization, and (2) specific methods of operationalizing such a plan.

Indeed, as new products appear, as the competitive environment shifts, as corporate strategies change, and as the demand for response time to problems and/or opportunities shortens, the priorities a company assigns to its various EUC applications appropriately evolve as well. This volatility underscores the need in today's organizations for a viable framework useful in the integration of EUC strategy formulation.

REFERENCES

1. Alavi, Maryam, End-User Computing: The MIS Managers' Perspective. *Information and Management,* 8, 3 (March 1985), 171–178.
2. Alavi, Maryam, and Weiss, Ira R. Managing the Risks Associated with End-User Computing, *Journal of Management Information Systems,* 2, 3 (Winter 1985-86), 5–20.
3. Cheney, Paul H,; Mann, Robert I.; and Amoroso, Donald L. Organizational Factors Affecting the Success of End-User-Computing. *Journal of Management Information Systems,* 3, 1 (Summer 1986), 65–80.
4. Keen, Peter G. W. A Policy Statement for Managing Microcomputers. *Computer World,* In Depth, May 1983.
5. Nolan, Richard. Managing the Computing Resource: A Stage Hypothesis. *Communications of the ACM* (July 1973).
6. Nolan, Richard L. Managing the Crises in Data Processing. *Harvard Business Review* (March-April 1979).
7. Gerrity, Thomas P., and Rockart, John F. Managing End-User Computing in the Information Era. CISR working paper No. 120, Sloan School of Management, MIT, October 1984.

8. Leitheiser, Robert L., and Wetherbe, James C. The Successful Information Center: What Does It Take? *Proceedings of the Twenty-First Annual Computer Personnel Research Conference,* Minneapolis, MN, May 1985.

9. Munro, Malcolm C., and Huff, Sid L. Information Technology Assessment and Adoption: Understanding the Information Center Role. *Proceedings of the Twenty-First Annual Computer Personnel Research Conference,* ACM, May 2–3, 1985.

10. Henderson, John C., and Treacy, Michael E. Managing End-User Computing. *Sloan Management Review,* 27, 2 (Winter 1986), 3–14.

11. Quillard, Judith A,; Rockart, John F.; et al. A Study of the Corporate Uses of Personal Computers. CISR working paper No. 109, Sloan School of Management, MIT, December 1983.

12. McFarlan, F. Warren, and McKenney, James L. *Corporate Information Systems Management: The Issues Facing Senior Executives.* Homewood, IL: Richard D. Irwin, 1983.

13. Nelson, R. Ryan, and Cheney, Paul H. Educating the CBIS User: A Case Analysis. *Data Base,* 18, 2 (Winter 1986).

QUESTIONS

1. Discuss the need for an organizational strategy vis-à-vis end-user computing.
2. Identify and describe five major strategies for the management of EUC.
3. Describe the relationship between an organization's EUC strategy and managerial activities, such as direction, support and control?
4. Do you agree with the premise that EUC technology adoption follows a learning curve phenomenon? Why or why not?
5. Describe McFarlan & McKenney's four phases of technological assimilation. How might the assimilation model be useful in determining the appropriate timing for EUC strategy implementation?

16

Organizational Factors Affecting the Success of End-User Computing

■

Paul H. Cheney
Robert I. Mann
Donald L. Amoroso

INTRODUCTION

Although end-user computing (EUC) is still in its early stages, signs of rapid growth are evident. Companies studied by Rockart and Flannery[1] experienced annual EUC growth rates of 50 to 90%, while their traditional data processing systems were growing at a much smaller annual rate of 5 to 15%. Benjamin[2] has predicted that by 1990 EUC will absorb as much as 75% of the corporate computer resource. Edlman[3] estimated that at least ten cents out of every revenue dollar is spent on the management of information, a far cry from the traditional management information systems (MIS) rule of thumb which places the MIS budget at 1% of sales. Edelman goes on to state that at RCA traditional data processing accounts for 10% of the MIS budget, administrative systems for 20%, and the white-collar contingent for 70%.

The increasing proliferation of EUC is obvious from the above evidence. If the concomitant problems in the areas of security, integrity, documentation, and accountability are not addressed quickly, we may see management imposing drastic cutbacks on the organizational use of EUC. Confusion, inefficiency, and a perceived or real lack of productivity may force management into constraining what we believe to be a major force in the manage-

Reprinted by special permission of the Journal of MIS, *Volume 3, Number 1, Summer 1986, pp. 65–80.*

ment of the information resource through the end of this century. For these reasons the identification of variables that may affect the success of end-user computing facilities (EUCF) within an organization is extremely important.

Nolan and Wetherbe[4] presented a research model which viewed MIS as an open system which transforms data, requests for information, and organizational resources into information within the *context of an organization*. Similarly, Ives, Hamilton and Davis[5] classified existing MIS research and generated illustrative hypotheses using a research model which described the interactions between three classes of variables: *the environment*, *the process*, and *the information system*. These researchers, among others,[6–11] recognize the importance of organizational characteristics as a potential influence on MIS success. This paper attempts to identify organizational variables affecting the success or failure of EUC within an organization. Propositions relating the variables to EUC success are presented and supported by logical arguments and previous research findings.

The source of data for this paper was a survey of the academic and trade literature. Only recently have EUC issues appeared in the literature with any regularity. Most of these publications contained conceptualizations about end-user computing based on practical experience; a smaller number represented empirical studies. To the extent that conceptualizations are based on experience, they are a valid source of data in an environment in which empirical data are in short supply. We will attempt to segregate conceptual and empirical findings whenever possible.

The literature review yielded a list of organizational context variables as well as data and opinions concerning those variables. Few of the concepts and opinions have as yet been tested; the results of this investigation are presented as a series of propositions that represent the dominant positions on the issues examined. The propositions are not intended to be formal hypotheses; rather, they are stated as general research questions which will require more extensive empirical investigation.

OUR VIEW OF ORGANIZATIONAL END-USER COMPUTING

We take a very broad view of EUC and basically adopt the Rockart and Flannery[1] categorization of end users. They defined six distinct types of end users within organizations.

☐ nonprogramming end users who access data through predeveloped menu-driven software packages;
☐ command level end users who generate unique reports for their own purposes, usually with simple query languages;
☐ end-user programmers who utilize command and procedural languages to access, manipulate, and process data for their personal information needs;

- ☐ functional support personnel who produce end-user software for managers within their functional area;
- ☐ end-user computing support personnel who develop application and/or decision support software within an information center environment;
- ☐ data processing (DP) programmers who accumulate knowledge concerning relevant hardware, software, communications, and management that will facilitate end-user computing within the organization.

The dependent variable for our propositions is end-user computing success. Previous literature has suggested several surrogate measures for information systems success. These include user information satisfaction, system utilization, decision effectiveness, organizational performance (e.g., return on investment, profitability), and the application of computer-based information systems to the major problems of the organization.[12] Critical success factors, if identifiable, have also been cited as a measure of information systems success.[13]

We assume that an end user will utilize EUC facilities only when they meet at least some of the criteria cited above. Unless use is mandatory, information systems are used extensively only when they are perceived to be of value to the end user. We, among others, believe that *utilization* is highly correlated with the other surrogate measures of MIS and EUC success.[14-17] Organizational performance and decision effectiveness are difficult measures to use due to the numerous intervening environmental variables that tend to influence them.

Several instruments have been developed and validated to measure user information satisfaction;[3,18-20] therefore, end-user information satisfaction and system utilization statistics provide readily available surrogate measures for EUCF success. If other criteria cited above are tractable, they should be used as well.

A CONCEPTUAL SCHEME

Ein-Dor and Segev[21] suggest a useful conceptual scheme for relating organizational context variables and MIS success. That scheme, which we adopt here, categorizes independent variables as uncontrollable, partially controllable, or fully controllable. The classification permits a stepwise analysis of the organizational context variables as they relate to EUC success, making the scheme useful for evaluating either existing or planned end-user computing facilities (see Figure 16.1).

The uncontrollable variables are those whose status is given with respect to the EUCF. They are uncontrollable because the information systems executive responsible for the EUCF has little or no control over the factors or because the time frame for change is longer than can be tolerated. The variables in this group are the task technology variables and the organizational

FIGURE 16.1
CONCEPTUAL SCHEME FOR EVALUATING ORGANIZATIONAL CONTEXT
VARIABLES

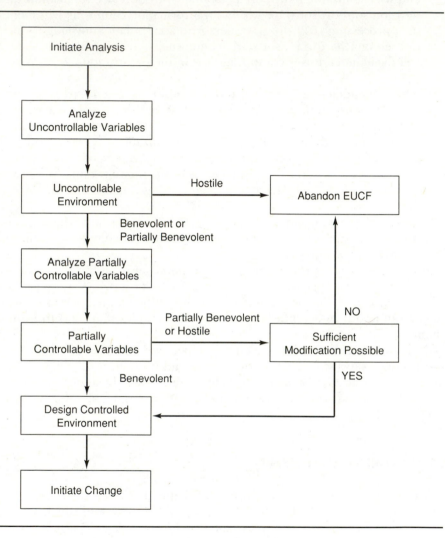

time frame. If analysis of the uncontrollable variables reveals a totally hostile environment, there is no point in continuing the operation of an existing EUCF or planning for the establishment of such facilities.

If the uncontrollable variables appear to be partially or wholly benevolent, then the partially controllable variables should be analyzed. The partially controllable variables are those in which change in the desired direction can be induced within an acceptable period of time. The variables in this group include the existing systems development backlog and the psychological climate (management attitudes toward EUC). The fully controllable variables are those that are totally under the control of management. They include the rank of the executive responsible for EUC, end-user training, and corporate end-user computing policies.

In order to establish the feasibility of using these variables, suggestions for operationalizing them are provided in Table 16.1. Interactions between variables are possible. All of the variables interact with EUC success, the dependent variable. In some cases there may be a feedback relationship where EUC success affects specific variables. This indicates that those variables

TABLE 16.1
SUGGESTED OPERATIONAL MEASURES FOR EUC VARIABLES

Variable	Operational Measure
Uncontrollable	
1. Task technology variables	
a. management activities	strategic planning executives; management control executives; operational control managers (classify by organizational chart and position title)
b. task structuredness	classify as unstructured; semistructured and structured via the task's description
c. task repetitiveness	how frequently is the task performed
d. task interdependence	classify the task as independent; pooled interdependent or sequential interdependent via its description
2. Organizational time frame	planning horizon; rate of technological change within the industry
Partially Controllable	
3. Psychological climate	attitudes toward EUC; expectations about EUC
4. Systems development backlog	mean number of months to begin a software development project once it is approved
Fully Controllable	
5. End-user computing (EUC) training	variety (tutorials, consultants, documentation, formal classes, programmed instruction, computer-assisted instruction (CAI), help command, external assistance) and availability of training
6. Rank of EUC executive	number of levels below CIO (Chief Information Officer)
7. EUC policies	existence and quality of EUC policy manuals

and EUC success are mutually dependent. Psychological climate and the systems development backlog in particular are affected by, and in turn impact, EUC success.

PROPOSITIONS: SUGGESTIONS FOR RESEARCH

The following propositions represent suggestions for future research in the area of end-user computing. Each of the variables and the interactions between them is discussed, and previous research in the area is cited. Table 16.2 summarizes the references and the propositions to which they relate. Each reference is categorized as an empirical study (E), a survey study (S), a case study (C), or a theoretical argument (T).

UNCONTROLLABLE VARIABLES

Task Technology

Proposition 1

The higher the level of management activity being supported, the more likely the success of an EUCF.

End-user computing can be considered as the ultimate user involvement in IS development. Several authors[9,10,22,23] have found a positive relationship between the perceived value of information systems and managerial position. Gingras and McLean[10] noted that managerial level is positively related to the amount and quality of system use. In addition Dickson and Simmons[24] noted that, the higher the managerial level, the less resistance to change is encountered. Schonberger[25] states that greater user involvement is needed at higher management levels due to the decision-oriented nature of the computer applications at the strategic planning level. Because top management recognizes the importance and value of information systems, they are less resistant to change and they recognize that their involvement is necessary if decision support aplications are to be successful. As a result they will be more involved with and concerned about the success of the EUCF. Although we suspect that the upper levels of management may have neither the time nor the inclination to develop their own software, they will in many cases interact closely with their support staff in order to acquire and use the EUCF to meet their needs.[9,18,22,24] To the extent that these needs are satisfied, the likelihood of a successful EUCF is enhanced.

Proposition 2

The more structured the tasks being performed by the end user, the more likely the success of the EUCF.

Although this proposition may appear to contradict the former, we are

TABLE 16.2
PROPOSITION-RELATED REFERENCES

Reference number	Author(s)	Background	Proposition number											
			1	2	3	4	5	6	7	8	9	10	11	12
22	Adams, 1975		E								E			
18	Ahituv, 1980	T												
38	Alexander, 1980							T						
30	Alloway, Quillard, 1983				E				E		E			
42	Argyris, 1971	E							T					
19	Bailey, Pearson, 1983	E				E								
35	Barkin, Dickson, 1977	T				T								
2	Benjamin, 1982	T				C			T			T		
6	Bennett, 1976	C			C									
32	Benson, 1983	E			E				E	T				
43	Brady, 1967									T				
46	Canning, 1981	E		E										
31	Carlson, Grace, Sutton, 1977					C								
7	Cheney, 1984	E												
34	Cheney, Dickson, 1982													
26	Culnan, 1983			E	E	E					E			
48	Davis, Olson, 1985											S/E		
39	Dearden, 1972													
36	DeBrabander, Edstrom, 1977					E		T						
44	Dickson et al., 1984													
24	Dickson, Simmons, 1970		S							S				
3	Edelman, 1981	T												
8	Edstrom, 1977	E						E						
21	Ein-Dor, Segev, 1978	T					T							
49	Ein-Dor, Segev, 1982										E			
41	Franz, Killingsworth, 1982							E						
9	Gallagher, 1974	E	E											
10	Gingras, McLean, 1982	E	E											
40	Ginzberg, 1978							C						
50	Guthrie, 1974												S	

TABLE 16.2 (Continued)

Reference number	Author(s)	Back-ground	Proposition number											
			1	2	3	4	5	6	7	8	9	10	11	12
27	Hammond, 1974	T/C		T			T							S
11	Heany, 1972	S												
53	Henderson, Treacy, 1984	T												
5	Ives, Hamilton, Davis, 1980	S												
12	Ives, Olson, 1984	S												
20	Ives, Olson, Baroudi, 1983	E												
37	Jenkins, 1977									E				
47	Johnson, 1984									C				
39	Lefkovits, 1979	T												
29	Lucas, 1973		E	S		S				S			S	
23	Lucas, 1975					E				E				
28	MacIntosh, Daft, 1978	E			E									
14	Maish, 1979	E				E								
51	Manley, 1975				T								T	
45	Mann, Watson, 1984				T									
33	McCartney, 1983				T									
37	McLean, 1979			E			E			E				
4	Nolan, Wetherbe, 1980	T												
49	Reimann, Waren, 1985	E												
52	Rivard, Huff, 1984	E											E	
15	Robey, 1979	T												
3	Rockart, 1979	E			E									
1	Rockart, Flannery, 1983	E									S/C	E		
54	Rockart, Treacy, 1982													E
25	Schonberger, 1980		S	S										
45	Sprague, Carlson, 1982									T/S				
16	Swanson, 1976	S												
17	Swanson, 1978	T												
59	Wegner, 1971										E			

S = survey
E = empirical research
T = theoretical
C = case

positing each independently of the others. Given the level of management activity, the more structured the task, the easier the development process. Hence the greater likelihood of success.

Several authors[26-28] have noted that additional tools, procedures, and techniques are necessary when developing systems to support unstructured task situations. The information needs of end users are much more difficult to identify and specifically define in unstructured situations.[25-29] Culnan[26] also states that the more unstructured the task, the more sophisticated the needed mode of access.

Proposition 3

The more repetitive the task being supported, the more likely the success of EUCF.

Although task repetitiveness does not appear to have any consistent relationship with user involvement in the development of a decision support system,[45] some authors believe that it is unlikely that end users will often develop software to support ad hoc, one-time tasks.[30,31] Others[1,32,33] contradict this point. The more repetitive the task, the clearer the frame of reference and the easier it is for the end user to formulate procedures to solve problems.[31] Even though there is no complete agreement on this point, we believe it requires further investigation. Information reporting, data base management, office automation, and institutionalized decision support systems represent the task more easily supported by end-user computing facilities.[6,28,32]

Proposition 4

The more interdependent the tasks being supported, the more likely the success of an EUCF.

Some evidence exists[6,34] that higher levels of task interdependence encourage higher levels of user involvement. Tasks that are highly interrelated have less well defined information needs initially and tend to evolve over time. Traditional systems development methodologies demand the specification of clearly defined requirements prior to system design. These requirements imply that interdependent tasks may be better supported as end-user-developed systems. Several authors[2,31] have noted that different users develop different problem-solving approaches. The approaches used by problem solvers depend upon the needed integration across organizational areas. Barkin and Dickson[35] state that the relationship of tasks to other tasks can positively affect information systems utilization. Others[23,28,29,36] state that strategic planners require a higher level of integration than the management and operational control management groups.

Organizational Time Frame

Proposition 5

The shorter the organizational time frame, the greater the likelihood of EUC success.

Ein-Dor and Segev[21] proposed that, the shorter the organizational time frame, the greater the likelihood of MIS failure. This would be likely because traditional systems development is a time-consuming process, whereas setting up an EUCF would take a shorter time. If the time frame for the development process is longer than the time frame of the organizational need, the traditional systems development approach is not capable of solving the organization's information problems. McLean[37] states that the systems development task can be transferred to the user subject to consideration of the organizational time frame, maintenance problems, and the scope and orientation of the applications developed. The overall organizational time frame is composed of a combination of individual time horizons. The shorter the time horizon, the more satisfied the user is with the EUCF, primarily because it is the only way such persons can get the systems they need.[21,27,37] Users have become impatient with the systems development backlog and the long development times once their projects are finally begun. EUC facilities, with their relatively short development time frames, are particularly useful in these situations, thus enhancing the likelihood of their success.[37]

PARTIALLY CONTROLLABLE VARIABLES

Psychological Climate

Proposition 6

The more realistic the expectations of top management, information systems professionals, and end users, the greater the likelihood of EUC success.

Every organization develops its own psychological climate with respect to EUC just as it does with every other aspect of MIS. This climate is established by the members of the organization including top management, information systems professionals, and end users.

Unrealistic expectations may be self-induced or they may be fostered by experts. In the unrealistically high direction, end users expect more from the EUCF than is reasonable. Management has often perceived that computer hardware and software products have been oversold. The products, in many cases, never performed as effectively as the salesperson had promised.

Alternatively, sources of low expectations concerning EUC are the less satisfactory EUC experiences of other organizations. The impact of horror stories has, in the case of MIS, deterred organizations from adopting specific systems or technologies.[8,38-40] If the system is adopted, managers often refrain from making any significant demands on the new system or they may not participate in the design, development, or implementation of the system. The lack of confidence and user involvement in the development process are indications of unrealistic user expectations. Unrealistic expectations (low or high) inhibit EUC success.

Franz and Killingsworth[41] noted that the users with the most training and experience will have formed expectations about an information system which are closer in line with those of the analysts and designers of the system. In these situations expectations tend to be more realistic.

Systems Development Backlog

Proposition 7

The larger the existing systems development backlog of projects, the greater the likelihood of EUCF success.

It is estimated that the formal systems development backlog in most organizations is three to four years.[32] These large backlogs stem primarily from the shortage of systems development personnel. A common user complaint is that there are not enough analysts and programmers to keep up with the demand for new systems. There are several alternative solutions to this problem including: (1) making analysts and programmers more productive, (2) increasing the utilization of software packages, and (3) transferring the development function from the systems staff to end users.[42] The latter alternative is appropriate when end users can do the task satisfactorily and have an adequate EUCF for applications development.

Another important systems development backlog consists of the applications that end users fail to propose formally because costs of these projects are difficult to justify and because the existing formal backlog is already so large that even if the project were approved it would be years before development could begin. This "invisible backlog" is reputed to be 4 to 5 years in length at most organizations and is in addition to the known formal backlog.[30,34] Alloway and Quillard[30] state that this "invisible backlog" is 784% greater for managerial support systems than for transaction processing systems. They also state that the actual backlog may be overstated if it includes projects which have not as yet been formally approved. Obviously, the larger these two backlogs (i.e., formal and invisible), the greater the propensity for establishing an EUCF. Once the system is established, the probability of the EUCF succeeding should also be enhanced.

FULLY CONTROLLABLE VARIABLES

EUC Training

Proposition 8

The availability of end-user training is positively related to the success of the EUCF.

Educational program development has received attention in the MIS literature for over two decades beginning with Brady's 1967 study, which suggested that lack of education is a major reason for the lack of MIS utilization.[43] A more recent study of the key information system issues for the 1980s ranked "user education" as the sixth most important issue.[44] A number of researchers have included the education of end users as a component in their research frameworks.[4,12,29] Lucas[23] notes that "the older and less educated member of the organization is most likely to resist a computer-based system." Sprague and Carlson[45] suggest several different educational techniques including tutorials (one student-one instructor); professional development seminars; programmed instruction; computer-assisted instruction; resident experts; and "help" components in software packages. Education is a major activity of the traditional MIS systems development process. It is also a major type of support provided by information centers.[46,47] Additional research into the most effective forms of end-user education is needed.

Rank of the Responsible Executive

Proposition 9

The likelihood of a successful EUCF *declines rapidly, the lower the rank of the executive responsible for the* EUCF.

Experience, supported by the findings of several studies, suggests that the likelihood of MIS success, including the success of EUC, declines rapidly, the lower the rank of the executive to whom the EUC or MIS chief reports. In the case of overall MIS activities the chief information officer (CIO) must be no more than two levels removed from the chief executive office (CEO).[34,48] As EUC becomes more important, we believe the same argument holds on a different scale. The domain of the CIO used to be primarily in data processing. Today he/she is often responsible for office automation; data, voice, and image communication; and decision support as well as the traditional data processing function.[22] Alloway and Quillard[30] state that the management of the information systems resource should occur at the very highest management levels if the MIS function is to be successful. Ein-Dor and Segev[49] found a significant correlation between the rank of the MIS director and MIS success. In our opinion it is imperative that the director of the EUCF report directly to the CIO if the maximum benefits from the facility are to be achieved.[16,30]

Corporate Policies

Proposition 10

The establishment of corporate policies covering the creation and operation of the EUCF *will increase the likelihood of* EUCF *success.*

It is not sufficient to merely build and support systems; these projects must meet overall organizational objectives and sustain a level of quality and completeness that is appropriate to the organizational unit and decision activity.[48] In the traditional development of information systems, the analyst provides an independent review of the information requirements and systems design specifications. The analyst also provides an organizational mechanism for enforcing appropriate standards and practices in the areas of testing, documentation, programming controls, operating controls, audit trails, and interfaces with other systems.[1,48] These same controls are needed when end users develop, maintain, and use their own systems. Benjamin[2] was among the first to recognize that the rapid growth in end-user computing will cause information systems management to develop policy and control mechanisms for the management of the EUCF. He states that the traditional policy and control methods may not work in this area and new ones will have to be developed.

INTERACTIONS BETWEEN VARIABLES

EUC Success and Psychological Climate

Proposition 11

EUC *success and psychological climate are mutually dependent.*

Attitudes and expectations play an important role in establishing the psychological climate in an organization before the installation of an MIS, whether it is developed by MIS professionals or by end users.[8,50] Once a system has been installed, the psychological climate is also affected by the end users' experiences with it. End-user attitudes are substantially affected. Lucas and others have found that the quality of the system determines the attitudes toward it.[29,51] Good experiences with the EUCF and EUC systems generate favorable attitudes and encourage continued widespread use of the EUCF.

Successful MIS efforts have been linked in several studies to a favorable psychological climate,[51,52] but little study has been done relative to EUC activity. Research in this area promises to add greatly to our understanding of EUC successes and failures and the ability of management to establish a favorable EUC organizational environment.

EUC Success and the Systems Development Backlog

Proposition 12

EUC *success and the systems development backlog are mutually dependent.*

The lack of enough analysts and programmers has been a principal reason for establishing corporate EUCFs. As the EUCF successfully designs, develops, operates, and maintains new systems this will reduce the existing systems development backlog. However, if the EUC systems do not work it will increase the systems development backlog.[1,53]

REMARKS

We have attempted to identify a set of organizational factors potentially affecting the success or failure of end-user computing in an organization. In doing so we have adopted a conceptual scheme within which these variables might be analyzed by management. The desired outcome from the analysis is either the abandonment of a doomed EUCF or the design of a controlled environment within which the EUCF may flourish.

In addition, we have advanced a set of propositions for research. Neither the set of organizational variables nor the set of propositions is expected to be complete. We encourage researchers to expand our set of variables and propositions, as well as to conduct empirical studies on the research questions raised by this paper.

References

1. Rockart, J.F., and Flannery, L.S. The Management of End User Computing. *Communications of the ACM*, 26, 10 (October 1983), 776–784.
2. Benjamin, R.I. Information Technology in the 1990s: A Long Range Planning Scenario. *Management Information Systems Quarterly*, 6, 2 (June 1982), 11–31.
3. Edelman, F. Managers, Computing Systems, and Productivity. *Management Information Systems Quarterly*, 5, 3 (1981), 1–19.
4. Nolan, R.L., and Wetherbe, J.C. Toward a Comprehensive Framework for MIS Research. *Management Information Systems Quarterly*, 4, 2 (June 1980), 1–9.
5. Ives, B.; Hamilton, S.; and Davis, G.B. A Framework for Research in Computer-Based Management Information Systems. *Management Science* (September 1980), 910–934.
6. Bennett, J. Integrated Users and Decision Support Systems. *Proceedings of the 6th and 7th Annual Conferences of the Society for Management Information Systems* (1976), 77–86.
7. Cheney, P.H. Effects of Individual Characteristics, Organizational Factors and Task Characteristics on Computer Programmer Productivity and Job Satisfaction. *Information and Management* (July 1984), 209–214.
8. Edstrom, A. User Influence and the Success of MIS Projects. *Human Relations*, 30 (1977).
9. Gallagher, C.A. Perceptions of the Value of a Management Information System. *Academy of Management Journal*, 17, 1 (March 1974), 46–55.
10. Gingras, L., and McLean, E.R. Designers and Users of Information Systems: A Study in Differing Profiles. *Proceedings of the 3rd International Conference on Information Systems* (1982), 169–182.
11. Heany, D.F. Education: The Critical Link in Getting Managers To Use Management Systems. *Interfaces*, 2, 3 (May 1972), 1–7.
12. Ives, B., and Olson, M. User Involvement and MIS Success: A Review of Research. *Management Science*, 30, 5 (1984), 586–603.
13. Rockart, J.F. Critical Success Factors. *Harvard Business Review* (March–April 1979), 81–91.
14. Maish, A.M. A User's Behavior Toward His MIS. *Management Information Systems Quarterly*, 3, 1 (March 1979), 39–52.
15. Robey, D. User Attitudes and Management Information System Use. *Academy of Management Journal*, 22, 3 (1979), 527–538.
16. Swanson, E.B. Measuring User Attitudes In MIS Research: A Review. *Omega*, 10, 2 (1976), 157–165.
17. Swanson, E.B. A Note on Interpersonal Information Systems Use. *Information and Management*, 1, 6 (1978), 287–294.
18. Ahituv, N.A. A Systematic Approach Toward Assessing the Value of an Information System. *Management Information Systems Quarterly*, 4, 4 (December 1980), 61–75.

19. Bailey, J.E., and Pearson, S.W. Development of a Tool for Measuring and Analyzing Computer User Satisfaction. *Management Science,* 29, 5 (May 1983), 530–545.

20. Ives, B.; Oson, M.; and Baroudi, S. The Measurement of User Information Satisfaction. *Communications of the ACM,* 26, 10 (October 1983), 785–793.

21. Ein-Dor, P., and Segev, E. Organizational Context and the Success of Management Information Systems. *Management Science,* 24, 10 (June 1978), 1064–1077.

22. Adams, C.R. How Management Users View Information Systems. *Decision Sciences,* 6 (1975), 337–345.

23. Lucas, H.C. Performance and Use of Information Systems. *Management Science,* 21, 8 (April 1975), 908–919.

24. Dickson, G.W., and Simmons, J.K. The Behavioral Side of MIS. *Business Horizons* (August 1970), 59–71.

25. Schonberger, R.J. MIS Design: A Contingency Approach. *Management Information Systems Quarterly,* 4, 1 (March 1980), 13–30.

26. Culnan, M.J. Chauffeured Versus End User Access To Commercial Databases: The Effects of Task and Individual Differences. *Management Information Systems Quarterly,* 7, 1 (March 1983), 55–68.

27. Hammond, J., The Roles of the Manager and Management Scientist in Successful Implementation. *Sloan Management Review,* 15, 2 (Winter 1974), 1–24.

28. MacIntosh, N.B., and Daft, R.L. User Department Technology and Information Design. *Information and Management,* 1, 3 (1978), 123–131.

29. Lucas, H.C., Jr. A Descriptive Model of Information Systems in the Context of the Organization. *Proceedings of the Wharton Conference on Research on Computers in Organizations* (1973). In *Data Base,* 5, 2 (1973), 27–36.

30. Alloway, R.M., and Quillard, J.A. User Managers' Systems Needs. *Management Information Systems Quarterly,* 7, 2 (June 1983), 27–43.

31. Carlson, E.D.; Grace, B.F.; and Sutton, J.A. Case Studies of End User Requirements for Interactive Problem Solving Systems. *Management Information Systems Quarterly,* 1, 1 (March 1977), 51–63.

32. Benson, D.H. A Field Study of End User Computing: Findings and Issues. *Management Information Systems Quarterly,* 7, 4 (December 1983), 35–45.

33. McCartney, L. The New Info Centers. *Datamation,* 29, 7 (July 1983), 30–46.

34. Cheney, P.H., and Dickson, G.B. Organizational Characteristics and Information Systems: An Exploratory Investigation. *Academy of Management Journal,* 25, 1 (March, 1982), 170–184.

35. Barkin, S.R., and Dickson, G.W. An Investigation of Information System Utilization. *Information and Management,* 1 (1977) 35–45.

36. DeBrabander, B., and Edstrom, A. Successful Information System Development Projects. *Management Science.* 24, 2 (October 1977), 191–199.

37. McLean, E.R. End Users as Application Developers. *Management Information Systems Quarterly,* 3, 4 (December 1979), 37–46.

38. Alexander, T. Computers Can't Solve Everything. *Fortune,* 80, 5.

39. Dearden, J. MIS Is a Mirage. *Harvard Business Review,* 50, 1 (January–February 1972), 90–99.

40. Ginzberg, M.J. Steps Towards a More Effective Implementation of MS and MIS. *Interfaces,* 8, 3 (May 1978), 57–63.

41. Franz, C.R., and Killingsworth, B. A Comparison of User and Analyst Perceptions of the User Involvement Process. *Proceedings of the 14th Annual Meeting of the American Institute for Decision Sciences* (1982), 186–188.

42. Argyris, C. Management Information Systems: The Challenge to Rationality and Emotionality. *Management Science,* 17, 6 (February 1971), 275–292.

43. Brady, R.H. Computers in Top-Level Decision Making. *Harvard Business Review* (July–August 1967), 67–76.

44. Dickson, G.W., Leitheiser, R.L., Wetherbe, J.C., and Nechis, M. Key Information Systems Issues for the 1980's. *Management Information Systems Quarterly,* 8, 3, 135–162.

45. Sprague, R.H., Jr., and Carlson, E.D. *Building Effective Decision Support Systems.* Englewood Cliffs, N.J.: Prentice-Hall, 1982.

46. Canning, R.G. Supporting End-User Programming. EDP *Analyzer,* 19, 6 (June 1981).

47. Johnson, J.W. The Infocenter Experience. *Datamation,* 30, 1 (January 1984), 137–142.

48. Davis, G.B., and Olson, M.H. *Management Information Systems: Conceptual Foundations, Structure, and Development,* 2nd ed. New York: McGraw Hill, 1985.

49. Ein-Dor, P., and Segev, E. Organizational Context and MIS Structure: Some Empirical Evidence. *Management Information Systems Quarterly* (September 1982), 55–68.

50. Gurthrie, A. Attitudes of User Managers Toward Management of Information Systems. *Management Informatics,* 3, 5 (1974).

51. Manley, J. Implementation Attitudes: A Model and a Measurement Methodology. Chapter 8 in Shultz, Randall T. and Slevin, Dennis P. , eds. *Implementing Operations Research-/Management Science.* New York: American Elsevier, 1975.

52. Rivard, S., and Huff, S.L. User Developed Applications: Evaluations of Success from the DP Department Perspective. *Management Information Systems Quarterly,* 8, 1 (March 1984), 39–50.

53. Henderson, J. C., and Treacy, Michael E. Managing End User Computing. CISR Working Paper No. 114, Cambridge, MA, MIT Center for Information Systems Research, May 1984.

54. Jenkins, A.M. An Investigation of Some Management Information Systems Design Variables and Decision Making Performance: A Simulation Experiment. Unpublished Ph.D. Thesis, University of Minnesota, Minneapolis, 1977.

55. Lefkovits, H.C. A Status Report on the Activities of Codasyl End User Facilities Committee (EUFC). *Information and Management,* 2 (1979), 137–163.

56. Mann, R.I., and Watson, H.J. A Contingency Model for User Involvement in DSS Development. *Management Information Systems Quarterly,* 8, 1 (March 1984), 27–38.

57. Reimann, B.C., and Waren, A.D. User-Oriented Criteria for the Selection of DSS Software. *Communications of the ACM,* 28, 2 (February 1985), 166–179.

58. Rockart, J.F., and Treacy, M.E. The CEO Goes Online. *Harvard Business Review* (January–February 1982), 82–88.

59. Wegner, P. Education Related to the Use of Computers in Organizations. *Communications of the ACM,* 14, 9 (September 1971), 573–588.

QUESTIONS

1. How can *EUC success* be measured within an organization?

2. (a) Identify at least two EUC variables within each of the following three categories: uncontrollable, partially controllable, and fully controllable.
   (b) Describe operational measure for each of the EUC variables identified in part (a).

3. Describe the interaction between (a) EUC success and psychological climate, and (b) EUC success and the systems development backlog.

PART

V

CASES AND APPLICATIONS IN EUC

∎

Perhaps the best way to learn about an applied subject such as EUC is through the experiences of others. Based on the evidence presented in previous readings, it is clear that (1) EUC applications are widespread, and (2) EUC applications vary considerably. Some are mainframe-based, and others run on a PC. Some are designed to serve a single end user, while others may support a number of different departments and cross functional lines. Indeed, a variety of EUC applications have been described throughout this book.

The final section provides in-depth descriptions of four additional EUC applications. It is designed to represent a cross-section of experiences with EUC in major organizations. These descriptions should enhance your understanding of how end-user systems can be effectively developed, implemented, maintained, and managed.

Since the early 1980's, personal computers have had a major impact on corporate America. Accordingly, management has been forced to ask a number of questions, such as: How are PCs and the related technology best introduced into the organization? Who should be assigned the day-to-day responsibility for managing EUC? What role does telecommunications play in the facilitation of EUC? These questions and others are addressed by "Liberty Labs: The PC Problem" (Reading 17).

In Reading 18, "Educating the CBIS User: A Case Analysis," Ryan Nelson and Paul Cheney describe the activities of four companies with unique approaches to the education of their user community. These four "minicases" provide additional insights into the role of organizations in promoting the integration and use of information systems among end users.

In Reading 19, James Senn does an excellent job of describing the problems surrounding the management of end-user computing currently being faced by virtually every organization. Unlike many organizations, however, the Morgan Corporation is recognizing the EUC trend and wrestling with such managerial issues as direction, support, and control at a relatively early stage in the growth of end-user computing.

As the information center at Quaker Oats approached its third birthday, IS management took a close look at the center's success. Although it concluded that the center was both successful and popular, it also discovered that the center had fulfilled its function. Once Quaker Oats' management accepted the fact that the IC's effective cycle had ended, it began to prepare for an orderly phaseout. In Reading 20, "When It's Time to Tear Down the Information Center," vice president of information systems Ronald Brzezinski provides a step-by-step account of how they broke down the walls of the IC at Quaker Oats. This reading raises a number of interesting questions concerning the life cycle of the information center and the future direction, support, and control of end-user computing.

17

Liberty Laboratories: the PC Problem

■

Brandt Allen

INTRODUCTION

"If we're the leader in personal computing, how come we have so may problems? From what I can tell—the more we spend, the worse it gets." With this statement, the president of Liberty Laboratories, a division of the well-known eastern consulting firm Liberty Research, captured the frustration experienced by the Labs' managing executives, consultants, and their staffs. As new technologies, particularly the personal computer (PC) and the local area network (LAN), were added to Liberty Labs' already broad inventory, even more complaints about incompatibility, placement of hardware, and need for support were heard by the president and his staff. The issue of technology growth and its attendant problems needed a quick and effective solution.

LIBERTY LABORATORIES

Liberty Labs' (LL's) major focus was its well-known research program in commercial applications of scientific research. The parent company (Liberty Research) was one of the best known research/consulting firms in the United States. Since its founding in 1900, it had been committed to the vision "that scientific findings emerging from academic research could be applied to business purposes with great benefit to both industry and society." The firm,

The material was prepared by Professor Brandt Allen. Copyright©1986 by The Darden Graduate Business School Sponsors, Charlottesville, Virginia.

based in Cambridge, Massachusetts, first became well known for developments in paper making, photography, textiles, and food processing. Later it expanded into marine research, life sciences, the space program, health service management, and economic research.

In this work, the firm was a leader in the use of microcomputers. Visitors to LL often stayed to see its computer facilities, and its local area network, reportedly the largest and most advanced among firms of its kind. LL consultants were occasionally invited to give presentations to learned society meetings on the Labs' program and were often engaged to advise other client firms in establishing systems of their own.

Liberty Labs, though of medium size by the standards of other consulting groups, was a busy place with highly active consultants and a hard-working staff. Eighty consultants or "professional officers" divided their time among research, consulting, and administrative responsibilities.

Consultants typically held masters or PhDs in their area of expertise; most had ten years work experience before coming to LL. Turnover among consultants was moderate, averaging 12 percent per year. LL was unique among consulting firms in that the permanent staff employed only senior-level consultants; there were no associates, juniors, or researchers. This function was performed at LL by assignees: employees of the client firm temporarily assigned to LL for the duration of the contract. Assignees worked in the "Pens," a large collection of interconnected offices and meeting rooms adjacent to the library. Many assignees lived in the company hotel and then returned to their homes on weekends. At times as many as 200 assignees could be found at LL. The atmosphere at the Labs, especially in the evenings, seemed more like that of a small college or university than a corporation with young men and women busily writing, reading, preparing graphics, working in small groups or socializing. The hotel even had its own pub.

About five-sixths of the officers were active computer users with an IBM PC or its equivalent in their office; more than half had home computers as well. Many worked long hours; most worked at home on the evenings and weekends. A few could regularly be found at the Labs on Saturdays and Sundays. Most of the assignees used micros as well; there were many PCs scattered throughout the Pens. Typical use was for word processing, Lotus 1-2-3, proprietary financial analysis or statistical analysis packages and presentation graphics.

In addition to the officers and assignees there were about 80 administrative executives and staff members, not counting maintenance personnel or the hotel staff. Included in this count were about 30 full-time secretaries each of whom was experienced in the use of at least one word processing system, typically Wang. Other professional and administrative personnel staff included the following areas:

Audio Visual

Center for Financial Studies (an area of the Pens for studies requiring special security)

Computer Support
Executive Hall (the Dining Room and Hotel)
Institute for Humanity
Library
Personnel, Financial Administration and Accounting
Government Relations
Public Relations
Archives and Publications

Computer use among people in these functions varied widely but all operated some computing equipment in their offices and were responsible for some computer applications. LL had its own library, for example, which used an IBM PC for access to various bibliographic search services. In LL's Archives and Publications office, records were maintained on current and completed research, contracts, proposals, LL reports and publications, and consultants' outside publications, using three of the firm's old Apple II micros.

The Labs had a rich mixture of technology, including, as of January 1, 1986:

22 Wang word processing terminals,
90 IBM PCs, ATs, XTs, and portables (and IBM-compatible computers),[*]
18 MacIntosh "FAT MACs,"
a Local Area Network (LAN) with 70 connected PCs,
connections to the parent firm's broad-band (Ungerman-Bass) LAN,
8 Conference room video projectors (also with PCs and network connections),
15 CRT terminals,

plus several older Apple II computers, Digital Rainbows, CPT word processors and several Wang minicomputers. Peripherals included various types of graphic and letter-quality printers, laser printers, and a plotter.

Part of this equipment was in common areas such as the Pens, demonstration suites, and rooms accessible to staff, consultants, and administration while the remainder was assigned to, or for all practical purposes was appropriated by a particular consultant or office. (Earlier, when micros were just being introduced, some "loaner" computers had been assigned to consultants who were to be the "keepers"; unfortunately that's just what they did.) The common areas were:

The Pens microlab . . . 40 IBM PCs (or IBM compatible computers)
MacIntosh lab . . . . 5 FAT MACs
CRT room . . . . .10 CRTs
Conference rooms . . . . 8 PCs and video projectors

---

[*] It was common to refer to any of these machines as a "PC".

FIGURE 17.1
LIBERTY LABORATORIES HARDWARE/SOFTWARE/APPLICATIONS AS OF JANUARY 1, 1986

Activity	Full- and Part-time People	Hardware	Primary Software	Primary Activity
Consultants	64	Mostly IBM or IBM-Compatible	Lotus, word processing, graphics	Consulting and research
Secretaries	15	2 IBM PC/XT 14 Wang terminals or Wang PCs	Word processing	Word processing
Government Relations	4	2 DEC Rainbows Wang 22 (mini) IBM PC/XT	Proprietary fimanical Lotus	Accounting
Audio Visual	2	Compaq	Lotus 1-2-3	Data base
Center for Financial Studies	3	CPT	CPT word proc.	Data base, inventory Word processing, data base
Institute for Humanity	4	IBM/PC/XT	dBase III	Data base management
Computer Support	2	IBM/PC/AT		
Executive Hall	9	IBM PC, Wang VS (5 terminals)	Word processing	
Library	7	IBM PC	Proprietary Visi Calc	Data base inquiries
Personnel, Financial Administration and Accounting	8	Wang PC, Apples, 2 IBM XT	1-2-3, Word processing dBase III, Advanced DB Master	Accounting, record keeping
Public Relations	2	IBM PC/XT, Apple	Word processing comm DB Master, Visi Calc	
Archives/Publications	5	3 Apple IIe, IBM XT	DB Master	Recordkeeping

316

The rest of the technology was located as shown in Figure 17.1. As indicated by this exhibit, every secretary had a workstation (either Wang or IBM PC). Every professional officer who requested one had a PC or its equivalent.

ADMINISTRATION/MANAGEMENT

Responsibility for information processing rested with many parties—especially the consultants, the vice-president for administration, the computer administrator, and the Labs' Computer Committee; in most instances there was only an informal understanding about these responsibilities as opposed to a formal, written assignment. Consulting firms typically were not managed in a hierarchical, top-down fashion, and Liberty Labs was no exception.

The consultants, project teams, assignees, and to some extent, administrators were responsible for their own computing support as required by their client contact and research needs. Consultants tended to be strong-willed and difficult to control, or as the saying went: "Managing consultants is like trying to herd cats." Almost every need was unique or seemed so: one consultant's major interest was connecting his computer (and some specially equipped staff PCs) on-line to the Salomon Brothers and Merrill Lynch financial service networks in New York where he conducted his research. Another's interest was expert systems and the use of automated text analysis software. Mouse-controlled, three-dimensional decision diagrams was one researcher's pet project. Another was an expert in project management. His next-door neighbor's research was on industrial innovation cycles. Many did all their writing at their PC. The only common thread was on the client-education side: most presentation or teaching materials used Lotus 1-2-3.

Consultants sought PCs and software from a variety of sources including: LL's Computer Committee and direct from clients. Money wasn't a major constraint for most consultants; there was almost always a way to get a PC or a new printer or a $500 software package. If all else failed, they petitioned the president or their group vice president or chief professional officer. The justification for some requests had been weak; a few seemed to want a computer just for office decoration.

Consultant expectations seemed to increase geometrically: first a simple PC was necessary. Then it was an XT or AT. Some consultants felt the Labs should provide everyone with a PC if they requested it; there was some argument for a home machine as well.

Things moved a little more slowly and with more deliberation when administrative technology was being considered. In general, the consulting and research programs tended to drive the Labs and its administrative decisions, so that administrative computing received second priority to client-related computing, even though efforts had been taken to avoid treating them separately. The vice president for administration had formal responsibility for information technology for administrative and technical staff or for everything except contract (i.e., consulting) computing. Besides the extensive Wang word processing facilities, he had secured a variety of micros for administrative support.

LL had a computer support staff of two full-time professionals: an administrator and a programmer assisted by one part-time secretary and numerous student aides from a local college; they assisted both professional and administrative computing. The computer administrator held a degree in mathematics and had worked as both a hardware and a software engineer before coming to the Labs in 1982. Because of her technical ability and experience she was involved in every issue related to the selection or management of information technology. She maintained her technical knowledge by extensive reading, attendance at conferences and professional associations, and through hands-on use, mostly helping others. From time to time, she lectured on technology and its use both at the Labs and for other organizations.

LL's Computer Committee consisted of several of the consultants most interested in computers, the vice president for Facilities and Office Services, the vice president for Management Consulting, and the computer administrator. They made operating decisions about equipment acquisition and tried to chart the technological direction the Labs would follow. The committee had been most active in securing new technology; committee members drafted many budget proposals for funds (the president rarely denied requests of the committee). The committee, in turn, had endorsed or supported every constant request for an office PC and nearly every software request.

There were no written policies as to what a consultant had to do to get a PC or other equipment. Usually the requests and the justification were in short memo form. Large expenditures were reviewed by the committee— the decision to add eight more consultants to the network, for example. A consultant needing an XT for some reason would approach the vice president for facilities, the computer administrator or the committee chairman with the request. The committee and the vice president's office would then work to meet that need by securing funds. Sometimes thy would insist the consultants use client funds. Occasionally, they would simply "forget" someone when they felt their request was unworthy.

They had not been so successful in solving some of the Labs' compatibility problems, such as the word processing conflicts, nor had they found an effective way to improve consultant and staff understanding of the technology and the software packages in any fashion short of one-on-one assistance. They had sponsored at least a dozen educational sessions in the preceding three years on Lotus 1-2-3, DOS, the network, word processing, graphics, basic computer concepts, and the like, but with limited attendance. The individuals most in need of education usually didn't show up; they preferred calling the computer administrator when they had a question.

Many of the problems experienced by Liberty were revealed by incidents that became well known; several of these incidents are summarized in the following section.

CONSULTANT RESISTANCE

Some consultants seemed to resist the computer or were slow in adopting micro-based models, data analysis, networking and word processing on their projects. These individuals were also the most frequent source of complaints. "Their" PCs seemed to experience more hardware problems than others'. Angry confrontations between these consultants and the computer support staff were commonplace. One consultant was just barely on speaking terms with the computer administrator due to a series of run-ins that began one morning when he asked for a personal micro for his office. "We don't have any extra ones right now," he was told. "Well, can't you take one out of Mr. X's office? He never seems to use it. Anyway, how come he gets one and I didn't? I'm a senior consultant. I want to get started learning this thing right now."

Some of the computer problems around Liberty Labs were no doubt exacerbated by the personalities of the computer administrator and the chairman of the computer committee. While both had cheerfully spent hours helping others and had received many sincere "thank you's," they could on occasion be impatient. This was a more serious issue for the administrator than the committee chairman, who was a former consultant and a senior vice president.

COMPATIBILITY

There were both software and hardware compatibility problems in the Liberty Labs building. The hardware conflicts were between the IBM PC's and the Wang word processing (OIS and VS) equipment, the Wang minis, and to a lesser extent the old Apple IIs still in the building (which were used in various administrative offices for spreadsheet and database chores). The software differences were just as significant. Somewhere in the building could be found:

Spreadsheets: Lotus, Visi-Calc, Symphony, Lotus Release 2, Jazz, Excel, IFPS/Personal

IBM word processing: PC Write, Officewriter, Multimate, Bank Street Writer, Wordstar, Wordperfect, IBM Writing Assistant, Easywriter

Database: DB Master, Advanced DB Master, dBase II, dBase III, R Base

Graphics: Storyboard, Picture It Videoshow, GEM, PC Paint, PC Paintbrush, Energraphics, PC Picture Graphics

Communications: PC-Talk, Smartcom

Utilities: Sidekick, Spotlight

STAT: SPSS/PC, SAS, LISRE, SORITEC, RISKCALC, LINDO, VINO, GINO

New packages were arriving weekly, sometimes daily. Clients suggested new software to the consultants, consultants bought new packages, new consultants arrived with them, and of course, assignees and staff came with their favorites.

One consultant commented: "True, there is great variety, but I believe actual usage follows a Pareto Distribution; i.e.:

Wordprocessing
Wordperfect 80%
PC Write 10%
Others 10%
Spreadsheets
Lotus 80%
IFPS 19%
Others 1%

and so forth."

CRIES FOR HELP

The computer support staff was inundated with requests for help from consultants, staff, and assignees. There was no tabulation of support requests, but a conservative estimate was that there were 10–20 requests a day for help. A day's requests might be:

☐ Consultant X had bought a new printer for his home computer but it wouldn't print. "What can I do? It's too big to be carrying back and forth and even if I brought it in here and you got it to work in my office it wouldn't necessarily work at home."

☐ A secretary called to say that the word processor wouldn't boot. Would someone come up to fix it? In the meantime there was no other word processor for her use.

☐ A senior consultant asked what kind of cable was needed for *his* new printer. A second was informed that their cable had arrived. "Would you hook it up for me? I'm afraid I'll screw it up."

☐ "Which is best, the Apple II C or the II E?"—from a staff member who was about to buy a computer for her son.

☐ An assignee stopped the computer administrator in the hall with: "The ribbon is out on the letter-quality printer. If you tell me where they're kept, I'd be happy to replace it for you." Before the first assignee was twenty steps down the hall, a second relayed a similar message. "Why can't you keep the printers ready to use? I have a document I need to print, and I need it now."

☐ "That new laser printer you put in Room X doesn't work from Lotus off the network from my AT."

☐ "Have you got a driver for an HP laserjet that I could use from Lotus on my 6300?"
☐ "Will you order me a copy of Superdrafter? It may be just what we need for our project. Can we get it by the weekend?"
☐ "What sort of database should I get for our new contract?"
☐ "That package came in, but we're having problems getting it to load. Will you...?"
☐ "Will you fix this new copy of Lotus so it will work on my computer?"
☐ "I saved it, but it didn't take."
☐ "It won't print anymore."

All of the consultants who used computers sooner or later asked for help. The most active often asked the most questions. Most calls or requests were to help somebody learn to use a piece of software. The software being used were mostly purchased packages. Some requests, directly or indirectly, were for guidance in selection of software or equipment. Actual hardware failures were rare. Some of the problems were complex because Liberty Labs often acted as a beta test site for packages. Another frequent request was to order a package, part, printer, modem, screen, or other piece of equipment.

Wang/IBM Word Processing

Almost every secretary had a word processing terminal connected to one of three shared-logic (dedicated) Wang word processors. Most offices had their own high-quality, high-speed Wang printer and diskette storage reader. In general the Wang word processing system was highly regarded by consultants, staff, and administration. The Labs had a substantial investment in Wang equipment as well as a staff skilled in its use. Over five years worth of proposals, reports, and research studies had been prepared (and still resided) on the Wang diskettes. These diskettes contained the primary copy of a substantial portion of the consultants' work product. Unfortunately, there was a basic incompatibility between the Wang technology and the IBM PCs used by the consultants, assignees, and many clients. Consultants tended to use Wordperfect, Officewriter, PC Write, Wordstar, or Bank Street Writer; three consultants had learned to use the Wang, but most of their work was done on PCs. This made it difficult to exchange documents between the two machine types although there was a limited capability to do this.[*] Over time the number of IBM PC word processing packages seemed to grow. Efforts to solve this conflict had all failed; two of these efforts were especially noteworthy.

The first attempt at change came about the same way most changes

---

[*]Files created by a word processor on the IBM PC were converted to ASCII text files. No underlining, emphasized characters, or other special effects could be used as each word processing program defined control characters to handle special effects. The text file was then loaded onto a Wang minicomputer through a Wang PC connected to that mini.

occurred; it began with a consultant's idea: "My secretary is willing to learn to use the IBM in addition to the Wang. Why don't we put an IBM PC in the secretarial bay, and we can take our diskettes back and forth to that machine."** The idea was expanded. "Perhaps all three secretaries would be able/willing to learn to use it. . . . If it works, it can be the beginning of a phaseout for the Wang." The experiment began in a careful fashion. The secretaries were first asked to join the effort. They agreed. They chose a word processing package (after all, they would be the big users). With some help from the computer support group, the secretaries chose Officewriter since it was so similar to the Wang. An IBM XT was purchased and installed. Lessons were given. The IBM keyboard was pronounced awkward; it was replaced with one from Keytronics. The noisy printer was replaced with a quiet laser printer. A special desk/table was purchased. Every effort was made to insure the ideas's success. This was a project that everyone backed: the secretaries, the consultants, the president's office, and the computer committee. There were no obvious detractors.

Six months later it was a failure. There were many possible explanations: for one, the secretaries had all left the company for one reason or another. No one blamed the computer but the people who had chosen the software, keyboard, and so forth were gone. Also, the consultants supported by that office had refused to switch to Officewriter. They kept right on with their old word processing packages. In explanation they reported that their new secretary really liked the other word processor better anyway. Soon there were several users of the old word processor including the secretaries. Indeed, there were several IBM word processors being used in the office. This incident raised afresh the issue of which word processor a secretary should learn, how many they should learn, and who should choose.

The second failure involved a "bridge" between the IBM PCs and the Wang. An XT was to be placed in another secretary's bay; the PC was to operate a new Wang product which involved a Wang-like keyboard for the IBM and a software package that was essentially the Wang word processor on the IBM PC. The concept was that this machine could be used by secretaries and consultants, especially those consultants who did their own word processing. It didn't work. The secretaries reported that it was too slow and the consultant didn't like it because it wasn't compatible with whatever word processor they were using.

PROBLEMS WITH NEW TECHNOLOGY

During the early part of September 1985 a local area network product called PC Network was installed that linked the assignees and the Pens PCs and the PCs of five consultants and two secretarial bays. It required using a new

** Secretaries were mostly grouped into offices or "bays" of three, each bay supporting 15 or 16 consultants.

operating system, DOS 3.1. A third secretarial PC was moved across the hall from the two bays to a more comfortable room and was connected to the network. Three problems immediately arose:

Wordstar. Almost the next day there was an angry consultant phone call to the computer support group: "My *Wordstar* doesn't work anymore on any secretary's computer. It worked before you moved it across the hall; now you fix it." And when it was resolved, "Now the margins are all screwed up."

Investigation established that it wasn't the move, but the new operating system that now had conflicting computer-to-printer commands. Anyone using that particular word processor under DOS 3.1 would have encountered that problem. Second, the new laser printer with a 12-pitch rather than a 10-pitch cartridge had caused his margin shift.

Laserprinter. One of the secretarial bays was outfitted with an IBM XT, an HP laser printer, and the Wang word processing software (IBM PC version) running under DOS 3.1. It didn't work either. Wang had shipped the wrong driver. Three weeks went by before everything worked as planned.

Quietwriter. A similar problem occurred to the letter-quality printer used on one of the secretarial machines. All of the pieces worked well separately (Quietwriter, DOS 3.1, Wang Word Processing, and PC Network) but not in unison.

Basic Programs. One prominent consultant had a long-term project that required the use of many Basic programs. These programs had been put together over many years and were quite valuable. Unfortunately, the command used in all of them to trigger printing off the screen to a printer didn't work under the network software. A memo from the support group to consultants and staff explaining why it didn't work and why it wasn't even good programming practice and setting forth two solutions only served to make matters worse. The consultant urged that the network be removed.

THE PERSONNEL OFFICE PROBLEM

The situation in Personnel was different. Most of the secretarial and professional staff were openly critical of the computer support group. "These database systems don't really do what we want and we don't know how to change them. Whenever we call for help, they say they're too busy or that we should fix it ourselves." The support group had a different story: "They call when the paper jams in the printer. They think we should drop everything we're doing and come running if they can't get a disk to boot. They won't try anything themselves."

Other factors helped explain part of this problem; the old personnel director who had designed the systems and had supported them with considerable personal investment of time had resigned. The computer support person who had actually built some of them and whose office was right beside Personnel had also left. His replacement's office was at the other end of the building. The new personnel director didn't have the same degree of experi-

ence with computers. One system was in Advanced DB Master on the IBM PC
(a predecessor version had once run on the old Apple II under DB Master).
Another system was in dBase III, a newer system with greater capacity and
extended features that seemed to be needed at the time. They were not at all
compatible.

THE GOVERNMENT RELATIONS OFFICE PROBLEM

A similar problem arose with the Government Relations office. Their big
application was a once-a-year proposal-tracking and evaluation program written in Fortran for the Labs' time-sharing system. Government Relations staff
entered data daily for about six weeks concerning government contracts while
consultants, secretaries, and assignees entered data on tips, rumors, and hard
intelligence they had gathered. It was an important and complicated process.
In the fall of 1985, the new Government Relations director called the computer administrator to ask when she (the computer administrator) could begin
keying data for processing of Federal contracts. The answer was: "That's your
responsibility." Another confrontation. The Government Relations director's
remarks were something to the effect, "I thought you were responsible for our
computer systems; you're the computer administrator. If I'm to be responsible for this thing, why wasn't I told before?" It was difficult to determine just
who was right.

The administrator's explanation was, "We taught your people to use the
system last year and showed them how to do it. It's their system, they've got
to be responsible for it. I don't do keypunching."

THE MACINTOSH ISSUE ON THE SECOND FLOOR

The computer seemed to generate fear in some quarters—witness the second-
floor MacIntosh experiment. Liberty Labs had received an incentive to purchase two MacIntosh micros for use by consultants. One was placed in the
third-floor common area and was busily used right from the start. The second
was placed in a secretarial office on the second floor; it wasn't used much.
One day a consultant, finding the third-floor MAC already used, walked an
assignee to the second-floor office and said, "Here, use this one." The secretary there reacted immediately and angrily: "He can't do that. He's not
supposed to be in here." Later it was learned that it was the computer that
was not wanted.

THE IBM PC PURCHASE

While at times Liberty Labs seemed to add technology with considerable
speed, at other times the bureaucracy was numbing, especially in Liberty

Research's purchasing department. In the spring of 1985, the Labs competed with other Liberty Research divisions for funds for special in-house research projects; they won the largest appropriation, for $110,000. The appropriation coincided with the Labs' June 1 purchase of 25 PCs from the IBM Corporation. It seemed a simple matter: use the appropriation to pay IBM. Unfortunately corporate headquarters intervened. They said the deal had to go to competitive bid. When bids came back in November, IBM was not the low bidder. Liberty Research had not permitted the Labs to specify a particular brand of microcomputers; therefore, vendors supplied bids for various types of PCs—Silent Partners, IDS PC, UNI PC, Equity I, Leading Edge, etc. LL refused to accept any equipment other than IBM because of compatibility problems. IBM had been patiently waiting; as of mid-January 1986 the contract was out for rebid and IBM was still waiting for its money.

On another purchase with corporate funds (supervised by Liberty Research) the LL division acquires several IBM PC/ATs. After numerous problems, it was discovered that the vendor had substituted boards and disk drives, and the only parts of the computers supplied by IBM were the main system board and the cover. The vendor was then forced to replace the boards and drives with ones specified by Liberty Research. Later, the vendor was dropped from conducting business with the entire firm and its divisions.

THE MACINTOSH OFFER

The Computer Committee chairman was interested in the MacIntosh computer: he liked the graphics capability and its other features and saw many potential applications for it at the Labs. He also liked the way IBM representatives reacted to its presence. He secured several MACs for assignee use and had hosted several corporate visitors from Apple Computer. In early December 1985 a phone call announced that Liberty Labs would receive a huge discount to install a network of MacIntosh micros, laser printers, and associated equipment and software. The chairman favored acceptance: it would add a graphics capability not available on the IBM PC; there would be more micros in the Pens; and the Apple laser printer would have many uses. The administrator had reservations: there'd be compatibility problems moving data/text from one kind of machine to another, a whole new set of staff and consultant questions would arise, and there would be many more requirements for support. The committee discussed the matter at length.

In the end it was decided to accept the offer subject to several conditions:

- ☐ they would not be used for spreadsheets or other functions already performed on the IBM PCs.
- ☐ only graphics, assignee word processing, certain consultant research, and certain projects that required MAC software would use the machines.
- ☐ some would be placed in consultant offices.
- ☐ others would go into a special MacIntosh lab in the Pens.

The machines arrived January 7. The boxes filled most of a small conference room. Within an hour, four people had asked the Chairman if they could have a MAC.

THE CORPORATE ROLE

There were limits to the help that Liberty Research could provide the Labs. Divisional computing was growing rapidly with many different kinds of minis and micros. Indeed, the corporation as a whole seemed to be going in several directions. It used IBM, CDC, Burroughs, DEC, and PRIME computers for various kinds of administrative, general time-sharing, and research computing. At the other end of the scale, Liberty Research and the AT&T Corporation had embarked on a major effort to introduce AT&T minis and the Unix operating system into the firm.

SOME OPINIONS

The casewriter solicited the opinions of several key individuals at Liberty Labs. The computer administrator:

> Everyone's expectations are very high right now. That's good . . . in fact it is great! However, there are a lot of problems when high expectations change to unrealistic goals. The microcomputers and our new network can improve our productivity and communications but on the other hand they are not always the solution. Some consultants and assignees want a push-button solution *today* and cannot understand why everything is not working smoothly. Some even insist they cannot live without the new technology ("project reports will have to be delayed if the network is not ready") when we have managed to exist without these items in the past.

A consultant who was one of the advanced users:

> This whole microcomputer mess is becoming a pain in the neck. On the one hand I am having a hard time keeping up with all that is going on at the Labs, for example, Apple MacIntoshes arriving, changes in the network, new versions of Lotus being available, etc.; but on the other hand I see too many of my colleagues who are unwilling to invest some time to figure out how to do some things for themselves. They expect too much support. At times they operate too much as a business manager by trying to delegate too many things to others . . . assignees, secretaries, staff, etc. They need to be more entrepreneurial.

> I am trying to operate as independently as possible by going along with the mainstream and learning how to do things for myself. I am very happy with the hardware and software support which is available. I use WordPerfect to do all my own correspondence, research writing, and project material preparation. As long

as I can get my stuff printed quickly and neatly, I will be satisfied. I need easy and immediate access to letter-quality printers which I am getting right now. I do most of my analysis with Lotus. The network has worked great for getting these materials to the assignees. Other than that I see little use or need for the network.

The Computer Committee chairman's reaction was:

Of course I agree with the president. We do have problems. But some we can't do much about. The software explosion, for example. I can't very well stop a consultant from using some new package if he needs it for a project. I do wish we could solve the Wang/IBM word processing problem—that does seem tractable. But we'd better decide pretty quick. I'm about to go after another budget for more micros and enough other stuff to put everyone on our network. Personally, I think the real problem here is on the human side. We've got a lot of people in the building who are afraid of these things. You know, it's amazing. I've seen consultants trying to use something new, a model, a hard disk, the network, whatever. When they can't get it to work, they take all their anger out on the support group. I've heard them curse the administrator (in her absence) when something goes wrong as if it was somehow her fault. There's a lot of fear and frustration out there. I wish I knew what to do about it.

We have embarked on a distributed or decentralized computing strategy because it seemed to be the best concept overall. This means each department and administrative area must look after its own. I'm not sure that a central machine, networked into these PCs would be all that useful, but I'm certainly willing to look at it. IBM has offered to practically *give* us a 4300, but I am not sure it would help. We've got to do something to reduce the noise around here.

QUESTIONS

1. Describe the frustration experience by the personnel of Liberty Labs.

2. To what extent do you feel the problems experienced at Liberty Labs can be attributed to their rather unique (research/consulting-based) environment? In other words, do you think that other firms are experiencing the same set of computer-related problems?

3. Evaluate the administration/management of information processing within Liberty Labs. If you were appointed president of LL, how (if at all) would you reorganize the information processing function?

4. Address the hardware/software compatibility issue within today's organizations by using LL as a case example.

5. Discuss LL's strategy to move toward a distributed or decentralized computing environment. What impact is this move likely to have on (a) the computer support staff, and (b) the LL user community?

6. Do you agree with the Computer Committee Chairman's statement: "I think the real problem here is on the human side."? Why or why not?

Educating The CBIS User: A Case Analysis

■

R. Ryan Nelson
Paul H. Cheney

INTRODUCTION

Experts have been calling for solutions to the problem of integrating computer-based information systems (CBIS) into the organization for over two decades. Indeed, the lack of success is disappointing, and to some extent may be attributed to a basic lack of computer-related education on the part of the user community. Therefore, fulfillment of the task termed "education integration" is an important consideration for the information systems department.

The research described in this study will begin to address this need by providing some descriptive evidence as to how a number of companies educate their CBIS users. A field research design was employed using a series of structured interviews with managerial users and CBIS professionals from a cross-section of firms.

EDUCATION AS AN INTEGRATIVE TOOL: PRIOR RESEARCH

There has been an ongoing effort to understand the managerial issues associated with developing and integrating computer-based systems into

Reprinted by special permission of Data Base, *Volume 18, Number 2, Winter 1987, pp. 11–16.*

organizations. Starting in 1958 with Whisler and Leavitt's article[1] on the predicted demise of middle management and progressing through Nolan and Gibson's stage hypotheses[2,3] and Argyris' espoused theory versus theories in action,[4] there have been a wide range of concepts on how to deal with the problem of getting individuals to appropriately use computer-based information systems.

For years managers of large institutions have been plagued by a recurring problem they often describe in these terms:

> We are beset by an endless stream of bright, talented, and impatient young people. Each confidently asserts that he is in possession of an intellectual product, a magic elixir of great potency. Without it, our organization cannot grow. Indeed, it may not even survive. Before this elixir can go coursing through our organization, senior managers must be educated. Through no fault of our own, we lack an understanding of proposed additions to our inventory of techniques or equipment. We have no choice but to find time in our busy schedules for personal development.[5]

Unfortunately, research efforts have largely ignored educational processes. Education is given lip service, of course, but actions indicate a lack of consensus that education is indeed the critical link in getting managers to use computer-based information systems.

In the late 1960's a pair of studies suggested several reasons why managers were not making maximum use of the computer. Churchman and Schainblatt described a fundamental breakdown in the relationship between the CBIS user and CBIS professional.[6] Brady[7] concluded that the computer can have a more significant positive impact on the organization if the organization attends to the executive development and educational needs of both the middle and top levels of management.

In 1984, the Society for Information Management (SIM) and the MIS Research Center (MISRC) at the University of Minnesota conducted a survey of leading information systems practitioners and academics. That survey ranked "the facilitation of organizational learning and usage of information systems technologies" as the sixth most important IS management issue.[8]

Recently, literature on the subject of end-user computing has devoted a fair amount of attention to the development of CBIS training programs. Benson[9] and Rockart and Flannery[10] address portions of their individual research efforts toward end-user education. In each of Benson's 67 end-user interviews, the interviewee was specifically asked what additional education he/she needed or wanted, and what education he/she felt was needed by company managers to make better use of computer technology. "A significant number of them expressed interest in further training for themselves, usually with the provision that it would not be too demanding on their time and that it would be financed by their employer . . . furthermore it is interesting to note that six of the seven top managers interviewed named upper management training as a primary need."[9] Over half of those interviewed by Benson reported being self-trained, while only 15% said they had received computer-related training by the company which employed them. Rockart and Flannery made five recommendations for the development of a substantial end-user education program, including the education of "top line management—or at the very least the steering committee members—as to the tools, techniques, and potential impacts of the end-user computing era so that the need for effective policies can be understood."[10]

THE STUDY

A field study methodology was chosen to obtain information about how firms actually educate their CBIS users. A sample of 20 companies in the southeastern United States was chosen, utilizing the McFarlan and McKenney Strategic Impact Matrix.[11] That is, only firms whose CBIS activities represented a *high strategic impact on existing operating systems* were chosen. First, each company's director of CBIS was interviewed for data related to characteristics of both the CBIS department and the organization in general, as well as existing CBIS educational programs. Where appropriate, training administrators and/or trainers were interviewed for additional information on educational policies and procedures. Second, managerial users of CBIS were interviewed for information concerning their individual utilization of information systems, satisfaction with those systems, computer-related abilities, and participation in training activities.

Survey Results

The companies were asked to describe their CBIS educational programs in terms of:

1. percentage of CBIS budget devoted to education/training,
2. number of employees devoted to computer-related education/training,
3. educational techniques utilized.

Table 18.1 presents a portion of the responses to these questions, as well as some demographic data about our sample. Companies are represented numerically to preserve confidentiality.

Overall, companies reported relatively small CBIS training budgets. Roughly 80% of the surveyed companies reported training budgets between zero and two percent of the CBIS budget. In terms of training staff (reported in man/years for full-time employees), the numbers ranged from zero to eight with 12 firms reporting two or less full-time CBIS trainers.

TABLE 18.1
SURVEY COMPANY DATA

Company Number	Sales (Millions)	Number of Employees	CBIS Budget (Thousands)	% Of Corporate Budget	% For Training	CBIS Staff	Training Staff
1	$ 327	112	$ 300	6%	0%	1	0
2	1,388	19,800	500	5%	5%	10	1
3	100	1,600	1,600	20%	8%	17	1
4	205	150	504	10%	0%	15	0
5	516	1,170	12,000	23%	1%	193	1
6	203	1,000	5,000	8%	1%	100	1
7	450	3,491	12,700	3%	2%	54	4
8	111	2,000	9,960	9%	2%	200	5
9	50	500	500	1%	1%	6	1
10	1,800	9,500	29,000	2%	1%	190	3
11	3,400	40,000	68,000	10%	1%	250	4
12	2,400	17,400	1,100	1%	0%	11	0
13	422	14,562	3,300	8%	4%	182	8
14	15,000	31,000	94,000	2%	1%	718	4
15	10,000	97,300	13,500	3%	1%	79	2
16	10,000	100,000	243,000	8%	3%	175	2
17	600	3,000	*	*	*	*	1
18	6,200	5,270	25,000	10%	2%	350	6
19	6,700	40,000	80,000	1%	1%	210	5
20	514	225	1,300	2%	1%	22	1
Averages:	3,019	19,404	31,645	7%	2%	146	1

* One company reported data as confidential.

Seven educational techniques[12] were fairly evenly represented in the surveyed companies:

Tutorial—each user is individually taught by an instructor or colleague.

Resident Expert—a passive version of the tutorial technique in that education via a consultant is user-initiated.

Course/Seminar—courses, lectures, or professional development seminars in which the instructor is usually an internal or external "expert" in CBIS.

External—education received external to the organization itself (e.g., one-week microcomputer seminar held at vendor's headquarters.)

PI/CAI—programmed instruction (PI) and its automated counterpart, computer-assisted instruction (CAI) (e.g., Lotus tutorial); the instructor prepares lessons which consist of three parts: content, questions, and answer/next lesson pairs.

Interactive Training Manual (ITM)—combination of tutorial and PI/CAI; an application-oriented CBIS and a guidebook are used together. The guidebook contains lessons and the application system provides the examples and the exercises.[13]

Help Component—here the resident expert is the CBIS itself in the form of an online training or guidance component.

In addition, managers were asked to describe all seven educational techniques in reference to both the quantity and quality of training received. Table 18.2 ranks, in ascending order, the seven techniques for both quantity and quality. Quantity is represented in terms of total hours. The interviewees were asked to estimate the total hours of training they had received since joining their present employer. Quality is represented via individual ratings (5-point scale with 1 = Very Low, 5 = Very High) by the 100 managers interviewed. The Resident Expert technique proved to be superior in terms of both quantity and quality, while ITM and the help components scored significantly lower than the other techniques in terms of quantity. The PI/CAI and the help component received the lowest quality ratings.

TABLE 18.2
RANKING OF EDUCATION TECHNIQUES

Quantity	Mean Total Hours	Quality	Mean Rating
1. Resident Expert	104.82	1. Resident Expert	3.96
2. Course/Seminar	44.11	2. ITM	3.42
3. External	35.63	3. Tutorial	3.33
4. PI/CAI	18.43	4. Course/Seminar	3.32
5. Tutorial	14.78	5. External	3.07
6. Help Component	9.41	6. PI/CAI	2.86
7. ITM	7.82	7. Help Component	2.73

CASE DESCRIPTIONS

The following section presents a series of four narrative descriptions of individual companies that exhibited (a) an interesting approach to the education of their CBIS user community, and (b) a willingness to share their experiences with the public.

Blue Cross and Blue Shield of North Carolina

Blue Cross and Blue Shield of North Carolina (BCBSNC) is a corporation authorized by a special enabling act of the North Carolina General Assembly to provide the people of North Carolina with an effective and efficient way to obtain needed health serviced on a voluntary prepayment basis. Formed January 1, 1968, with a current enrollment of more than 2.7 million members, BCBSNC covers 36% of the state's total population. Earned fees were approximately $516 million and they employed 1,709 people in 1983. BCBSNC began using computer-based technology immediately upon their formation for accounting functions. Recently, the information systems department has succeeded in implementing a series of new claims processing systems, automating a group rating system, and installing an integrated telecommunications network.

The CBIS department operates on a budget of $12 million (23% of corporate budget) with a staff of 193. The CBIS hardware configuration evolves around 3 mainframes (IBM 3033's), 3 minicomputers, and 96 microcomputers. Approximately 1,000 CRT's access the system from both internal and external (e.g., hospitals and doctors' offices) locations. The CBIS software library consists of a wide variety of languages and packages including IMS, EASYTRIEVE, PANAUDIT, SAD and LOTUS 1-2-3.

Blue Cross approached the education of their CBIS user community from two directions. First, the CBIS department offers a host of technically-oriented courses geared primarily at mainframe users. Second, the corporate training department is responsible for providing micro-related training.

Less than one percent of the CBIS budget is allocated under the general heading of "training." One full-time training administrator is responsible for identifying corporate training needs and then seeing that those needs are addressed. Once training needs have been established, Blue Cross employs a rather innovative method of delivering the training service.[14] Technical seminars, coordinated by the training administrator, are conducted by "expert employees," an employee who displays some level of expertise in a particular subject area. According to the training administrator the expert is usually more than willing to teach for a couple of reasons: "It is an ego boost to be asked to teach or speak to a group, and the prospective teacher has an opportunity to head off potential problems long before they happen, since training will show end users the correct (i.e., company preferred) ways of performing certain tasks."[15]

Seminars last approximately an hour and a half and are held once a week for as many weeks as necessary. This method has several advantages over a single, all-day class. Managers are more willing to let their people attend since loss of staff time in class is more spread out, reducing the impact on projects. If an employee is having difficulty understanding some of the subject matter presented in a seminar, he or she has the opportunity to learn the material prior to the next seminar. In a one- or two-day class that same employee might be hopelessly lost or might hold others back. Subjects frequently taught are:

- ☐ IMS batch programming
- ☐ IMS TP programming
- ☐ advanced IMS calls
- ☐ EASYTRIEVE/IMS
- ☐ the linkage editor
- ☐ COBOL interval sorts and reportwriter
- ☐ MVS dump reading
- ☐ OS job control language

The second training approach taken by Blue Cross is geared more for the non-technical types of users (the majority of the end-user population). The corporate training department is responsible for providing micro-related training (e.g., LOTUS 1-2-3, dBASE, WORDSTAR, etc.). The funding for this training comes out of the corporate budget.

In addition to courses and seminars, Blue Cross offers computer-related training through all six of the other techniques described above. External coursework is obtained through North Carolina State University or at vendor-sponsored programs.

Durham Life Insurance Company

Based in Raleigh, North Carolina, Durham Life markets life, health, disability, automobile and homeowners insurance, and annuities to individuals; life, health, dental, and disability insurance to groups; and life and disability insurance to banks, automobile dealers and other credit institutions. Presently, annual revenues are $200 million and employment is slightly over 1,000.

Since the 1960's, Durham Life has been using computer systems to increase its operational efficiency. Recent system enhancements include: (a) training agents in the use of "The Financial Needs Analysis," a marketing system produced by the Vernon Publishing Company; and (b) enhancement of the distribution of individual life products through their licensed Personal Producing General Agency network via the purchase of a software illustration system that is considered to be the finest in the industry. This software package is offered to those independent agents who have their own personal computers, thus enabling them to illustrate to their clients a variety of marketing concepts—using Durham Life's "Universal Life" products.

Durham Life presently invests about 8 percent ($5 million) of their total budget in CBIS operations. Approximately 10% (100) of all Durham Life employees work within the CBIS functional area. Fifteen IBM PC's provide the majority of the end-user hardware support.

Computer-related training is a relatively new phenomenon at Durham Life. Currently, training seminars on several computer-based topics (e.g., LOTUS 1-2-3, WORDSTAR, PC-DOS, IBM Assistant Series, CHART and PC DRAW) are being offered. DELTAK courseware is also used. DELTAK offers a wide variety of instructional material, including: (a) "teach yourself" diskettes that give users help with their IBM PC or related software, (b) mainframe computer-based training (CBT) that teaches productivity software such as SAS, FOCUS and ADRS II, and (c) video journals—videotaped courses designed to familiarize managers with new technology and computer concepts. Training activities are the responsibility of a one person staff with the title of "Personal Computer Coordinator," who works without a budget. The PC Coordinator commented that a lot of her job involves "hand-holding" . . . getting the end user started on a particular tutorial and then continually responding to their questions. To date approximately 10 to 15 managers have made use of the PC Coordinator's services. External vendor-sponsored training is also available.

The Manager of Information Support expressed a desire to formally develop the concept of the Resident Expert (RE), e.g., "If somebody in accounting is an RE in LOTUS, corporate resources might be more efficiently utilized by directing questions to that person. It is a distribution of the educational responsibility."[6] The problem in creating such a program at Durham Life seemed to be politically based. "Approval from the Accounting Manager is hard to get due to the difficulty in accounting for the time expended by an employee in answering LOTUS questions, as opposed to doing the job he/she was hired for in the first place."[16]

> It is purely a financial reason, when you buy a piece of hardware you capitalize it and depreciate it over a five-year period of time; in other words the philosophy is that hardware is free. Hardware is not going to get sick, strike, or quit. We've just purchased a $2 million computer and that decision was made in a one hour meeting. On the other hand, I've been through three hour arguments over whether or not we were going to send somebody to a $500 class. The biggest fear is that we will spend several thousand dollars training somebody in a leading-edge technology only to lose him to some other company. We (CBIS), for example, will not hire anyone of a technical nature with less than 2 years experience on hardware similar to our own.[16]

Nuclear Regulatory Commission

The Nuclear Regulatory Commission (NRC) licenses and regulates the use of nuclear energy to protect the public health and safety and the environment. It does this by licensing persons and companies to build and operate nuclear reactors and to own and use nuclear materials. The NRC makes rules and sets standards for these types of licenses. The NRC also carefully inspects the activities of the licensed companies to ensure that they do not violate the safety rules of the Commission. The NRC was established as an independent regulatory agency under the provisions of the Energy Reorganization Act of 1974. Transferred to the NRC were all licensing and related regulatory functions formerly assigned to the Atomic Energy Commission.

The NRC budget was $450 million in 1985, and they employed 3,491 people. Three percent of that budget (12.7 million) is directed toward the CBIS function, which covers internal, as well as external (e.g., time-sharing and hiring of consultants) computer-related support.

In October 1984, the Information Technology Services (ITS) training laboratory was created, the first of two facilities to support end-user computing at the NRC. The training lab serves NRC personnel by providing customized classroom instruction to computer users on a regularly scheduled basis. Three fully equipped classrooms are available for NRC use, one complete with eight IBM PC's. Classes include data processing concepts and terminology as well as hands-on instruction on the use of NRC standard hardware and software.

A second facility, the ITS support center, was officially opened in January 1985. Designed to compliment the activities of the training lab, the support center provides ongoing guidance and assistance to end users of NRC-accessible administrative data processing facilities, including mainframes, minicomputers and PC's. In addition to a full-time staff of ADP specialists providing telephone and walk-in consulting, the support center contains terminals and microcomputers for demonstration, trial use and individual self-instruction.

The support center also serves as an organizational clearinghouse—focal point to disseminate information of interest to CBIS users through the ITS Newsletter, CBIS Services Guide and ITS Reference Library. In addition, software and data sharing is encouraged by providing a software locator service, helping users to access shared corporate data, and lending support to user groups.

The ITS training lab and support center received approximately two percent ($250,000) of the CBIS budget during the last budgeting cycle. During the first six months of operation more than 500 NRC employees at headquarters and in the regions have been trained by the ITS training lab and support center staff (approximately 5 full-time employees).

Northern Telecom

Northern Telecom, Ltd. is a leader in the telecommunications industry. Starting out as a manufacturing arm of Bell Canada, the historical development of Northern Telecom, Ltd, (NTL) is much the same as the spinoff of Western Electric from AT&T. NTL recorded sales of $3.4 billion in 1984. Slightly over 12% of NTL's 40,000 employees are located in the Research Triangle Park, North Carolina. These 5,000 employees are responsible for producing the number one central office switch in the world and, as a result, account for one quarter of NTL's total sales.

Perhaps due to the company's desire to stay ahead of its competition, Northern Telecom places a high priority on internal utilization of CBIS technology. Ten percent of the budget is devoted to CBIS, which employs a staff of 250 people. As the Director of Business Systems and DSS stated: "We're in a very fortunate position here in that we get tremendous help from our senior executives . . . including our general manager who is stressing automation everywhere. In a recent review, 80% of the corporate-level objectives were directed at automated systems . . . and this is cascading down throughout the organization."[17] In addition, it is the view of Northern Telecom's top management that "to make these business systems effective you've got to educate the people."[17] By "people," the interviewee meant both the CBIS professional and the managerial user. "Although it's not really called 'training' a key to effectively getting information systems utilized is to understand the user's problems, enabling us to come back to them with a solution that's user-understandable."[17]

Training at Northern Telecom is approached from three directions:

Application Systems—This approach is directed at the users of the typical development functions (e.g., manufacturing, finance, human resources, marketing and engineering). The responsibility for this training falls on the Development Manager, whose staff "train users on what the application was all about . . . e.g., here's the information that's in the system . . . and here's how you can get it out."[17]

Executive Data Base—A relatively new project at Northern Telecom trains senior-level managers how to access an "executive data base." Through this approach, managerial users will be trained to download data from the data base for subsequent manipulation on personal computers.

Information Center—This approach is directed at training the ever increasing number of end users from all levels of management. It is estimated that 3,000 users will have been trained in 1985 by this approach alone. A staff of three full-time employees make up the training arm of the information center, which is called the Personal Productivity Learning Center (PPLC). The stated objective of the PPLC is to provide the user with improved computer skills so he/she can increase their personal productivity.

PPLC training is both mainframe- and microcomputer-oriented. Mainframe coursework consists of OMNIWORD, RAMIS, CMS, QUIZ, SCRIPT and Powerplan. In 1984, micro coursework began with three eight-hour courses. Following a needs analysis, a number of other courses soon developed to meet increased demand; such as LOTUS 1-2-3, Symphony, dBASE and PC Graphics, as well as a general course for senior executives in "computer awareness." Each quarter a detailed course catalogue is distributed among Northern Telecom employees with course numbers, descriptions, dates offered, registration deadlines, prerequisites and estimated fees.

The chargeback method is employed for the funding of PPLC. The PPLC operates as a profit center in order to pay for facility-enhancements, as well as current operations. Estimates were for an $80,000 profit in 1985.

Discussion

This study has focused on the current training practices of a number of different firms. While the findings indicate low resource allocation for computer-related training, they also point toward the development of some rather innovative methods of educating today's end user.

In closing, we would like to emphasize the need for companies to view education as a means for operationalizing corporate strategies on CBIS integration. Therefore, it is incumbent on organizations to change their training strategies as their level of technological absorption and associated corporate strategies change. Top-line management (e.g., the corporate steering committee) is urged to formalize a set of evolving educational policies and procedures by periodically seeking answers to the folowing questions:

1. Who is in need of computer-related training/education? As a first step, organizations need to carefully identify the various end user factions (i.e., levels and/or types of users). For example, Rockart and Flannery[10] introduce a six-level categorization of end users ranging from nonprogramming end users to DP programmers—each of which requires a distinct program of education.
2. What abilities/skills are required by the end-user community? Based on varying ability levels within and between the various end-user factions, trainers are encouraged to assess individual training needs across the organization prior to program design.
3. How should end users be trained/educated? Following a proper analysis of the end-user community, specific training methods/techniques can be employed (individually or in combination) to ensure an effective learning environment.

References

1. Whisler, T.L. and Leavitt, H.J. "Management in the 1980's," *Harvard Business Review*, Volume 36, Number 6, November–December 1958, pp. 41–48.
2. Gibson, C.F. and Nolan, R.L. "Managing the Four Stages of EDP Growth," *Harvard Business Review*, Volume 52, Number 1, January–February 1974, pp. 76–88.
3. Nolan, R.L. "Managing the Crisis in Data Processing," *Harvard Business Review*, March–April 1979, pp. 115–126.
4. Argyris, C. "Double Loop Learning in Organizations," *Harvard Business Review*, Volume 55, Number 5, September–October 1977, pp. 115–125.
5. Heany, D.F. "Education: The Critical Link in Getting Managers to Use Management Systems," *Interfaces*, Volume 2, Number 3, May 1972, pp. 1–7.

6. Churchman, C.W. and Schainblatt, A.H. "The Researcher and the Manager: A Dialectic of Implementation," *Management Science,* Volume 11, Number 4, February 1965, pp. B69–B87.

7. Brady, R.H. "Computers in Top-Level Decision Making," *Harvard Business Review,* Volume 45, Number 4, July–August 1967, pp. 67–76.

8. Dickson, G.W., Leitheiser, R.L., Wetherbe, J.C. and Nechis, M. "Key Information Systems Issues for the 1980's," *MIS Quarterly,* Volume 8, Number 3, September 1984, pp. 135–159.

9. Benson, D.H. "A Field Study of End User Computing: Findings and Issues," *MIS Quarterly,* Volume 7, Number 4, December 1983, pp. 35–45.

10. Rockart, J.F. and Flannery, L.S. "The Management of End User Computing," *Communications of the ACM,* Volume 26, Number 10, October 1983, pp. 776–784.

11. McFarlan, F.W. and McKenney, J.L. *Corporate Information Systems Management,* Richard D. Irwin, Inc., Homewood, Illinois, 1983.

12. Sprague, R.H., Jr. and Carlson, E.D. *Building Effective Decision Support Systems,* Prentice-Hall, Inc., Englewood Cliffs, New Jersey, 1982.

13. Grace, B.F. "Training Users of a Decision Support System," *DataBase,* Volume 8, Number 3, Winter 1977, pp. 30–36.

14. Johnson, M. "A Training Alternative," *Datamation,* Volume 31, Number 2, January 15, 1985, pp. 156–157.

15. Pickard, M. Personal Communication, Blue Cross Blue Shield of North Carolina, Durham, North Carolina, March 1985.

16. Cullipher, L. Personal Communication, Durham Life Insurance, Raleigh, North Carolina, March 1985.

17. Downer, J.A.H. Personal Communication, Northern Telecom, Inc., Research Triangle Park, North Carolina, March 1985.

18. Nelson, R.R. "Education of the CBIS User Community: An Exploratory Study." Ph.D. dissertation, University of Georgia, Athens, Georgia, 1985.

FOR FURTHER READING

1. Ackoff, R.L. "Management Misinformation Systems," *Management Science,* Volume 14, Number 4, 1967, pp. B147–B156.

2. Dickson, G.W. and Simmons, J.K. "The Behavioral Side of MIS," *Business Horizons,* Volume 13, Number 4, August, pp. 59–71.

3. Ginzberg, M.J. "Early Diagnosis of MIS Implementation Failure: Promising Results and Unanswered Questions," *Management Science,* Volume 27, Number 4, April 1981, pp. 459–478.

4. Lucas, H.C., Jr. *The Analysis, Design and Implementation of Systems,* McGraw-Hill Book Co., New York, New York, 1981.

5. Lucas, H.C., Jr. *Toward Creative Systems Design,* Columbia University Press, New York, New York, 1974.

QUESTIONS

1. Discuss BCBSNC's bi-directional approach to mainframe and microcomputer-related training.

2. What are the pros/cons of BCBSNC's method of involving "expert employees" in computer-related training. Would this be a viable alternative in all organizations? Why or Why not?

3. Discuss the implications of the statement made by Durham Life's Manager of Information Support (i.e., regarding the low priority placed on training).

4. How might computer-related training differ in the public vs. private sectors?

5. What impact can top-level management support have on training within the organization? What can the information systems department do to solicit better management support?

6. Discuss the implications of a chargeback mechanism for training. How might *timing* be an important consideration?

The Morgan Corporation

■

James Senn

Bob Short, chief information officer for Morgan Corporation, is reviewing the latest proposal from the end-user committee. This committee has been meeting for several weeks to discuss strategies, policies, and procedures for facilitating end-user computing. At the same time the committee has carefully considered the need to establish controls over end-user computing activities. This is the heart of the entire concern, as Bob sees it. The MIS Department, while generally supportive, expressed concern over the lack of control that would result as end-user computing became more predominant. The analysts raised questions about how quality control procedures would apply to user-developed systems and whether they would even be aware when user managers or their staff developed and installed applications. Bob has been placed in a position where he now must decide the future of end-user computing and strategies for managing and facilitating it within the Morgan Corporation.

HISTORY OF THE MORGAN CORPORATION

The Morgan Corporation was founded in 1912 by Thomas Morgan. From the beginning it manufactured high quality tools at its northern Maryland location. Morgan purchased 150 acres in this region because it was near water and rail lines and not far from the industrial heartland of the northeast. As manufacturing and heavy industry in the northeast and midwest grew, so too did the Morgan Corporation. When the nature of heavy industry in the United States changed, the Morgan Corporation adapted to stay with the changing industrial complex. The company was not affected by foreign competition or the bad economic times that the steel industry and other parts of the United States industrial complex faced.

Reprinted by permission. Originally appeared in Information Systems in Management *(Third Edition), Wadsworth Publishing Company.*

The Morgan Corporation is still a family-owned company and currently employs 3500 employees. In 1957 Thomas Morgan, Jr. became chief executive officer and in 1967, when Thomas Morgan retired, Thomas Morgan, Jr. ascended to the position of chairman of the board. He immediately appointed Earl Dennison as president of the corporation. Dennison was succeeded in 1974 by the current president, Myron Stern.

Although the company is family owned, Thomas Morgan is careful to ensure that the best employees are always hired for the job. His own son, Gordon Morgan, has held a variety of positions within the company in order to gain the necessary experience. Currently he is vice-president of sales and oversees an annual sales volume of $74 million. Prior to his current position he was vice-president of engineering, where he learned firsthand the importance of having quality products designed and manufactured in a manner that provides the best possible value to the customer at the best return for the company.

The Morgan Corporation has been successful because it continually provides high-quality industrial tools at fair market prices. The staff continually monitors its own costs and prices very carefully. While this has always been true and is an important part of Morgan's history, it has become even more effective since the introduction of time sharing systems in the 1960s and personal computers in the 1980s.

The Morgan Corporation is proud of the fact that it has never had an employee strike. Union stewards are involved in all manufacturing, safety, and labor management decisions. When problems arise, both management and labor always seek the most effective ways in which to resolve the dispute. All agree that Morgan is a good place to work and both management and staff want to keep it that way.

MIS DEPARTMENT AT MORGAN

The MIS Department grew as the company evolved. It uses state-of-the-art equipment and is organized to provide quality assurance for all of its applications.

Organization of the Department

The MIS Department consists of 61 people, including programmers, operations staff, quality control personnel, and information services staff members (see Figure 19.1 for the organizational breakdown). Day-to-day operations are handled by a 21-person staff that works in three shifts, six days a week. This group is responsible for running the company's IBM mainframe and maintaining the library of over 8,000 magnetic tapes. The operations manager, Bill Parks, is very proud of the fact that his group is responsible for the systems' 98% "up-time" record. There is very little turnover among the

FIGURE 19.1

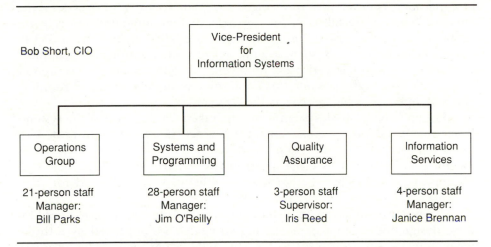

operations staff. Many of the people have been there for 10–15 years and take a great deal of pride in "their system." They work diligently to ensure production schedules are met and all jobs and reports are completed on time.

Jim O'Reilly, manager of the Systems and Programming Department, oversees 28 programmer/analysts. All are well versed in the COBOL language and some also have extensive training in assembly language. Approximately 18 months ago, Jim O'Reilly also acquired the FOCUS fourth-generation language for use in selected applications. Approximately one-third of the programming staff has become very familiar with FOCUS, and uses it when it is necessary to develop information retrieval applications quickly or when new applications are first prototyped. Jim is currently considering acquiring PC/FOCUS so that it may be installed in the company's information center and made available to end users.

Unlike most information systems groups, O'Reilly's staff has experienced very little turnover. During the last year three programmers were added to the staff, but only one person left. Jim feels this results from the fact that Morgan is a good company to work for and the information systems group itself has much to offer. This group uses the latest computer and software technology, and it is centered around the concept of team building. When large development projects must be undertaken, Jim carefully establishes a team whose individuals complement each other. The team takes full responsibility for developing requirements specification, formulating the overall design, and then seeing the design through to its implementation.

Like most information systems staffs, the systems development group expends at least half of its effort maintaining existing systems, some of which have been placed for over 10 years. Its staff members agree that the current backlog of requests from users is at least 18 months of work.

The MIS Department operates under a charge-back policy. Whenever an application is developed, or changes are made to an existing system, the costs of doing so are billed to the department that submitted the request. Personnel costs, the largest cost component, are billed at rates from $35 to $60 per hour. Other costs, such as computer test time, or unusual equipment purchases, are also charged back. however, users do not pay for computer time or any other expenses once the application is implemented and running. The MIS operations budget covers these expenses.

Morgan's charge-back system is closely linked with the size of the systems development staff. It is expected that the budget transfers from user departments will cover 75% of the cost of the development staff salaries. (The other portion is attributed to internal needs of the department.) Thus new staff position are justified by whether there is adequate user demand for their services.

All development activities, including statement of requirements specifications, design specifications, and testing strategies are approved by a three-person quality control group within the MIS Department. This group is responsible for ensuring that requirements for new systems or modified systems are met and for seeing that all software is appropriately tested before it is implemented. It maintains precise documentation standards and oversees the development, use, and maintenance of testing libraries. The library for each major application area contains both artificial and live data; these data are used as a database to test any new application. That is, data are read from the testing library and processed with the applications software so that the results generated can be verified for accuracy and correctness. Both the quality control group and Jim O'Reilly feel this is one of the reasons why the software development by the programming group is so reliable. (Approximately 70% of all software running at the Morgan Corporation was developed internally. Large scale, generalized applications such as payroll and MRP were purchased from commercial vendors.)

The Information Services Group was established in 1984 to develop and operate the company's end-user oriented information center. At that time Janice Brennan, a senior analyst in the programming group, was selected to develop and launch the center. Her enthusiasm for working with staff members in the functional areas of the company (such as marketing, accounting, and personnel), coupled with her understanding of the overall development process followed at Morgan, were responsible for her selection as information services manger. The group currently consists of four other persons. The center is equipped with a number of personal computer as well as video display terminals that are connected to the mainframe system. End users make extensive use of the information center for hands-on information processing.

Morgan Corporation Computing Complex

The heart of the computing system includes two IBM 3481 mainframe systems that were installed in 1986. Each system includes 16 megabytes of main memory and 4 1/2 gigabytes of disk storage (IBM 3380 disk drives). Over 100 IBM 3278/3279 display terminals (or the equivalent) are attached to the system. The majority of the terminals are located in the functional areas of the company; about 40 are in the systems development group for use by programmer/analysts.

In addition to the applications software that is either purchased or developed by the systems group, Morgan also runs the PROFS personal support system, and the IDMS/R database management system.

Other computer systems are installed at various locations within the company. The Production Department operates its own System 36 and uses Wang office systems for word processing and departmental computing. The Research and Development group relies heavily on a VAX system for CAD/CAM and for meeting its engineering/computing requirements. Each group is very dependent on the departmental systems. The Marketing, Finance, Accounting, and Personnel departments rely on the 4381 mainframes and are hardwired to the systems. In the past they have used only the mainframe system; however, personal computers have been popping up in these departments for use in budgeting, evaluating marketing strategies, and personnel management activities. The end users appear very content with the personal computers and anticipate greater use of them in the future.

Bob Short, Chief Information Officer

Bob Short became the chief information officer approximately 9 months ago. Prior to that time he served for two years as vice-president for manufacturing. He has been with the company for eleven years in various management capacities and has proved to be an effective manager in each instance. Thomas Morgan has personally commented that he feels Bob will be a candidate for president of the company in the near future.

Short is not a technician and thus he views management information systems from a functional viewpoint. That is, his concern is how information systems can best be used to support the overall mission of the company; he does not get bogged down in technical details such as which programming language to use of how much memory should be purchased on a new mainframe system. Those decisions are the responsibility of his functional managers.

His extensive business background, which began after graduation from the University of Virginia with a degree in business, gives him important insight into the value of information systems from a business perspective. Two months after becoming CIO, he also enrolled in an MBA program with a concentration in MIS.

Short feels that any decision made concerning information systems is first and foremost a business decision and that the technical issues should be addressed in that light. Consequently, he is not as concerned with having the newest, latest, or fastest equipment available as he is in ensuring that it will meet the needs of Morgan Corporation. Similarly, even if a project cannot be fully justified on a cost/benefit basis, if it appears that it is in line with the company's growth direction, Short is likely to endorse it and put the plan into action. As a result of these types of decisions, Bob Short has in a very short time developed a great deal of credibility with Morgan's MIS Operations Committee, the steering committee that oversees the approval of all major information systems applications for the company.

Because Short has been a member of the corporate management team for several years his office is located in the corporate suite area, rather than in the MIS Department. This location is more than symbolic in that it allows him to constantly interact with other corporate executives and to be continually aware of new planning activities and possible new developments in the company. For example, when the new Baltimore plant was under consideration, Short was an active participant in planning for the facility. His involvement ensured that MIS considerations were included in the decision process. As a result there was much closer integration between the new facility management and the information processing group than might otherwise have occurred.

Short is always careful to spend time in the MIS group even though his busy schedule of meetings at the corporate level sometimes makes this difficult. He is aware that his role is to facilitate the use of information systems in corporate activities and to link information systems plans and business activities, and he knows that the information he receives form the MIS staff is essential in achieving this objective.

MIS Operations Committee

The Morgan Corporation management team has been concerned for several years about linking information systems and corporate strategies. Therefore it was not a surprise to management when three years ago Thomas Morgan endorsed the establishment of the MIS Operations Committee. This committee reviews all project requests originated within the corporation, whether from functional area managers or from information systems staff members.

Whenever a manager believes a new application is needed or significant changes must be made to an existing application, a project request form must be completed and submitted to the Operations Committee. This form is reviewed by the committee, which has the authority to endorse or disapprove the development of this application. All information systems application must be approved by the Operations Committee before the systems and programming group can undertake work on them. The form, shown in Figure 19.2, indicates that managers must briefly describe the application and why it is needed. The Operations Committee then receives estimates from the Information Systems Department about the feasibility of the project and the amount of time it will take for requirements specification, systems design, programming, and testing.

The importance of and priority for the application is established by the

MIS Operations Committee, not the information systems group. This committee also oversees the development backlog and establishes the priority for new requests within that backlog. Based on the information provided by the requesting manager and the committee's knowledge of existing applications, it may decide to group several applications together and improve their priority or it can consider a request as a separate application that must stand on its own merit.

Although individual managers may disagree with a particular decision about their project request, overall they feel the Operations Committee has done an effective job in maintaining applications priorities. "They have made the best of a bad situation," according to Vern Josephson, vice-president for marketing. "Managers request many more computer applications than it is physically possible for MIS to develop and maintain. Therefore, the committee has had to sort out our requests based on their individual justifications, not on political tests or technological elegance. Like any other department, we would like to do much more than we have and we would like to meet all development requests; however, that is unlikely to occur."

Since its inception three years ago, the MIS Operations Committee has focused entirely on applications for Morgan Corporation's mainframe complex. It has had little involvement with the MAPICS manufacturing planning system that runs on the Production Department's System 36 and it has not been involved in the CAD/CAM project for the R & D group. However, committee members are wondering more and more about their responsibilities for the management of end-user computing. The increasing proliferation of personal computers has raised questions for the MIS staff members and the Operations Committee participants.

The MIS Operations Committee consists of nine members; two are from the MIS department and the remainder are from other parts of the Morgan Corporation. Bob Short and Jim O'Reilly participate from the MIS Department. Other committee members include the vice-presidents of manufacturing, personnel, and R & D, as well as department managers for materials control, safety, sales, and financial accounting. June Parsons, vice-president for personnel, currently serves as chairperson of the Operations Committee. Each person on the committee serves for one calendar year. However, the committee is established so that people rotate on and off at six-month intervals. At no time does a majority of the committee's membership change. This provides continuity in all decisions and preserves the objectivity of the committee. June is approximately halfway through her one-year term as chairperson of the committee.

All participants on the committee are at the vice-president or senior management level in the corporation. This is no accident. When the committee was established corporate management decided that the committee should be given the full authority to approve or disapprove proposals and to commit corporate and information systems resources to projects. But management also recognized that to make decisions of this nature the participants needed to be at a level in the company where they would naturally have information

FIGURE 19.2
COMPUTER SERVICES PROJECT PROPOSAL

COMPUTER SERVICES PROJECT PROPOSAL

Routing

PROPOSAL FOR BUDGET PURPOSES

1. _____
   originator

2. _____
   comp. serv.

PROPOSAL FOR CURRENT IMPLEMENTATION

3. _____
   corp. dept. head

4. _____
   comp. serv.

5. _____
   committee

ORIGINATING DEPARTMENT

Requested by _____ Department _____ Location_____

Request date _____ Required date _____

Request summary

Benefits: Explain how this request will reduce expenditures, reduce manpower, or enhance company operations. Include estimated dollar savings/costs.

COMPUTER SERVICES DEPARTMENT
Computer Services Analysis of Request

Analysis by _____ Date _____

1. Is request for:
    a) New system or function _____Yes _____No

    b) Correction of an existing system   _____
                                                  System or Program

    c) Addition/modification of an existing system   _____
                                                      System or Program

    d) System or function development:
        Description of work to be done:
        _____
        _____
        _____

2. Required computer services resources:
    a) Estimated system analysis man-hours _____
    b) Estimated programming man-hours _____
    c) Estimated debug and test man-hours _____
    d) Estimated documentation man-hours _____
        Total man-hours _____
    e) Estimated development and test computer time _____ hours
    f) Estimated production CPU time _____per_____
    g) Special system requirements _____

3. General:
    a) Is request consistent with long-range systems objectives? _____
    b) Comments: _____
        _____
        _____
        _____

_____

_____

Approval: _____BUDGET   _____IMPLEMENTATION

Minor project:

_____   _____   _____   _____
Requesting Corp Dept Head   Date   Mgr-Computer Svcs   Date

Request scheduled for completion by _____

Major project:

_____   _____   _____   _____
Requesting Staff Dept Approval   Date   Computer Priorities Comm.   Date

about corporate plans and activities. Thus senior members of the committee were selected for membership. This decision has turned out to be wise and as a result the Operating Committee format works well.

Information Center Services

The Information Center Services Group was created by Janice Brennan and currently includes four other persons. Its mission is to facilitate end-user computing within the company, which is interpreted to mean supporting managers and staff members who have computing requirements that do not merit development within the MIS group. Often these are one-time requirements for information or applications that do not require high-volume transaction processing support. Applications developed through the information center also need not be submitted to the Operations Committee for review or approval.

The center currently includes twenty IBM personal computers, each equipped with 3278/3279 emulation boards. These boards allow the PCs to interconnect with the mainframe systems if needed or to operate on a stand-alone basis as a simple personal computer. The information center provides four IBM PC/AT 3270 computers that are connected to the 4381 systems. These computers support high resolution graphics and allow users to run multiple sessions at the same time with up to four different windows on the display. There are also twelve 3278 terminals in the information center. Each is connected to the mainframe complex.

Several mainframe applications were developed specifically with information center users in mind. For example, a project management system runs on a mainframe and is accessible to end users through IBM 3278 terminals or PCs with emulation boards. This system allows individuals to establish project milestones and monitor the actual and planned performance. Individuals enter the data about this project as it becomes available to them. Users are charged only for the connect time during which they are using the application. There are no development costs for these applications. Another information center application running on the mainframe assists the marketing and sales staff in preparing product quotations for customers. By interacting with the system they can examine the impact of manufacturing quantities, production costs, and profit to derive a selling price acceptable to customer and company. This application is used extensively by the sales staff.

The information services group maintains a library of personal computer software that is effective in meeting end-user needs. Among the most widely used software are such packages as dBase III, Lotus 1-2-3, Symphony, Framework, and the Harvard Project Manager. Several word processing packages, including WordStar and Multimate, are also available through the information center. A newsletter, prepared each month by Janice Brennan, informs people in the company of new facilities in the information center, communicates user experiences, and provides tips about end-user computing. Brennan feels that the newsletter has been valuable in informing Morgan employees of the capabilities within the center as well as encouraging end-user computing in general.

END-USER COMPUTING COMMITTEE RECOMMENDATIONS

The end-user computing committee, established to look at necessary guidelines for encouraging the development of selective computer applications by end users, includes representatives from each or the functional areas of the Morgan Corporation as well as the MIS Department. It is chaired by Jane Mandell, Associate Director of the information center. The committee met several times over the past three weeks and submitted a set of recommendations, which are attached as Figure 19.3.

Among the issues of greatest importance to the Morgan Corporation are determining what controls, if any, should be placed on the development of end-user applications, and defining the MIS Department role in developing, supporting, and maintaining applications for which their department is not wholly responsible. The philosophy of the end-user computing committee is that users should be responsible for ensuring that the application is correct. That is, they feel that all risk and responsibilities should be placed on end users, and not on the MIS Department.

Members of the MIS Department, whose opinions Bob Short greatly respects, have reviewed these recommendations and have expressed significant concerns. Bob must now deal with these concerns since ultimately he must make the recommendation to adopt or to ignore the memo from the end-user committee.

The systems development staff feels it is politically naive to assume that they will not be held responsible if there are end-user computing fiascos. Therefore, they want the quality control group to certify *any application* before it is put into use. This means that the group must know in advance when an application is going to be developed, what software will be used, and how it will be applied. The programmer/analysts want each application, and the data source for the application, registered with the MIS Department. Furthermore, they want agreement and a statement in the new guidelines that any applications not developed by the MIS Department will not be maintained by the department.

Great concern is also expressed regarding the establishment of hardware, software, and data standards. While the majority of programmer/analysts strongly support the notion of end-user computing and privately work with individuals to help them develop applications and get them into operation, they fear that standards they have worked hard to evolve in fact will be ignored. For example, they feel that a standard personal computer should be selected for predominant applications throughout the corporation. The

FIGURE 19.3
MEMORANDUM ON MANAGEMENT OF END-USER COMPUTING

Memorandum on Management of End-User Computing

MEMORANDUM: Robert Short, Vice-President for Information Systems
FROM: Jane Mandell, Chair, End-User Computing Committee
SUBJECT: Recommendations for Management of End-User Computing

The End-User Computing Committee has carefully examined the opportunities and concerns of providing managers and staff members with personal computers and other computing resources that are not directly within the scope of either the MIS Department or the Morgan Information Center. It is our opinion that the Morgan Corporation can receive important benefits from the judicious use of computing resources by end users. However, we believe these activities must be managed carefully to ensure that there is no risk to the company.

This memo summarizes the recommendations formulated by the End-User Computing Committee. It outlines the basis for our recommendations and lists those types of applications that we believe are suitable for end-user development.

The issue of adequate supervision for end-user computing was discussed at length and from many angles. The committee recommends seven guidelines that will provide acceptable levels of flexibility and control.

There is not agreement by all committee members on all issues. However, each item has been recommended by at least two-thirds of the seven-person committee.

MANAGEMENT OBJECTIVES

Two objectives guided our activities and form the basis for our recommendations. They are to:

* Encourage and facilitate the use of computer resources by managers and staff members to raise personal productivity and enhance the effectiveness of decisions and departmental actions.
* Improve the timeliness with which applications suitable for direct use by managers and staff members are developed.

We recognize that there are many computer applications that should be developed by the MIS Department. It is explicitly noted that those computer systems suitable for end-user development are not ones normally prepared by the department's programmer/analysts, but rather new categories that current staff members are unable to support due to time constraints and workload requirements.

SUITABLE APPLICATIONS

The committee believes those applications suitable for end-user development:
* Use commercially available generalized software packages (e.g., dBASE III, Lotus 1-2-3, and Microsoft Chart)
* Do not process high volumes of data or demand large storage capacities
* Do not interact with the financial control systems of the Morgan Corporation
* Produce limited quantities of printed output
* Produce information used within the originating department
* Interact with mainframe systems and databases for data retrieval only (data from

end-user applications are not submitted to the mainframe systems and do not modify corporate data)
* Will be used a limited number of times and do not result in ongoing application systems

Additional characteristics may be recognized as new computer hardware and software products emerge or as experience with end-user computing provides us with new insights.

MANAGEMENT RECOMMENDATIONS

To obtain the greatest possible advantages from personal computers and end-user computing, while providing suitable management controls, the committee has determined that managers and staff members must take responsibility for the applications they develop or cause to be developed. It is unreasonable to expect that the MIS Department can be responsible for errors or inefficiencies in applications they do not prepare.

In addition, the committee believes the increased use of the Information Center demonstrates its usefulness within the company. We have placed a greater burden on the center to assist in managing end-user computing.

The following management guidelines are recommended:

1. All computer applications that are used in decision making or involve the commitment of Morgan Corporation financial and personnel resources must be approved by the Information Center.

2. Managers and staff members who develop their own computer applications, whether involving personal computers, department computers, or Information Center facilities, are responsible for ensuring that their application is correct and that it contains no errors.

3. The Information Center director must be notified, in writing, when managers or staff members develop and put into effect any application that was not developed by the MIS Department or Information Center personnel.

4. Any computer application developed through the Information Center will be developed without cost for assistance.

5. Computer applications that modify the corporate databases or require high-volume transaction processing must go through normal approval and development processes. These applications should not be developed by managers or staff members.

6. Computer applications and computer equipment that will incur a continuous cost for maintenance (such as for ongoing license or maintenance fees) or for which the total software cost is greater than $2500 must be submitted to and approved by the MIS Operations Committee.

We hope these recommendations will be openly and widely discussed by Morgan employees. Changes and additions will be welcomed. We also anticipate that the guidelines will evolve with experience. Thus, the above recommendations should not be considered final.

We also feel it is appropriate to develop an approval request form for all end-user applications.

Please contact me if any item in this statement needs clarification. I look forward to your comments and suggestions.

creation of a mixed vendor environment would make it virtually impossible to standardize applications support of any form. Many end users counter this by saying that there will be a mixed environment anyway, and that standards are impossible, so let's go with it.

There have been instances of improper decisions due to lack of data or improper manipulation of data through end-user developed applications. Therefore the concerns of the MIS Department are real. They see the benefits of end-user computing and the opportunity to manage the backlog in a more effective way. But they are very uncomfortable with turning the development of any applications software over to nonprofessionals unless adequate controls are placed on them.

Bob Short is pondering his action. He wants to support end-user computing because he believes it is a valuable resource for the firm. But he knows also that the risks of errors, missing controls, and careless projects are real. "The questions are tough," he is thinking to himself. "The MIS group is already working continuously and cannot take on additional development tasks. Yet they don't want to see information systems quality get out of hand. Is there a way to achieve both objectives and not offend either group? For that matter, are there even *two sides*?"

Bob must also decide whether the end-user committee is recommending too much responsibility—and too much power—to the information center. Is the center taking on a role that may hinder the original service?

Short has been heard to ask "*Can* end-user computing be managed?" Now he must answer his own question.

QUESTIONS

1. If the end-user computing and management plans proposed in the committee's memo are followed, what, if any, problems do you foresee?

2. Are the management guidelines defined in the memo adequate? What do you feel should be added, eliminated, or changed?

3. Project Morgan's end-user computing situation in 5 years. Will the issues or objectives then be different from now? What specific impact will this have on the management and control policies for end-user computing?

4. Are the hardware and software procurement policies outlined in the memo adequate for the situation? Rather than a required approval for purchases with recurring costs or purchases over a certain dollar value, do you feel there should be specific hardware or software standards, or authorized vendors? Justify your answer.

5. Is there any way to prevent users from purchasing whatever hardware and software they want, and developing applications without notifying the Information Center Group? Give specific recommendations to prevent this.

6. Bob Short is not a technician. What would be the difference in his approach to end-user computing if he did not have a functional business background and were not tied in to top management?

20

When It's Time To Tear Down The Info Center

■

Ronald Brzezinski

At the Quaker Oats Co., we recently celebrated our information center's third anniversary in an unusual way. We began tearing it down.

It is not that the info center wasn't doing a good job bringing micros to our Chicago staff. In fact, the info center had done so much to upgrade everyone's microcomputing skills that we no longer needed a separate department to support desktop technology.

By all industry measures, Quaker's info center was very successful. From its very inception, the center's 2,000 users—employees in marketing, distribution, manufacturing, accounting, and sales—complimented and applauded the information center's staff for their cooperation, professionalism, and dedication to making technology work for the user—or client, as we say. During the past three years, the success of the information center at Quaker has surpassed all expectations.

When our info center opened in May of '84 we celebrated in the traditional way. We held a ribbon-cutting ceremony to inaugurate the newly constructed facility, which was housed next to the information services department. The info center's charter was to act as an arm of the information services department dedicated to providing technical support and services to Quaker's staff and management in acquiring and using personal computers.

In three years, the info center has accomplished much. The information center staff managed the orderly introduction of over 1,200 desktop computers into the business. They trained over 2,000 employees in the fundamental

Reprinted from DATAMATION, *Volume 33, Number 21, November 1, 1987, pp. 73–82.* ©*1987 by Cahners Publishing Company.*

and advanced concepts of desktop computing. By installing over 3,000 software packages, they achieved cooperation and standardization throughout the company for tools such as word processing, spreadsheets, and database systems. Through a hot-line service, they provided on-the-spot expert advice to clients. They implemented and later enhanced an executive information system that is used by the company's senior management, including chief executive officer William Smithburg.

The information center staff was so adept at transferring personal computing technology ownership and responsibility to the clients that many users have become expert in the use of the new desktop and interactive technologies. Largely as a result of the efforts of our info center staff, many standalone and networked desktop and portable computers are now used throughout Quaker in a variety of applications, from tracking commodity purchases to measuring product performance. Several hundred imaginative business solutions have been developed by the clients and are now supported by them.

Following the center's success, we in information systems management began to ask, "What can the info center do for an encore, and how can the IS department leverage the talented information center staff resources?"

Many of our preliminary answers focused on expanding existing education, coaching, and technology support activities. Not surprisingly, these solutions required increasing the information center's size and budget to keep pace with the expanding client base. But as we began to evaluate the budget, it became clear that these added expenses could not be justified by a corresponding added value to the business.

As we began to analyze the directions the info center could take, we defined the relationship between the info center and the information services department. The info center's effectiveness is indirectly related to the IS department's commitment and capability to build an integrated data, communications, and technology infrastructure. Essentially, the effectiveness of the information center lessens as the technology infrastructure expands. Maintaining a separate information center contradicts the integration activities that the information systems department is struggling to achieve.

Knowing when to dismantle an information center is always difficult. It's easy to say, "If it ain't broke, don't fix it." Confusing the matter further is the trendiness of the info center. Many industry "experts" are still proclaiming the merits and benefits of information centers. Consequently, mixed messages are continually being sent to the clients, to IS staff, and to management regarding the importance and benefits of the information center.

At Quaker Oats, these mixed messages prompted us to look more closely at the information center work loads, its effectiveness, and its recent accomplishments. After observing the info center for a few weeks, several factors convinced us that it was time to dismantle and reintegrate it with IS.

Out talented information center staff was rapidly evolving into a maintenance mode, which didn't leverage their skills effectively. New administrative procedures—like chargeback systems and technology management processes—had evolved within the information center that duplicated existing IS department procedures. In many ways, the info center had evolved into a small business with its own set of technology inventory systems, chargeback processes, and service request procedures. The result was that the information center analysts, in their quest to be responsive to clients, were unknowingly propagating fragmented technology solutions. These "solutions" began hampering the IS department's applications and technology integration efforts.

Hindsight indicated that similar telltale signs had been surfacing for several months. Unfortunately, we in IS management did not recognize that these changes were symptomatic of an organization approaching the end of its effective life cycle.

In addition to our own observations, we began hearing complaints from the information center staff and their clients. The staff complained of being overworked. Requests came in for additional personnel. Clients began voicing concerns regarding service response; the hot line, they said, was not covered consistently.

The sheer volume of calls to the hot line—300 to 500 calls each week for less than 1,000 clients—indicated that clients were increasingly dependent on the center's staff. They found it easier to call the hot line than to read their manuals.

Like most info centers, Quaker's was instituted to help change how the business uses new technologies. Although nobody ever officially declared it as such, the information center was designed to be a transition department. We broke the function out of information services and established the info center as a separate department in response to a particular problem—the introduction of personal computers.

When we built the info center, we didn't know how long the transition period would last. What we did know, but overlooked, is that major organizational changes occur in three- to five-year waves. We should have anticipated that the information center's effective life cycle would be between three and five years. In Quaker's case, the information center life cycle is right on target.

It's important to remember that dismantling the information center is more than just knocking down the walls. You must address several important factors before you can begin the process:

□ Transfer to another IS department the continued support for several key functions, such as executive management support, limited hot-line service, and training.
□ Identify new career opportunities to leverage the info center staff skills.
□ Prepare the clients to rely less on information center staff.
□ Prepare the info center staff for new challenges.

At Quaker, we found it helpful to think in terms of phasing out the information center, with an emphasis on "phasing." Four separate shutdown phases are required:

- ☐ Refocus the purpose. Instead of helping the clients understand the technology, shift the emphasis to assisting the clients in accessing and manipulating computer-based data.
- ☐ Reorganize. Give the info center staff new objectives, direction, and management. At Quaker, the information center staff no longer reports to the vice president of information systems. Now, the staff reports to the director of information resource management. The organizational change reinforced the shift in the information center's purpose.
- ☐ Change the physical setting. Break down the walls that isolate the group from their coworkers in the information systems department.
- ☐ Phase out. Shift the support and coaching functions to the clients while still maintaining a centralized approach to investigate, standardize, and coordinate the use of personal and desktop technologies in the business. This phase will require moving the information center analysts into new applications support roles in order to more effectively leverage their skills. This can be accomplished by expanding and upgrading existing support functions in other information systems groups and/or by adding new job categories.

As an element of the phaseout process, Quaker's information center analysts were invited to explore new career opportunities in the business and technology functions. Several information center analysts already have been promoted and/or transferred to user or client organizations. They have assumed key responsibilities to help integrate new technologies into complex business processes. Some of them are now responsible for the implementation of the use of handheld computers by sales representatives.

In addition, we've opened up technology career paths to the information center analysts. During the past several months, some of them were temporarily reassigned to information systems applications and technology development projects to take advantage of their technology, applications, and business skills. Because of their backgrounds, they provided the necessary expertise to effectively design new technologies into new business applications. We intend to continue leveraging the information center skills by establishing an architectural assurance function, which will help ensure that appropriate technologies are effectively designed for new business systems.

Because of the rapid changes taking place in the high technology industry, the new functions and jobs that former information center analysts are now fulfilling may also be transition services. We don't know low long the new services will be required, but we do know that support and service groups should not be isolated from the rest of the information systems department. The information center has taught us how to tear down the walls.

QUESTIONS

1. Describe the accomplishments of the information center (IC) at Quaker Oats.
2. What factors were involved in the decision to dismantle the information center at Quaker Oats?
3. Why did Quaker Oats view the IC as a "transition department." Do you agree with this view? Why or why not?
4. What factors must be addressed before beginning the dismantling process?
5. How does the life and death of the IC at Quaker Oats compare with the life cycle hypothesized in "Nolan's" stage model?

ADDITIONAL CASES

Three additional EUC-related cases are listed below. These cases may be obtained by contacting HBS Case Services, Harvard Business School, Boston, MA 02163.

Corning Glass Works (B): Personal Computing—The Implementation of Change
Harvard Business School, 9-183-015, 1982

QUESTIONS

1. Describe when and how end-user computing became prevalent in Corning Glass Works (CGW).
2. How did John Parker and CGW make use of the traditional four-stage "Nolan" growth model in relation to EUC?
3. What did Dennis Lockard, manager of the information center, do to help market EUC within CGW? Whom did he hire and why? Describe the three-step plan.
4. At the time this case was written, what technology was beginning to impact corporate America. How did John Parker plan to introduce this new technology within CGW?
5. What role did/does telecommunications play in the facilitation of EUC? Where was the management function for telecommunications located? What are the implications of such a location?
6. What was the fate of the information center within CGW? Evolution or Dissolution?

Air Products and Chemicals, Inc.—MIS Evaluation of End-User Systems
A. Nedzel and J. Cash
Harvard Business School, 9-182-005, 1981

Questions

1. How was Air Products and Chemicals organized to support end-user computing?
2. What impact did on-line systems (vs. batch) have on the spread of EUC?
3. What issues were (a) the catalyst for, and (b) created by, the Industrial Gas Division's (IGD) procurement of Tank and Material Control Systems?
4. Describe the process Air Products underwent in the selection of a database inquiry product. Do you feel the evaluation process was adequate? Why or why not?
5. Assume that you are Peter Mather, what is your decision regarding the selection of FOCUS vs. RAMIS II? Explain your decision.

General Foods Information Services Department
L. R. Porter
Harvard Business School, 9-183-013, 1982

Questions

1. Utilizing the traditional four-stage "Nolan" growth model, identify what stage(s) of development General Foods is currently in (i.e., at the time this case was written). Justify your answer.
2. Assume that you are Ed Schefer and the group vice-president, Mr. Tappan, has asked you to prepare an evaluation of how cost beneficial personal computers have been to General Foods in the past year. What will you include in your report?
3. Evaluate the policy statement and the General Foods Information Services Department's strategy for implementing the policy. Would you initiate any more policy requirements? If so, what?
4. Should the Information Services Department control personal computer use or should unit departments be allowed to purchase personal computers at their own will? Discuss the implications of (a) too much and (b) too little control over PC usage.
5. Discuss the impact (realized and/or potential) of computer-related educational efforts on behalf of General Foods. Be sure to include in your discussion: (a) impact on both ISD personnel and non-ISD personnel, and (b) your suggestions for improvement.
6. How do *you* feel IS activities/responsibilities will change at General Foods, or "corporate America" for that matter, over the next five/ten years? How might these changes affect *you*, personally?

EUC Bibliography

A large body of EUC writings can be found in books, articles, conference proceedings, and the like. This diversity can be seen in the varied sources of materials included in this book of readings. To help you find other materials of interest, the following EUC bibliography is provided. While it contains references to what is felt to be the most important and interesting materials *primarily* focused on EUC, it includes only a small percentage of what has been written. There are many other excellent EUC writings, particularly of a "secondary nature" (e.g., writings on user satisfaction, individual differences, user involvement in the systems development process, etc.), with more appearing daily. This bibliography should provide assistance, however, as you strive to learn more about EUC.

The bibliography contains both books and articles. The articles have been categorized by their major topic(s): (1) general overview; (2) management of EUC; (3) development process; (4) EUC support; (5) the end-user community; (6) the IS/DP department and EUC; (7) evaluation of EUC; (8) EUC's impact on productivity/competitive advantage; (9) EUC and DSS; (10) EUC and OAS; (11) technological issues; (12) EUC research; (13) cases and applications of EUC; and (14) the future of EUC. Many of these categories are subdivided. The numbers shown for each category or subcategory reference the numbered articles in the bibliography. In addition, Figure A.1 presents a histogram depicting the number of EUC articles that have appeared over the last twenty years by, year (based on this bibliography). As depicted in the graph, a significant increase in the number of EUC articles published occurred in the early 1980's, coinciding with the introduction of the personal computer to corporate America.

BOOKS

1. Carr, H. H., *Managing End User Computing*, Englewood Cliffs, N.J.: Prentice-Hall, (1988).
2. Jarke, M., (ed.), *Managers, Micros and Mainframes: Integrating Systems for End Users*, New York: John Wiley & Sons, (1986).
3. Martin, J., *Application Development Without Programmers*, 1st Edition, Englewood Cliffs, N.J.: Prentice-Hall, (1982).
4. Martin, J., *End-User's Guide to Data Base*, 1st Edition, Englewood Cliffs, N.J.: Prentice-Hall, (1981).

FIGURE A.1

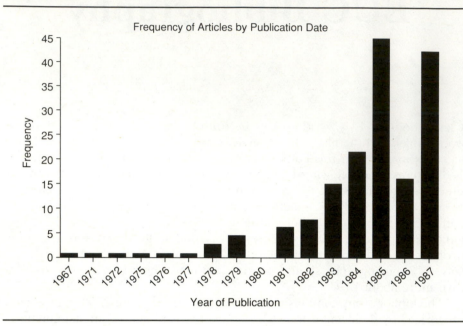

Frequency of Articles by Publication Date

5. Martin, J., *An Information Systems Manifesto*, 1st Edition, Englewood Cliffs, N.J.: Prentice-Hall, (1984).

6. Martin, J., *Fourth Generation Languages: Principles*, Vol. I, Englewood Cliffs, N.J.: Prentice-Hall, (1984).

7. Martin, J., *Fourth Generation Languages*, Vol. II, Englewood Cliffs, N.J.: Prentice-Hall, (1984).

8. Martin, J., *Fourth Generation Languages*, Vol. III, Englewood Cliffs, N.J.: Prentice-Hall, (1984).

9. Panko, R., *The Management of End-User Computing*, New York: John Wiley & Sons, (1988).

10. Perry, William E., *The Information Center*, Englewood Cliffs, N.J.: Prentice-Hall, Inc., (1987).

REFERENCE TO THE EUC ARTICLES

General Overview

17, 30, 68, 75, 93, 106, 115, 132, 135, 142, 144, 145, 146, 167.

Management of EUC

☐ Managerial issues—6, 7, 9, 13, 17, 35, 37, 39, 49, 56, 65, 66, 76, 80, 83, 86, 87, 93, 103, 121, 127, 135, 136, 145, 168

☐ Planning for EUC—14, 82, 84

☐ Control issues—8, 9, 19, 29, 49, 90, 94, 121, 127

Development Process

- ☐ Design—18, 70, 95, 96, 97, 107, 115, 122
- ☐ Organizational variables—36, 37, 109, 139
- ☐ Others—13, 53, 112, 116, 120, 123, 133, 140, 141, 142, 149, 156

EUC Support

- ☐ Information centers—11, 20, 22, 23, 28, 29, 31, 32, 38, 45, 62, 72, 74, 77, 85, 89, 98, 103, 104, 105, 109, 110, 114, 117, 120, 123, 155, 158, 160, 165, 166
- ☐ Training end users—17, 18, 33, 34, 52, 58, 61, 63, 64, 79, 88, 108, 113, 124, 125, 126, 128, 129, 150, 151, 153, 159, 164
- ☐ Other—25, 81, 99, 161, 163, 168

The End-User Community

1, 8, 10, 16, 17, 21, 22, 27, 36, 46, 50, 51, 75, 84, 107, 111, 118, 142, 144, 146, 149, 156

The IS/DP Department and EUC

2, 4, 32, 44, 59, 68, 106, 139, 143, 152

Evaluation of EUC

2, 5, 48, 69, 71, 83, 91, 92, 94, 134, 141, 143

Impact of EUC on Productivity/Competitive Advantage

7, 24, 43, 47, 55, 67, 80, 118, 127, 147

EUC and DSS

16, 21, 27, 35, 57, 69, 91, 92, 112, 116, 128, 140, 146, 163

EUC and OAS

18, 40, 42, 46, 57, 69, 78, 108, 118, 119, 130, 148, 157, 159, 162

Technological Issues

- ☐ Personal computer—3, 14, 19, 39, 40, 41, 60, 63, 73, 76, 78, 86, 90, 93, 99, 100, 101, 102, 131, 136, 137, 138, 153
- ☐ Mainframe—101, 102

- ☐ Telecommunications—54, 59, 81
- ☐ Other—15, 26, 47, 67, 107, 116, 120, 133, 147

EUC Research

12, 17, 132, 154, 161

Cases and Applications of EUC

2, 3, 27, 38, 41, 42, 65, 87, 124, 155, 166

The Future of EUC

15, 51, 148

ARTICLES

1. Adams, C. R., "How Management Users View Information Systems," *Decision Sciences*, Vol. 6, No. 2, (April 1975), pp. 337–345.
2. Air Products and Chemicals, Inc.: MIS Evaluation of End-User Systems, Harvard Business School, Case #9-182-005, (1982).
3. Air Products and Chemicals, Inc. (B): Personal Computers, Harvard Business School, Case #9-183-014, (1982).
4. Alavi, M., "End-User Computing: The MIS Managers' Perspective," *Information & Management*, Vol. 8, No 3, (March 1985), pp. 171–178.
5. Alavi, M. "Some Thoughts on Quality Issues of End-User Developed Systems," *Proceedings of the 21st Computer Personnel Research Conference*, Minneapolis, MN, (May 2–3, 1985), pp. 200–207.
6. Alavi, M., R. R. Nelson, and I. R. Weiss, "Strategies for End-User Computing: An Integrative Framework," *Journal of Management Information Systems*, Vol. 4, No. 3, (Winter 1987–88), pp. 28–49.
7. Alavi, M., R. R. Nelson, and I. R. Weiss, "The Management of End-User Computing: Critical Attributes for Organizational Success," *20th Annual Meeting of the Hawaii International Conference on Systems Sciences*, Kona, Hawaii, (January 6–9, 1987).
8. Alavi, M., J. S. Phillips and S. M. Freedman, "Strategies for Control of End-User Computing: Impact on End Users, *Proceedings of the Seventh International Conference on Information Systems*, San Diego, CA, (December 15–17, 1986), pp. 57–66.
9. Alavi, M. and I. R. Weiss, "Managing the Risks Associated with End-User Computing," *Journal of Management Information Systems*, (Winter 1985-86), pp. 5–20.
10. Alloway, R. M. and J. A. Quillard, "User Managers' Systems Needs," *MIS Quarterly*, Vol. 7, No. 2, (June 1983), pp. 27–43.

11. American Management Association, *1985 AMA Report on Information Centers*, New York, cited in CRWTH Computer Coursewares, "The Second CRWTH Information Center Survey," *CRWTH News for Better Training*, Vol. 3, No. 1, 1985.

12. Attia, A. and T. C. Richards, "End-User Computing: A Call for Research," *Proceedings of the 1985 Annual Meeting of the American Institute for Decision Sciences*, Las Vegas, Nevada, (November 11–13, 1985), pp. 325–327.

13. Beheshtian, M. and P. D. Van Wert, "Strategies for Managing User Developed Systems," *Information & Management*, Vol, 12, No. 1, (January 1987), pp. 1–7.

14. Belohlav, J. and L. Raho, "Developing Strategic Directions: The Personal Computer Policy," *Proceedings of the 1985 Annual Meeting of the American Institute for Decision Sciences*, Las Vegas, Nevada, (November 11–13, 1985), pp. 350–352.

15. Benjamin, R. I., "Information Technology in the 1990s: A Long Range Planning Scenario," *MIS Quarterly*, Vol. 6, No. 2, (June 1982), pp. 11–31.

16. Bennett, J., "Integrated Users and Decision Support Systems," *Proceedings of the 6th/7th Annual Conference of the Society for MIS*, (1976), pp. 77–86.

17. Benson, D. H., "A Field Study of End User Computing: Findings and Issues," *MIS Quarterly*, Vol. 7, No. 4, (December 1983), pp. 35–45.

18. Bikson, T. K. and B. A. Gutek, "Training in Automated Offices: An Empirical Study of Design and Methods. In J. I. Rignsdorp and T. Plomp, *Training for Tomorrow*, Proceedings of IFAC/IFIP 1983 Symposium, (1983), pp. 129–143.

19. Boockholdt, J.L., "Security and Integrity Controls for Microcomputers: A Summary Analysis," *Information & Management*, Vol. 13, No. 1, (August 1987), pp. 33–41.

20. Bracy, M., "Info Center Success 'Centers' Around the DP Manager," *Data Management*, Vol. 22, No. 2, (February 1984), pp. 26–37.

21. Brady, R. H., "Computers in Top-Level Decision Making," *Harvard Business Review*, Vol. 45, No. 4, (July-August 1967), pp. 67–76.

22. Brancheau, J.C., D. R. Vogel, and J. C. Wetherbe, "An Investigation of the Information Centre From the User's Perspective," *Data Base*, Vol. 17, No. 1, (Fall 1985), pp. 4–17.

23. Brzezinski, R., "When It's Time to Tear the Information Center Down," *Datamation*, Vol. 33, No. 21, (November 1, 1987), pp. 73–82.

24. Canning, R. G., "The Challenge of Increased Productivity," *EDP Analyzer*, Vol. 19, No. 4, (April 1981), pp. 1–12.

25. Canning, R. G., "Supporting End User Computing," *EDP Analyzer*, Vol. 19, No. 6, (June 1981), pp. 1–12.

26. Canning, R. G., "Programming By End Users," *EDP Analyzer*, Vol. 19, No. 5, (May 1981), pp. 1–12.

27. Carlson, E. D., B. F. Grace, and J. A. Sutton, "Case Studies of End User Requirements for Interactive Problem-Solving Systems." *MIS Quarterly*, Vol. 1, No. 1, (March 1977), pp. 51–63.

28. Carr, H. H., "An Empirical Investigation of the Formal Support for End User Requirements from the Information Center Concept," Unpublished dissertation at the University of Texas at Arlington, (1985).

29. Carr, H. H., "Charging for Information Center Services," University of Georgia, EUCRC WP#15, Athens, GA, (April 1986).

30. Carr, H. H., "End-User Computing and General Systems Theory," University of Georgia, EUCRC WP#8, Athens, GA, (June 1985).

31. Carr, H. H., "Information Centers: The IBM Model vs. Practice," *MIS Quarterly*, Vol. 11, No. 3, (September 1987), pp. 325–338.

32. Carr, H. H., "What is the Best User-to-Staff Ratio for an Information Center?," University of Georgia, EUCRC WP#23, Athens, GA, (February 1987).

33. Carroll, J. M., "Minimalist Training", *Datamation*, Vol. 30, No. 18, (November 1, 1984), pp. 125–136.

34. Carroll, J. M., and C. Carrithers, "Training Wheels in a User Interface," *Communications of the ACM*, Vol. 27, No. 8, (1984), pp. 800–806.

35. Chen, H. C., and C. Y. Lin, "The Management of End User Computing in Distributed Decision Support Systems Environment," *Proceedings of the 1987 Annual Meeting of the Decision Sciences Institute*, Boston, MA, (November 23-25, 1987), pp. 297–300.

36. Cheney, P. H., "Effects of Individual Chracteristics, Organizational Factors, and Task Characteristics on Computer Programmer Productivity and Job Satisfaction," *Information & Management*, (July 1984), pp. 209–214.

37. Cheney, P.H., R. I. Mann, and D. L. Amoroso, "Organizational Factors Affecting the Success of End User Computing," *Journal of Management Information Systems*, Vol. 3, No. 1, (Summer 1986), pp. 65–80.

38. Christy, D. P. and C. E. White, Jr., "Structure and Function of Information Centers: Case Studies of Six Organizations," *Information & Management*, Vol. 13, No. 2, (September 1987), pp. 71–76.

39. Chrysler, E. "Managing the Micro Invasion," *Journal of Systems Management*, Vol. 36, No. 1, (January 1985), pp. 34–36.

40. Collins, F., and T. Moores, "Microprocessors in the Office: A Study of Resistance to Change", *Journal of Systems Management*, Vol. 34, No. 11, (November 1983), pp. 17–21.

41. Corning Glass Works (B): Personal Computing–The Implementation of Change, Harvard Business School, Case #9-183-015, (1981).

42. Corning Glass Works: Office Worker Productivity, Harvard Business School, Case #9-184-017, (1983).

43. Cron, W. L. and M. G. Sobol, "The Relationship Between Computerization and Performance: A Strategy for Maximizing the Economic Benefits of Computerization," *Information & Management*, Vol. 6, No. 3, (June 1983), pp. 171–181.

44. *Computerworld*, "End User Computing: MIS Answers the Call," (August 18, 1986), pp. 41–55.

45. CRWTH Computer Coursewares, "The Second CRWTH Information Center Survey," *CRWTH News for Better Training*, Vol. 3, No. 1, (1985).

46. Culnan, M. J., "Chauffeured Versus End User Access to Commercial Databases: The Effects of Task and Individual Differences," *MIS Quarterly*, Vol. 7, No. 1, (March 1983), pp. 55–68.

47. Curley, K. F., and P. J. Pyburn, "Intellectual Technologies: The Key to Improving White Collar Productivity," *Sloan Management Review*, Vol, 24, No. 1, (Fall 1982), pp. 31–39.

48. Davis, F. D., Jr., "A Technology Acceptance Model for Empirically Testing New End-User Information Systems: Theory and Results." Unpublished doctoral dissertation, MIT, (1985).

49. David, G. B., "Caution: User Developed Systems Can Be Dangerous to Your Organization," MISRC Working Paper #82-04, (February 1984), pp. 1–28.

50. David, J. G., "A Typology of Management Information Systems Users and Its Implications for User Information Satisfaction Research," *Proceedings of the 21st Computer Personnel Research Conference*, Minneapolis, MN, (May 2–3, 1985), pp. 152–164.

51. Dearden, J., "SMR Forum: Will the Computer Change the Job of Top Management," *Sloan Management Review*, Vol. 25, No. 1, (Fall 1983), pp. 57–60.

52. Dight, J., "Training & Technology = Profits," *Datamation*, Vol. 29, No. 11 (November 1983), pp. 202–208.

53. Doll, W. J. and G. Torkzadeh, "The Quality of User Documentation," *Information & Management*, Vol. 12, No. 2, (February 1987), pp. 73–78.

54. Duxbury, L. E., C. A. Higgins and R. H. Irving, "Attitudes of Managers and Employees to Telecommuting," *INFOR*, Vol. 25, No. 3, (August 1987), pp. 273–285.

55. Edelman, F., "Managers, Computing Systems, and Productivity," *MIS Quarterly*, Vol. 5, No. 3, (September 1981), pp. 1–19.

56. El Sawy, O., "Implementation by Cultural Infusion: An Approach for Managing the Introduction of Information Technologies," *MIS Quarterly*, Vol. 9, No. 2, (June 1985), pp. 131–140.

57. El Sawy, O., "Personal Information Systems for Strategic Scanning in Turbulent Environments: Can The CEO Go On-Line? " *MIS Quarterly*, Vol. 9, No. 1, (March 1985), pp. 53–60.

58. Eriksson, I., R. Kalmi and M. I. Nurmien, "A Method for Supporting Users' Comprehensive Learning," *Proceedings of the Eighth International Conference on Information Systems*, Pittsburgh, PA, (December 6–9, 1987) pp. 195–211.

59. Ferratt, T. W. and L. E. Shrot, "Work-Unit Environments of Information Systems and Non-Information Systems People: Implications for End-User Computing and Distributed Processing," *Proceedings of 21st Computer Personnel Research Conference*, (May 2–3, 1985), pp. 126–133.

60. Flavell, R. B., "Management and the Micro," *Omega*, Vol. 12, No. 5, (1984), pp. 419–284.

61. Galletta, D., "A Learner Model of Information Systems: The Effects of Orientating Materials, Ability, Expectations and Experience on Performance, Usage and Attitude." Unpublished doctoral dissertation, University of Minnesota, (1984).

62. Garcia, B., "The Second CRWTH Information Center Survey," *CRWTH News for Better Training*, 3, 2, (1985).

63. Gattiker, U. E., "Teaching Micro-Computer Skills to Management Students: Academic Achievement, Gender, Student Effort on Homework, and Learning Performance," *Proceedings of the Eighth International Conference on Information Systems*, Pittsburgh, PA, (December 6–9, 1987), pp. 368–382.

64. Gattiker, U. E. and D. Paulson, "The Quest for Effective Teaching Methods: Achieving Computer Literacy for End Users," *INFOR*, Vol. 25, No. 3, (August 1987), pp. 256–272.

65. General Foods: Information Services Department, Harvard Business School, Case #9-183-013, (1982).

66. Gerrity, T. P. and J. F. Rockart, "End-User Computing: Are You a Leader or Laggard?," *Sloan Management Review*, Vol. 27, No. 4, (Summer 1986), pp. 25–34.

67. Green, J., "Productivity in the Fourth Generation," *Journal of Management Information Systems*, Vol. 1, No. 3, (Winter 1984–85), pp. 49–63.

68. Gremillion, L.L. and P. Pyburn, "Breaking the Systems Development Bottleneck," *Harvard Business Review*, Vol. 61, No. 2, (March–April 1983), pp. 130–137.

69. Gremillion, L. L. and P. Pyburn, "Justifying Decision Support and Office Automation Systems," *Journal of Management Inforamtion Systems*, Vol. 2, No. 1, (Summer 1985), pp. 5–17.

70. Guimaraes, T., "Prototyping: Orchestrating for Success," *Datamation*, Vol. 33, No. 23, (December 1, 1987), pp. 101–106.

71. Guimaraes, T., "The Benefits and Problems of User Computing", *Journal of Information Systems Management*, (Fall 1984), pp. 3–9.

72. Guimaraes, T., "The Evolution of the Information Center", *Datamation*, Vol. 30, No. 11, (July 15, 1984), pp. 127–130.

73. Guimaraes, T. and V. Ramanujam, "Personal Computing Trends and Problems: An Empirical Study," *MIS Quarterly*, Vol. 10, No. 2, (June 1986), pp. 179–187.)

74. Hammond, L. W., "Management Considerations for an Information Center," *IBM Systems Journal*, Vol. 21, No. 2, (April 1982), pp. 133–161.

75. Harold, F. G., "Certification Comes of Age: End Users Are Now Eligible," *Proceedings of the 21st Computer Personnel Research Conference*, Minneapolis, MN, (May 2-3, 1985), pp. 50–55.

76. Harrison, W. L. and M. E. E. Dick, "An Investigation of Microcomputer Policies in Large Organizations," *Information & Management*, Vol. 12, No. 5, (May 1987), pp. 223–233.

77. Head, R. V., "Information Resource Center: A New Force in End-User Computing," *Journal of Systems Management*, Vol. 36, No. 2, (February 1985), pp. 24–29.

78. Healey, M., "What is a Workstation", *Datamation*, Vol. 33, No. 2, (January 15, 1987), pp. 55–57.

79. Heany, D. F., "Education: the Critical Link in Getting Managers to Use Management Systems," *Interfaces*, Vol. 2, No. 3, (May 1972), pp. 1–7.

80. Henderson, J. C. and M. E. Treacy, "Managing End User Computing For Competitive Advantage," *Sloan Management Review*, Vol. 28, No. 2, (Winter 1986), pp. 3–14.

81. IBM Series Management of End-User Computing (1), "Access to Data," 1st Edition, White Plains, New York: IBM, (1985).

82. IBM Series Management of End-User Computing (2), "Executive Direction," 1st Edition, White Plains, New York: IBM, (1985).

83. IBM Series Management of End-User Computing (3), "Justification," 1st Edition, White Plains, New York: IBM, (1985).

84. IBM Series Management of End-User Computing (4), "Planning for Users' Needs," 1st Edition, White Plains, New York: IBM, (1985).

85. IBM Series Management of End-User Computing (5), "Support Organization," 1st Edition, White Plains, New York: IBM, (1984).

86. IBM Series Management of End-User Computing (6), "Workstation Management," 1st Edition, White Plains, New York: IBM, (1984).

87. IBM Series Management of End-User Computing, "Managing End User Computing at Dow Corning Corporation," 1st Edition, White Plains, New York: IBM, (1984).

88. Jarvenpaa, S. L., and N. M. Ray, "End-User Learning Behavior in Data Analysis and Data Modeling Tools," *Proceedings of the Seventh International Conference on Information Systems*, San Diego, CA, (December 15-17, 1986), pp. 152–167.

89. Johnson, J. W., "The InfoCenter Experience," *Datamation*, Vol. 30, No. 1, (January 1984), pp. 137–142.

90. Kahn, B. R., and L. R. Garceau, "Controlling the Microcomputer Environment", *Journal of Systems Management*, Vol. 35, No. 5, (May 1984), pp. 14–20.

91. Kasper, G. M., "The Effect of User-Developed DSS Applications on Forecasting Decision-Making Performance in an Experimental Setting," *Journal of Management Information Systems*, Vol. 2, No. 2, (Fall 1985), pp. 26–39.

92. Kasper, G. M. and R. P. Cerveny, "A Laboratory Study of User Characteristics and Decision-Making Performance in End-User Computing," *Information & Management*, Vol. 9, No. 2, (September 1985), p. 87–96.

93. Keen, P. G. W. and L. A. Woodman, "What to Do With All Those Micros," *Harvard Business Review*, Vol. 62, No. 5, (September–October 1984), pp. 142–150.

94. Klepper, R. and E. G. McKenna, "Support for Quality Assurance in End-User Systems, *Proceedings of the 1987 Annual Meeting of the Decision Sciences Institute*, Boston, MA, (November 23–25, 1987), pp. 356–358.

95. Kozar, K. A. and J. M. Mahlum, "A User Generated Information System: An Innovative Development Approach," *MIS Quarterly*. Vol. 11, No. 2, (June 1987), pp. 163–174.

96. Kraushaar, J. M. and L. E. Shirland, "A Prototyping Method for Applications Development by End Users and Informations Systems Specialists," *MIS Quarterly*, Vol. 9, No. 3, (September 1985), pp. 189–197.

97. Langle, G. B., R. L. Leitheiser, and J. D. Naumann, "A Survey of Applications Systems Prototyping in Industry," *Information & Management*, Vol. 7, No. 5, (October 1984), pp. 273–284.

98. Lefkowitz, H. C., "A Status Report on the Activities of CODASYL End User Computing Facilities Committee (EUCF)," *Information & Management*, Vol. 2, No. 4, (October 1979), pp. 137–163.

99. Lee, D. M., "Usage Patterns and Sources of Assistance for Personal Computer Users," *MIS Quarterly*, Vol. 10, No. 4, (December 1986), pp. 313–325.

100. Lehman, J., "Personal Computing Versus Personal Computers," *Proceedings of the 21st Computer Personnel Research Conference*, Minneapolis, MN, (May 2–3, 1985), pp. 97–102.

101. Lehman, J., J. Van Wetering, and D. Vogel, "Mainframe and Microcomputer-Based Business Graphics: What Satisfies Users? ," *Information & Management*, Vol. 10, No. 3, (March 1986), pp. 133–140.

102. Lehman, J. and D. Vogel, "Mainframe and Microcomputer-Based Business Graphics: End User Computing Comparisons and Trends," *Proceedings of the 21st Computer Personnel Research Conference*, Minneapolis, MN, (May 2–3, 1985), pp. 66–73.

103. Leitheiser, R. L. and J. C. Wetherbe, "Service Support Levels: An Organizational Approach to End-User Computing," *MIS Quarterly*, Vol. 10, No. 4, (December 1986), pp. 337–349.

104. Leitheiser, R. L. and J. C. Wetherbe, "The Successful Information Center: What Does It Take? ," *Proceedings of the 21st Computer Personnel Research Conference*, Minneapolis, MN, (May 2–3, 1985), pp. 56–65.

105. Lind, M. R., "Facilitating End-User Computing," *Proceedings of the 1987 Annual Meeting of the Decision Sciences Institute*, Boston, MA, (November 23–25, 1987), pp. 303–305.

106. Lucas, H. C., "The Evolution of an IS: From Key-Man to Every Person." *Sloan Management Review*, Vol. 19, No. 2, (Winter 1978), pp. 39–52.

107. MacIntosh, N. B. and R. L. Daft, "User Department Technology and Information Design," *Information & Management*, Vol. 1, No. 3, (May 1978), pp. 123–131.

108. Mack, R. L., C. H. Lewis, and J. M. Carroll, "Learning to Use Word Processors: Problems and Prospects," *ACM Transactions on Office Information Systems*, Vol. 1, No. 3, (July 1983), pp. 254–271.

109. Magal, S. and H. H. Carr, "An Investigation of the Effects of Age, Size and Hardware Option on the Critical Success Factors Applicable to Information Centers," University of Georgia, EUCRC WP#22, Athens, GA, (February 1987).

110. Magal, S., H.H. Carr, and H. J. Watson, "Critical Success Factors for Information Center Managers," University of Georgia, EUCRC WP# 21, Athens, GA, (November 1986).

111. Maish, A. M., "A User's Behavior Toward His MIS," *MIS Quarterly*, Vol. 3, No. 1, (March 1979), pp. 39–52.

112. Mann, R. I. and H. J. Watson, "A Contingency Model for User Involvement in DSS Development," *MIS Quarterly*, Vol. 8, No. 1, (March 1984), pp. 27–38.

113. Mayer, R. E., "The Psychology of How Novices Learn Computer Programming," *Computing Surveys*, Vol. 13, No. 1, (March 1981), pp. 121–141.

114. McCartney, L., "The New Info Centers," *Datamation*, Vol. 29, No. 7, (July 1983), pp. 30–46.

115. McLean, E. R., "End Users As Application Developers," *MIS Quarterly*, Vol. 3, No. 4, (December 1979), pp. 37–46.

116. Meador, C. L. and R. A. Mezger, "Selecting an End User Programming Language for DSS Development," *MIS Quarterly*, Vol. 1, No. 4, (December 1984), pp. 267–281.

117. Melymuka, K., "The Information Center," *PC Week*, (December 3, 1985), pp. 77–79.

118. Millman, Z. and J. Hartwick, "The Impact of Automated Office Systems on Middle Managers and Their Work," *MIS Quarterly*, Vol. 11, No. 4, (December 1987), pp. 479–491.

119. Moore, G. C., "End User Computing and Office Automation: A Diffusion of Innovations Perspective," *INFOR*, Vol. 25, No. 3, (August 1987), pp. 214–235.

120. Munro, M. C. and S. L. Huff, "Information Technology Assessment and Adoption: Understanding the Information Centre Role," *Proceedings of the 21st Computer Personnel Research Conference*, Minneapolis, MN, (May 2-3, 1985), pp. 29–37.

121. Munro, M. C., S. L. Huff and G. Moore, "Expansion and Control of End-User Computing," *Journal of Management Information Systems*, Vol. 4, No. 3, (Winter 1987–88), pp. 5–27.

122. Naumann, J. D. and A. M. Jenkins, "Prototyping: The New Paradigm for Systems Development," *MIS Quarterly*. Vol. 6, No. 3, (September 1982), pp. 29–44.

123. Necco, C. R., C. L. Gordon and N. W. Tsai, "The Information Center Approach for Developing Computer-Based Information Systems," Vol. 13, No. 2, (September 1987), pp. 95–101.

124. Nelson, R. R. and P. H. Cheney, "Educating the CBIS User: A Case Analysis," *Data Base*, Vol. 18, No. 2, (Winter 1987), pp. 11–16.

125. Nelson, R. R. and P. H. Cheney, "Training End Users: An Exploratory Study," *MIS Quarterly*, Vol. 11, No. 4, (December 1987), pp. 547–559.

126. Nelson, R. R. and P. H. Cheney, "Training Today's User," *Datamation*, Vol. 33, No. 10, (May 15, 1987), pp. 121–122.

127. O'Donnell, D. J. and S. T. March, "End-User Computing Environments—Finding a Balance Between Productivity and Control," *Information & Management*, Vol. 13, No. 2, (September 1987), pp. 77–84.

128. Olfman, L., "A Comparison of Construct-Based and Applications-Based Training Methods for DSS Generator Software." Unpublished doctoral dissertation, Indiana University, (1987).

129. Olfman, L., M. Sein, and R. P. Bostrom, "Training for End-User Computing: Are Basic Abilities Enough for Learning?", *Proceedings of the Twenty-Second Annual Computer Personnel Research Conference*, Calgary, AB., (1986).

130. Olson, M. H. and J. A. Turner, "Rethinking Office Automation," *Proceedings of the Sixth International Conference on Information Systems*, Indianapolis, IN, (December 16–18, 1985), pp. 259–269.

131. Painter, W. J., "Introducing Micros Into Large Organizations—A Checklist of Problems and Solutions," *Journal of Information Systems Management*, Vol. 5, No. 1, (Winter 1988), pp. 29–31.

132. Panko, R. R., "Directions and Issues in End User Computing," *INFOR*, Vol. 25, No. 3, (August 1987), pp. 181–197.

133. Parker, J., "A Program Development System for the Casual Programmer," *Proceedings of the 21st Computer Personnel Research Conference*, Minneapolis, MN, (May 2-3, 1985), pp. 172–180.

134. Parker, M. M. and R. J. Benson, "Information Economics: An Introduction," *Datamation*, Vol. 33, No. 23, (December 1, 1987), pp. 86–96.

135. Porter, L. R. and J. L. Gogan, "Coming to Terms with End-User Systems Integration," *Journal of Information Systems Management*, Vol. 5, No. 1, (Winter 1988), pp. 8–21.

136. Pyburn, P.J., "Managing Personal Computer Use," *Journal of Management Information Systems*, Vol. 3, No. 3, (Winter 1986-87), pp. 49–70.

137. Quillard, J. A., J. F. Rockart, E. Wilde, M. Vernon, and G. Mock, "A Study of the Corporate Use of Personal Computers," CISR Working Paper No. 109, Center for Information Systems Research, Massachusetts Institute of Technology, Sloan School of Management, 77 Massachusetts Avenue, Cambridge, MA., (December 1983).

138. Quillard, J. A. and J. F. Rockart, "A Study of the Corporate Use of Personal Computers," CISR Working Paper #109, MIT Sloan School of Management, (1983).

139. Raymond, L., "The Presence of End-User Computing in Small Business: An Exploratory Investigation of its Distinguishing Organizational and Information Systems Context," *INFOR*, Vol. 25, No. 3, (August 1987), pp. 198–213.

140. Reimann, B. C. and A. D. Waren, "User-Oriented Criteria for the Selection of DSS Software," *Communications of the ACM*, Vol. 28, No. 2, (February 1985), pp. 166–179.

141. Rivard, S. and S. Huff, "User Development of Applications: A Study Model of Success," *Proceedings of the 21st Computer Personnel Research Conference*, Minneapolis, MN, (May 2–3, 1985), pp. 81–90.

142. Rivard, S. and S. Huff, "An Empirical Study of Users as Application Developers," *Information & Management*, Vol. 8, No. 2, (February 1985), pp. 89–102.

143. Rivard, S. and S. L. Huff, "User Developed Applications: Evaluations of Success from the DP Department Perspective," *MIS Quarterly*, Vol. 8, No. 1, (March 1984), pp. 39–50.

144. Rockart, J. F., "Chief Executives Define Their Own Needs," *Harvard Business Review*, Vol. 57, No. 2, (March–April 1979), pp. 76–88.

145. Rockart, J. F. and L. S. Flannery, "The Management of End User Computing," *Communications of the ACM*, Vol. 26, No. 10, (October 1983), pp. 776–784.

146. Rockart, J. F. and M. E. Treacy, "The CEO Goes On-Line," *Harvard Business Review*, Vol. 60, No. 1, (January–February 1982), pp. 82–88.

147. Rockart, J. F. and M. S. Scott Morton, "Implications of Changes in Information Technology for Corporate Strategy," *Interfaces*, Vol. 14, No. 1, (January–February 1984), pp. 84–95.

148. Roessner, J. D., "Market Penetration of Office Automation Equipment: Trends and Forecasts," *Proceedings of the Sixth International Conference on Information Systems*, Indianapolis, IN, (December 16-18, 1985), pp. 270–284.

149. Rushinek, A. and S. Rushinek, "What Makes Users Happy?," *Communications of the ACM*, Vol. 29, No. 7, (July 1986), pp. 594–598.

150. Sein, M. K., "Conceptual Models in Training Novice Users of Computer Systems Effectiveness of Analogical vs. Abstract Models and Influence of Individual Differences," Unpublished doctoral dissertation, Indiana University, (1987).

151. Sein, M. K., R. P. Bostrom and L. Olfman, "Training End Users to Compute: Cognitive, Motivational and Social Issues," *INFOR*, Volume 25, No. 3, (August 1987), pp. 236–255.

152. Severson, E. and K. A. Kozar, "A Business Approach to Cracking the Applications Backlog," *Journal of Information Systems Management*, Vol. 5, No. 1, (Winter 1988), pp. 17–21.

153. Sharrow, J., V. Weaver, and K. Kilduff, "Appreciation and Confidence: A Study in Micro Training," *Information Center*, (December 1985), pp. 44–47.

154. Sipior, J. C. and G. L. Sanders, "End User Computing in Groups: A Conceptual Framework and Model for Research, *Proceedings of the 1987 Annual Meeting of the Decision Sciences Institute*, Boston, MA, (November 23–25, 1987), pp. 300–302.

155. Sumner, M. R., "Organization and Management of the Information Center: Case Studies." *Proceedings of the 21st Computer Personnel Research Conference*, Minneapolis, MN, (May 2-3, 1985), pp. 38–49.

156. Sumner, M. R., "The Impact of User-Developed Applications on Managers' Information Needs, *Proceedings of the 1985 Annual Meeting of the American Institute for Decision Sciences*, Las Vegas, Nevada, (November 11–13, 1985), pp. 328–330.

157. Swanson, E. B., "A Note on Interpersonal Information Systems Use," *Information & Management*, Vol. 1, No. 6, (December 1978), pp. 287–294.

158. Swider, G. A., "Ten Pitfalls of Information Center Implementation," *Journal of Information Systems Management*, Vol. 5, No. 1, (Winter 1988), pp. 22–28.

159. Thiel, C. T., "Office Automation—Training Starts with Top-Down Acceptance", *Infosystems*, (May 1984), pp. 60–64.

160. Vacca, J. R., "The Information Center's Critical Post-Start-Up Phase," *Journal of Management Information Systems*, (Spring 1985), pp. 50–55.

161. Vijayaraman, B. S. and S. E. Harris, "End-User Computing Support in Organizations: Some Implications for Research and Practice, *Proceedings of the 1987 Annual Meeting of the Decision Sciences Institute*, Boston, MA, (November 23-25, 1987), pp. 362–365.

162. Vogel, D. R. and J. C. Wetherbe, "Office Automation: End User Impact," *Proceedings of the 21st Computer Personnel Research Conference*, Minneapolis, MN, (May 2–3, 1985), pp. 165–171.

163. Watson, H. J. and H. H. Carr, "Organizing for DSS Support: The End-User Services Alternative, *Journal of Management Information Systems*, Vol. 4, No. 1, (Summer 1987), pp. 83–95.

164. Wegner, P., "Education Related to the Use of Computers in Organizations," *Communications of the ACM*, Vol. 14, No. 9, (September 1971), pp. 573–588.

165. Wetherbe, J. C. and R. L. Leitheiser, "Information Centers: A Survey of Services, Decision, Problems, and Successes," *Journal of Information Systems Management*, Vol. 2, No. 3, (Summer 1985), pp. 3–10.

166. White, C. E. and D. P. Christy, "The Information Center Concept: A Normative Model and a Study of Six Installations," *MIS Quarterly*, Vol. 11, No. 4, (December 1987), pp. 451–458.

167. Zink, R. A., "The Tilt to End-User Programming," *Computerworld*, Vol. 18, No. 7A, (July 1984), pp. 5–14.

168. Zmud, R. W. and M. R. Lind, "Linking Mechanisms Supporting End-User Computing," *Proceedings of the 21st Computer Personnel Research Conference*, Minneapolis, MN, (May 2–3, 1985), pp. 74–80.

Index